WARSHIPS
OF THE WORLD

WARSHIPS
OF THE WORLD

ANTONY PRESTON

Bison Books

First Published in 1983 by
Bison Books Corp., 17 Sherwood Place,
Greenwich, CT 06830, U.S.A.

Copyright © 1983 Bison Books Corp.

ISBN 0 86124 102 9

Printed in Hong Kong

CONTENTS

INTRODUCTION

by S.L. Mayer

The development of the ironclad warship revolutionized the art of naval warfare and in the 19th century required the naval powers of the world to scrap their sailing fleets and literally start from scratch. Although the French introduced the first ironclads in the 1850s, the otherwise inconsequential battle between the *Monitor* and the *Merrimack* during the American Civil War in 1862 proved to every major naval power that the age of the sail, the principal means of propulsion of vessels afloat, was over. Within two decades the race for naval supremacy in building, first ironclads, and then soon after, ships with steel hulls, was going forward full tilt, with the leading nations of the sailing age in the forefront, Britain and France, followed closely by new entrants such as Imperial Germany, Italy, Russia, Austria-Hungary and the United States. By the turn of the century the leader in the race to build bigger and better battleships was Britain, challenged in Europe by Germany, Japan in Asia, and in the Western Hemisphere the United States. Britain's mastery of the seas, once challenged by France in the 18th century, and unchallenged since Trafalgar in 1805, was now under attack on all sides.

New naval weapons were introduced, often by Britain, to maintain her waning naval supremacy in the early years of the 20th century. Submarines, first used experimentally during the War of the American Revolution, were launched, and soon both Germany and Britain boasted of major submarine fleets which could damage and even curtail all shipping, commercial and otherwise, on the surface of the world's oceans. This presented a particularly dangerous situation for Britain, as she was entirely dependent upon international shipping for most of her food and raw materials, which in turn were converted into exports which left Britain's ports by sea. In order to protect maritime commerce, destroyers were introduced, and they became vital escorts for merchant shipping during both world wars against their undersea predators. Cruisers replaced the ancient corvettes and other smaller sailing craft. As whole new fleets were introduced, it was inevitable that they should be given trials so that naval architects could see their brainchildren in action. The Battle of Manila Bay between the emerging American fleet of Admiral George Dewey and the rather pathetic collection of miscellaneous ships sailing Asian waters under the Spanish flag proved little, but seven years later, at Tsushima, in the straits between Japan and Korea, one of the most significant of modern naval battles took place between Imperial Japan and the ships of Admiral Rozhdestvenski of Czarist Russia. In some ways this was the only battle fought between the British and French Navies in the 20th century, if one timorously avoids mention of the fiasco at Mirs-el-Kebir in 1940 between the Royal Navy and the recently Vichy-controlled French forces off the Algerian coast. In 1905 the Russian Fleet was almost entirely made in France; the Japanese Fleet was almost entirely constructed in British shipyards. The overwhelming Japanese victory proved more than merely the beginning of the end of European supremacy in the world. It also showed that superior tactics as well as greater firepower and versatility by modern navies could propel hitherto inconsequential powers, such as Japan, onto the world stage. Russia's removal from the Far Eastern naval scene left the way free for Japan to dominate the northern

The nuclear-powered attack submarine USS *Scamp* (SSN-588) seen operating off the coast of Oahu, Hawaii in August 1961. The *Scamp* and her sisters of the *Skipjack* Class were the first nuclear submarines to incorporate the teardrop hull form. This helped them attain a submerged speed probably in excess of 30 knots. The *Skipjack* Class was the third class of nuclear attack submarine built for the US Navy.

A Seasprite antisubmarine helicopter prepares for takeoff from the guided missile destroyer USS *William Pratt* during a 1978 exercise.

Pacific, and therefore, inevitably, China, Korea and subsequently, the entire western Pacific.

This lesson was not lost on the Royal Navy, which was the backbone of the farflung British Empire. Any nation could easily challenge British maritime and commercial supremacy if it concentrated only a portion of its national will on the construction of modern ships. The challenge of Germany was paramount as Britain withdrew her fleet from American and Asian waters to concentrate her naval power in the North Sea. In addition, the race for a new class of battleship was introduced with the launching of *HMS Dreadnought* in 1906. Germany quickly began to construct her own dreadnoughts. By 1914 each nation had a formidable fleet of submarines, battleships and other craft.

Most naval personnel are proud of their ships, and there is a tendency to become so proud that one refuses to risk damage to one's prizes by sending them into battle. Such was the attitude of the Germans in 1914, but in order to break Britain's will to fight, the Imperial Navy was sent into the North Sea in 1916 to challenge the Royal Navy. Many millions of words have been written about who won the Battle of Jutland. Certainly the Germans sank more British tonnage than the British damage to the Imperial Fleet. But the Germans slunk back to their North Sea ports, seldom to venture out again. The challenge to British supremacy in the North Sea was met and matched, and the Germans resorted to submarine warfare to attack merchant shipping, Britain's imperial lifeline. At first British destroyers were unequal to the task of convoying materiel from North America, principally foodstuffs, and the entry of the United States into the war in April 1917 was the turning point in the war at sea, as both President Wilson and Prime Minister Lloyd George pointed out at the time. American destroyers convoyed goods part of the way across the Atlantic, and British destroyers protected shipping the rest of the way. The loss of the war at sea

by Germany in 1917 was the first step in the defeat of the Central Powers by the Entente Powers in World War I.

As Europe prepared for Round Two of their self-destructive pair of world conflicts, the lessons of the First World War were not lost on the men who prepared for the Second. Aircraft carriers, first lethargically introduced during the latter stages of World War I, were critical, for cruisers and destroyers as well as merchant vessels could be easily attacked from the skies. The combination of undersea warfare and aerial attack could devastate any surface navy. Therefore, Japan, the United States and Britain raced to build new fleets between the wars, while Nazi Germany concentrated on the construction of new, more modern and more lethal U-Boats than they ever had in World War I. When World War II broke out in 1939, and particularly after Germany gained the use of French submarine pens in June 1940, Britain was again challenged across the entire North Atlantic by the subs of Admirals Raeder and Doenitz.

However, it was in the Pacific that the greatest innovations in naval warfare took place. Aircraft launched from Imperial Japanese carriers opened the conflict in 1941 by wiping out most of the American surface fleet in the Pacific at Pearl Harbor. The Battles of the Coral Sea and Midway showed that the existence and sinking of aircraft carriers decided both battles. But if aircraft carriers made a war spread across thousands of miles of the world's largest ocean possible, the recapture of islands quickly overrun by the Japanese in the first six months of the war required newer, smaller and more maneuverable forces: strike craft. LSTs, LCTs, PT boats and other tiny vessels assaulted Guadalcanal, New Guinea, the Philippines, Okinawa and Iwo Jima once the larger craft had softened up the islands targeted for invasion. These strike craft, learning the lessons of the Pacific War even while it was in progress, were launched against European invasion sites, such as Salerno, Sicily and finally the Normandy and Provençal coasts in the D-Day and Anvil invasions of the summer of 1944. Battleships, once the pride of every navy, became increasingly obsolete, as submarines and destroyers dominated the war of the Atlantic while aircraft carriers and strike craft dominated the war in the Pacific.

After World War II, the American and British navies glowed in the aftermath of total victory while the Soviet Union built its modern navy in the 1960s and 1970s, concentrating on aircraft carriers and submarines as its principal weapons. By the late 1970s the Americans woke up to the fact that their naval power was being seriously challenged by the Soviets. The British had to wait until the Falklands Crisis of 1982 before the basic truths learned by generations of Britons in the past became clear to the new generation. Again, almost too late, as it was prior to the two world wars, the British and American peoples became aware of the vital importance of sea power and that their standard of living, indeed, their very existence as free peoples, depended to a large extent on their ability to exercise their naval power throughout the world.

In this major addition to the literature of war at sea, Antony Preston, Britain's leading naval historian, discusses the use of the six major classes of warships. Author of over a dozen major works, and sometime editor of *Navy International* and *Defence* magazines. He has appeared more recently on television as the authority on the Falklands War in both Britain and the United States. In this work he traces the modern history of battleships, destroyers, submarines, cruisers, aircraft carriers and strike craft, showing their changing roles during the naval conflicts of the 20th century. In each case, one fundamental truth is made plain. The role of various ships may change with the decades, but the importance of sea power for any commercial nation remains constant. *Warships of the World* is more than a study of naval forces. It is a continuing chapter in the history of the Anglo-American alliance. The liberty of the English-speaking peoples continues to depend on the maintenance of sea power.

Greenwich, Connecticut
December 1982

Battleships

Battleships

Previous page: A Sea Knight helicopter brings supplies to the battleship *New Jersey* during operations off Vietnam in 1968. As well as the helicopter pad, New Jersey was given new communications and electronic warfare equipment before being sent to Vietnam.
Page 9: The *New Mexico* leading the *Oklahoma, Nevada* and other US battleships in line ahead shortly after World War I.
Below: The *Colorado* saw service in many shore bombardment operations during World War II.

WOODEN WALLS AND IRONCLADS

No ship has ever achieved the aura of power of the battleship. Other warships have been more powerful, but throughout their short reign battleships were publicly equated with power. In days gone by national strength was reckoned in dreadnoughts and even as late as 1982, long after the battleships has ceased to count as a unit of strength, the US Navy is recommissioning a battleship to provide heavy-gun support.

To understand where it all started we have to go back five centuries to the time when it became feasible to mount heavy guns on board ships. A Frenchman called Descharges is traditionally regarded as the inventor of a method of cutting gunports in the lower deck and fitting them with hinged lids, about 1500. It was not long before a complete tier of guns was possible, and the first English man o'war with a complete lower gundeck appeared sometime after 1515. This transition was also being made in other navies of Europe, away from fighting with land-weapons between opposing groups of *men*. From now on the emphasis would be on damaging the enemy *ship*. Boarding and

hand-to-hand fighting would last for another four centuries but, from the sixteenth century, anti-ship weapons assumed ever more importance.

The following century saw greater discipline in tactics, with the ships fighting in a 'line of battle' to increase the strength of the 'battery' or 'broadside.' The need for more gunpower forced designers to add a second tier of guns, and by the early years of the seventeenth century three-deckers were being built. Gun design was improving, and some of the bewildering nomenclature of the previous century had been weeded out. Cannon

Above: Nelson falls mortally wounded on the deck of the *Victory* at Trafalgar.
Below: HMS *Brunswick* locked in combat with *L'Achille* and *Le Vengeur du Peuple* at the Glorious First of June, 1794.

became known as 42-pounders, demi-canon as 32-pounders, culverins as 18-pounders and demi-culverins as 9-pounders.

During the eighteenth century the steady growth in size and fighting power went on. The 1st Rate of 100 guns was expensive to build and man, and relatively few could be afforded. Thus a much greater number of three-decked 2nd Rates (90 to 98 guns) and two-decked 3rd Rates (64 to 84 guns) made up the balance of the fleet.

The line of development which had started in the early 1500s reached its peak at Trafalgar in 1805, when the main British Fleet under Vice-Admiral Lord Nelson met and destroyed a superior French–Spanish Fleet under Admiral Villeneuve. Nelson had three 100-gun ships, the *Victory*, *Royal Sovereign* and *Britannia* as well as two 98s while Villeneuve had the giant 130-gun *Santisima Trinidad*, the 112-gun *Santa Anna* and *Principe de Asturias* and the 100-gun *Rayo*. But the battle was decided by the 2nd and 3rd Rates, from the 98-gun *Dreadnought* and the 80-gun *Bucentaure* down to the elderly 64-gun *Agamemnon*, *Africa*, *Polyphemus* and *San Leandro*.

This slow majestic progress was interrupted by an innovation that was ultimately to destroy the wooden walls. In 1822 the French artilleryman Henri Paixhans published a treatise on how the French Navy could avenge its recent shattering defeat. He argued that France must find a technological answer, an 'equalizer' which would wipe out the British lead in warships. His solution was merely an adaptation of an old idea; the hollow cast-iron bomb (which had been around since the seventeenth

Above: A French two-deck ship of the line is dismasted during an engagement with the British in 1758.

century) could be redesigned to be fired from the 'long' ship-gun. If such a shell was to lodge in an enemy ship's timbers it would tear an enormous hole and probably start a fire. There was nothing that a contemporary sailor feared as much as fire, for with her mass of tarred cordage and dry timbers a wooden man o' war was likely to become a fiery death-trap.

Paixhans had little trouble in getting his ideas accepted, but instead of a fleet of small steamers with shell guns demolishing the Royal Navy, he had to endure the depressing sight of the British equipping their ships with his shell-gun. The French introduced their *canon-obusier* in 1824 and the British issued their first 8-inch shell guns two years later, but both navies continued to make solid-shot guns for the simple reason that they were more accurate over longer ranges. By the end of the 1830s most three-deckers carried about 60 per cent of the standard type to 40 per cent shell guns. The method of ignition was primitive but effective: the wooden fuze was ignited by the flash of the black powder charge as the gun fired, and a simple time-delay prevented detonation until (it was hoped) the shell struck the target.

The Royal Navy tried to propel a small sloop by steam as early as 1814 and seven years later the first paddle sloops were ordered from the Royal Dockyards. There was no attempt to build a steam powered battleship at this stage for one very simple reason: no new ones were laid down in the years after Waterloo, because so many hulls were already on the stocks. In the late 1820s a new class of 120-gun 1st Rates was begun, whose armament was to be six 68-pdrs and 114 32-pdrs. Even bigger ships followed, for the Royal Navy had a huge investment in wooden shipbuilding.

It was only a matter of time before steam power was installed in a big warship. The paddle wheel was only suited to small warships because it would interfere with too large a percentage of the broadside of guns. As early as May 1840 the Admiralty decided to build a screw steamship, the sloop *Rattler*. In November 1845 work started on converting the incomplete 3rd Rate *Ajax* into a 'screw blockship' and when she went to sea on 23 September 1846 she was the world's first seagoing steam battleship. As she and her sister *Edinburgh* carried only 58 guns they were theoretically inferior to other two-deckers but it was recognized that they could out-maneuver any sail-powered warship afloat and so they were given the vague designation of 'screw blockships.'

The pace now accelerated as both the French and British put steam engines into all new ships of the line and converted as many of the existing hulls as they could afford. By 1853, on the eve of the Crimean War, the screw propeller and the shell-gun were firmly established. The small actions of the 1840s had shown that shells were effective but it was not until November 1853, when a Russian squadron of six ships of the line and four smaller ships trapped and sank a Turkish squadron of eleven ships at Sinope, that the major navies took the threat to their ships seriously. What made Sinope important was that all the Turkish ships had been set on fire, and the fact that the British and French, with their large fleets of wooden sailing ships, had just let themselves be drawn into a war with the Russians.

The Anglo-French fleet was to experience the new technology when it tried to support the land attack on Sevastopol with a bombardment of the forts. On 17 October 1854 the lumbering two-deckers and three-deckers went into action, the sailing ships each being towed by a small steamer. After about an hour and a half the *Albion* had been set on fire twice and sustained severe casualties from four shell hits. She was towed out of action stern first, and then it was the turn of the *Queen* to be set on fire by red-hot shot and the frigate *Arethusa* to be knocked about. The French *Ville de Paris* also suffered from a mortar shell under the poop which caused many casualties, but apart from the *Albion* all damaged ships were ready for action next day.

Although the Allies had not suffered heavily they took energetic steps to make sure that the next engagement would be on more favorable terms. The French Navy's *Directeur du Matériel*'s immediate suggestion was to fill the hollow sides of a ship with cannon balls, but the Royal Navy came up with a more sensible idea in 4-inch wrought iron plating. Both countries had experimented with wrought iron warship hulls in the 1840s but had lost interest when it became obvious that iron splintered when struck by solid shot. But by 1854 the science of metallurgy had advanced and wrought iron now had sufficient

elasticity to be able to absorb the energy of a hit without shredding into lethal splinters.

The French and British collaborated on the hurried design of ten 'floating batteries,' with a single gun deck, 4-inch plating on the sides and a simple barque rig and a steam engine to drive them at four knots. They could hardly steam or sail adequately, but they were intended to be towed to their theater of operations. The French ships, called *Congréve*, *Devastation*, *Foudroyant*, *Lavé* and *Tonnant* were ordered shortly after the Sevastopol bombardment and were ready the following summer, and the British *Aetna*, *Glatton*, *Meteor*, *Thunder* and *Trusty* were ready in April 1855. A series of small delays prevented the British floating batteries from getting out to the Black Sea in time for a big assault on the forts at the mouths of the Dnieper and Bug Rivers, and so the honor for the first action fought by armor-plated ships goes to the French. On 17 October 1855 the five French batteries opened fire against Kinbourn Kosa, a group of five forts guarding the approaches to Odessa. An hour and a half later the forts surrendered, having seen that the ships were impervious to the rain of red-hot shot and shell. Despite being hit repeatedly the only casualties suffered were from splinters entering through the embrasures or the overhead hatches.

The Crimean War came to an end before the floating batteries could prove themselves in a massive assault on Kronstadt planned for the spring of 1856. With it ended very quickly that brief *entente* between Great Britain and France for almost immediately the government of Napoleon III embarked on a program to expand the Navy. By March 1858 preparations had been completed for building four 'ironclad' battleships and the Press was full of heady speculation about the end of British naval supremacy. The British, with the lessons of Sinope, Sevastopol and Kinbourn very much in mind, looked for some answer to the French threat.

The French were lucky in having the leading naval architect of the day, Dupuy de Lôme. He took the design of his outstanding steam two-decker *Napoleon*, built in 1850, and modified it to carry iron side plating capable of keeping out the newest 16-cm (6.5-in) explosive shell fired by the 50-pdr rifled muzzle loading gun. What resulted was hardly a beautiful ship, for *La Gloire* was squat and ugly, but she was soundly executed and fully justified the fame of being the world's first armored *seagoing*

Above: The British floating battery *Terror* seen just before her launch in 1856, too late for the Crimean War.

battleship. She was to be followed by two sisters, *L'Invincible* and *La Normandie* and a slightly larger ship, *La Couronne*.

For a while the British appeared to be paralyzed by the specter of resurgent French naval power, but behind the scenes there was feverish activity. During the summer of 1858 trials were carried out on test-samples of iron plates fitted to the side of the old ship of the line *Alfred* and two floating batteries. No fewer than a dozen shipyards and designers were asked to submit designs for ironclads, for the one trump card the Admiralty could play to beat the French was the ability of the British shipbuilding industry to outbuild the French. In November 1858 the Naval Estimates presented to Parliament included a sum for the construction of two armored 'frigates.'

Once mobilized the mighty British shipbuilding industry

Below: The stern of the first British ironclad HMS *Warrior* as seen in a modern model.

swung into action with its usual efficiency. The first ironclad, the *Warrior* was laid down at Blackwall on the River Thames in May 1859 and launched the following December, not long after the completion of *La Gloire*'s trials. The *Black Prince* was slightly later, being launched on the Clyde in February 1861, and the two ships entered service in October 1861 and September 1862 respectively. They were not only seagoing ironclads but also the world's first iron-hulled ironclads, for the British had already built a class of iron-hulled floating batteries in 1855–56 and in addition had the best-equipped iron shipbuilding resources. In any race of this sort the French could not compete for they lacked the industrial capacity. Their first iron-hulled ship, *La Couronne*, although laid down more than a year ahead of the *Warrior* was launched a month after her.

There were important advantages in using iron. Most important was the possibility of providing watertight bulkheads, but it also produced a much stiffer hull which could carry the weight of heavier guns as well as the armor. The hull could be made longer for speed without undue risk of 'hogging' and 'sagging' as wooden hulls were likely to. Another weakness of a wooden hull was the need to keep the gunports close together (because the hull had to be kept short), which made it easier for a hit from a large-caliber shot to punch in the armor plates and so disable several guns in the battery.

The appearance of the slim and graceful *Warrior* and *Black*

Left: The rather unprepossessing profile of the *Gloire*.
Above right: The dented turret of the *Monitor* after the Battle of Hampton Roads.
Right: Section through *Monitor*'s turret.
Below: The *Monitor* as seen in a contemporary engraving.

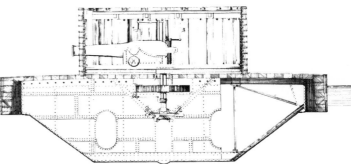

Prince in the Channel Squadron in 1862 did much to dispel the panic and helped to restore Anglo-French cordiality to some extent. The 'black snakes of the Channel' created a tremendous impression for unlike *La Gloire* they were remarkably handsome ships. Nor were they the only British ironclads. By 1866 another nine were completed, during which time the French Navy completed only two. Not only did French arsenals and shipyards lack the capacity for building rapidly but the demands for increased expenditure on the Army tended to siphon off the money which could have been spent on modern equipment for rolling armor plates and building steam machinery.

Neither *La Gloire* nor *Warrior* enjoyed their prestige for long. The following classes were even bigger and better protected, so big in fact that they became too unwieldy. Clearly the broadside ironclad could not develop much further and so designers turned to other means of providing the gunpower needed. One such idea was the cupola or turret, proposed in 1854 by John Ericsson, a Swedish engineer and also stumbled on in the Black Sea in 1855 by a Royal Navy captain, Cowper Coles. Coles had put a 32-pdr gun on a crude turntable on a raft, nicknamed the *Lady Nancy*, and in 1859 he produced plans for a gun-raft protected by an iron shield or cupola. The Navy liked his ideas and installed a prototype turret on the deck of the floating battery *Trusty* for firing trials in 1861. It was hit 33 times by heavy shells but continued to function. The Admiralty was convinced and drew up plans for turret-armed ironclads.

Events overtook the Admiralty's plans, for in 1861 the American Civil War broke out. The new Federal Navy's problems were acute, for by April 1861 it had not only lost the cream of its officers but also its main dockyard at Norfolk, Virginia. The Confederates found the new steam frigate *Merrimack*, lying

Above and top: The interior views of the monitor *Catskill*, an officer's cabin and the emergency steering position in the engine room.

engineer John Ericsson was on hand with his ideas for a turret-ship (last heard of in 1854). The Navy Department accepted his proposals promptly, and as speed was essential, Ericsson simplified the design as much as he could. His solution was the antithesis of the battery ship, an armored raft surmounted by a single revolving turret containing two 11-inch guns. Her name was to be *Monitor* 'that she might serve as a warning to others.'

The *Monitor* was commissioned on 25 February 1862, just four months after the contract had been signed. Even so she was nearly too late, for on the day she was due off Hampton Roads the *Merrimack* put to sea. The Confederate ironclad destroyed the wooden frigates *Cumberland* and *Congress* with apparent ease, showing just how helpless an unarmored sailing warship was against an ironclad.

Next morning the *Merrimack* reappeared, intent on finishing off the big screw frigate *Minnesota*, which had escaped destruction the previous day by running herself aground. At first she ignored the *Monitor* mistaking her for a water-tank when she was sighted alongside the *Minnesota*, but as soon as the 'cheese-box on a raft' opened fire with her 11-inch guns the Confederate ironclad switched targets and tried to dispose of this impudent intruder. Firing continued for about three and a half hours, the *Monitor* firing her guns every seven or eight minutes and the *Merrimack* taking 15 minutes for each broadside. The baffled Confederates eventually tried to ram but the little turret ship could turn in a sixth of the length needed by the clumsy *Merrimack*. When several attempts failed the *Merrimack* withdrew to her anchorage in the James River, and the Battle of Hampton Roads was over.

The two doughty opponents met again on 11 April but did not engage as Admiral Goldsborough had strict orders not to risk the *Monitor*. Just what might have happened if the *Monitor* had used a heavier charge than the scanty 15 pounds of powder allowed for her unproofed guns, or if the *Merrimack* had fired solid shot against her armor can only be guessed at, but the result of the action on 25 February confirmed the value of both armor plating and the revolving turret. Although often claimed to

burnt out and scuttled in the dockyard, but when the water-logged hulk was raised they were delighted to find that the machinery was still in good condition.

The problem faced by the Confederate Navy was the reverse of the position in the Crimean War; it was blockaded in its harbors by Union ships and under bombardment from land artillery. If the *Merrimack* could be turned into an armored battery she would be able to run the gauntlet of the Union artillery and smash her way through the unarmored blockading squadron and clear the approaches to the port.

By June 1861 work had started at Norfolk on rebuilding the ship, using railroad iron to build up a sloping casemate housing a battery of nine guns. Although renamed CSS *Virginia* she remained better known by her original name, and the work on her was completed by the early spring of 1862. The Federal authorities, aware of her existence, had in August 1861 authorized the construction of ironclads to match her but the problem remained of what to build. Fortunately the Swedish

21

have been the reason why other navies became enthusiastic, Hampton Roads merely provided public proof. Some days before the battle the Admiralty had in fact given approval to build two turret ships. Admiralty records mention their Lordships' pleasure at the news of Hampton Roads, for it meant that their decision was less likely to be publicly challenged.

In America there was understandable enthusiasm to build more and more *Monitors*, for the little ship gave her name to a new type. The Southern States could not match this with their primitive industries, but succeeded in building a second *Virginia* (to replace the *Merrimack* burned in May 1862) and the *Tennessee*. The *Virginia* was scuttled when Richmond was abandoned but the *Tennessee* fought Farragut's fleet at Mobile Bay in 1864, surrendering after being disabled by the monitor *Manhattan*. The monitors proved very useful on the big rivers but they were barely sweaworthy; the *Monitor* very nearly foundered on the way down to Hampton Roads and did actually founder in a gale off Cape Hatteras at the end of 1862, while the *Weehawken* foundered in 1865. Although much bigger monitors were built, culminating in the 4400-ton *Dictator* armed with two 15-inch guns, they were no substitute for a seagoing fleet. Anti-British feeling in the North ran high as long as sympathy for the Southern cause persisted in Britain, but wild talk of sending the monitor fleet to settle scores with John Bull was ludicrous for they could never have fought their guns in the Atlantic.

Although most navies built monitors of various kinds the British were already moving to the next step, an ocean-going turret ship. In 1866 they ordered the *Monarch*, an 8000-ton fully rigged ship armed with four 11-inch guns in twin Coles turrets. Ever since the Battle of Hampton Roads the inventor had demanded that a turret battleship should be built, but when he saw the *Monarch* he was still not satisfied. Being a gunnery officer he could not accept her high freeboard, and wanted the lowest possible freeboard to give a 360 degree arc of fire. The Admiralty supported the Chief Surveyor, Edward Reed, in his claim that it was impossible to reconcile Coles' ideas with adequate seakeeping and stability but they reckoned without public opinion. By carefully orchestrating Parliamentary and Press support Coles was able to persuade the First Lord to let him design a second turret ship, to be called HMS *Captain*.

Not unnaturally Edward Reed, widely regarded as one of the two greatest living naval architects, took it as a slur on his department's competence, especially as Coles had no technical qualifications. The Navy's attitude was that Coles would have a free hand to advise and consult with the builders, the Laird brothers, but the customary supervision of construction by Admiralty overseers would not be allowed. In such an atmosphere the *Captain* took shape, and when she was launched in March 1869 it was discovered that she was considerably overweight. Coles was not particularly perturbed and showed no inclination to reduce the great spread of canvas the ship was to carry. Finally she went to sea in January 1870, and to show official approval the First Lord of the Admiralty Sir Hugh Childers announced that his only son would sail in her as a midshipman.

All went well for the first three months and the ship's officers expressed great satisfaction with her. But suddenly on the night of 6 September 1870, while the Channel Squadron was beset by a gale, HMS *Captain* was swept over on her beam ends and then capsized. So rapid was the disaster than only seven out of the 473 men aboard escaped. Among those who went down with her were Captain Coles and the midshipman son of Hugh Childers.

In the uproar that followed a searching enquiry revealed that HMS *Captain* had foundered from the 'pressure of sail assisted by the heave of the sea.' Edward Reed, however, was amply vindicated when his *Monarch* proved an outstanding success, but what was really at stake was the need to take professional ship-designers seriously. The process was already moving slowly and the loss of the *Captain* did no more than hasten it, but 1870 marked the end of the first experimental phase in the evolution of the battleship.

Below: The *Roanoke*, the only US monitor built with three turrets. The monitors were not suitable for long ocean voyages.

SOVEREIGNS OF THE SEAS

The *Captain* disaster did nothing to slow up developments, and throughout the 1870s navies built a bewildering variety of types in an effort to find the best solution. The spur was the need to protect ships against the newest guns, for with metallurgy making rapid advances it was just as easy to improve guns as it was to improve armor. As early as 1853 the British had introduced a rifled gun, in which the shell was forced into the rifling by the explosion of the charge. Their worst drawback was the amount of 'windage' or the gap between the shell and barrel needed to allow the shell to be loaded, but they were cheap and simple to operate.

Breech-loading offered the chance to overcome windage and in 1859 William Armstrong demonstrated his system to the Admiralty. He used a removable breech-block to close the chamber behind the charge and then rammed it tight by means of a hollow screw, through which the shell and charge had already been passed. There was strong support from Press and Parliament once again and the Armstrong gun was adopted promptly the same year. But once again things went wrong, not as disastrously as with HMS *Captain*, but demonstrating just as clearly what happens when public pressure takes over from professional judgment.

The disaster was the bombardment of Kagoshima on 15 August 1863 when a British squadron tried to exact an indemnity from the Daimyo of Satsuma for the murder of an English merchant. The action was distinguished by a series of gun-accidents which showed that the Armstrong was unreliable. In an action lasting two hours 21 Armstrong guns fired 365 rounds and suffered an aggregate of 28 accidents, the worst being when a 7-inch gun in the flagship blew out its breech-block and concussed the entire gun crew.

The answer was to change to the French system of 'shunt rifling' and muzzle-loading, for the Royal Navy could not afford any more expensive experiments which might involve reequipping the entire fleet. The French themselves had decided to change to breech-loading but they had adopted a hinged threaded block, without the separate breech block which had caused all the problems in the Armstrong gun. The threaded block took so many turns to open and shut that the logical improvement was to cut away every sixth part of the threads; it needed only a sixth-turn to shut it and yet it retained the strength of the fully threaded block. Friedrich Krupp preferred to use a sliding block breech-loading system but all three systems, British, French and German now strengthened their gun barrels by shrinking hoops on them, as first proposed by Armstrong.

Guns now got much bigger. At the end of the Crimean War the biggest gun afloat was a 10-inch 84-pdr. Armstrong produced a 13-inch 600-pdr and at the end of the Civil War the monitor *Puritan* was going to receive two 20-inch Dahlgren guns. The breech-loaders also grew rapidly in size and weight; the 7-inch 110-pdr Armstrong weighed a mere 4 tons whereas the 13-inch 600-pdr weighed 22 tons, causing many more problems in handling. A whole variety of devices came into use to control the recoil of such monsters and steam and hydraulic training were developed for the mountings.

The French did not favor the turret, preferring to develop the *barbette*, a circular iron shield inside which the guns

Right: The forward 12-inch turret of the USS *Mississippi* pictured in 1908. The *Mississippi* carried two such turrets.
Below: A painting of the battleship USS *Iowa*, showing her as she would have appeared in 1898.

revolved. Its advantage was that it weighed less than the turret since the training machinery was only turning the guns rather than the whole mass of the armored turret. In turn this meant that guns could be carried higher above the waterline than in turret ships, and from the end of the 1860s a number of French ships were fitted with four single guns in barbettes disposed 'lozenge' fashion (one forward, one aft and two port and starboard amidships). The British found a different solution, in the 'central battery,' shortening the side armor in order to give heavier protection to a central 'casemate' amidships. This arrangement not only saved length but with recessed gunports allowed the guns to fire closer to the centerline. One of the weaknesses of the older broadside ironclads was this lack of end-on fire, and many expedients were adopted to provide bow- and stern-chase guns.

The biggest problem was lack of experience on which practical design ideas could be based. The Civil War was recognized to have been a special case never likely to recur, while the Crimean War had even less relevance. But on 20 July 1866 the Austrians and Italians fought off the Island of Lissa in the Adriatic, and this action was to have as much influence as Hampton Roads. Not only was it the first full fleet action fought in European waters since Trafalgar but also the first battle involving sea-going ironclads. The newly unified Italian state had joined Prussia in furthering Bismarck's plans to acquire part of the Austro-Hungarian Empire. The Austro-Hungarian Fleet under Rear-Admiral Wilhelm von Tegetthoff had only seven armored ships out of a total of 27, against Count Carlo Pellion de Persano's 12 out of a total of 34, but there was a vast difference in the standard of leadership and training. The Italians had spared no expense to create a new fleet, including a new turret ram, the *Affondatore*, and could bring 200 modern rifled guns into action aginst the 74 in Tegetthoff's fleet.

Below: HMS *Agincourt* was built with the unusual number of five masts but is seen here after two had been removed.

Faced with such opposition Tegetthoff could either avoid action or trust in superior seamanship and tactics. He chose the latter, knowing full well that Persano was an indecisive leader with poorly trained men. He ordered his ships to close the range so that the older muzzle-loaders could penetrate the Italians' armor and instructed them to ram enemy ships whenever possible, to throw the Italian battle-line into confusion: 'ironclads will dash at the enemy and sink him.' Tegetthoff's three divisions attacked in an arrowhead formation and achieved his primary objective by slipping through a gap in the Italian line. Although ramming proved almost impossible because of the clumsiness of the ships and the dense clouds of powder-smoke the attempts produced a fierce melée.

The decisive moment came when Tegetthoff in his flagship *Ferdinand Max* sighted the *Re d'Italia* through a gap in the smoke. The big Italian frigate had been disabled by a shell-hit in the rudder and could do nothing to escape her fate as the *Ferdinand Max* bore down on her. The iron spur under the forefoot struck the *Re d'Italia* full amidship and tore an enormous hole on the waterline. The *Ferdinand Max* then reversed her screws and pulled away, ripping an even larger hole. The doomed Italian ship sagged slowly over to starboard as hundreds of tons of water rushed into her hull, righted momentarily and then rolled the other way and capsized, taking 662 men with her. The only other casualty of the battle was the ironclad *Palestro*, which blew up after being set on fire by the *Ferdinand Max* early on, but the Italians had had enough. After a show of bravado by hoisting a signal for 'General Chase' Persano withdrew to Ancona and left the field to Tegetthoff.

The real lesson of Lissa was that poor maneuverability and inaccurate guns made it very difficult to sink ships in battle, but the world's navies seized on the ramming of the *Re d'Italia* as proof that the ram would be decisive. For another 30 years battleships would be built with massive reinforced stems for ramming tactics, achieving little apart from spectacular collisions with their squadron-mates. And yet we can now see

Above: HMS *Inflexible* tried to combine ahead and astern fire with a
small area of armor by mounting the two turrets *en echelon* amidships.
This arrangement was not successful.
Left: HMS *Devastation*, the most successful 1870s design.

that Lissa actually proved the opposite. Over and over again
ramming attempts by Tegetthoff's ships had been defeated, and
the solitary success had only been achieved because the victim
was unable to steer.

There was very little to help the designer in formulating
requirements, and a confused and contradictory battle like
Lissa was very little guidance. The two lessons learned, the
need for end-on fire and a strengthened ram bow, were the
wrong ones, but indirectly they proved a positive influence.
More emphasis was placed on handiness and inevitably the
revolving turret was vindicated as it offered the widest arcs
of fire. But there were to be many quaint compromise solutions
to the problem during the 1870s; turret rams, casemate ships,
box-battery ships and more of the monitor type. All of them
looked like the freaks that they were, often with huge exagge-
rated rams. There were ships with two turrets side by side on
the forecastle, turrets *en echelon* amidships and combinations
of central batteries and barbettes, in a bewildering profusion
of types. There was no war nor even a serious threat of a war (in
Europe at any rate) and this 'fleet of samples' was more a reflection of the industrial growth of Europe than any expression of
tactical doctrine.

Battleship design, with its need for even harder armor plate,
bigger forgings for guns and the most powerful machinery, made
heavy demands on technology. At first the British had dominated

the field, followed by the French, but before long both Germany
and Russia developed the capacity to build ironclads. For the
time being the other industrial giant, the United States, was
content to ignore these developments, as the aftermath of the
Civil War focussed energies on developing internal resources
rather than maritime power. There was also the understandable
tendency to assume that the large fleet of monitors was sufficient
investment in sea power for the time being. The magnitude of
that error would become apparent later, but without the threat
of a naval war to disturb the complacency of the politicians in
Washington there was little that anyone could have done to
change matters.

It was left to the British to show the way ahead. In 1869, while
the *Captain* was still fitting out and the *Monarch* had just gone
to sea, Parliament voted for three more large turret ships.
With the reputation of the US Navy's monitors standing very
high, Sir Edward Reed chose a low freeboard ship with two
large twin turrets protected by an armored 'breastwork' and
no sails of any sort. The arrival of the USS *Miantonomoh* at
Portsmouth in 1867 lent some credence to American claims
of the big monitors' seaworthiness but eyewitness accounts
testify to the hellish conditions aboard when she first arrived.
Then came the disaster of the *Captain*, a year after the keels of
the first two of the new turret ships were laid, and a storm of
protest arose. To settle doubts about their design the First Lord
of the Admiralty appointed a Committee on Designs. When
it met in January 1871 Reed had already resigned as Chief
Constructor, to take up a job in industry and so it had little
difficulty in recommending certain changes to the design of
the new ships. But what was much more important was the
recommendation that sail power should be abolished for large
warships. It was recognized that a 'very high degree of offensive
and defensive power' could not be combined with real efficiency
under sail. Although later ships were to carry masts and yards
they did so to save coal on long cruises by 'easing' the engines;
the age of fighting under sail was over.

HMS *Devastation* went to sea in the spring of 1873 under a
cloud of suspicion and pessimism never seen before or since.
An anonymous hand even placed a notice by the gangway on
the day of her commissioning: 'Letters for the *Captain* may
be posted here.' But she confounded the critics when she was

sent out into the Eastern Atlantic with the old broadside iron-clad *Agincourt* and the new central battery ship *Sultan*. She behaved as well or better in a variety of sea states and she was in no danger of capsizing. Naturally her low freeboard imposed some limitations, for it was impossible to prevent water from finding its way down below the forecastle, but there was no doubt that she could steam and fight in the Atlantic. She and her sister *Thunderer* also carried nearly 2000 tons of coal and could steam some 5000 miles at cruising speed. The lack of sail power gave the guns maximum arcs of fire ahead and on the beam and reduced the size of the crew considerably. Without the weight of heavy masts and standing rigging the hull was also steadier and a greater proportion of weight could be devoted to armor, coal and habitability.

In 1872 the Italian Navy laid down two large battleships, the *Duilio* and *Dandolo*, intended to have the thickest armor and the largest guns. The designer, Benedetto Brin had considerable talent and his first proposal for ships with four 38-ton 12.5-inch guns would have given the Italians two ships well able to deal with any opposition in the Mediterranean.

Problems only started when Armstrongs offered the Italian Navy its latest 60-ton 15-inch gun. No sooner was the offer accepted than Armstrongs raised the bidding with a 100-ton 17.7-inch, and Brin was told to alter his design accordingly. He was forced to recast the design entirely, choosing a 'raft body' underwater, on which the ship would be able to float if the remaining two-thirds of the ship were flooded. The basic concept was sound enough but the immense size of the guns made nonsense of it. The light hull could not take the stresses of continuous firing, and as the 100-tonners fired so slowly and inaccurately the ship could easily be riddled by shells from lighter and faster-firing guns before she could reply. The Italian answer to these criticisms was beguilingly simple: they knew that the *Duilio* and *Dandolo* would not show up too well in a ship-to-ship combat but if given sufficient speed they might be able to stay out of trouble.

In 1874 the official 'reply' to the Italian ships, HMS *Inflexible* was laid down. She resembled the *Duilio* in having two turrets *en echelon* amidships, a raft body and central 'citadel' protected by 24 inches of compound steel and iron armor. The Admiralty did not try to match the Armstrong 100-ton gun, preferring the Woolwich 80-ton 16-inch. This gun marked the peak of rifled muzzle-loader development. The

Above: The German turret ship *Friedrich der Grosse* (1877) carried four 10.2-inch guns and could steam at 14 knots.
Above right: HMS *Thunderer* in 1891 after being rearmed with breechloading 10-inch guns.
Below right: The *Andrea Doria* and her sisters were slight improvements on the *Duilo* and *Dandolo*.
Below: The armored corvette *Baden* and her sisters were built in 1875–83. They carried six 10.2-inch guns.

had thought out any task for her to perform, her sole claim to fame was to be commanded by Captain John Fisher at the bombardment of Alexandria in 1882. She fired 88 rounds and was hit by a single 10-inch shell which inflicted considerably less damage than the blast of her own 16-inch guns.

Undaunted by the shortcomings of the *Duilio* and *Dandolo*, Benedetto Brin went on to build much improved versions, the *Italia* and *Lepanto*. This time the guns were 103-ton 17-inch breech-loaders, and instead of two turrets he sited them in a heavily armored 'redoubt' resembling the French barbette system. They were technical masterpieces but were overtaken by two events, the introduction of high explosive shells and quick-firing guns. Now it was possible to inflict great damage on unarmored structures with comparatively light guns (mostly 4-inch to 6-inch). Ships like *Italia* and *Inflexible* would be put out of action even if they could not be sunk.

There was a revolution brewing in the world of big guns as well. In 1878 Sir Andrew Noble and Professor Abel began a series of experiments which proved that ballistics would be improved with slower-burning gunpowder. This in turn called for longer barrels to ensure that the powder burned for as long as possible. Other improvements were to make the gunpowder in large or 'pebble' grains and to chamber the breech to improve combustion. All this led to agitation for a return to breech-loading, for longer guns were very difficult to load from the muzzle-end. In 1875 Krupp had introduced his 'mantle-ring' system, shrinking a jacket over the breech-end to provide much

barrels were too long to be run back into the turret for loading and instead the muzzles were depressed below an armored 'glacis' on the deck to allow first the charge and then the shell to be rammed upwards.

Inflexible was a triumph of mechanical ingenuity, the first battleship lit by electricity, the first with anti-rolling tanks, the thickest armor ever, and above all, the first design to be thoroughly tested and discussed before building started. And yet she was a failure; because there was no Naval Staff nobody

greater strength than before, and no muzzle-loader could match the extra power. Excessive parsimony had prevented the Royal Navy from considering such innovations for the best part of a decade, but a growing awareness that the European navies could overtake the British loosened the purse strings at last.

In April 1879 a committee was set up to consider a revival of the breech-loader and at the same time a group of technicians went to Meppen to witness trials of the new Krupp guns. They returned full of enthusiasm and the Admiralty wasted no further time in ordering a new breech-loading 12-inch. The French interrupted screw method was adopted rather than the Krupp sliding breech, with several safety interlocks in an effort to prevent accidents.

Once the decision was made to revert to breech-loaders the Royal Navy planned a new series of ships to match the latest French barbette ships. The first was HMS *Collingwood* which used the layout of the *Devastation* with the four 12-inch breech-loaders in twin barbettes on the French style. The protection was limited to a short but thick belt on the waterline, closed at either end by a transverse bulkhead. The ends were left 'soft' or unarmored, on the assumption that as long as the central 'citadel' remained intact the ship would float with both ends flooded. Although her 12-inch guns looked somewhat less imposing than the older muzzle-loaders they were much more efficient and enhanced her neat, functional appearance. Five more improved *Collingwoods* were built, four with four new 30-ton 13.5-inch guns and one, HMS *Benbow*, with two 111-ton 16.25-inch guns. The decision to go for another 'monster gun' was a mistake, for with one round fired every 3–4 minutes the *Benbow* was less likely to score a hit than a ship armed with twice as many lighter guns.

Below: Sir William White's *Royal Sovereign* established the layout used for all British battleships up to the revolutionary *Dreadnought* design.

The 1880s and 1890s saw a remarkable upsurge of public interest in naval affairs, in Great Britain, Europe and the United States, with naval yearbooks and journals providing more information about warship designs, armaments and fleet strengths. The debates about design had hitherto been confined to the administration and technicians, except when a disaster brought the problems into the public arena, but from now until World War I respective naval strengths would be a matter of public concern. Newspapers and books bombarded their readers with information about trials of new guns and armor plates, and as all the underlying tensions came closer to the surface a note of strident nationalism pervaded it all. The closing years of the nineteenth century became the Age of the Battleship, with rival strengths reckoned in numbers of battleships, but little thought given to broader strategic and technical matters.

There was, for example, the question of the Whitehead torpedo, a self-propelled explosive device which could blow a hole in a ship's side. The Royal Navy had enthusiastically snapped up the invention in the early 1870s without thinking too hard about how best to use it. But, by the mid-1880s, small fast torpedo boats had been built in sufficient numbers to threaten any battleships trying to lie off an enemy harbor. This made any repetition of the classic blockade of the French Fleet by Cornwallis a thing of the past, and some supporters of the torpedo boat even dared to predict that the battleship had no future.

Despite these criticisms the 'Admiral' Class was chosen as the basis for a new class of big ships to be built under a massive program authorized by the 1889 Naval Defence Act. Growing public agitation about the alleged weaknesses of the Royal Navy had forced the Conservative Government's hand. Had the critics known, the British position was not as bad as they had assumed, for the French Chamber of Deputies had been told in 1886 that only ten battleships were ready to go to sea. Out of six ships started between 1878 and 1881 only one was nearing completion and another was less than 40 per cent complete after five years'

Above: SMS *Kurfurst Friedrich Wilhelm* (1893) saw service in the early months of WWI but was then laid up and her crew transferred to more modern ships.
Right: The USS *Illinois* (BB.7) seen being prepared for docking in January 1902.

work. The French still had most of their timber-hulled ironclads from the 1860s on the strength whereas such ships as HMS *Warrior* had virtually been pensioned off.

The new design, the *Royal Sovereign* Class, matched the scale of the program, with the freeboard which the 'Admirals' lacked. Seven were barbette ships, carrying their four 13.5-inch guns in open-topped mountings, but as a stop to the objections of the elderly First Sea Lord, Sir Arthur Hood, an eighth unit was built with turrets instead of barbettes. The case was finally proven; the *Hood* had less freeboard and so could never make the speed of her half-sisters in bad weather.

The impetus given by the Naval Defence Act was not lost, and the next class of nine ships, the *Majestics*, were even more impressive. The layout of the *Royal Sovereigns* was retained but

Below: The USS *Kearsarge* had her secondary guns mounted directly over her main armament – an unusual and unsuccessful arrangement. She is seen here in 1899.

the barbettes were given armored hoods – the term 'hooded barbette' eventually became 'turret' when the old pillbox-type had disappeared – and all the 6-inch guns were protected by armored casemates. The *Majestics* were even better-looking than the previous ships, so much so that the US Navy paid them the compliment of copying the look for their *Alabama* Class. It was not only the fighting qualities of the *Majestic* Class that amazed other navies; the lead-ship was built by Portsmouth Dockyard in under 22 months, a world record. In less than ten years the Royal Navy was strengthened by 16 first-class battleships, whereas France and Germany completed only 6, and Russia and the United States 4 each.

The French Navy went into comparative decline at the end of the century, partly because of the patent hopelessness of trying to outbuild the British, partly because of mischievous political meddling, but largely because of the influence of the 'Young School' or *Jeune Ecole*. There were influential naval officers who believed that torpedo boats had made the battleship obsolete and that destruction of commerce was a more certain way to beat the British than fighting their Fleet. But in place of the French appeared a much more dangerous rival, the German Navy. Starting from a coast defense force, its strength was built up by a series of Navy Acts intended to provide a firm basis for replacing obsolescent tonnage. Dreams of naval expansion pandered to nationalist sentiments in a way that mere totals of money could not. They also alarmed the British, who saw clearly that the enlarged German Navy could only threaten their own position. With jingoism and tension rampant in all the leading nations of Europe it was not the moment to start a naval arms race but Admiral Tirpitz could not see this. Protesting all the while that the new battleships were essential to protect German interests, he ordered 20 large battleships between 1890 and 1905. The argument was quite simply that battleships were a measure of national prestige, and as Germany was a strong industrial nation she needed a fleet of appropriate size. A second reason

Below: HMS *Caesar* of the *Majestic* Class, regarded as the best of
Sir William White's designs. She is seen in the standard Victorian
color scheme of black hull, white upperworks and buff funnels.
Far right, top: The monitor USS *Amphitrite* (1895) and her sisters
were totally unsuited for any but the shortest-range operations.

was Germany's desperate need for powerful allies; Tirpitz reasoned that a big enough fleet would make Germany a desirable ally.

The US Navy had expanded very little since 1866 for Congress refused consistently to sanction any major warships, on the grounds that battleships and big cruisers would lead to 'international adventures.' Far-sighted officers and administrators tried as early as 1874 to get some measure of new building put in hand but they were only able to get grudging permission to repair old monitors. To circumvent this they used money voted to repair five Civil War monitors to build five new ships. As material had to be ordered surreptitiously the work took from 17 to 22 years to complete.

The first battleships allowed to be built were the small 2nd class units *Texas* and *Maine* (the latter was first conceived as an armored cruiser) ordered in 1886. Four years later three battleships, *Indiana*, *Massachusetts* and *Oregon* were ordered, but with only 12 feet of freeboard and 400 tons of coal they were hardly fit for more than coastal defense. The next ship, the *Iowa* was hardly any better, and until the three *Alabama* Class were laid down in 1896–7 the US Navy could not boast a single battleship capable of facing the latest European models.

Russia was in a worse state than France, with a slow building rate and a tendency to pack too many features into a small hull. Recognition of some of the basic weaknesses led the Russians to seek French advice on design, and from them they acquired many theories of design. The Russian sailor and his officers were brave but lacked good professional training, while the innate corruption of the system made the task of reform hopeless.

To an outside observer the front-line navies at the end of the century appeared marvels of precision and smartness. There was as yet no suggestion that color-schemes should be chosen for anything but appearance, and the long lines of black hulls,

white upperworks and buff funnels impressed civilians. After 30 years of peace, 'spit and polish' had been given too much priority over such matters as gunnery and tactics, but we should not underestimate the seamanship and skills of late nineteenth century battleship captains. Gunnery was practised at no more than 4000 yards, little more than the extreme range of Nelson's 32-pounders at Trafalgar, but this was because irregular-burning powders produced a wide scatter of shots at extreme ranges. At a range of 7000 yards or more the only thing visible with the naked eye was a plume of smoke from the target's funnels and the 100-feet high splash of a 12-inch shell.

Much nonsense has been written about officers throwing shells overboard to avoid the tedium of gunnery drills, and the facts are that by the end of the century the front-line navies were all in a state of reasonable efficiency. But it was all to be made to look obsolescent by a veritable hurricane of change which was to transform them beyond recognition.

GUNNERY AND THE DREADNOU

The problem of all nineteenth century battleship-designers was that they were denied all but a few tantalizing fragments of experience. All their theories of gun layout and armor distribution rested on the experience of the Crimean War, Lissa and half a dozen minor actions. Not until 1904 did modern warships meet their equals, when the Japanese clashed with the Russians over which one was to dominate Manchuria. At the end of the war the Russian Pacific Fleet had been sunk at its moorings by long-range gunfire and the Baltic Fleet had been annihilated at the Battle of Tsushima in May 1905, the first full fleet action since Lissa.

The Japanese had deliberately courted war for they were determined to stop Russia from establishing a foothold in Manchuria. The powerful fortified base at Port Arthur was a constant thorn in their flesh and when it was announced that the Port Arthur fleet would be increased from seven to thirteen battleships by the end of 1905 the Japanese decided to strike first. They had only six modern battleships and it seemed foolish to wait until the Russian superiority was doubled.

On the night of 8 February 1904 ten destroyers attacked Port Arthur and damaged two battleships and a cruiser with torpedoes. This foretaste of Pearl Harbor gave the Japanese Fleet only a temporary advantage and a great fillip to their confidence. The Russians never gained the iniative thereafter, and when the energetic Admiral Makarov was drowned in his flagship *Petropavlovsk* after she had struck a mine, the fighting spirit of the Port Arthur squadron seemed to wither away. Not even the sinking of two Japanese battleships in a minefield tempted the Russians; an attempt to break out in August 1904 was the last sign of any activity and four months later 11-inch howitzers belonging to General Nogi's besieging army sank the surviving ships at their moorings.

Meanwhile the Russian Baltic Fleet had begun its incredible odyssey, steaming around the world to try to save Port Arthur. Vice-Admiral Rozhdestvenski's fleet ploughed on around the Cape of Good Hope and despite the dispiriting news of the surrender of Port Arthur continued its seven-month journey

The Russian battleship *Oslyabya* was sunk at Tsushima. This photograph gives a good impression of the high sides and tumble-home which were a feature of many late nineteenth century designs.

and approached the Japanese islands with the intention of either brushing past Admiral Togo's fleet to reach Vladivostok or bringing it to action and destroying it. With eight battleships, three coast defense ships, three big armored cruisers, six light cruisers and ten destroyers Rozhdestvenski seemed to have a powerful advantage over Togo's four battleships, seven armored cruisers and seven light cruisers. But Togo's ships could steam together at 15 knots whereas the Russians had a combined speed of only 12 knots and there was no comparison between the standards of training in the two fleets.

Early on the morning of 27 May 1905 Togo's scouts sighted the Baltic Fleet entering the Straits of Tsushima but it was noon before Togo decided to bring his big ships into action. The Russians were already in line ahead, the four modern ships leading, and Togo turned to port to bring his own line around on a course nearly parallel. The Russians replied with fierce but inaccurate fire at a range of about 6500 yards, and failed to prevent Togo from concentrating his fire against the head of the line. By 1400 the flagship *Kniaz Suvorov* was under heavy fire from several ships and Vice-Admiral Rozhdestvenski had been badly wounded by a shell-splinter. The Russian second division, comprising four older battleships, was under heavy fire from the Japanese armored cruisers and eventually the *Oslyabya* was reduced to a sinking condition by numerous hits.

The flagship drifted off from her consorts, shrouded in smoke from internal fires. A hit from a destroyer's torpedo failed to stop her and three hours later she was still fighting off attacks. At about 1730 a destroyer took off the badly wounded Admiral but still the smoke-blackened wreck fired her light guns and

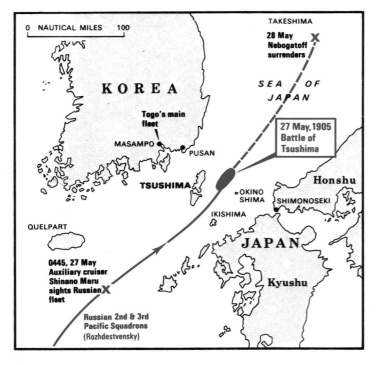

Above: Rozhdestvensky's advance to Tsushima.
Below: The 12,900 ton *Tsarevitch*, sister ship of the *Borodino*.

kept the Japanese destroyers and torpedo boats at bay. Finally at 1920 a division of torpedo boats scored two or three hits and ended the agony; the *Kniaz Suvorov* rolled over on her side and went down with all 928 officers and men.

Meanwhile the *Borodino* led the survivors of the battleline in a forlorn attempt to break out of the trap. At about the same time as the sinking of the flagship she was set on fire and her magazines blew up. The *Alexander III* had already capsized after repeated hits from 12-inch shells, leaving only the *Orel* and a handful of older ships circling aimlessly. The Japanese steamed around them firing at will, hampered only by the dense clouds of smoke. When the sun rose next morning the *Orel* and the other survivors could do nothing more and so they surrendered. The only ships to escape were a few which had chosen internment in neutral ports. It was the first complete victory since Trafalgar, the tactician's dream of a 'battle of annihilation.' Japan suddenly became a world power and the Russians were reduced (albeit temporarily) to second-class status.

There were many lessons to be learned from Tsushima, but as always many wrong conclusions were drawn. The outstanding feature to most commentators was the 'immense' range at which fire had been opened, 7000 yards instead of half that distance, as had been customary. However, all but a few observers failed to notice that Japanese gunnery had been rapid rather than accurate and only when the range came down considerably and the target had been disabled did the number of hits start to increase.

Another popular misconception was the psychological effect of high-explosive or 'common' shells exploding. Many naval observers claimed that the concussion alone would demoralize an enemy and even advocated using them in place of armor-piercing shells. Not for another 11 years would it be rediscovered that superficial damage does not sink ships, and only penetration below the waterline or a hit in a magazine can sink a ship quickly. Another point overlooked was that the aggressive tactics used so successfully by the Japanese depended largely on the slow speed of the Russians and their inability to maneuver in unison.

The surrendered Russian ships and those raised in Port Arthur after the capture of the fortress yielded much valuable information, and even the Japanese ships damaged in action showed several shortcomings in design. British technical experts were allowed to inspect some of the ships in Japanese dockyards and the reports drew attention to the need for better pumping arrangements to prevent progressive flooding. Another fault which came to light was the poor quality of the Japanese armor-piercing shell; its Shimose burster was so sensitive that it detonated the shell when it struck the armor, rather than after penetration. The defect had been spotted earlier and was supposed to have been rectified but many of the Tsushima prizes showed that Japanese shells had burst outside the armor.

The excellent work done by the Japanese armored cruisers obscured the fact that they had been dealing with slow and weakly protected old battleships. A modern armored cruiser was in many ways superior to some older battleships and Admiral Kamimura's big cruisers had done sterling work against Rozhdestvenski's second and third divisions, composed of ships inferior in almost every aspect. It is doubtful if they would have had such a free hand if the Russian battleline had been properly screened by a mixed force of destroyers and cruisers.

The main reason for paying too little attention to the lessons of Tsushima was the conviction held by the major navies that they were already moving into a new era of technology. Certainly the ships engaged at Tsushima were obsolescent in comparison with the latest battleships on the drawing board in Britain, Germany and the United States and so it was understandable that less attention was paid to their behavior in battle. Many of the new concepts were apparently vindicated by Tsushima and the minor details were dismissed as irrelevant; unfortunately it was these 'minor' details which in the long run caused more trouble than anything else.

The new ideas were basically connected with the need to hit at longer range. Improvements in powder had already made it possible to increase the length of guns and so improve their ballistics, but at the end of the century there was another technological change, which went almost unnoticed.

The torpedo had been in service since 1870 but while it had a range of only 800 yards at 30 knots it held very few terrors for battleships on the high seas. The introduction of the heater system, however, pushed up range enormously to 3000 yards and more. This corresponded roughly to contemporary battle-ranges, making it necessary for the first time to open fire at much longer ranges. This effect on battle tactics is very rarely mentioned in connection with the sudden increase in battle ranges which took place in all leading navies at the turn of the century and yet it was by far the most important factor. The only drawback was that contemporary gunnery training methods and fire control lagged far behind and the first attempts to fire at longer ranges were disappointing.

Vital reforms in training were needed to push up the Royal Navy's average performance dramatically. There were no radar sets and only comparatively crude optical rangefinders so there was only one way to range on a distant target; spotting the shell-splashes of each salvo. With a battleship firing her four 12-inch guns every 2–3 minutes it was clearly difficult to range on a target if either or both ships were moving at high speed. It was also very hard to distinguish the splash made by a 6-inch shell from a 12-inch at great distances since both shells made very large splashes.

The first solution was to strengthen the main armament by

Right: Plan of the early phase of the Battle of Tsushima.
Below: The Japanese *Hatsuse* seen in 1901. She was sunk by a Russian mine in May 1904.

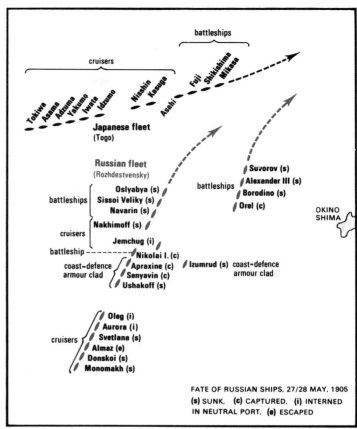

FATE OF RUSSIAN SHIPS, 27/28 MAY, 1905
(s) SUNK, (c) CAPTURED, (i) INTERNED
IN NEUTRAL PORT, (e) ESCAPED

Above: Admiral Togo, victor at Tsushima.
Below: Togo's flagship *Mikasa* was the newest Japanese battleship and resembled contemporary British designs with twin funnels and casemated secondary armament.

installing an 'intermediate' battery of guns – these ranged from 6.7-inch in German ships to 7-inch and 8-inch in US ships, and finally in 1901 the British followed the trend by putting 9.2-inch in the *King Edward VII* Class. This caused more headaches because the shell-splash was even harder to distinguish from a 12-inch and because the blast from such large guns tended to make it hard to man searchlights and light guns nearby. The British went one better in the *Lord Nelson* and *Agamemnon*, omitting all the 6-inch guns and increasing the secondary armament to ten 9.2-inch but the Americans went even further ordering two ships with eight 12-inch guns and no intermediate guns of any sort.

This was the best solution of all. With four twin turrets a battleship could fire salvos from alternate guns, keeping up a good rate of fire to compensate for the 'rate of change' in relative positions. Four shells in a salvo offered a reasonable chance of hitting, provided the salvo was 'bracketed' around the target. The two ships, the USS *Michigan* and *South Carolina*, were given a most logical arrangement of guns, four twin turrets on the centerline, two forward and two aft with No 2 and No 3 superimposed to fire over No 1 and No 4 respectively. Quite by chance the 1903 edition of *Jane's Fighting Ships* published an article by the Italian designer General Cuniberti, proposing an 'ideal ship for the British Navy' armed with twelve 12-inch guns, protected by 12-inch armor and steaming at 23 knots.

The decision to order the two American ships in 1903, coming on top of the increase in torpedo-range and the recommendations of gunnery experts had considerably more influence on the British Admiralty than a sketch design in *Jane's*. Determined not to be left behind, in total secrecy the British designed a revolutionary new battleship to be called *Dreadnought* and hoped to be able to use their superior shipbuilding capacity to regain the lead. The leading influence in this plan was the new First Sea Lord, Sir John Fisher, who wished to enlarge the Royal Navy to meet the challenge from the rapidly growing German Navy. He followed the American lead in restricting the secondary armament to a battery of light guns to fight off torpedo craft but he went much further in adopting the new steam turbine in place of the old reciprocating engines.

The argument in favor of the turbine really rested on power

Above: The *Shikishima* and her sister *Hatsuse* were built in Britain. She survived as a training hulk until 1947.

output. True, reciprocating engines had once been run in conditions which made the engine room a 'cross between an inferno and a snipe marsh' but they were now economical and clean thanks to forced lubrication and balanced crankshafts. The real problem was that any major increase of power to give higher speed (say 3 knots) would need nearly 50 per cent more power, and such an increase would increase the volume of the machinery enormously. Fortunately the British were in the lead of turbine development, having put the Parsons turbine in four destroyers and a light cruiser. The Cunard line was about to instal Parsons turbines in a big transatlantic liner and the Engineer-in-Chief was confident that the *Dreadnought* could reach 21 knots; three knots more than the *Lord Nelson*.

To pull together all the diverse strands Fisher appointed a very highly qualified Committee on Designs, whose terms of reference were to consider the design of a battleship armed with 12-inch guns and anti-torpedo boat armament, no intermediate guns, and 21 knots' speed and 'adequate' armor. From the first meeting on 3 January 1905 it was clear that Fisher had already decided what sort he wanted, and there was very little real discussion about alternatives. Yet Fisher seems to have had little idea of the implications of long-range gunnery as he still maintained that hits at 6000 yards and more would only be obtained by firing single shots slowly. Several arrangements of guns were considered in an attempt to get six twin 12-inch but in each case size and cost proved prohibitive. Finally design 'H' was accepted, and reciprocating engines were replaced by turbines at the last minute. When the Committee handed in its report on 22 February it had finalized the most revolutionary warship design since the *Warrior* in just seven weeks.

There were surprisingly few mistakes for such a hurriedly designed ship. Siting the boats between the two funnels meant that the masthead control platform stood directly over the fore-funnel and was usually blanketed by smoke when the ship steamed at full speed. Political pressure to keep size down elimi-

nated a strake of 8-inch side armor above the main 11-inch belt which had been provided in the *Lord Nelson*, making the new ship vulnerable to shellfire when the side belt was immersed at maximum draught. Against these criticisms she had several minor innovations and there was much internal weight saving. As it was intended to build the ship as quickly as possible structures were kept simple. The variety of steel sections was kept to the minimum and wherever possible standard-sized plates were used. Finally a large amount of material was prepared in advance and the four 12-inch turrets already building for the *Lord Nelson* and *Agamemnon* were requisitioned.

With such elaborate attempts to cut down building time it was to be expected that the new battleship would be built in record time, but even so the rate of construction was staggering and it constitutes a record which has never been broken. The keel was laid on Monday 2 October 1905 and only a week later the main deck beams were in place. By the end of December the hull was almost complete and she was launched and christened *Dreadnought* on 10 February 1906. Amid a fanfare of publicity she was credited with completion on 3 October, 366 days after keel-laying but these were only 'basin trials' and the *Dreadnought* was not actually ready to go to sea until December. The results were a great credit to the designers and the builders for the turbines gave virtually no trouble and the hull suffered no ill effects from the concussion of such a large number of guns.

The *Dreadnought* put the naval world in a ferment. Although only a logical response to tactical and technical pressures she was immediately seen as a ship which must be copied. The German *Marineamt* was taken completely unawares by her speed of construction and the massive jump in fighting power, and ordered a halt to battleship construction to give their designers time to absorb the new ideas. In the prevailing Anglo-

German tension the newspapers proclaimed that henceforward all comparisons of naval strength must be in 'dreadnoughts' as the 'pre-dreadnoughts' had been made obsolescent. This was nonsense, for the *Dreadnought* was simply a more efficient battleship and would in some circumstances have been at a disadvantage if faced by two smaller ships. But in the age of rampant 'navalism' the British Navy League and the German *Flottenverein* did not bother their heads with such hair-splitting. Nevertheless the arms race between Britain and Germany was given a tremendous fillip, for instead of the Royal Navy's 40 older battleships ranged against 20 German ships of smaller size and weaker armament there was now a margin of only one.

Fisher's Committee on Designs also had to consider the design of a new armored cruiser. As soon as the broad outlines of the *Dreadnought* were settled the Committee started to examine sketch designs but this was like no cruiser yet seen, with 12-inch guns in place of the 9.2-inch carried by the previous *Minotaur*

Class. The design chosen bore a strong resemblance to the *Dreadnought* but had nearly double the horsepower to provide 25 knots. Even so this massive increase in power was only possible because the armor-scale was to be the same as the *Minotaur*'s 6-inch side armor, and only four twin 12-inch turrets were to be mounted instead of five. These were the new 'dreadnought armored cruisers' *Invincible*, *Inflexible* and *Indomitable*, destined to provoke even more controversy than HMS *Dreadnought*. On a displacement of nearly 17,000 tons and armed with eight 12-inch guns there was a natural tendency to equate them with battleships and they were soon unofficially dubbed 'battleship cruisers' and finally in 1912 'battlecruisers.'

The problem was that their proper role was never worked out. Internally they showed very little difference from the *Minotaur* Class, and they were in no sense fast battleships. But Fisher had been greatly impressed by the success of the Japanese armored cruisers at Tsushima and wanted ships which could reconnoiter

Above: The *Nassau* Class dreadnought *Westfalen*.

for the battle fleet, pushing past any small cruisers which tried to stand in their way. For this purpose the 12-inch guns made sense as they would allow the big cruiser to get close enough to the enemy battle-line to count numbers and estimate course and speed. Such a ship could not be dealt with easily by small cruisers and in the closing stages of a fleet action would also be able to swoop on crippled battleships. So far so good, but in the second role of the armored cruiser, protection of commerce, the 12-inch guns were far too big and slow-firing to be of use against small fast moving targets. The new type was therefore a big and expensive solution to that problem. Fisher maintained that the *Invincible* was fast enough to catch anything smaller or escape from anything more powerful, but this presupposed that no other navy had similar ships.

The real weakness of the battlecruiser was that its heavy armament lent it a spurious 'capital' rank, and an admiral would always be tempted to use it to reinforce his battleships. In fact

within a year or two of their completion the term 'capital ship' was introduced to cover both battleships and battlecruisers. The wide disparity between the Russian and Japanese fleets at Tsushima was overlooked, and nobody seems to have thought of what might have happened to Admiral Kamimura's armored cruisers if they had been opposed by a better trained enemy. A ship with a 6-inch armor belt would be vulnerable if she attempted to fight a modern battleship on equal terms, but Fisher airily dismissed this question by saying that 'Speed is Armor.' In one sense that dictum was perfectly valid, but only if the battlecruiser used her superior speed to stay out of trouble. A fast battleship would have been the ideal means of gaining a tactical advantage in battle but a 25-knot ship protected with 12-inch armor would have had to be 50 per cent bigger, and this was not politically or financially acceptable.

Above, above left and below: Four views of the *Dreadnought* under construction. Far left, 2 October 1905, some keel plates and frames already in position. Above left, 28 October, less than one month later, the armored deck being laid. Above, 11 August 1906, nearly complete. Below, mid-February 1906, shortly after launch with funnels but no turrets.

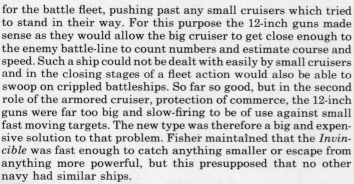

The Germans replied to both the *Dreadnought* and the *Invincible*, the former with the 20,000-ton *Nassau* Class and the latter with the 19,000-ton *Von der Tann*. The battleships were not an outstanding design, quite well protected but carrying their six 11-inch guns in a cramped arrangement of centerline and wing turrets. The new battlecruisers were a major improvement over the *Invincible*, with good protection and layout. The German designers got closer to the ideal of the fast battleship because they were prepared to sacrifice some speed and gunpower to provide more armor; the 11-inch gun was retained to allow 8-inch armor and the extra tonnage was used to provide better protection against torpedoes.

The British relied on their superior shipbuilding capacity to increase their lead over the Germans, and deliberately made no major alterations to the succeeding classes of dreadnoughts in order to avoid delays. In this way they had seven dreadnoughts of nearly identical design in service by early 1910, *Dreadnought* herself, three *Bellerophon* Class and three *St Vincent* Class, as well as three *Invincible* Class battlecruisers. In the same period

Below right: The stokehold of a British dreadnought. Normally it would be crowded with stokers sweating to feed the fireboxes.
Below: The *Thüringen* of the German *Helgoland* Class. Built 1908–12, this class carried twelve 12-inch guns.

the German Navy commissioned four *Nassau* Class and the *Von der Tann* was still completing. Even the next three British dreadnoughts, the *Neptune* and the two *Colossus* Class and the three *Indefatigable* Class battlecruisers were very similar to their prototypes apart from a modified layout of guns to improve their arcs of fire. In their second class of dreadnoughts, the *Helgoland* Class the Germans decided to adopt a 12-inch gun to match the British gunpower but the British had already decided to put a 13.5-inch gun into the *Orion* Class of 1909.

The race was now an open one, with each class of ship intended to match the latest on the other side of the North Sea. It was useless for the diplomats to try to negotiate any 'holiday' to slow down the tempo of this arms race, for the answer was always 'national survival is at stake.' The cost of a dreadnought at £1–£2 million sounds absurdly cheap today, but in modern terms it represents at least 100 times that figure.

The building of dreadnoughts can be equated with the space program in the 1960s and 1970s, in the sense that it fuelled a crucial area of economic growth and demanded the very best

of contemporary technology, and was also inextricably linked with national prestige. A battleship provided work in the shipyards and in the steelworks and gun foundries of the nation. Heavy engineering was still the motor force of industrial expansion and the battleship's needs for better armor plate, shells, guns and machinery all stretched various sciences to the limit.

The last chance to effect a reconciliation between German and British interests probably came in 1908. The architect of German naval expansion, Admiral Tirpitz, had successfully fought for his Navy Laws back in the 1890s, legislation which provided for regular replacement of obsolete tonnage instead of the annual haggling between the Navy and Treasury and Parliament, such as went on in Britain. In this Tirpitz was only doing his duty towards his country, to prevent later governments from hamstringing a long-term program by neglect or sudden whims. But by 1908 the small ineffective coast defense ships had been replaced by ocean-going battleships clearly capable of fighting their opposite numbers in the Royal Navy, and the British did not like the implications. In 1908 Tirpitz used a loophole in the current Navy Law to make a major increase in strength to the German Navy; a provision for replacing eight *grosse Kreuzer* (large or armored cruisers) was interpreted as permitting the building of eight battlecruisers. Although the precedent had been established when Fisher referred to the *Invincibles* as 'dreadnought armored cruisers,' the German move came at a time when German naval expansion was under particularly close scrutiny in Britain. The Liberal government was under strong pressure from its Radical wing to reduce 'bloated armaments' but equally torn by fear of losing popular support if it allowed the Royal Navy to be overtaken by the German Navy as a result of unilateral disarmament. There was also the fear of industrial unrest if the tempo of construction should slacken. In Germany too, the situation was not straightforward as the military hierarchy was constantly worried by the threat of a Socialist majority in the Reichstag.

The *Dreadnought* did not cause the First World War but she and her successors were an integral part of the last decade of the old order that passed away in 1914. They were only a symptom of the fever in the veins of Europe, not the fever itself, but there can be no doubt that the endless comparisons of strength and the forecasts of future trends inflamed public opinion and played on deep-rooted fears. The British navalists' slogan, 'We Want Eight and We Won't Wait' expressed the fears and hopes of xenophobes in all the major maritime nations.

READY FOR WAR

The outbreak of war in August 1914 came as something of an anti-climax to the vast fleets which both sides had created. The Germans lay secure behind thick minefields and the guns of the Heligoland fortress while the British battle squadrons had been sent to a pre-arranged rendezvous in the Orkneys, the huge natural harbor of Scapa Flow.

Moving the Home Fleet, given a more ancient and resounding name, the Grand Fleet, on the outbreak of war from its peacetime southern bases to Scapa Flow was a mighty task of logistics and planning. Fortunately July 1914 had seen an experimental full mobilization of the whole fleet to test the arrangements for calling up reservists, and when the First Lord of the Admiralty, Winston Churchill, prudently cancelled leave because of the crisis following the Sarajevo murders virtually the whole strength of the Royal Navy in home waters was ready and fully armed.

Although the British showed none of the recklessness which German plans had counted on, the first use of their capital ships was a piece of opportunism which amply justified the risks taken. On 28 August 1914 a force of light cruisers and destroyers pushed into the Heligoland Bight to attack the German outposts, and ran into stiff opposition from light cruisers. Vice-Admiral Sir David Beatty and four battlecruisers were outside the Bight waiting to cover the withdrawal, but when he heard that the British forces were likely to be overwhelmed he took the *Lion*, *Tiger*, *Queen Mary* and *Princess Royal* in at high speed, ignoring the threat from U-Boats and minefields. The arrival of these powerful ships brought the action to a dramatic end when their 13.5-inch guns sank the light cruisers, *Ariadne* and *Köln*, turning the tables on the Germans and extricating the British light cruisers and destroyers.

In the Mediterranean things went badly, when, by a series of misunderstandings, the German battlecruiser *Goeben* escaped from two of the Mediterranean Fleet's battlecruisers, the *Indomitable* and *Indefatigable*. The *Goeben* and her escorting light cruiser *Breslau* eluded their pursuers and their arrival at the Dardanelles helped to force Turkey from her uneasy neutrality into the arms of the Central Powers. The sinking of Rear-Admiral Cradock's two old armored cruisers off Coronel by a

German squadron under Vice-Admiral Spee on 1 November 1914 led to a swift counterstroke. Three days later Vice-Admiral Sturdee hoisted his flag in the battlecruiser *Invincible* and she and her sister *Inflexible* left Cromarty Firth to go south to Devonport to take on stores. After only a week the two battle-cruisers left for South America, arriving at Port Stanley in the Falkland Islands on 7 December. There they found the old battleship *Canopus* and a scratch force of cruisers under Rear-Admiral Stoddart.

The two big ships immediately started the arduous task of coaling and next morning, while they were still engaged on the task, lookouts sighted two German cruisers approaching Port Stanley. The *Canopus* had been put aground on a mud flat to provide a steady gun-platform and soon she was able to open fire to deter the attackers from any attempt to pick off the British ships as they left the harbor. Once the battlecruisers worked their way clear of the harbor the fate of the German squadron was sealed. It was the job for which the battlecruisers had been designed, and as the armored cruisers *Scharnhorst* and *Gneise-nau* had not been docked for some time they were bound to be overtaken sooner or later. Sturdee knew this and settled down to a long stern chase, the two battlecruisers belching clouds of coal smoke as they worked up to full speed. Shortly before 1300 the first shots were fired at 16,000 yards. Spee gallantly hauled his flagship and her consort around to give battle and at the same time cover the flight of his three light cruisers, but with four British cruisers in company their freedom would be short-

Above: The old French battleship *Charlemagne* served in the Dardanelles campaign, and for the rest of the war in the Mediterranean.
Above left: Polishing the guns on a German dreadnought.

lived. As the range came down the shooting steadied, and even though both battlecruisers were hit by German shells of all calibers they suffered only slight damage. Both *Scharnhorst* and *Gneisenau* sank after a hopelessly one-sided fight.

Meanwhile the Grand Fleet was learning to live with the soul-destroying routine of life at Scapa Flow. On October 1914 there was a submarine scare in the Flow itself when one of the patrolling destroyers thought she sighted a periscope. Immediately the C-in-C Admiral Sir John Jellicoe ordered the Grand Fleet to be dispersed to a series of temporary bases in Northern Ireland and the west coast of Scotland until permanent net defences and minefields could be provided. For an anxious month the exit to the Atlantic was unguarded but the High Seas Fleet was not inclined to take advantage. Instead Admiral Hipper was instructed to lead his battlecruisers on a raid across the North Sea to bombard Yarmouth in November 1914, followed by a similar bombardment of the Yorkshire coast the following month. The idea behind these pinprick raids was to force the British to divide their fleet and so permit the High Seas Fleet to pounce on a weaker portion of it and fight at favorable odds. It worked, but only partially, to the extent that public outcry forced the Admiralty to move Beatty's battlecruisers from Scapa Flow to Rosyth, where they were better placed to intercept such raids.

Intelligence of a similar raid led the Admiralty to order the Grand Fleet battleships and the Rosyth battlecruisers to meet off the Dogger Bank. This time a light cruiser sighted Hipper's battlecruisers and the result was the brief skirmish known as the Battle of the Dogger Bank, on 24 January 1915. In a hectic stern-chase the flagship *Lion*, the *Tiger*, *Princess Royal*, *New Zealand* and *Indomitable* slowly overhauled Hipper's flagship *Seydlitz*, the *Moltke* and *Derfflinger* and the armored cruiser *Blücher*. The full weight of British fire disabled the *Blücher* bringing up the rear but as a result of a signalling error the British ships halted the chase to concentrate on the sinking *Blücher* although the other German ships were being caught at that time.

The mix-up came at the moment when the *Lion* was badly hit by German gunfire. In all she was hit by 17 shells, one of which burst on the waterline and caused extensive flooding. Although this was brought under control the ship listed to port and slowed down, until finally all light and power failed, bringing the ship to a dead stop. Beatty transferred his flag as quickly as he could but by the time he had resumed control of the action Hipper's

Above: Predreadnoughts of the US Atlantic Fleet in 1917.
Below: The German battlecruiser *Lützow*.

Above: A fine view of the French predreadnought *Saint Louis* showing the pronounced tumble-home favored by French designers. *Saint Louis* served at the Dardanelles.
Below: The *Suffren* (completed 1903) was heavily damaged in March 1915 by Turkish gunfire and sunk in November 1916 by a U-Boat.

ships were drawing out of range and it was hopeless to continue the pursuit. The *Indomitable* took the crippled *Lion* in tow and the whole force returned to Rosyth. The *Blücher* had been sunk but a magnificent opportunity had been wasted.

The adventures of the *Goeben* merit a book to themselves. She had propelled a reluctant Turkey into war with Russia by bombarding Sevastopol at the end of October 1914, despite being nominally Turkish-manned as the *Yawuz Sultan e Selim*. On 18 November she fought a brief action against the Black Sea Fleet, hitting the *Evstafi* four times and receiving one hit in return before escaping in fog. Then on 26 December 1914 she struck two Russian mines off the Bosphorus and this damage prevented her from playing a more prominent part in fending off the Allied attacks in March 1915. On 10 May she met the Black Sea Fleet again, and this time the Russians did much better. The *Evstafi* hit the *Goeben* three times at the creditable range of 16,000–17,500 yards. On 8 January 1916 she met the new dreadnought *Imperatritsa Ekaterina* and was considerably discomforted to find that the Russian 12-inch guns could elevate to 25 degrees and range out to 28,000 yards.

Shortage of coal kept the *Goeben* in harbor from October 1916 so that she could not take advantage of the declining morale of the Russian Fleet. Not until 20 January 1918 did she venture forth again, this time to strike at the British forces guarding the exit to the Dardanelles. At Imbros she disposed of the monitors *Raglan* and *M.28* with little difficulty but when she and the *Breslau* headed for Mudros both ships struck mines. For the *Goeben* it was the second mine, for she had been slightly damaged by one just after leaving the Dardanelles, but then *Breslau* struck four more and sank. The *Goeben* tried to re-enter the Straits but struck a third mine. She was now being bombed from the air by British aircraft and in the confusion she ran aground off Nagara Point at 15 knots. There she lay for six days while more bombing raids were made on her until finally the old battleship *Torgud Reis* and two tugs came down the Straits to get her afloat again. The bombs were too light to inflict any damage but the mine damage was not fully repaired until long after the war, and she was effectively put out of action until the Armistice.

When the Allies became involved in Greek affairs in 1916 the battleships were withdrawn to Salonika and subsequently four British pre-dreadnoughts were sent to bolster the Italian Fleet at Taranto. The Italians, uneasy at having parity with the Austro-Hungarian Fleet, demanded dreadnoughts but the War Council treated this request with some acerbity. Italians made good use of their ships for shore bombardment in the Northern Adriatic and pushed ahead with the development of motor torpedo boats. On the night of 9–10 December 1917 Captain Luigi Rizzo took *MAS.9* and *MAS.13* into Muggia Bay near Trieste to attack the old battleships *Wien* and *Budapest*. The two 18-inch torpedoes from *MAS.9* struck the *Wien* amidships and she sank quickly but the two fired by *MAS.13* missed the *Budapest* and hit a jetty.

Rizzo scored another outstanding success when in broad daylight on 10 June 1918 his *MAS.15* attacked the dreadnought *Szent Istvan*. The battleship was in company with her sisters about ten miles west of Premuda Island when *MAS.15* and *MAS.21* approached unobserved and fired four torpedoes. The fate of the *Szent Istvan* is well known for as she rolled over she was filmed from another ship, and as the only World War I action movie of a ship sinking it features in many film libraries around the world. The Italian main fleet achieved very little but the efforts of Luigi Rizzo showed that given the right conditions and a vital element of daring the battleship was just as vulnerable as the torpedo boat specialists had prophesied 30 years earlier.

LINE OF BATTLE

Jutland, or Skagerrak to the Germans, remains one of the most fascinating sea battles of all time. The reason is that the result was a baffling paradox; the Germans scored more material successes and cheated the British of a crushing victory, and yet it did them no good whatsoever. Jutland was the first major clash of fleets in European waters since Lissa and the only full-scale battle between the two fleets in the entire war. It was also the largest sea-battle to date, with 252 ships engaged, and the last one in which all the classic ship-types played their parts, battleships, battlecruisers, armored cruisers, light cruisers and destroyers. Ironically it was also the first battle in which aerial reconnaissance played any sort of role.

The two sides had shadow-boxed in the North Sea since August 1914 largely because the German high command was only prepared to sanction hit-and-run raids on the east coast of England. But there was a faction inside the German Navy which wanted a more positive policy and when in February 1916 Vice-Admiral Reinhard Scheer was appointed to command the High Seas Fleet he brought with him a new offensive spirit. This time he planned a coordinated trap for the Grand Fleet, sending U-Boats to mine the exit routes from Scapa Flow and Rosyth and then sending Hipper's First Scouting Group to lure Beatty's battlecruisers into the grip of the whole High Seas Fleet. It might have worked but for the fact that since the end of 1914 the Admiralty had been reading the majority of German cipher messages and when it was realized in London that the High Seas Fleet would be at sea Admiral Jellicoe was ordered to take the Grand Fleet out and rendezvous with Beatty's battlecruisers off the Skagerrak. The composition of the two forces was slightly different from usual because three of Beatty's older battlecruisers had been sent north to Scapa Flow for gunnery practice, and to strengthen the Battlecruiser Fleet it was given four of the *Queen Elizabeth* Class fast battleships.

Everything still depended on chance, but when on 31 May two groups of light cruisers turned to investigate a Danish steamer blowing off steam it was the prelude to a major action. The light cruisers were attached to their respective battlecruisers and each admiral closed the range eagerly in the belief that he could lure the enemy into the arms of his Commander in Chief. Fire was opened at over 24,000 yards, with six British battlecruisers against five German, for in his haste to get into action Beatty had left his 5th Battle Squadron of *Queen Elizabeths* behind. They had deliberately been stationed ten miles astern because Beatty did not want Hipper to refuse action in the face of greatly superior odds but it meant that these four powerful ships were late in coming into action.

The sea was calm but visibility was hazy when the first salvoes thundered out. Beatty had turned east to put himself between Hipper and the German bases while Hipper had turned southeast to draw Beatty back on the High Seas Fleet. Beatty's move was strategically sound but it put him at a disadvantage for the sun was sinking behind his ships, silhouetting them clearly while leaving the German ships merging into the haze. To make matters worse dense clouds of coal smoke and cordite fumes began to roll across the water, adding to the difficulty of reading signals. By an error in signals from the flagship the British ships found themselves firing at the same target while the weakest ship, HMS *Indefatigable* was unsupported in a duel with the *Von der Tann*.

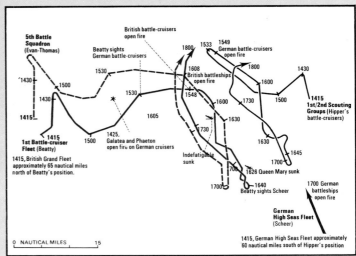

5th Battle
Squadron
(Evan-Thomas)

British battle-cruisers
open fire

1533

1549 German battle-cruisers
open fire

1800

Beatty sights
German battle-cruisers

1530

1800

1430

1608
British battleships
open fire

1600

1430

1500

1430

1530

1548

1500

1415
1st/2nd Scouting
Groups (Hipper's
battle-cruisers)

1415

1605

1600

1730

1415
1st Battle-cruiser
Fleet (Beatty)

1500

1425,
Galatea and Phaeton
open fire on German cruisers

1630

1630

1415, British Grand Fleet
approximately 65 nautical miles
north of Beatty's position.

730

Indefatigable
sunk

1645

1700

1626 Queen Mary sunk

1700

700

1700 German
battleships
open fire

1700

1640
Beatty sights Scheer

**German
High Seas Fleet**
(Scheer)

0 NAUTICAL MILES   15

1415, German High Seas Fleet approximately
60 nautical miles south of Hipper's position

Above: HMS *Indefatigable* seen minutes before she blew up.
Right: Chart of the first phase of the Battle of Jutland.
Bottom: A hurried snapshot taken from HMS *New Zealand* shows the
remains of the *Indefatigable* sinking.
Below: SMS *Von der Tann*, the first German battlecruiser, was clearly
superior to contemporary British designs.

The action developed rapidly, with the *Moltke* scoring two hits on the *Tiger*, *Derfflinger* finding the range of the *Princess Royal* and the *Lutzow* hitting the *Lion*. At the rear of the line the *Von der Tann* and *Indefatigable*'s fierce duel reached a climax at about 1600 when the German ship scored three hits aft. The British battlecruiser lurched out of the line with smoke pouring from her and sinking by the stern but before she could indicate the extent of her damage another hit landed near the forward 12-inch turret and another hit the turret itself. Suddenly she blew up in a tremendous cloud of brown smoke and sheets of orange flame as her magazines detonated, and when the shower of debris cleared the *Indefatigable* had disappeared with nearly all hands. In only twenty minutes Hipper's ships had evened the odds.

Worse was very soon to follow. The *Derfflinger* shifted fire from the *Lion* to the *Queen Mary* and quickly straddled her. A 12-inch shell hit 'Q' turret amidships and put the right-hand gun out of action and about five minutes later another two shells hit, one near 'A' and 'B' turrets and the other on 'Q' turret. Once again there was a huge explosion as the forepart of the *Queen Mary* vanished in a sheet of flame and smoke. Horrified onlookers saw the remains of the ship listing to port and sinking with the propellers still revolving, and then another explosion obliterated her. Nine men survived out of 1285.

Some clue to the cause of the disaster was gleaned from the experience of the *Lion*. She was hit on 'Q' turret just above the left-hand gun port by a shell which burst above the gun and killed or wounded all the gun crew. A fire broke out among the cordite charges near the guns but a fire party quickly ran a hose over the face of the turret and soused the wrecked turret with water. Yet a full 28 minutes after this the cordite in the turret burst into flame again and spread to the working chamber below. The combustion of the eight full cordite charges was so violent that 'Q' magazine bulkheads were buckled and a venting plate blew out, allowing flames to enter the magazine. Fortunately the magazine had already been flooded by a gallant Royal Marine turret-officer, for if the magazine crew had merely closed the doors they would not have remained flash-tight. When the ship was examined later the burn marks in the hoist showed that the flame had jumped 60 feet, grim proof of how badly unstable cordite could behave.

Help was at hand for the hard-pressed British battlecruisers, however, for the 5th Battle Squadron had caught up and was now able to open fire at extreme range. Within six minutes the flagship *Barham* was hitting the *Seydlitz* at nearly 19,000 yards and HMS *Valiant* was ranging on the *Moltke*. The German ships could not reply at this colossal range, and the only remedy was to make small shifts in course to throw off the British range-takers but this had little effect. To make matters worse Beatty's destroyers launched a torpedo-attack and hit the *Seydlitz*, tearing a huge hole in her side. Yet such was the stout construc-

tion of German battlecruisers that she was able to keep up full speed for a while.

The situation changed dramatically when Beatty learned from his light cruisers that battleships had been sighted and two minutes later he saw for himself the mass of masts, funnels and smoke of the High Seas Fleet. This was just the way it was meant to happen, and he ordered his ships to turn about and go north, secure in the knowledge that the Grand Fleet was hurrying south at top speed to meet him. Yet again, however, the flagship's signal staff were too hasty and omitted to pass on the fresh instructions to the 5th Battle Squadron, leaving them to carry on firing at the German ships until they noticed Beatty's ships turning away. By the time they could be pulled around they were within range of the German battle line and suffered concentrated fire from Hipper's ships as well as the head of Scheer's line. The *Barham* and *Malaya* took several hits and suffered casualties but they and their sisters *Valiant* and *Warspite* fought back and avoided serious damage.

Relief for Beatty's hard-pressed ships was, however, almost at hand for Jellicoe had ordered the 3rd Battle Cruiser Squadron under Rear-Admiral Hood to hurry ahead of the main fleet to reinforce Beatty. The three ships, *Invincible*, *Indomitable* and *Inflexible* came into action just as Beatty was starting to turn to the east across Hipper's bows in a deliberate attempt to prevent him from sighting the Grand Fleet too soon. Now the visibility favored the British for the first time and in order to take the pressure off, Hipper ordered his destroyers to attack the British capital ships. But just as the light craft started to deploy Hood's three battlecruisers appeared out of the haze, 12-inch guns firing. Hood handled his big ships with great skill and within minutes they had inflicted crippling hits on the *Lützow*, reduced the light cruiser *Wiesbaden* to a wreck and damaged the *Pillau* seriously.

It must be remembered that it was now evening and in the worsening visibility the rival commanders were working by guesswork and intuition. For Jellicoe in the Fleet Flagship *Iron Duke* the most urgent problem was to know just *where* the High Seas Fleet would be when it was sighted, and in which direction it would be steaming. From the flag-bridge he could see only seven miles, and if his own fleet was caught in the wrong formation or heading in the wrong direction his superiority in numbers and gunpower would be thrown away. The Grand Fleet was cruising in six columns 'line abreast', a box formation to reduce the risk from submarine attack, and it had to deploy into 'line ahead' to bring every available gun into action. Finally the fog of conflicting and garbled sighting reports resolved itself, the diminutive admiral studied the plot for no more than ten seconds and then gave series of orders for deployment on his port column. It was the right decision for at one stroke he interposed his fleet between the High Seas Fleet and its bases and had brought his most powerful squadrons into action first.

Far right, top: The *Royal Oak* (left) and *Hercules* of the 1st Battle Squadron after the British deployed.
Far right: HMS *Iron Duke*, Jellicoe's flagship.
Below: The Grand Fleet in cruising formation, nearest the camera are ships of the *Iron Duke* Class.

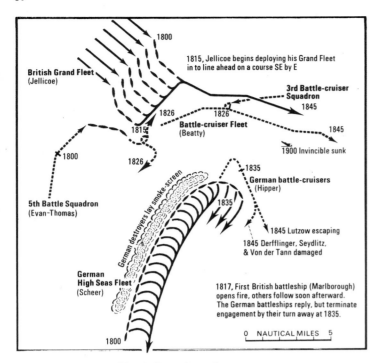

Above: The German 'Battle Turn Away.'
Below: HMS *Invincible*'s 'Q' magazine blows up.

As the majestic columns of ships wheeled in turn the two fleets finally sighted one another and ripples of orange flashed down the lines as the first ranging salvoes were fired. Jellicoe had put the Grand Fleet in an ideal position, crossing Scheer's 'T' and concentrating fire on the head of the German line. The British battlecruisers and the *Queen Elizabeths* also appeared out of the murk and took up their allotted position at the ends

of the battle line but during this phase a sudden shift in visibility left the *Invincible* silhouetted against the setting sun, a perfect target for the *Derfflinger* and *Lützow*. At 10,500 yards she was an easy target and was hit five times. The fifth hit blew the roof off 'Q' turret, and once again those ominous clouds of cordite smoke and coal dust billowed up as the *Invincible* broke in two.

In direct contrast to the brilliant performance of Hood's 3rd Battle Cruiser Squadron the armored cruisers of the 1st Cruiser Squadron now immolated themselves in a totally pointless attack. Passing down the engaged side of the battle line and incidentally masking its fire with dense clouds of smoke, Sir Robert Arbuthnot led the *Defence* and three others in a headlong attack on the disabled light cruiser *Wiesbaden*. He paid for his stupidity with his life as the *Defence* blew up while the *Warrior* was reduced to a sinking condition, all to achieve a few hits on a ship which was already sinking. The *Warrior* and the other two were only saved from a similar fate by the arrival on the scene of the battleship *Warspite*, of the 5th Battle Squadron. She and her squadron were trying to follow Beatty's battlecruisers in taking the place at the end of the line but at a crucial moment her steering jammed, causing her to turn a complete circle near the *Warrior*. The German battleships at the head of the line could not resist the chance of sinking a superdreadnought and immediately switched fire from the cruiser. While the *Warspite*'s people struggled to cool down her overheated steering machinery she continued to circle, surrounded by shellsplashes. The scene was nicknamed 'Windy Corner' by onlookers who were certain that she would be sunk, but in fact she escaped serious damage and was able to get under control again. The distraction also gave the *Warrior* time to crawl away to safety, although she later sank.

The battle was now between the Grand Fleet and the High Seas Fleet, and the German gamble had failed. Jellicoe's insistence on constant gunnery practice showed in his flagship's shooting against the *König*. The German ship's diary shows that the *Iron Duke* fired nine salvoes in less than five minutes, of which seven shells hit. One Common shell pierced the lower

edge of the main belt armor and set fire to a number of 5.9-inch charges in a magazine. As with most German cordite it did not explode, in marked contrast to the behavior of British cordite. The loss of the *Indefatigable*, *Queen Mary* and *Invincible* might never have occurred if British propellant had been of the same standard.

The High Seas Fleet had only one course left, its 'Battle Turn Away,' in which all ships turned 180 degrees simultaneously and steamed back on a reciprocal course. It achieved its aim of breaking contact but Jellicoe hauled his Grand Fleet around to the south-east and again to the south twelve minutes later to keep it between the High Seas Fleet and its escape route. At 1908 Scheer blundered into the same trap and this time his position was desperate, with the horizon apparently filled with hostile battleships. He ordered Hipper's battlecruisers on a 'death ride' supported only by the destroyers, to give the main fleet time to make another Battle Turn Away. The destroyers were very roughly handled and the battlecruisers took terrible punishment. The *Lützow* was hit five times and had two turrets out of action; five 15-inch hits on the *Derfflinger* disabled two turrets and started ammunition fires. Three hits on the *Grosser Kurfurst* caused severe flooding. By now the German ships could hardly see the enemy, and the only hits scored were two by the *Seydlitz* on the *Colossus*, which caused minor damage.

The breakaway was successful and the two fleets drew apart for the last time but there was to be one more engagement between heavy ships. Beatty's battlecruisers fired briefly at portions of the High Seas Fleet but at such long range as to be relatively ineffective.

Up to this point Jellicoe could be assured of a handsome victory, for his fleet had proved superior in gunpower and tactics to Scheer's. The loss of life in the *Defence* and the three battlecruisers was tragic but the loss of the four ships had not affected the relative position. Twice the High Seas Fleet had been forced to turn away from the Grand Fleet's guns and still the British were firmly in position across the route back to the German bases. Jellicoe's plan was to station his destroyers well astern of the

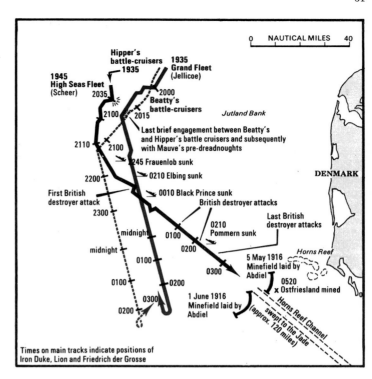

Above: The night action and the German escape.

battle fleet to prevent any attempt by Scheer to double back, and to maintain a cruising formation until daylight, when he hoped to continue the destruction of the High Seas Fleet. British tactics did not favor night action, for the very sound reason that it was a risky business, but they failed to take account of the Germans' absolute necessity to fight at night in order to

escape an annihilating battle in the morning. Furthermore the German Navy had trained for night action whereas the British had not, with the result that when their ships met the British destroyers their reactions were quicker. What also helped was that one of the British battlecruisers had imprudently signalled the correct night challenge and reply to a sister ship, with a German light cruiser watching from the mist. The Germans had only part of the challenge but this was enough to make many British ships hold their fire for fear of hitting a friendly ship.

In spite of these advantages the High Seas Fleet had a frightening ordeal before it finally smashed through the British light forces. When the pre-dreadnought *Pommern* was hit by a single torpedo from HMS *Onslaught* her magazines exploded and she blew up with all hands. The light cruiser *Rostock* was torpedoed and the *Elbing* was rammed by the battleship *Posen* while twisting and turning to avoid torpedoes. The *Lützow* had strained her bulkheads by trying to keep up with the other battlecruisers, and when Scheer learned that she was drawing 70 feet of water forward and was unable to steam he ordered her to be torpedoed.

Once clear of the British flotillas the High Seas Fleet had a clear run home, apart from a mine which damaged the *Ostfriesland*. Although it had performed very creditably it had not won a victory of any sort, except in the sense of avoiding destruction. For the British it was a strategic setback; their fleet had been built at great expense to achieve an overwhelming victory and because that victory eluded them they had to continue with the ruinously expensive war on the Western Front. In relative strength they were hardly affected by the outcome; apart from the *Queen Mary* the losses had been in weak ships and these were replaced very quickly by much more powerful new construction. In the tactical sense they had won; Jellicoe was in possession of the battle area with his fleet intact while Scheer was hurrying back to base as fast as he could. The real blow for the British was to their pride, reputation and confidence. The press and public had been educated to believe that some sort of Trafalgar would happen, a battle of total annihilation, and when the Admiralty unwisely released the text of Scheer's report on the battle because Jellicoe's was not complete, it was construed as proof of a British catastrophe. The losses were impressive but against them could be set the *Lützow* and the *Pommern* and the light cruisers and the virtual sinking of the *Seydlitz* outside Wilhelmshaven. What was alarming was the weakness of training and command, for it soon became apparent that subordinates had rarely shown any initiative in reporting sightings of enemy ships, assuming that the C-in-C already had the information. There had been plenty of gallantry but far too many mistakes and failures to interpret the spirit of the orders as well as the letter.

On the material side the worst shortcoming was undoubtedly the violent behavior of cordite propellant. The root cause of the explosions was that the system for preventing flash from reaching magazines was nowhere near adequate to cope with the unforeseen violence of the flash. Ironically the precautions in British ships were more elaborate than in German ships but because German cordite was more stable it never created an explosion.

A less obvious material failure was the weakness of the British armor-piercing shell, for this meant that the high-quality gunnery of the Grand Fleet during the later phases of the action did much less damage to the German ships than it should have. In all there were 17 hits on German armor varying from 10 to 14 inches in thickness; of these one HE and three glancing Armor-Piercing Capped (APC) had no chance of penetrating, but only one of the remainder penetrated the armor (*Derfflinger*'s barbette) and burst inside. Five more holed the armor without doing more than send fragments through and the other seven shells did not hole the armor. Against lighter armor British shells fared no better, and only one 15-inch APC shell penetrated the *Moltke*'s 8-inch upper belt armor at 18,000 yards.

The cordite and shell problems were tackled energetically by the Admiralty but inevitably it took time for new shells to be manufactured in quantity and for improvements to be made to magazines.

Both fleets completed their repairs as fast as they could but there was to be no second fleet action in the North Sea. The Grand Fleet continued its monotonous sweeps to no avail, but on the one occasion that both fleets were at sea, in August 1916, two of the Grand Fleet's escorting light cruisers were torpedoed and as soon as Scheer learned that Jellicoe was at sea he returned to harbor.

Frustrated and bored the men of the Grand Fleet might be but

Top: A *Queen Elizabeth* Class ship seen during a 'throw-off' gunnery exercise. In such exercises the crew would aim normally at a real target but the equipment would be set to introduce a standard error so that efficiency could be judged safely.
Below: HMS *Superb* (left) and *Canada* seen at Jutland.

ultimately their morale survived intact, whereas that of the High Seas Fleet crumbled. There were two reasons, first the tedium of inactivity in bases never designed to handle such large numbers of men and second, the steady drain of what might be called 'middle management,' the younger officers and qualified petty officers and sailors for service in U-Boats and torpedo boats. The gaps were filled by conscripts and reservists but inevitably the gap between officers and men grew wider and with so little time spent at sea there was plenty of time for grievances to fester. Nor could anyone be unaware of the worsening state of the civilian population as the Allied blockade steadily reduced the quality of foodstuffs. The pressure on the Navy to 'do something' to support their Army comrades fighting in the east and in France was there all the time but as the Grand Fleet was more powerful than it had been before Jutland there was little that Scheer could do without risking a second and more disastrous encounter. The first rumblings of discontent were heard towards the end of 1917 and when at the end of the war Scheer and Hipper tried to take the fleet to sea the sailors mutinied against what they believed to be a suicide mission.

When the end came it was almost unexpected. When the German Army requested an Armistice the British insisted that the High Seas Fleet must be handed over, and this was granted. On 21 November the might of the Grand Fleet mustered off Rosyth to see the unforgettable sight of 14 battleships and battlecruisers steaming in to give themselves up. Between the long lines of ships they went, before being escorted to Scapa Flow for internment until the peace conference at Versailles should decide their fate. Beatty's signal was appropriately curt, 'The German flag will be hauled down at sunset and will not be hoisted again without permission.'

Once at Scapa Flow the German ships were cut off from the outside world, receiving only basic rations and letters from Germany. The British newspaper's available gave very lurid accounts of the progress of negotiations at Versailles, and it was even suggested that the ships should be taken over by the Royal Navy and used to bombard the German coast if the German delegation refused to accept the terms of the peace treaty. Already humiliated by their surrender and aware that the Navy had apparently shown less concern for its professional honor than the Army, the Imperial Navy officers decided on one last token gesture. Taking advantage of the temporary absence of the British battle squadron guarding them, the entire High Seas Fleet scuttled itself at its moorings on 21 June 1919. Boarding parties were able to save only the *Baden* and a few destroyers, but the rest went to the bottom. It marked not only the end of a fleet but the end of the heyday of the battleship. There would be bigger and better ships but never again would the battleship have the unchallenged prestige that she had enjoyed in August 1914.

THE WASHINGTO

Such is the folly of mankind that the victorious Allies of 1918 were embroiled in a new naval arms race within a year. The balance of power was a thing of the past, with the German Navy eliminated and the United States emerging very rapidly as an industrial giant to whom all the other Allies except Japan were heavily in debt. There was only one sane way out, a negotiated mutual reduction of the naval programs, and the United States convened an international naval disarmament conference to meet in Washington in November 1921.

The Washington Conference had far-reaching influence on the development of capital ships. The British accepted that there should be parity with the United States but the Japanese were furious when they were bracketed with the French and Italians as inferiors of the British and American navies. Both the Japanese and the Americans wanted above all to save what they could out of their huge programs; Japan wanted to avoid scrapping one large battleship while the United States wanted to keep four. All three navies agreed on 16-inch as the maximum gun-caliber, and after some debate 35,000 tons was chosen as the future maximum displacement. Finally the Washington Treaty for the Limitation of Armament was signed in Washington on 13 December 1921.

With a 10-year 'holiday' or moratorium on battleship-building the leading navies turned their minds to modernizing the capital ships left to them under the Treaty. Oil fuel replaced coal and by installing lighter boilers more armor could be used.

Right: The USS *California* seen fitting out at Mare Island Navy Yard in 1920.
Far right, top: The *New Mexico* in dry dock in June 1919. Only US battleships of this vintage featured the clipper bow.
Far right: The British battlecruiser *Hood* was fast and well-armed but was long overdue for a refit to improve her protection when she was sunk by the *Bismarck* in 1941.

N TREATY

Below: In an attempt to reduce the area of heavy armor necessary the *Nelson* and her sister *Rodney* carried all nine of their 16-inch guns forward.

ATLANTIC AND MEDITERRANEAN

When Winston Churchill said, 'We are fighting this war with the ships of the last' he was speaking no more than the truth. Fortunately for the Royal Navy there was no High Seas Fleet across the North Sea, only the nucleus of the big fleet that Admiral Raeder had wanted to build. The British could look forward to a pair of new battleships in 1940–41, whereas the German *Bismarck* was unlikely to be ready until early 1941. Even if Italy came into the war the British hoped that the French fleet would keep the Mediterranean under Allied control.

The British followed the strategy that had proved so successful in World War I, moving the Home Fleet to Scapa Flow to block the exits to the Atlantic, but this time the great fleet base did not prove immune to attack. On the night of 13–14 October 1939 *U.47* under *Kapitänleutnant* Prien penetrated the line of blockships in Kirk Sound and found the old battleship *Royal Oak*

lying at anchor. Prien's salvo of three torpedoes, fired from ahead, failed to do any damage for the one torpedo which hit apparently struck an anchor cable or detonated only partially. After an interval to reload Prien fired another salvo and this time there was a loud explosion underneath the *Royal Oak* and she rolled over and sank 13 minutes later.

As in 1914 the Home Fleet was sent away to bases on the west coast of Scotland until the defenses of Scapa Flow could be strengthened. During this time the *Nelson* was damaged by a magnetic mine while entering Loch Ewe and the *Barham* was hit by a torpedo but the *Kriegsmarine* was not able to take advantage of the Home Fleet's weakness, and it was not until the invasion of Norway in April 1940 that the respective heavy units came into contact. The *Renown* narrowly missed intercepting the German invasion forces on 6 April but three days later in

Above: Jutland veteran HMS *Warspite* served throughout WW2 at Narvik, in the Mediterranean and in support of the D-Day landings. Below: HMS *Renown* seen in 1940 after a refit. For much of the war she served with Force H at Gibraltar.

shocking weather she surprised the battlecruisers *Scharnhorst* and *Gneisenau* some 50 miles from Vestfjord. The British ship's lookouts spotted the Germans through the snow squalls and closed to within nine miles before opening fire. The *Renown* put *Gneisenau*'s forward fire control out of action but she and her sister used their superior speed to get away in the murk. Hitler's orders were quite specific that capital ships were not to expose themselves to damage and so Admiral Lütjens felt obliged to break off the action.

In the second Battle of Narvik the veteran *Warspite* distinguished herself by following a force of nine destroyers up Ofotfjord to hunt down a force of German destroyers. It was hardly an ideal setting for a battleship, with a risk of grounding or being torpedoed but Admiral Whitworth's gamble paid off. Her Swordfish floatplane was able to reconnoiter for the whole

Above: The *Littorio* maneuvering under full helm. The ships of this class were fast and graceful and carried nine 15-inch guns. *Littorio* was badly damaged at Taranto. Renamed as the *Italia* she was surrendered to the Allies in 1943.

force and her 15-inch guns completed the destruction wrought by the destroyers' guns and torpedoes. At the end of the day the entire German force of eight destroyers had been wiped out, and the *Warspite* had begun a career of extraordinary luck.

Norway showed that air attack was dangerous to battleships. The *Rodney* was damaged and several smaller ships sunk by Ju 87 Stuka dive-bombers and it was at last realised that gunfire alone could not defend ships. Multiple light guns broke up massed attacks and heavier guns could force bombers to keep high but fire control was not yet sufficiently advanced to ensure more than random hits. The vulnerability of aircraft carriers was also demonstrated when during the closing stages of the campaign the *Scharnhorst* and *Gneisenau* caught HMS *Glorious* after she had evacuated the last RAF aircraft and aircrew from Norway. The only opposition came from the destroyer *Acasta*, which managed to hit *Scharnhorst* with a torpedo before being sunk.

The next action involving capital ships was the tragic destruction of the French fleet at Mers-el-Kebir in July 1940. After the fall of France the old battleships *Paris* and *Courbet* had escaped to England and the incomplete *Richelieu* and *Jean Bart* managed to reach North Africa, but four of the remaining capital ships, the *Dunkerque*, *Strasbourg*, *Bretagne* and *Provence* had been instructed by the new Pétain Government to remain at Mers-el-Kebir near Oran, under the terms of the Armistice

negotiated with Hitler. The British were understandably alarmed at the collapse of the joint strategy in the Mediterranean, for Italy had chosen this moment to join the war. To guard against any French move the Admiralty immediately formed 'Force H' under Admiral Somerville, including the *Hood*, *Valiant* and *Resolution* and the new carrier *Ark Royal*.

The result was that on 3 July 'Force H' opened fire on the crowded harbor. The 15-inch salvoes quickly overwhelmed the French ships and the *Bretagne* blew up, while the *Dunkerque* and *Provence* were badly damaged. The only large ship to escape the carnage was the *Strasbourg*, which got clear behind the dense clouds of smoke. The *Hood* was only capable of 28 knots and could not catch the French battlecruiser, but Somerville had carried out his orders and the bulk of the French Fleet was now immobilized. But of course as a consequence French opinion was outraged and the French Navy in particular became violently anti-British. Any hopes that individual ships might desert the Vichy cause to join General de Gaulle's Free French Forces in England were dashed. Nor did the failure to take Dakar in September improve relations, for the *Richelieu* was damaged twice by British attacks. This did not stop her from firing on the attacking force with her 15-inch guns, and when HMS *Resolution* was damaged by a torpedo from the submarine *Bévéziers* the attack was cancelled.

For a while it looked as if the powerful Italian Fleet might force the British to abandon the Mediterranean but this gloomy view took no account of the difference in temperament between

Above: An Italian battleship opens fire during the Battle of Cape Spartivento. The British cruiser *Berwick* was damaged before the Italians broke off the action.
Below: HMS *Nelson* down by the bow after being hit by an Italian aerial torpedo while escorting a Malta convoy.

the British and the Italians. Admiral Cunningham was given the *Warspite* as his flagship and the unmodernized *Royal Sovereign*, *Ramillies* and *Malaya* as well as the old carrier *Eagle*. With this force Cunningham had no hesitation in giving battle to the Italians, and the result of the action off Calabria on 9 July showed that his confidence was justified. Both the Italians and the British were at sea to cover the passage of convoys when Admiral Campioni's squadron was sighted by the British. A torpedo-attack by the *Eagle*'s Swordfish was unsuccessful but the *Warspite* was at extreme gun-range. As the Italian ships worked up to full speed, heading for the horizon, the *Warspite*'s guns fired their first salvoes in anger since Jutland 24 years earlier. Suddenly an orange flash appeared on the flagship *Giulio Cesare* as a 15-inch shell landed alongside her funnels. That was the end of the action for the Italians retired under cover of a smokescreen and used their higher speed to get away. The British were naturally disappointed but the action showed that they had little to fear from the Italian fleet. Incidentally the *Warspite*'s record of a hit at 26,400 yards still stands, the greatest range at which naval guns have scored a hit on a moving target.

The next action, between 'Force H' and Campioni off Cape Spartivento on 27 November was inconclusive but Cunningham had already inflicted a serious defeat on the Italians. With a new carrier, HMS *Illustrious* and another modernized battleship, the *Valiant* he was able to attack the enemy in his main base at Taranto. On the night of 11–12 November a force of 21 Swordfish biplane torpedo-bombers attacked Taranto, sinking the *Conte di Cavour* and severely damaging the new *Littorio* and the *Duilio*. Although the damaged ships would be repaired the attack meant that three out of six battleships were out of action. More important the Italians had lost the initiative to the British, who could now send convoys through the Mediterranean to reinforce their forces in Malta and Egypt. Ever since 1918, when it had been planned to use Sopwith Cuckoo torpedo-bombers to attack the High Seas Fleet, the Fleet Air Arm had hoped for such an opportunity, and now it had made history. Among the interested parties who studied the results of Taranto were the Japanese, who were at that moment thinking of ways to do much the same thing to the Americans at Pearl Harbor.

Early in 1941 Cunningham at last had his chance to strike a blow at the Italian Fleet. On 28 March the carrier *Formidable*'s torpedo-bombers put two torpedoes into the new battleship *Vittorio Veneto*, giving the Mediterranean Fleet a chance to cut

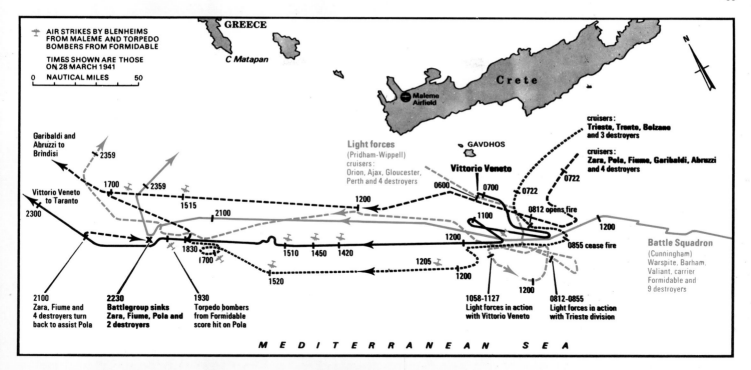

Above: Chart of the Battle of Matapan.

her off. At dusk Cunningham's ships were still 65 miles astern but he had already made up his mind to risk a night action and pressed on. Since Jutland the Royal Navy had learned a lot and although only a few ships had radar they were equipped with such aids as flashless cordite and the drills had been practiced endlessly. In contrast the Italians were badly equipped, with no radar but above all lacking any sort of training for night-fighting.

The object of the pursuit, the *Vittorio Veneto* had actually escaped and was heading for home but just before dusk a stray aircraft torpedo had hit one of her escorting cruisers, the *Pola*. Admiral Iachino ordered two of her sisters, the *Fiume* and the *Zara* to go back and try to tow her home. It was while these two ships were looking for their stricken consort that they appeared as echoes on the British radar screens. Suddenly they realized that they had fallen into a trap, but too late.

The Battle of Cape Matapan, or Gaudo Island to the Italians, was a massacre. The *Warspite*, *Barham* and *Valiant* sank the *Fiume* and *Zara* in minutes, despite a gallant attempt by the escorting destroyers to defend them. Then the British destroyers hunted down the crippled *Pola* and torpedoed her after taking off as many survivors as they could.

Cunningham did not regard Matapan as anything more than a skirmish for he had intended to sink the *Vittorio Veneto* but its strategic value came to light two months later. During the evacuation of Crete the Mediterranean Fleet was exposed to merciless dive-bombing and was suffering heavy losses. Now was the time for the Italian Fleet to put to sea but somehow it failed to grasp the opportunity to avenge Matapan. Even after German U-Boats sunk the carrier *Ark Royal* and HMS *Barham* and Italian frogmen had put the *Queen Elizabeth* and *Valiant* out of action in Alexandria, the memory of Matapan continued to inhibit the Italian high command, and they lost their last chance to dominate the Mediterranean.

Back in home waters the British faced a serious threat from the German heavy surface ships. In 1939–40 and again in 1941 the *Scharnhorst* and *Gneisenau* had sortied into the North Atlantic, sinking the armed merchant cruiser HMS *Rawalpindi* and 22 merchant ships totalling over 115,000 tons gross. To counter the threat to the Atlantic convoys the Admiralty reinforced each convoy with an old battleship. Although these veterans were totally outclassed, on the two occasions that the

German ships made contact the sight of a tripod mast and control top was sufficient to make them sheer off. Hitler's orders had to be obeyed, even when they ran counter to common sense.

A much more dangerous threat was the battleship *Bismarck*, which completed her training and shakedown by April 1941. With a margin of 6000 tons over the Washington Treaty limit the designers had been able to produce a balanced design, fast, well-armed and well-protected. When the Admiralty learned of the movement of two large ships westward out of the Baltic it was obvious that the *Bismarck* and the new heavy cruiser *Prinz Eugen* were ready to break out into the Atlantic. On 21 May they sailed from Bergen and disappeared but already two heavy cruisers, HMS *Norfolk* and HMS *Suffolk* were patrolling their most likely exit-route, the Denmark Strait between Iceland and Greenland. As the *Suffolk* was equipped with radar she was able to make contact in spite of the bad visibility on 23 May. The old battlecruiser *Hood* and the new battleship *Prince of Wales* had already sailed from Scapa Flow. They intercepted the German ships shortly after dawn on the 24th.

The action opened briskly with *Hood* firing well on ranges supplied by her Type 284 radar. Her first three salvoes were right for distance but off line, and in the opinion of the *Bismarck*'s surviving 3rd gunnery officer the next salvo looked likely to hit. But instead, just as the *Hood* turned to port to bring her full broadside to bear she vanished in a huge explosion. When the smoke cleared the two halves of the ship could be seen disappearing, just like the battlecruisers at Jutland. Then a tornado of fire burst about the *Prince of Wales* as both *Bismarck* and *Prinz Eugen* concentrated their fire on her. She was hit seven times by four 15-inch and three 8-inch shells, the worst hit being a 15-inch shell which passed through the compass platform without detonating. It scattered fragments of the

binnacle around, killing or wounding everyone except Captain Leach. The *Prince of Wales* fought back gamely coping with a crop of teething troubles as well as the disastrous hit on the compass platform. Straddles were obtained, and it was later learned that two 14-inch shells hit the *Bismarck* below the waterline, a creditable achievement for any new ship.

The Admiralty now mustered all its resources to hunt down the *Bismarck*. The carrier *Ark Royal* and the *Renown* had already left Gibraltar and the battleship *Rodney* left her convoy to join the Home Fleet. The C-in-C Home Fleet, Admiral Tovey was at sea in the *King George V*, heading for the last known position of the German ships, and all available aircraft and ships were searching, for the heavy cruisers *Norfolk* and *Suffolk* had lost radar contact. Late on the night of 24 May the *Bismarck* had been hit by an 18-inch aerial torpedo from one of the *Victorious'* Swordfish but this had exploded on the armor belt amidships and had not slowed her down. What nobody knew was that the two hits from the *Prince of Wales* had damaged the *Bismarck*'s fuel tanks, contaminating a large part of her oil and leaving a long slick.

Finally on 26 May a Catalina flying boat sighted the oil slick and identified the *Bismarck*. She was now heading for Brest in Brittany, for Admiral Lutjens had realized that the Atlantic sortie would be impossible without the full load of fuel. But the nearest British heavy ships would not be able to close the distance before the *Bismarck* came under the shelter of shore-based aircraft. It was essential to slow her down before this happened and so the *Ark Royal* was ordered to fly off a torpedo-strike.

The first wave of Swordfish nearly sank HMS *Sheffield*, one of the Home Fleet cruisers in the area, but the second strike was a success. In spite of withering fire from the guns the Swordfish managed to get two hits, one on the armor and one right aft. The second wrecked the steering gear and jammed the rudders, leaving the giant ship careering helplessly in circles until she could be slowed down and steered on the pro-

Below: The 'pocket battleship' *Graf Spee* on fire after being scuttled in Montevideo harbor. Ships of this type were designed as commerce raiders but were not a success.

pellers. Throughout the night the *Bismarck*'s crew worked to free the rudders for their lives depended on it. Divers might have gone over the side with explosives to blow the tangled wreckage away but the rough weather put it out of the question.

Early next morning the Home Fleet hove into sight, the flagship *King George V* and the *Rodney* and at 2047 the British fired their first salvoes. The first German salvoes were accurate, straddling the *Rodney* but thereafter *Bismarck*'s gunnery fell off rapidly and within half an hour she was silenced. Admiral Tovey ordered the flagship out to 14,000 yards to get more plunging hits and sent the *Rodney* in to 4000 yards to fire full broadsides at the superstructure but still she would not sink.

By now the battleships were running short of fuel after their long chase and Tovey decided to break off the gun action, leaving the job of sinking the tortured wreck to the torpedoes of the heavy cruiser *Dorsetshire*. Three torpedoes hit the starboard side and then the *Dorsetshire* moved around to fire a fourth into the port side, and at 1036 the *Bismarck* sank.

The sinking of the *Bismarck* put an end to the *Kriegsmarine*'s plans to disrupt Atlantic shipping with surface forces. Thereafter the *Scharnhorst*, *Gneisenau* and *Prinz Eugen* remained at Brest, subjected to heavy if inaccurate high-level bombing by the RAF. Sooner or later they were likely to be hit and so in January 1942 Hitler ordered Naval Group Command West to bring the three ships back to Germany. The plan for Operation Cerberus had all the hallmarks of Hitlerian genius, a daylight dash through the English Channel in the teeth of coastal guns, air attacks and surface ships. Once again Hitler had divined his opponents' weakness: nobody *believed* that heavy units would dare to go through the Channel, and as long as a heavy 'umbrella' of fighters was provided by the Luftwaffe the risk was small. And so it turned out on 12 February 1942 when the three ships managed to get through the Channel unscathed, apart from striking mines at the end of the day.

Above: The main armament of HMS *Rodney*.

After her escape the *Scharnhorst* was sent to join the *Tirpitz* and the surviving cruisers and destroyers in Northern Norway, where they could at least threaten the convoys taking supplies to Murmansk. Although the *Tirpitz* played a major part in the destruction of convoy PQ.17 it was merely a false report that she had left harbor which did the damage. For the rest of the time the heavy ships played the part of a 'fleet in being.' When the *Tirpitz* was immobilized by British midget submarines in September 1943 it was left to the *Scharnhorst* to make some sort of effort to stop the convoys getting through. The new Commander in Chief, Dönitz, obtained permission from Hitler to mount a major operation but on condition that Hitler refrained from interfering. Northern Group was commanded temporarily by Admiral Bey, who was under the impression that a destroyer-raid was all that was intended, but at the last minute he was told that the *Scharnhorst* ought to be sent out as well.

With the British reading many of the top-level signals the circumstances were hardly favorable, but on Christmas Day the *Scharnhorst* and five destroyers sailed from Altenfjord. Their objective was a convoy outward bound for Murmansk, for reconnaissance had failed to detect a second convoy, homeward bound from the Kola Inlet to Loch Ewe. The two convoys were escorted by cruisers and destroyers, with a distant escort provided by the battleship *Duke of York*, the cruiser *Jamaica* and four destroyers. The C-in-C Home Fleet, Admiral Fraser, was sufficiently certain of German intentions to transfer some escorts from one convoy to the other strengthening it to 14 destroyers. Admiral Bey was taking his force into a hornet's nest, and when he lost contact with his destroyers early next morning disaster became certain. Unaware that the *Duke of York* and *Jamaica* were only 200 miles away, closing at a steady

17 knots the *Scharnhorst* continued on course to intercept the convoy.

At 0840 the cruiser *Belfast* picked up the *Scharnhorst* on radar at 30 miles, and three-quarters of an hour later she fired star-shell into the Arctic gloom. Then the *Norfolk* opened fire and an 8-inch shell smashed into the *Scharnhorst*'s foretop, destroying the fire control director. Badly shaken, the battlecruiser turned away, her bulk enabling her to outstrip the cruisers in the heavy seas. Admiral Burnett, flying his flag in HMS *Belfast*, ordered the three cruisers to return to the convoy. It was feared for a time that the *Scharnhorst* would return to base but just after mid-day she reappeared and opened fire on the cruisers at 11,000 yards. The *Norfolk* was hit in an 8-inch turret and had most of her radar sets knocked out but the three cruisers fought back and forced the battlecruiser to turn away.

The *Scharnhorst* had unwittingly turned in the direction of the *Duke of York* and at 1617 the Home Fleet flagship picked her up on radar. When the range came down to 12,000 yards the *Duke of York* opened fire, taking the *Scharnhorst* completely by surprise. She sheered away sharply but the duel continued at ranges of 17,000–20,000 yards as she used her speed to open the range. Her gunnery improved but the two hits on the *Duke of York* went through masts without exploding. The *Duke of York*'s gunnery was excellent, and even when the *Scharnhorst* made small alterations of course to avoid the salvoes radar-plotting was able to allow for them. One or more of the 14-inch hits damaged a propeller shaft but this was not enough to cripple the *Scharnhorst* and eventually Admiral Fraser ordered his destroyers to attack. They achieved four hits.

Below: The battleships *Nevada, Texas, Arkansas, Warspite* and *Ramillies* led the D-Day bombardment operations.

The *Duke of York* opened fire again at 10,400 yards and within half an hour the *Scharnhorst*'s speed was down to 5 knots. She was burning furiously and shrouded in smoke and when the *Jamaica* closed in for the *coup de grace* with torpedoes she reported that all she could see was a dull glow in the smoke. Nobody saw the end of *Scharnhorst* at around 1945 and only 36 survivors were found in the icy water. She had gone down with nearly 2000 men on board, a victim of an outdated strategy and poor intelligence.

With the *Scharnhorst* gone it remained only to account for the *Tirpitz* which had survived many attempts to sink her. The problem was basically one of topography, for it was almost suicidal to make a low-level bombing run against a ship moored close to the side of a fjord. On the one occasion that a 750-pound bomb hit it penetrated all the decks but failed to burst. Next the X-Craft attack in September 1943 damaged her machinery and turrets severely. This forced the Germans to move her to a more southerly base for repairs, and once at Kaafjord she was within reach of RAF bombers flying from Northern Russia. On 15 September 1944 a force of 27 Lancasters attacked carrying new weapons, the 12,000-pound 'Tallboy" bomb and 400-pound JWII buoyant bombs. One hit forward caused great damage to the forepart of the ship and two near misses put the machinery out of action.

Time was running out for the Third Reich and the high command decided that the best use for the *Tirpitz* was as a floating fortress to defend Tromsö. With her damaged bow temporarily repaired the *Tirpitz* was moved from Kaafjord to Haakoy Island, three miles west of Tromsö in mid-October. Here she was at last within range of Lancasters flying from the far north of Scotland, and, after an unsuccessful attempt on 29 October, 32 Lancasters attacked with Tallboys on 12 November. The aircraft

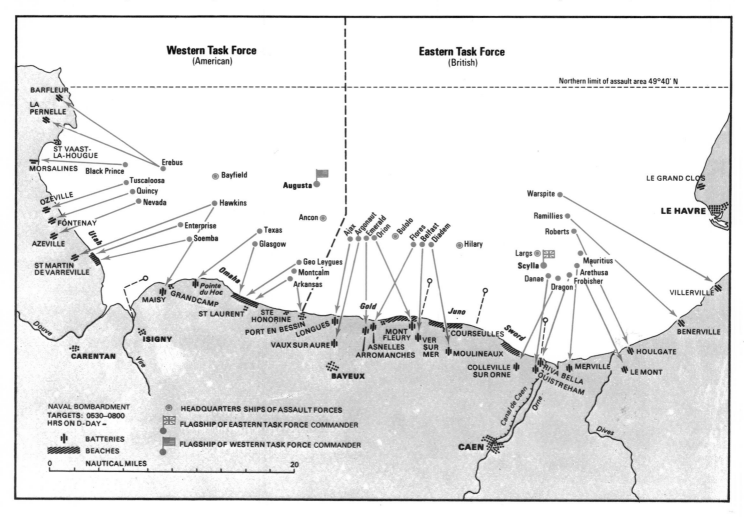

Above: The panzerschiff *Deutschland* was the first of her class to be built. Her name was later changed to *Lützow* on Hitler's orders.

had it all their own way, evading radar cover until they were only 75 miles away and not meeting any defending fighters. In clear weather the bomb-aimers were able to achieve what they had been planning for three years and three hits were observed. Although still firing her antiaircraft guns the *Tirpitz* began to list heavily and ten minutes after the attack had begun she rolled over and sank. It had taken 13 air attacks by 600 aircraft and an attack by midget submarines to finish off the last German capital ship.

The last duty for battleships in the European theatre was to provide covering fire for the big amphibious landings, starting with Torch and ending at Normandy. In June 1944 seven US and British battleships provided fire support for the D-Day landings, blasting concrete emplacements on the Atlantic Wall and disrupting German movements in response to calls from troops ashore. It was the last moment of glory for the older ships such as the USS *Arkansas* and *Nevada* and HMS *Warspite*, no longer able to take their place in the battle line but still capable of accurate shooting. They were only part of the massive effort which went into the liberation of Europe but they symbolized the way in which sea power had been the final deciding factor.

Right: The USS *Texas* is straddled by fire from a German shore battery whole bombarding Cherbourg, 25 June 1944.
Below: The *Littorio* Class *Vittorio Veneto* at speed.

VULNERABLE GIANTS

War in the Pacific had been brewing for many years for as Japan grew in military and industrial power she grew more aware of just how flimsy the Western colonial empire was. But the overriding need for Japan was raw materials, tin, rubber and oil to sustain her economic growth. Apart from coal the Japanese Home Islands lacked most of the important raw materials, and as these existed in abundance in the East Indies it was inevitable that Japanese thoughts should turn to conquest.

Standing in the way of expansion was the United States, and in particular her Pacific Fleet based on Pearl Harbor. The British were fully engaged in fighting the Germans and Italians and so were unable to spare reinforcements but the US Navy would have to be neutralized before any action could be taken in the East Indies. By 1940 the plans were ready for a daring strike to knock out the American Fleet and then occupy a huge defensive perimeter of island bases across the Pacific. Behind this 'island barrier' the Japanese hoped to be able to absorb any counterattacks and reduce enemy strength by attrition from submarines. The British attack on Taranto was studied with great interest, for the Japanese intended to repeat it on a much larger scale, using more modern aircraft in greater numbers.

At the end of November 1941 a fleet of six aircraft carriers, two battleships and three heavy cruisers put to sea for the attack on Pearl Harbor. Avoiding shipping routes the task force was in position 375 miles north of Hawaii by the night of 6–7 December without being detected. At 0700 next morning the first wave of aircraft left the carriers, and only two hours later the raid was over. The impossible had happened; the great base had been taken by surprise and eight battleships had been sunk or badly damaged. Most of the damage had been done by the first wave, for the aircraft were able to identify 'Battleship Row' easily. At 0810 a hit by a 1600-pound bomb on the *Arizona* detonated her forward magazines and she was blown apart. The *Oklahoma* capsized and the *California*, *Maryland*, *Tennessee* and *West Virginia* were badly damaged. The *Nevada* was set on fire and was nearly sunk in the harbor entrance but managed to put herself ashore out of the fairway. The only battleship to escape serious damage was the *Pennsylvania*, but even she required extensive repairs and to all intents and purposes the US Pacific Fleet had been wiped out.

There were a few compensations. The carriers had all been away exercising on the fatal Sunday and in their enthusiasm the Japanese pilots had omitted to destroy the huge tank farms. If the 4.5 million barrels of oil fuel stored there had been destroyed Pearl Harbor would have been finished as a base, no matter how many ships had survived.

The next to feel the weight of Japanese air power were the British, who had finally sent the *Prince of Wales* and the *Repulse* to the Far East at the eleventh hour in the hope that this might intimidate the Japanese. The attack on Pearl Harbor robbed the ships of any strategic value but in any case they were doomed for there was only rudimentary air cover from a few obsolescent RAF fighters. Three days after Pearl Harbor as the two ships were searching for a reported amphibious landing on the east coast of Malaya they were attacked by a mixed force of 30 bombers and 50 torpedo-bombers. The *Repulse* was slightly damaged by a bomb but the *Prince of Wales* was hit aft by a torpedo. Within minutes the ship had taken on some 2500 tons of water in the machinery compartments and was listing 11½ degrees. Then the shock of near-misses knocked out all the electric generators and the antiaircraft mountings lost power. A second wave of attacks missed both ships but the third wave put four more torpedoes into the starboard side. By now the *Prince of Wales* was doomed for her pumps could not cope with the progressive flooding but she could still steam. She made off slowly to the north and survived a further bomb hit at 1244 but at 1320 she suddenly lurched further to port and capsized.

The *Repulse*, despite her age, showed great skill in dodging the attacks but the third attack scored a hit aft. Unable to steer, she was helpless and took three more torpedoes, before capsizing. Destroyers were able to rescue Captain Tennant and 796 crew. It was the end of nearly a century of Western supremacy in the Far East, and also the end of the battleship's supremacy. Even if it could be argued that none of the other ships were modern, the *Prince of Wales* was a new-generation ship designed specifically to survive air attacks.

In retrospect the destruction of the battle fleet at Pearl Harbor was a blessing for it freed the American naval aviators from pre-war concepts of operating carriers as an adjunct to the battle squadrons. Now the fast carrier task group had to be the main striking force because there was no other, and the first big battles in 1942, Coral Sea and Midway, were decided by rival air groups without the surface fleets making contact at all. Particularly at Midway, when the Japanese C-in-C Admiral Yamamoto had seven battleships, including the giant *Yamato* and yet was powerless to defeat three American carriers. In 1942 both sides finally concluded that the battleship was no longer relevant and all work on battleships was downgraded in favor of greatly expanded carrier programs.

Freed from the treaty restrictions the US Navy could now build the ships that it wanted, and in 1939–40 six 45,000-ton *Iowa* Class were authorized, followed by five *Montana* Class displacing 56,000 tons. The *Iowas* were magnificent ships, fast and long-legged to keep up with the carriers. But in the meantime the burden had to be borne by the veterans. With a tremendous effort the Pearl Harbor casualties were repaired, apart from the *Arizona* and *Oklahoma*, some to be sent back into service with only updated antiaircraft batteries and others after total rebuilding.

When US forces landed on Guadalcanal on 7 August 1942 powerful Japanese surface forces were thrown in to try to dislodge them. On the night of 12–13 November 1942 the fast battleships *Hiei* and *Kirishima* attempted to bombard the US Marines' strip at Henderson Field but were surprised by a force of US cruisers and destroyers. In a fierce short-range action the *Portland* and *San Francisco* inflicted severe damage on the *Hiei*, and after she took a probable torpedo-hit she withdrew to the north. Her sister *Kirishima* escaped with only one 8-inch hit but planes from the carrier *Enterprise* found *Hiei* next day and harried her mercilessly. Finally she was abandoned and sunk by her escorting destroyers.

The following night another bombardment was attempted but

Above: The USS *New Mexico* is hit by a suicide plane. Kamikazes damaged *New Mexico* twice, in January and May 1945.
Right: The battleship *Colorado* in 1942. She carried the old-fashioned 'cage' masts until modernized in 1944.

this time the battleships *Washington* and *South Dakota* were in support. At 2316 both battleships opened fire on a Japanese light cruiser, only to suffer the sort of unpleasant surprise the British had suffered at Jutland. The Japanese were experts at night-fighting and they opened fire immediately with guns and torpedoes. All four American destroyers were put out of action before they could fire their own torpedoes, and to add to the confusion the *South Dakota* suddenly went out of control. About 17 minutes after the action had started the concussion from one of her twin 5-inch gun mountings caused a short-circuit in the electrical system. Although the power-loss lasted only three minutes the entire ship was in darkness and there was no power for guns, gyros or fire control. She turned to avoid the blazing destroyers but blundered off towards the Japanese line. At a range of only 5800 yards she was silhouetted against the glow and was fired on by the *Kirishima* and the heavy cruisers *Atago* and *Takao*.

The *South Dakota* was saved from serious damage because the *Washington* had prudently kept her searchlights switched off. Firing on radar the *Washington* was able to close to 8400 yards before riddling the *Kirishima* with nine 16-inch hits. The Americans withdrew to lick their wounds, leaving the Japanese destroyers to save the survivors of the *Kirishima* before sinking her with torpedoes. Although tactically an American victory it had revealed serious weaknesses in their organization.

As the new battleships joined the Fleet the older ships were relegated to bombardment duties in support of the various amphibious landings. The role of the newer fast battleships was

Above: Quadruple 40mm Bofors antiaircraft mountings were fitted to all US battleships from 1942 onward.
Above left: Opening the breech of a 16-inch gun on a US battleship.

not merely to ward off surface attacks on the carriers but to provide additional antiaircraft firepower. Being designed as steady gun-platforms their fire control was better than a cruiser's or a destroyer's, so that their effectiveness 'per barrel' was greater. In the Battle of the Philippine Sea in June 1944 Admiral Willis A Lee's seven fast battleships, were disposed in a battle line 15 miles east of the nearest carriers. Their task was to put up a 'wall of fire' to thin out any Japanese carrier planes trying to attack Admiral Spruance's forces, and this they did superbly, inflicting many casualties.

The last battle of the Pacific was also the biggest in history. The Battle of Leyte Gulf, in reality four separate battles, saw all types of warship functioning as designed; battleships, cruisers and destroyers were all involved in possibly the last conventional surface actions ever fought. The battle came about because the Japanese, in spite of the losses that they had

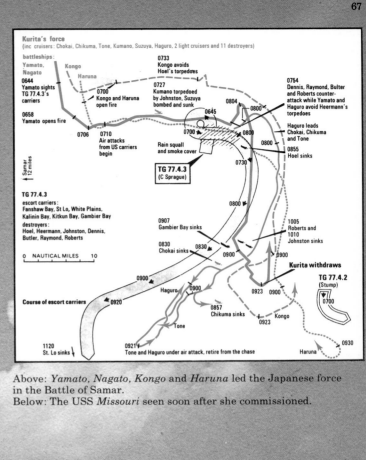

Above: *Yamato, Nagato, Kongo* and *Haruna* led the Japanese force in the Battle of Samar.
Below: The USS *Missouri* seen soon after she commissioned.

taken since the heady days after Pearl Harbor, still hankered after an annihilating battle between the two fleets. The demolition of their island perimeter and dwindling oil reserves made it imperative to do something decisive, and the invasion of the Marianas in mid-1944 finally forced their hand. It did not take a genius to predict that the next American thrust would be in the Philippines, and to defeat this the *Sho-1* or Victory Plan was conceived. It was to be a final gambler's throw with the entire surface fleet committed to tempt the Americans into a full-scale action. It was crude but simple; without sufficient carrier aircrews to fly from the carriers the surface forces would have to force their way through to the invasion areas. Faced with this threat the Americans would have to bring in their main fleet and give battle.

Command of the Mobile Force was entrusted to Vice-Admiral Ozawa and comprised four carriers and the two hybrid battleship-carriers *Hyuga* and *Ise* (but without aircraft), as well as three cruisers. Vice-Admiral Kurita had Forces 'A' and 'B', the heavy striking force, comprising the 64,000-ton *Yamato* and *Musashi*, the *Nagato*, *Haruna* and *Kongo* and 12 cruisers. Force 'C' was divided into a Van Squadron under Vice-Admiral Nishimura, with *Fuso* and *Yamashiro* and a single heavy cruiser, and a Rear Squadron under Vice-Admiral Shima, with three heavy cruisers. To the Americans these formations were identified by their location: the Mobile Force was labelled the 'Northern Force,' Forces 'A' and 'B' became the 'Center Force' and Force 'C' the 'Southern Force.'

Ozawa's role was that of decoy to draw Admiral Halsey's Fast Carrier Task Force away from the invasion fleet. Forces 'A' and 'B' would then join Force 'C' to destroy the invasion fleet, brushing aside any opposition. Against the 18-inch guns of the *Yamato* and *Musashi* and the fearsome Long Lance torpedoes of the cruisers and destroyers would be ranged only six old battleships, the *Mississippi*, *Maryland*, *West Virginia*, *Tennessee*, *California* and *Pennsylvania* for all the fast battleships were with Halsey's Third Fleet. Decoying Halsey would also reduce the threat from air attack, it was hoped, for the attackers would only be faced by the Seventh Fleet's escort carriers. It was accepted that Ozawa's force would probably be destroyed but, faced with the risk of certain defeat within a few months, the Japanese felt that the sacrifice would be worthwhile.

As soon as the first assault waves were reported moving into Leyte Gulf *Sho-1* was put into action, Ozawa sailing from Japan and Kurita, Nishimura and Shima from Brunei. But things went wrong almost immediately for Kurita's heavy units were sighted by two US submarines as they passed through the Palawan Passage. After sending off the vital news the two submarines made a brilliant attack, torpedoing three heavy cruisers. The Japanese air forces in the Philippines had wasted their strength in largely unsuccessful attacks on American carriers rather than provide a combat air patrol over Kurita's ships and so they now felt the full weight of air attack. Over 250 planes from Task Force 38 mounted five separate attacks.

The *Yamato* and the *Nagato* were each damaged by two bomb hits but the *Musashi* bore the brunt. An estimated 13 torpedoes hit her on the port side and seven more on the starboard side, as well as 17 bombs and 18 near-misses. Even her massive protection could not stand up to such punishment and Kurita was forced to leave her behind. She finally sank about eight hours after the attacks had begun, but the fifth attack was the last. Kurita was not to know it, but Halsey had taken the bait and the whole of his Fast Carrier Task Force was in hot pursuit of Ozawa, leaving the invasion armada off Samar undefended. To the appalled Americans it was a nightmare come to life, the giant *Yamato* and her consorts attacking flimsy escort carriers and their destroyer escorts. Nor were the CVEs' aircraft armed with weapons for attacking battleships; their job was to provide support for the troops ashore, and no dive-bombers were embarked. And yet the impossible happened – the Japanese withdrew without achieving the destruction of the invasion fleet,

although they sank an escort carrier, two destroyers and a destroyer escort.

As predicted, Ozawa's force was devastated when Halsey's planes caught up with it off Cape Engano. All the carriers were sunk but the converted carrier-battleships *Hyuga* and *Ise* both escaped and made their way back to Japan. But the most devastating defeat of all had overtaken Nishimura when he entered Surigao Strait just after midnight on 24–25 October. His force, comprising two destroyers leading the flagship *Yamashiro*, the *Fuso* and the heavy cruiser *Mogami* in line ahead with two more destroyers guarding the flanks, brushed aside attacks by PT-Boats and was then attacked by destroyers, Nishimura appears to have taken no evasive action, and at 0207 a spread of probably five torpedoes hit the *Fuso* amidships. Oil fuel caught fire and then a series of explosions tore the ship in half, but instead of sinking the two burning halves drifted apart. Both Japanese and American lookouts reported two blazing ships, and the after section took an hour to sink.

Behind the destroyers and PT-Boats was waiting Admiral Jesse B Oldendorf's Battle Line, old battleships but equipped with the latest fire control and radar. At 0253 they opened fire at 22,800 yards, first the *Tennessee* and *West Virginia* and then the *Maryland* and the flagship *Mississippi*. Incredibly the *Yamashiro* seemed impervious to broadsides of 14-inch and 16-inch shells, and even torpedoes, but finally she slowed to a dead stop and lay blazing furiously in the water. No ship could take that sort of pounding indefinitely and at 0319 she finally rolled over and sank. Surigao Strait was a fitting swansong for the battleship, particularly as both the Japanese and the American ships were veterans of an earlier generation. They may have been overtaken by the carriers in importance but when it came down to a question of stopping a strong force of ships, just as the British had found with the *Bismarck* the battleship's guns were the final arbiter.

The Imperial Japanese Navy was all but wiped out at Leyte, for although aircraft remained there were no trained pilots to fly them and no carriers; there were still surface ships but no fuel to enable them to put to sea. As the remnants of the Air Force immolated themselves in *kamikaze* attacks on the invasion fleet around Okinawa the Navy planned the biggest suicide of all. The giant *Yamato* was ordered to use the remaining oil fuel (there was only enough for a one-way trip) for a last sortie against the invaders. Although there was talk of blasting her way through the ring of Allied ships and then beaching herself

Above: The US *Mississippi* during a bombardment operation.
Left: The quarterdeck of the USS Massachusetts (BB.59).
Below: The massive US invasion fleet off Leyte, October 1944.
The battleships *Colorado* and *Texas* are among the ships in the
foreground.

on Okinawa as a huge gun-emplacement, the real purpose was
to act as live bait. By drawing off as many carrier planes it was
hoped to leave the air-space around Okinawa clear for a gigantic
kamikaze attack on the transports. Code-named *Ten-Go*, the
force comprized the *Yamato*, the light cruiser *Yahagi* and eight
destroyers under the command of Vice-Admiral Ito.

At 1600 on 6 April 1945 the *Ten-Go* force slipped away from
Tokuyama Bay and headed towards Okinawa in a ring formation with the *Yamato* in the centre. At 1220 the next day the
Yamato signalled that she could see large numbers of aircraft
33,000 yards off her port bow. At 1232 she opened fire, using even
the 18-inch guns to fire a 'splash barrage' against low-flying
attackers. At 1240 the first bombs hit her and ten minutes later
she was hit on the port side by torpedoes. After another eight
torpedoes on the port side and two on the starboard side the
flooding got out of control and the list could no longer be
corrected. After the last torpedo hit at 1417 the giant ship was
listing 20 degrees and the order 'abandon ship' was given. She
finally capsized and erupted in a huge explosion, probably
caused by internal fires reaching the magazines.

Although the fast carriers had dominated the Pacific War
the battleship retained her prestige to the end. When General
MacArthur and Admiral Nimitz witnessed the unconditional
surrender of Japan it was on the quarterdeck of the USS
Missouri, while HMS *Duke of York* was moored nearby repre-
senting the British Pacific Fleet.

THE END OF AN ERA?

The battleship was officially dead but she would not lie down. A surprising number remained in commission after the Second World War, mainly because their large hulls provided useful accommodation for sailors and cadets under training. Their spaciousness also made them ideal flagships.

The US Navy now had four of the magnificent *Iowas* in commission. All the old battleships were rapidly decommissioned and laid up for disposal, with the exception of the *Mississippi*, which was earmarked for conversion to a gunnery training and trials ship. Even the two *North Carolinas* and the four *South Dakotas* went into the 'mothball fleet' early in 1947.

The battleship might have remained in limbo, rather like a domesticated dinosaur, had it not been for the Korean War. When the North Korean Army crossed the 38th Parallel in 1950 the *Missouri* was the only US battleship in commission. In September that year she was sent to South Korea and served three tours of duty between 1950 and 1953. She was joined by her three sisters and they proved invaluable for shore bombardment. Again and again the battleships were able to give rapid and precise fire support to ground troops, their biggest advantage being their ability to 'loiter' and resume the bombardment if the enemy showed signs of further activity. No matter what weight of ordnance could be delivered by aircraft they always had to return to base after a short interval whereas the battleship could usually be called up to provide more gunfire.

The four *Iowas* remained active until 1955–58. In 1953 the *Iowa* and *Wisconsin* joined the last British battleship HMS *Vanguard* in the big NATO exercise 'Mariner' in the North Atlantic. All three showed off their enormous endurance by refuelling all the escorting destroyers in the task force. When the *Wisconsin* decommissioned on 8 March 1958 at Bayonne, New Jersey it seemed that end of the story had been reached, the first time since 1895 that the US Navy had no battleship in service. But soon the Vietnam War was absorbing an increasing American military effort and there was a vociferous demand from the US Marine Corps for something heavier than 8-inch gunfire support. Finally in 1967 permission was granted to bring a battleship forward from reserve.

The choice fell on the *New Jersey*, last in commission exactly a decade earlier. She was taken in hand at Philadelphia Navy Yard in August 1967 and recommissioned the following April. The *New Jersey*'s comeback was short but effective. On the 'gun line' in Vietnam she spent 120 days in all, of which 47 days were continuous. During the Second World War she had fired a total of 771 16-inch shells, during the Korean War she had fired nearly 7000 rounds, but this time she fired 5688 rounds and 15,000 rounds of 5-inch as well. Sadly she was taken out of commission in December 1969 but in 1981 her reactivation was again authorized. There is even talk of rearming her sisters with Cruise missiles to serve as flagships. The battleship is not yet finished.

Right: A Sea Knight helicopter lands on the *New Jersey* while the battleship is alongside the ammunition ship *Mount Katmai*, off Vietnam in July 1968.
Top left: The *New Jersey* and the carrier *Coral Sea* return to the US from Vietnam in April 1969.
Top right: The USS *Idaho* bombards Okinawa in 1945.

Below: The USS Alabama (BB.60) seen in Puget Sound, Washington in March 1945, shortly before leaving to take part in the Okinawa invasion.

DESTROYERS

DESTROYERS

Previous page: An escorting destroyer passes an aircraft carrier of the US task forces operating off Okinawa in 1945.
Page 73: The USS *Martin Ray* (DE.338) on convoy duty in the Atlantic late in World War II.
Below: The USS *Moffett* (DD.362) in the South Atlantic in January 1943. The *Moffett* served in South American waters throughout 1943.

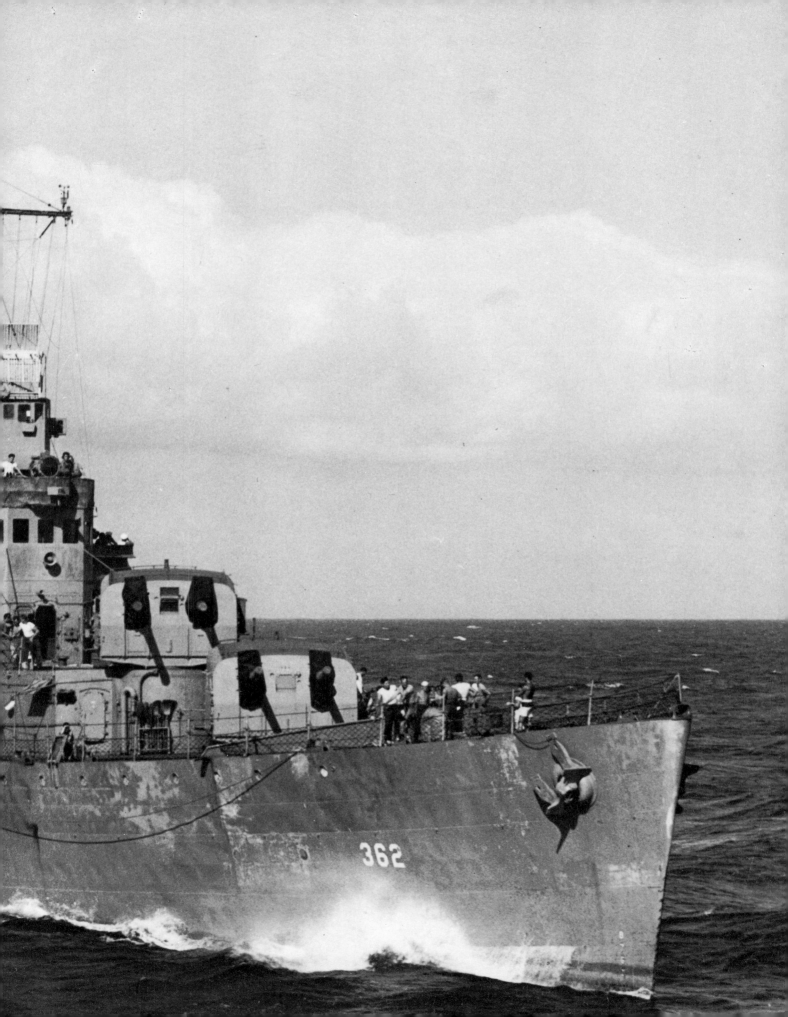

DOVER PATROL TO JUTLAND

The first shot of the naval war was fired by the British destroyer *Lance* on 5 August 1914, a unit of the 3rd Flotilla, led by the light cruiser *Amphion*.

On receipt of a report that a steamer had been seen 'throwing things overboard' the 3rd Flotilla weighed anchor and left Harwich. At midday they sighted smoke, and the *Lance* and *Landrail* gave chase. The steamer hoisted the German ensign, and was quickly stopped and sunk by the two destroyers. She turned out to be the auxiliary minelayer *Königin Luise*, and she had been caught only 13 hours after the declaration of war. The *Amphion* led her destroyers back to Harwich, but early next morning she ran into the minefield laid by the *Königin Luise*.

Destroyers played a major part in the first big operation of the war, a raid on the German outposts off Heligoland, which led to the Battle of the Heligoland Bight on 28 August. It involved the submarines at Harwich as well as the destroyers. The plan was to use an outer patrol line of submarines to decoy the German torpedo boat patrols out to sea, where they could be trapped by the Harwich Force destroyers and their light cruiser leaders. Both sides had a lot to learn. First the British betrayed their intentions by sending too many radio messages, and then poor staffwork at the Admiralty prevented the two commodores, Keyes and Tyrwhitt, from being told that the Admiralty had decided to send more powerful reinforcements, in the shape of a cruiser squadron and four battlecruisers. The Germans, on the other hand, were caught completely unawares, and their heavy units were lying in the Jade River without steam up and unable to cross the bar until high tide. It had not occurred to the Ger-

man High Command that the British would send such strong forces into the Bight, almost within range of the guns on Heligoland, and their light forces were at a disadvantage.

At about 0700 the *Laurel* opened fire on the German *G.194* and within an hour British destroyers and the light cruisers *Arethusa* and *Fearless* were in action with the torpedo boats guarding the German inner patrol line. Destroyer gunfire could never be very accurate, and although the range fell to 7000 yards the thick haze meant that the heavy fire was largely ineffective. Suddenly the cruisers *Stettin* and *Frauenlob*, which had been lying at anchor off Heligoland and had raised steam when they heard the gunfire, arrived on the scene. They took on the British cruisers and were able to silence the *Arethusa* with 35 hits. The British destroyers left the cruisers to fight it out, and concentrated on punishing the torpedo boats *D.8* and *T.33*, which had found themselves caught up in the battle. The *Fearless* and her destroyers later managed to trap the *V.187*, which went down fighting.

The *Arethusa* had been badly knocked about, and although the sweep should have been over, at 1030 her destroyers were still standing by while she stopped to make urgent repairs to her machinery and guns. Every minute that passed made it more likely that German reinforcements would appear from the Ems and Jade. When the first of these appeared, the light cruiser *Strassburg*, she was mistaken for a much larger cruiser and Commodore Tyrwhitt signalled to Vice-Admiral Beatty and his battlecruisers, 'Respectfully submit that I may be supported. Am hard pressed.' But long before any help could arrive the

destroyers would have to face heavy punishment. Just as the *Laurel* turned away after firing her torpedoes a salvo of 10.5-cm shells hit her. One hit in the engine-room killed four men and injured others; a second hit near the forward 4-inch gun killed most of the crew and another wrecked the after funnel and wounded her captain. Her next astern, the *Liberty*, lost her captain and signalman when a shell burst behind the bridge, and the last in line, the *Laertes*, was hit in the boiler-room.

Suddenly the cruiser *Mainz* shuddered as one of the British torpedoes hit her. In total darkness, with every piece of glass between decks smashed, the ship began to sink slowly by the head. She had already been set on fire, and the arrival of the first British reinforcements, a squadron of light cruisers, sealed her fate. The *Arethusa* was still limping home at 10 knots, and it seemed that she might yet be cut off and sunk, as the German reinforcements were now arriving. But suddenly five large ships came into sight from the west. They were Admiral Beatty's battlecruisers, the *Lion*, *Princess Royal*, *Queen Mary*, *Invincible* and *New Zealand*, steaming at full speed, with dense clouds of coal-smoke billowing from their funnels.

Heading between the burning wreck of the *Mainz* and the *Arethusa* the big ships turned their guns on the *Köln* and brought her to a stop. Then the luckless *Ariadne* blundered out of the mist and crossed the *Lion*'s bows, to be shattered by

Above left: HMS *Swift* at Dover. She was the flotilla leader in a frantic action against German torpedo boats in the Channel in 1917.
Above: HMS *Broke* was also involved in the action and rammed and sank a German torpedo boat.

repeated hits. Pausing only to finish off the *Köln*, the battle-cruisers drew off to cover the light forces' withdrawal.

It had been a risky action, but the risks had been justified by the bold handling of the British destroyers, which had repeatedly held off light cruisers and had saved the *Arethusa* from being sunk. It was to be the last major destroyer action for nearly two years, but the Harwich Force in particular was to be embroiled in many skirmishes with the opposing German cruisers and destroyers through the next four years. However much time the big ships on both sides might spend in harbor, the destroyers were constantly in action. The Harwich Force became more and more important as the chief offensive squadron in the North Sea, well placed to intercept raids by German surface ships and to mount offensive patrols in the southern North Sea.

The other important squadron was the Dover Patrol, which was based on Dover to guard the vital cross-Channel supply route between Britain and France. As the armies on the Western Front expanded, an ever-increasing number of troops had to be transported across the Channel, accompanied by vast quantities

Below: In the Mediterranean German and Austrian pressure forced the Allies to call in whatever help was available. These Japanese destroyers are lying off Corfu, April 1917.

of war material such as coal for French industry and ammunition for the guns. In the first weeks, when German troops swept through Belgium, the Dover Patrol destroyers showed how adaptable they were by joining in the bombardments of the German right flank.

The cross-Channel convoys were a tempting target for raids by German torpedo boats, particularly when the Germans were able to establish forward bases at Zeebrugge and Ostend. Fortunately for the Allies the northern French port of Dunkirk was still on their hands, and it became an equally useful forward base. Some idea of the problem, and also the size of target presented, is indicated by the fact that the average number of cross-Channel sailings was about 700 each year. Between August 1914 and December 1917 nearly six million troops were carried in addition to some 120,000 east-west transits of the English Channel. During the same period a further 800,000 casualties

were brought back from France. Yet, in all this time only one hospital ship and an empty transport were mined and another empty transport was sunk by German torpedo boats. The other casualties were all sustained by the warships and small patrol craft.

The most famous action of the Dover Patrol occurred on the night of 20 April 1917, when two large destroyers intercepted a force of German torpedo boats in the Channel. The flotilla leader *Swift* and the ex-Chilean *Broke* were patrolling off Dover when they heard firing off Calais and saw gun-flashes. When shells began to fall on Dover they knew for certain that a raid was in progress; they steered for Calais, but took care not to be drawn away from what they rightly interpreted as the enemy's main objective, the large collection of shipping which was sheltering in the Downs. In fact two large torpedo boats had bombarded Calais to draw off the patrols while four more had slipped in to bombard Dover before joining forces again.

About seven miles east of Dover the *Swift* and *Broke* sighted six vessels steaming fast off the port bow in the opposite direction. The strangers opened fire and the two British boats replied immediately. The *Swift* put her helm hard over to ram, but Commander Peck and his staff on the bridge were dazzled by the flash of the 6-inch gun forward and she passed just astern of the German line, firing a single torpedo as she went. Commander Evans, astern in the *Broke*, held his fire to allow the torpedo director a clear moment to aim. This torpedo or the one fired by the *Swift* a moment earlier, hit the *G.85* full amidships in a huge plume of smoke and spray. Evans, seeing his intended victim hit, altered course to ram the torpedo boat astern. It was the *G.42*, and she tried frantically to escape with sparks pouring from her funnels but her captain had left it too late, and with a screech of grinding steel the *Broke*'s bow tore into the thin side plating and flung her over on her beam ends.

Above right: The ill-fated Allied landings at Gallipoli in 1915 suffered from extended lines of supply. Here, HMS *Wolverine* guards the transports at 'W' Beach.
Right: Destroyers could be uncomfortable in rough weather but the task of protecting the Fleet had to be continued. Royal Navy 'M' Class destroyers escort a squadron of the Grand Fleet.

Below: German torpedo boats were a constant threat to the troop and supply ships which steamed back and forth across the Channel. However, they managed to sink only one transport during the war, thanks largely to the efforts of the destroyers of the Dover Patrol.

Above: German torpedo boats, with their low freeboard, also fared badly in a rough sea.

It must have been a nightmare scene, with the *Broke*'s guns pouring shells into *G.42* at point-blank range. Several of the German seamen had clambered onto the forecastle of the British destroyer, and the survivors of the forward gun crews assumed that they were boarders and armed themselves with rifles, bayonets and cutlasses. A murderous fight took place, at a range so close that even the officers on the bridge were using their personal side-arms. The *Broke* herself was in danger, for a box of cordite cartridges was burning, and illuminating her in a lurid red glow. One of the surviving German torpedo boats slid past out of the darkness and fired shells indiscriminately into the inferno. In seconds the *Broke*'s decks were running with blood, as a quarter of her crew were killed or wounded by 10.5-cm shells.

With her bows still locked into the hull of the sinking German

torpedo boat she was a sitting target until the unknown torpedo boat disappeared. Painfully she ground her way clear and tried to follow the *Swift*, which was in full pursuit of two enemy torpedo boats, but a shell had damaged the main steam pipe and soon she was losing feed-water to the boilers, so she steamed slowly back to the scene of the action. The *Swift* was soon back, for she had also been damaged severely by shellfire, and could not maintain full speed. It had been a brief and bloody engagement, but two large torpedo boats had been sunk and it effectively put an end to raids from the Flanders torpedo boat flotillas for the time being. Both commanders were awarded the DSO, and 'Evans of the *Broke*' rose to become a colorful Admiral in later years.

The destroyer's most valuable contribution in World War I was her unexpected efficiency as an antisubmarine craft. Until specially-designed escorts were built only the destroyer had the speed, maneuverability and armament to sink a submarine before she submerged.

The threat from submarines had not been taken seriously in

the early weeks of the war, but after several large ships had been torpedoed it was realized that no formation of warships should move anywhere without an escort of destroyers. After the inconclusive Battle of the Dogger Bank early in 1915, in which the destroyers had little to do but finish off the battered German cruiser *Blücher*, their work became almost entirely monotonous patrolling.

There was the ever-present danger from mines and the risk of collision between ships maneuvering at high speed in fog or darkness, without lights or radar. Out of 67 British destroyers lost between 1914 and 1918, collisions accounted for 18 and another 12 were wrecked.

The great trial of strength between the British Grand Fleet and the German High Seas Fleet eventually came at the end of May 1916. The Battle of Jutland was the first and in a sense the only test of the theories of destroyer tactics, for both sides had large numbers of torpedo craft present; 80 British destroyers and flotilla leaders and 62 German torpedo boats. The battle divided itself into two distinct parts, the day action on 31 May, in which

Below: Battleships of the Grand Fleet are escorted by the 11th Destroyer Flotilla. HMS *Marmion* is followed by *Marne*, *Prince*, *Kempenfelt* and *Morning Star*.

Above: HMS *Tipperary* took part in the night action at Jutland. She was a flotilla leader built for the Chilean Navy but taken over by the Admiralty at the beginning of the war.

the rival torpedo craft duelled with one another in vain attempts to take the pressure off their capital ships, and the night action on 31 May–1 June, in which British destroyers faced the entire German Fleet alone.

It was two German torpedo boats, *B.109* and *B.110* which unwittingly started the battle. At about 1600 they were ordered to examine a small Danish steamer, and while they were doing so two British light cruisers arrived on the same mission. Shots were fired and each group returned to its main body flashing the message 'Enemy in sight.' A fierce action developed between Admiral Beatty's battlecruisers and the German battlecruisers under Admiral Hipper, and when the British lost HMS *Indefatigable* and the flagship *Lion* was badly hit, the destroyers were ordered to attack to relieve the pressure. At almost the same time 15 German torpedo boats were ordered to attack the

Above: Destroyers played a vital role in the Battle of Jutland (1916) with 80 taking part. Here HMS *Badger* approaches the wreck of the battlecruiser *Invincible*.

British capital ships, as Hipper's line was coming under heavy fire. A fierce action developed in 'no man's land' between the two battle lines, in which the British *Nestor* and *Nomad* and the German *V.27* and *V.29* were crippled and left in a sinking condition. But the British destroyers' heavy gun-armament enabled them to keep the German boats off, and forced them to fire their torpedoes at too great a range to score any hits. The British destroyers fired their torpedoes at a range of 5000–7000 yards, and although most were dodged by a timely turn away by Hipper, one from the *Petard* exploded against the armor of the *Seydlitz*, tearing a hole 13 by 39 feet in her side. Although taking in water, she was able to keep her place in the battle line.

In the next phase of the day-action the two battlecruiser forces fell back on their main fleets. Visibility was deteriorating, partly because of haze but mainly from the dense clouds of smoke from the scores of coal-burning ships present. Both commanders were holding their light forces in check, knowing that a general fleet action was imminent, but this did not prevent HMS *Onslow* from attacking the cruiser *Wiesbaden* on her own initiative. Lieutenant-Commander John Tovey (a future Commander in Chief of the Home Fleet) decided that the damaged cruiser was a 'target of opportunity' and approached her. Suddenly he saw enemy ships looming out of the haze and realized that his destroyer was only 8000 yards from Admiral Hipper's battlecruisers. Tovey was unperturbed and turned to fire his four torpedoes at them, but just as the first torpedo leapt from its tube a heavy-caliber shell hit the *Onslow* in the boiler-room. With steam billowing from No. 2 boiler-room and her speed dropping rapidly, the *Onslow* limped past the *Wiesbaden* and fired a second torpedo, which exploded under the cruiser's conning tower. Then Tovey saw a line of battleships, Admiral Scheer's High Seas Fleet, deploying into action, and decided that the destruction of one destroyer was worth the chance of scoring a torpedo-hit. Although making only ten knots and listing heavily the 1000-ton *Onslow* crawled across the sea and launched her last two torpedoes at a range of 8000 yards.

It would be pleasing to report that such heroism was rewarded by at least one torpedo-hit on a battleship, but both the *Onslow*'s torpedoes missed, and her hit on the *Wiesbaden* did not prevent that sorely battered ship from continuing the fight later. The destroyer eventually came to a dead stop when her boilers ran out of feed-water. For a time it looked as if she might be sunk by the German ships, which were within gun-range, and her anxious crew had a grandstand view of an action between the battleship *Warspite* and the head of the German line, but the battleships swept on and ignored her. She was eventually taken in tow by her fellow-destroyer HMS *Defender*, which had the dubious distinction of having an unexploded 12-inch shell in the ashpit of one of her boilers. The two cripples fell in with the damaged *Warspite*, making her way back to Rosyth, but the battleship dared not loiter to help the destroyers, and left them. After a nightmare journey across 350 miles in a rising sea the two ships arrived safely. Both captains received the DSO, Tovey for his gallant attack and Commander Palmer of the *Defender* for his outstanding seamanship and determination.

Meanwhile the Grand Fleet was deploying into action, and Admiral Jellicoe, the Commander in Chief, pushed his three battlecruisers, *Invincible, Indomitable* and *Inflexible*, forward to support Beatty's ships. Escorting these ships were four destroyers, led by Commander Loftus W Jones in HMS *Shark*. The *Shark* and *Acasta* attacked a German light cruiser and a battlecruiser with torpedoes, but the divisional leader was badly damaged by gunfire. Refusing a tow from the *Acasta*, Loftus Jones was preparing to abandon ship when two German torpedo boats appeared. Although only the midships 4-inch gun was still working the crippled *Shark* fought back until she was hit by a torpedo. A handful of men, including the desperately wounded captain escaped on a raft, but during the night he and eight others died, leaving only six survivors out of a ships's company of 77 officers and men. The *Acasta* narrowly escaped the same fate, but she was towed by another destroyer and made port.

As darkness fell the fleet action died away, leaving the British apparently well placed between the High Seas Fleet and its bases. The capital ships were grouped into cruising formation once more, to provide a more compact defense against a night attack by torpedo boats, which was expected. Admiral Jellicoe stationed his destroyers five miles astern of the main fleet, partly to screen his big ships against such an attack but also to give them the opportunity to attack the enemy fleet if it should pass to the south on its way home. But these destroyers had very little idea of the whereabouts of much of their own fleet, let alone the enemy, apart from the knowledge that the battle fleet was five miles ahead. In the confusion of the fighting that had just ended the staff had overlooked the fact that the destroyers had no way of knowing whether they were attacking friend or foe. If they flashed the recognition signal they could expect to be lashed by gunfire, and if they fired first they ran the awful risk of sinking one of their own ships. The truth of the matter was, of course, that no-one had ever imagined such a large number of destroyers gathered together, with so little concrete information about everybody's position.

To summarize, the High Sea Fleet decided to take its chance in a night action, and try to drive its way through the screen of destroyers. In this decision Scheer had been helped by two strokes of good fortune: an intercepted signal told him that the destroyers were well astern of Jellicoe's fleet, and a rash visual exchange of the night challenge and reply between two British

Right: The US shipbuilding industry broke all construction records in 1918. Here USS *Belknap* (DD.251) makes a high speed trial.
Far right: In 1918 HMS *Walker* was one of the new 'V & W' Class which was much imitated by other navies.

battlecruisers at dusk had been partially read by a German light cruiser. The first piece of information gave Scheer the assurance that he was only facing light forces, against which the German night-fighting organization had more than a fair chance of success, and the second meant that British ships would be dangerously unsure in those vital opening minutes of night action, whereas the Germans would know immediately that they had been challenged by an enemy ship.

The first clash came at 2205, when the 11th Flotilla was challenged by ships which gave the first two letters of the

Above: The flotilla leader *Anzac* at high speed.

challenge for the day, followed by two incorrect letters. Before anyone could decide what to do, searchlights were unmasked by the cruisers *Hamburg* and *Elbing*, followed by a withering fire. The light cruiser *Castor* fired back, and she and two of her destroyers each fired a torpedo, but the rest of the flotilla held their fire, convinced that a mistake had been made. The torpedoes missed and the two hostile cruisers disappeared into the darkness as rapidly as they had appeared.

The leader *Tipperary* and her 4th Flotilla had seen the gun flashes and searchlights of the *Castor*'s action, and so were alerted. This was not enough, however, for as soon as the *Tipperary* challenged what she mistook for a force of friendly cruisers, she was blasted by gunfire. The 4th Flotilla had in fact run into the head of the German battle fleet, and the puny destroyers were about to take on dreadnoughts 20 times their size. The *Spitfire* swung to starboard to avoid the blazing wreck of the *Tipperary*, but her captain was blinded by the searchlights, and failed to see the ram bow of a big ship looming overhead. To avoid being cut in half he chose to collide with his opponent, port bow to port bow, and the *Spitfire* ground down the side of the other ship. The big ship's forward turret swung round and fired a salvo at her, but the destroyer was so small that the shells roared overhead; even so, the blast was enough to flatten the bridge and demolish the mast and fore-funnel.

When the *Spitfire* drew clear she had on board 20 feet of steel plating and part of some anchor gear wedged into her messdeck. Lieutenant-Commander Trelawny thought that the enemy 'light cruiser' was probably not a new ship because of the thick paint, but his opponent was actually the dreadnought battleship *Nassau*, displacing 20,000 tons and armed with twelve 11-inch guns.

The German ships were not having it all their own way, and the head of their line was thrown into confusion as a result of the British destroyers' torpedo attacks. The *Elbing* was one of a number of cruisers which were forced to weave between the battleships in an attempt to dodge the torpedoes, and while doing this she was rammed by the *Posen*. Then the *Rostock* did the same, and was hit by a torpedo as she squeezed through astern of the *Westfalen*. But the 4th Flotilla had been destroyed as a fighting formation without being able to stop the High Seas Fleet's breakthrough. Four destroyers had been sunk and four more seriously damaged while 390 officers and men had been killed, and 72 wounded.

The next obstacle in Admiral Scheer's path was a mixed force of destroyers, mainly the 13th Flotilla, and some of the 9th and 10th Flotillas. Although casualties were not as heavy as in the 4th Flotilla, the German battle-line again smashed its way through, damaging the *Petard* severely and literally blowing the *Turbulent* apart with gunfire, without suffering any loss. Then the 12th Flotilla attacked, and this time one of their torpedoes found its mark. Suddenly the predreadnought battleship *Pom-*

Above left: Destroyers were used as fast minelayers. Here a stoker contemplates the port mine-rail of HMS *Walker*.
Below: The arrival of US destroyers at Queenstown, Ireland, in May 1917 greatly helped spread the load of convoy duties. USS *Davis* (DD.65) is the leading ship.

Above: USS *Allen* (DD.66) was typical of the American destroyers of World War I. She also saw service in World War II.

mern of the 2nd Squadron was illuminated by a flash which spread along her waterline. She heeled over, torn apart by a series of further explosions, and quickly disappeared in flames as her ammunition detonated. All 844 men on board were lost.

Jutland showed that the destroyers had been overrated. Although both Commanders in Chief had repeatedly turned away rather than face torpedo attacks, the gunfire of defending cruisers and the battleships themselves had been sufficient to drive off daylight attacks. At night destroyers had found it very difficult to operate against a well-coordinated defense. There were 252 warships present at the battle, and of these only the German *Seydlitz* and the British *Marlborough* were damaged by torpedoes in daylight, while night attacks had accounted for two light cruisers and the old *Pommern*.

For many years the experience of Jutland was to dominate destroyer tactics in all navies, which is why the fighting has been described at some length. What the British learned was that, above all, each group of destroyers must be given as much information as possible about dispositions of both friendly and hostile ships. The second lesson was that flotillas were too large, as had been predicted as long ago as 1887. The large flotilla was retained for the time being as an administrative unit but for tactical purposes it was broken down into two divisions of eight. There was to be no second meeting between the British and German Fleets, and the growing need to divert destroyers to hunting U-Boats meant that any serious revision of destroyer tactics had to be deferred.

By the time of the second unrestricted U-Boat campaign of 1917 destroyers had become indispensible as escorts. Hitherto formations of warships had always moved with their screen of destroyers, but now merchant ships needed escorting as well when convoys were introduced in May 1917. Thus, when the United States entered the war the US Navy was asked to send destroyers as the most urgent priority, and a Japanese offer to send eight of their own to the Mediterranean was gratefully accepted.

On 24 April 1917 six destroyers of the US Atlantic Fleet, the *Wadsworth*, *Conyngham*, *Porter*, *McDougal*, *Davis* and *Wainwright* weighed anchor and left for Europe. They were the first massive reinforcement sent by the US Navy, and they were to prove crucial. Only 26 destroyers had been authorized between 1911 and 1914, and it was out of this group that the first reinforcements for Europe were drawn. In the interim a new type of destroyer was laid down, based on the 1913–14 designs but with a flush deck from bow to stern to give greater longitudinal strength, in place of the conventional raised forecastle. Although the last 50 of this giant program were not completed by the Armistice, the rate at which the others were built meant that they were all in time.

In World War I destroyers changed rapidly from being small, specialized craft to a warship type which was an integral part of the fleet. No other type proved so adaptable to the changes brought about by submarine and mine warfare, and no other type saw so much action. In every navy destroyers were hard-worked and indispensable. Valuable lessons had been learned about design and methods of employment, but above all a tradition of bravery, skill and determination had been forged in battle.

Above: Completed in 1918, USS *Ward* was the first US warship in action in the Pacific in World War II when she sank two Japanese midget submarines just off Pearl Harbor, before the air attack.
Below: *V.99* was a large 1200-ton German destroyer, seen here on trials.

Above: The Queenstown base allowed the US Navy to carry out maintenance without returning to the USA. A spare part for a 4-inch gun is made on a portable forge.

BATTLE OF THE ATLANTIC

The naval war began in earnest only hours after the expiry of the Anglo-French ultimatum to Germany on the morning of 3 September 1939. Two weeks later, on 14 September, the new carrier HMS *Ark Royal* was cruising in the Western Approaches with a hunting group of four destroyers. Suddenly tracks passed close astern of the carrier as *U.39* fired a salvo of four torpedoes. The destroyers pounced, and their Asdics soon picked up the echo of the U-Boat; after a short hunt the U-Boat was destroyed, the first of many to fall to destroyers. Three days later, however, the carrier *Courageous* was sunk by *U.29* in very similar circumstances, and her destroyers failed to find the attacker.

German destroyers played an important part in the seizure of Narvik on 9 April 1940. With a mixture of treachery and bluff 10 of them entered the fjord to land troops, and parleyed with the Norwegian ships defending the harbor. Commodore Bonte's flagship, the *Wilhelm Heidkamp*, broke off negotiations and without warning fired two torpedoes into the old coast defense battleship *Eidsvold*; a few minutes later the *Bernd von Arnim* put seven more into the *Norge*. But Bonte's flotilla was not to be allowed to savor its easy victory for long, for the British 2nd Destroyer Flotilla was already on its way, four H Class boats led by Captain Bernard Warburton-Lee in the flotilla leader *Hardy*. Warburton-Lee knew that Narvik was in German hands, and had decided to attack the transports, but he only knew of six destroyers, rather than the 10 which were actually there. The weather was atrocious with continuous snow squalls and poor visibility, but it allowed the five British destroyers to reach Narvik by 0400 on 10 April without being spotted.

At 0430 three of the destroyers swept into action, taking the Germans completely by surprise. No sooner had the alarm sounded than a torpedo hit the *Wilhelm Heidkamp* killing the Commodore and sinking her. Two more torpedoes blew the *Anton Schmidt* in half and shells damaged the *Diether von Roeder* and *Hans Lüdemann*. All five destroyers came in a second time and shot up the transports, but a third attack ran out of luck. Lieutenant-Commander Erich Bey had been given sufficient warning to get his three destroyers out of the neighboring Herjangs Fjord, while further down the main fjord Lieutenant-Commander Fritz Berger brought out the remaining two to cut off the British retreat. Warburton-Lee's destroyers were now caught between two fires. A 5-inch shell wrecked the *Hardy*'s bridge and killed Warburton-Lee, and then the ship ran aground out of control. The *Hunter* was also sunk and the *Hotspur* badly damaged, but the *Hostile* and *Havock* turned back to support their flotilla-mates. The German destroyers were also being hit, however, and were unable to prevent the crippled *Hotspur* from escaping. Even though two British destroyers had been sunk Warburton-Lee's attack had sealed

Above: The Royal Navy goes to war as destroyers steam through the waters of the North Sea in line.
Below: The veteran 'V & W' Class HMS *Walker* showed that she still had her teeth when she sank *U.99* and captured her ace commander, K/Lt Otto Kretschmer, in Spring 1944.

Above: In 1943 HMS *Vanoc* had already been at sea for 25 years. Her captain and some of her officers and crew pose for a Silver Jubilee photograph.

the fate of the eight German destroyers left at Narvik. On the way down the fjord HMS *Havock* sank an ammunition ship bringing 5-inch shells for the German flotilla, and as they had fired away nearly all their ammunition and torpedoes they were now unable to face further action with any hope of success.

On 13 April the blow fell. Vice-Admiral Whitworth, flying his flag in the battleship *Warspite*, was ordered to recapture Narvik and wipe out the remaining enemy destroyers. Taking nine destroyers with her, the battleship thrust up Narvik Fjord, with her floatplane reconnoitering for the destroyers and using her 15 inch guns with terrible effect. The destroyer *Eskimo* had her bows blown off by a torpedo but all eight of the German flotilla were sunk. The two Battles of Narvik did more than finish off the destroyers which had taken Narvik; with 10

destroyers sunk, the *Kriegsmarine* destroyer-strength was now reduced to nine vessels, and in the precarious months after Dunkirk, when the German Naval Staff was asked to support the Army's Sealion invasion plan, lack of destroyers to screen the big ships was one of the most crucial problems. Three of them were still under repair in August 1940, leaving only six destroyers to face the Royal Navy in the English Channel.

The Royal Navy had 162 destroyers left after the evacuation from France but only 74 of these were undamaged. The British Prime Minister had already asked the United States' President to consider lending 50 of the old flush-deckers to tide the RN over until its big building program began to produce new destroyers in 1941, but now destroyers were desperately needed to fight off the threatened invasion of the British Isles. On 5 September the two governments agreed to the exchange: 50 old destroyers in return for a 99-year lease on bases in British territory abroad. Captain Taprell Dorling ('Taffrail') is credited with the happy idea of naming the ships after towns common to

Below: Although built to fill an order for Brazil, HMS *Havant* was taken on by the Royal Navy when war broke out. She was sunk by German bombs off the Dunkirk beaches in May 1940.

Above: Flotilla leader HMS *Onslow* and the Tribal Class destroyer *Ashanti*.
Right: The distinctive four funnels of a flush-decked ex-United States, Lease-Lend destroyer.

the USA and the United Kingdom, but to the RN they were always known as the 'four-pipers.' They were delivered to the Canadian base at Halifax, Nova Scotia, and there they were commissioned into the RN and the Canadian Navy.

Despite the grumbles the British and Canadians achieved a lot with their flush-deckers. Several accounted for the sinking of U-Boats in the Battle of the Atlantic and on 28 March 1942 the *Campbeltown* (ex-USS *Buchanan*) was used to blow up the giant Normandie dock at St Nazaire to deny it to the battleship *Tirpitz*. Eight were lost, including one lent to the Soviet Navy in 1944. Toward the end of the war they were reduced to humbler duties, often serving as training ships or aircraft targets.

94

The Battle of the Atlantic was the most gruelling test for destroyers, whether ancient flush-deckers, their British veteran equivalents, the 'V&Ws', or the latest fleet destroyers. The winter conditions varied from grim to fearful, and tested human endurance to its limits. Although destroyers were effective submarine hunters they were far from ideal for the task. Even in normal weather they were lively, and would 'roll on wet grass'; in foul weather their slim bows tended to plough through waves rather than lift to them, so that they were battered far more than the tubby little corvettes and trawlers. Life under such conditions was endured but nothing more, and the only consolation was that the U-Boats were equally hampered by bad weather.

The transfer of 50 destroyers to the RN in 1940 was only the beginning of the United States' involvement in World War II. In March 1941 the Lend-Lease Bill was enacted to allow more warships to be built and 'lent' to the RN to ease the shortage of escorts. In April the Defense Zone, in which US freighters could be escorted regardless of whether they were carrying war material to Britain or not, was extended to longitude 26 degrees West. In the middle of the year the US Government took responsibility for guaranteeing the 'neutrality' of Iceland by putting American troops in place of the British and Canadians who had been there for a year. As Iceland was used by British and Canadian warships for refuelling there was now the likelihood of a U-Boat mistaking a USN destroyer for a hostile escort. The flush-decker's distinctive silhouette was common to both navies, and the latest *Benson* and *Bristol* Classes were similar in general build and layout to the British 'A to I' types.

From the spring of 1941 three destroyer squadrons were operating in the North Atlantic, DesRons 7, 30 and 31. The first 'hostile' action seems to have been an attack on a sonar contact by the destroyer *Niblack* in April, but the first serious provocation was the '*Greer* Incident' on 4 September 1941. The old flush-decker belonged to DesRon 30 but was proceeding independently, carrying supplies and mail to Reykjavik, when a British maritime patrol aircraft signalled to warn her that a U-Boat had been sighted 10 miles ahead. The *Greer* slowed down to allow her sonar operator to track the U-Boat, purely as a precaution, but one which was inevitably taken by the U-Boat to mean that the *Greer* was hunting her. For nearly four hours the destroyer tracked the U-Boat, during which time the British patrol plane dropped four depth-charges. Eventually the U-Boat commander, exasperated at what he regarded as highly 'unneutral' tactics, fired a torpedo. To this the *Greer* replied by

Below: The elderly flush-decker HMS *Claire* was converted to a Long Range Escort by the replacement of two boilers with extra fuel tanks.

dropping depthcharges, but when it was clear that the U-Boat had escaped she continued on her way to Iceland. The outcome was that US warships were given clear instructions to defend shipping in the North Atlantic, the 'shoot on sight' order which permitted USN escorts to attack German or Italian submarines.

The next incident was more serious, for on 17 October the new destroyer *Kearny* (DD.432) was torpedoed by *U.568*. Once again the US destroyers were hopelessly mixed up with British, Canadian and even Free French escorts, all trying to cope with a Canadian convoy which had been heavily attacked by a wolfpack. It was about 0200 and she had just dropped depth-charges (US destroyers were permitted to drop charges to 'embarrass' or frighten off U-Boats). In the intermittent glare from a burning tanker the U-Boat fired a spread of three torpedoes, and one of these caught the *Kearny* in the forward fire-room. There was a tremendous explosion, which tore up the deck and 11 men were killed and 24 wounded. The ship had been at battle stations, so the flooding could be contained as long as the forward fire-room bulkhead held up under strain.

The *Bensons* were the first destroyers built with machinery on the 'unit' system with turbines and boilers alternated to reduce the risk of the entire steam plant being knocked out by one hit, and the *Kearny*'s experience showed how important it was in enabling destroyers to withstand action damage. Certainly the unit system saved the *Kearny*, and she was able to limp to Iceland under her own power, escorted by the *Greer*. There she was secured alongside the repair ship *Vulcan* and patched up for the journey back to a proper repair yard.

The old four-stacker *Reuben James* (DD.245) was not so lucky. Exactly two weeks after the torpedoing of the *Kearny* she was escorting an eastbound convoy near the 'MOMP' or Mid-Ocean Meeting Point at which US destroyers handed over convoys to British and Canadian escorts. Just before dawn on 31 October

Above: Russian destroyers of the Baltic Fleet at the port of Kronstadt.

Above: USS *Gleanes* skirts the ice floes in the North Atlantic.

she was torpedoed on the port side and her entire fore-part disappeared in a massive explosion. Evidently the forward 4-inch magazine had detonated because all that was left of the *Reuben James* was the after-part from the fourth funnel to the stern. The shattered remnant of the hull stayed afloat for about five minutes, and as it sank the depth-charges exploded, killing many of the survivors. More than two-thirds of her complement including her captain, were killed or drowned, but even this was not enough to end isolationism in the United States. President Roosevelt immediately sought approval from Congress to transfer the Coast Guard to the control of the Navy and within two weeks further amendments to the Neutrality Act were passed but it was to take Pearl Harbor to convince the Americans that World War II had arrived.

Paradoxically, once the United States was at war with Germany the confrontation between US destroyers and U-Boats in the Atlantic diminished. The reason was simply that destroyers were desperately needed for the Pacific, and so it was agreed that the main contribution to the Battle of the Atlantic would be maritime aircraft for the RAF and destroyer escorts (DEs) for the Royal Navy.

The destroyers earmarked for Atlantic duties were more urgently needed to convoy troopships to the British Isles, but in August 1942 the *Emmons* and *Rodman* escorted the cruiser *Tuscaloosa* to North Russia. In September 1942 a South Atlantic Force of four old light cruisers and eight destroyers was created, to protect Brazilian shipping against U-Boats, and some of the old destroyers operated in the Caribbean to cope with the U-Boats' *Paukenschlag* ('Drumroll') offensive against American shipping.

In the last week of May 1941 the 4th Flotilla of the Home Fleet, comprising four Tribal Class, the *Cossack, Maori, Sikh* and *Zulu* and the Polish *Piorun* (ex-HMS *Nerissa*) was escorting a troop convoy when the news came that the German battleship *Bismarck* had broken out through the Denmark Strait, and had sunk the battlecruiser HMS *Hood* and shaken off the battleship *Prince of Wales* and two shadowing cruisers. On 26 May Captain Vian was ordered to join the Home Fleet, but when he intercepted a PBY Catalina's sighting report he altered course for the *Bismarck* on his own initiative, with the intention of slowing her down by torpedo attack.

Taking station on the cruiser *Sheffield*, which was in radar contact with the *Bismarck*, Vian led his destroyers through heavy seas to take up positions for a night attack. So bad were conditions that his own leader, HMS *Cossack*, and her next astern, the *Maori*, were swung right around at a speed of 26 knots. The two destroyers missed one another by a matter of feet and found that they had changed places in the line, but in the heat of the moment nobody paused to draw breath. At about 2200 the massive bulk of the *Bismarck* was sighted by the *Piorun*, silhouetted by the flash of her own guns. Vian wanted his destroyers to box her in before launching a coordinated attack, but the weather was so bad that even when easing down to 18 knots the lookouts were blinded by spray. There was no moon either, so Vian decided to allow his destroyers to attack independently. At ranges which varied from 6000 down to as little as 4000 yards the five destroyers dodged and weaved, while the tired gun-layers aboard the battleship tried to blast them out of the water. It was probably only their wild gyrations which saved the destroyers from being hit by anything bigger than splinters, but for all their efforts they could not hit the *Bismarck*. During the action the worried radar operator aboard the *Cossack* reported a number of shapes on his screen; it was realized that the air-warning radar had picked up the *Bismarck*'s 2000-pound shells in mid-flight.

At about 0300 the battered destroyers lost touch with the *Bismarck*. Although her radio aerials were shot away the *Cossack* had been able to broadcast a series of bearings to the

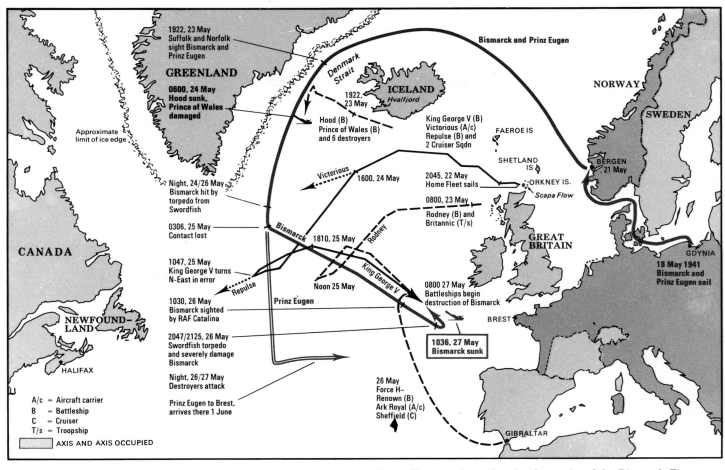

1922, 23 May Suffolk and Norfolk sight Bismarck and Prinz Eugen

GREENLAND

0600, 24 May Hood sunk, Prince of Wales damaged

Approximate limit of ice edge

Denmark Strait

1922, 23 May

Hood (B) Prince of Wales (B) and 6 destroyers

Bismarck and Prinz Eugen

ICELAND
Hvalfjord

King George V (B) Victorious (A/c) Repulse (B) and 2 Cruiser Sqdn

FAEROE IS

SHETLAND IS

NORWAY

SWEDEN

BERGEN 21 May

Victorious

1600, 24 May

2045, 22 May Home Fleet sails

ORKNEY IS.
Scapa Flow

Night, 24/26 May Bismarck hit by torpedo from Swordfish

0800, 23 May Rodney (B) and Britannic (T/s)

CANADA

0306, 25 May Contact lost

Bismarck

1810, 25 May

Rodney

GREAT BRITAIN

GDYNIA

1047, 25 May King George V turns N-East in error

King George V

Repulse

Noon 25 May

18 May 1941 Bismarck and Prinz Eugen sail

NEWFOUND-LAND

1030, 26 May Bismarck sighted by RAF Catalina

Prinz Eugen

0800 27 May Battleships begin destruction of Bismarck

BREST

2047/2125, 26 May Swordfish torpedo and severely damage Bismarck

1036, 27 May Bismarck sunk

HALIFAX

Night, 26/27 May Destroyers attack

26 May Force H– Renown (B) Ark Royal (A/c) Sheffield (C)

A/c = Aircraft carrier
B = Battleship
C = Cruiser
T/s = Troopship

Prinz Eugen to Brest, arrives there 1 June

AXIS AND AXIS OCCUPIED

GIBRALTAR

Above: The map shows the nine-day cruise of the *Bismarck*. Five destroyers under Captain Vian made a night attack on the mighty ship shortly before she was smashed by the battleships HMS *Rodney* and *King George V*.
Left: Impressive though it looks, the 4-inch forecastle gun of a destroyer would have been woefully ineffective against a capital ship.

Commander in Chief, Home Fleet. Although a final attempt was made by the *Maori* and *Sikh* to attack at 0700, the battleships *King George V* and *Rodney* were in sight, and so Vian's destroyers hauled off and left it to the big ships to play out the final act of the drama. Although they had not damaged the *Bismarck* they had carried out the destroyer's traditional role of shadowing and harassing an enemy capital ship, and the constant alarms and expenditure of ammunition did nothing to improve her chances of surviving the fleet action next morning.

Destroyers also put paid to the career of the battlecruiser *Scharnhorst* in December 1943. The immediate cause of this had been Hitler's understandable anger when a force of eight British destroyers had fought off an attempt by the pocket-battleship *Lützow*, the heavy cruiser *Admiral Hipper* and destroyers to attack their convoy. This action, known as the Battle of the Barents Sea, was fought in December 1942. One of the destroyers fought a brilliant delaying action to give time for the distant escort of two cruisers to come up and drive away the *Lützow* and *Hipper*. It was at this point that the destroyer *Friedrich Eckholdt* closed with the cruisers *Jamaica* and *Sheffield* under the impression that they were friendly, only to be blasted with 6-inch shells.

Hitler was not prepared to allow the Allies to run convoys to North Russia or to deploy their heavy ships in other theaters, and so another operation against a convoy was planned in 1943. A proposal to use the big destroyers alone was amended to include the *Scharnhorst*, but the greatly superior British radar would count against the Germans during the long hours of Arctic night.

Admiral 'Achmed' Bey, the man who had turned the tables on Warburton-Lee's destroyers at the First Battle of Narvik in 1940, commanded Northern Group's destroyers, and he took over as Flag Officer Northern Task Force when Admiral Kummetz went on leave in November. When his flagship sailed from Alten Fjord at 1900 on Christmas Day he was not to know that all the assumptions made by his staff were wrong. There was not one convoy but two, JW.55B homeward bound for England, and RA.55A bound for Murmansk. Aerial reconnaissance had detected only JW.55B, covered by a close escort force of three cruisers and destroyers, and although the Home Fleet had been detected leaving Iceland, the Luftwaffe report had been vaguely worded. It mentioned the possibility of a battleship being included, but in accordance with the rule that only facts were to be passed on to the Navy, this afterthought was deleted. But there was a battleship, the 38,000-ton *Duke of York*, flagship of the Commander in Chief Home Fleet, Admiral Fraser. Fraser was very well-informed about the *Scharnhorst*'s intentions, almost undoubtedly as a result of Ultra cryptanalysis, and had already ordered four destroyers to transfer from the undetected convoy to JW.55B's close escort. Bey was moving into a trap, with a battleship, a cruiser and four destroyers moving up at high speed to cut off his retreat and a total of 14 destroyers actually with the convoy, in company with three modern cruisers.

As a destroyer man himself, Bey must have had misgivings when he allowed his own destroyers to turn back, but they could not keep station with the flagship in the worsening weather. The Luftwaffe reconnaissance aircraft were now grounded as well, and the *Scharnhorst* was without any information apart from what could be seen by her radar and the eyes of her lookouts. U-Boats had given him reasonable estimates of the size, speed and course of the convoy, but they failed to sight the Home Fleet. Fraser's signals to his scattered forces were concise, to minimize the risk of attacks on friendly forces, whereas the German destroyers lost contact with the *Scharnhorst* early on the morning of 26 December and there was no way to recall them.

At 0840 on 26 December the cruiser flagship *Belfast* picked up a large 'blip' on her radar screen, which indicated that the *Scharnhorst* was only 30 miles away. As the *Duke of York* was still 200 miles away, the cruisers had to fight a holding action, which they proceeded to do in masterly fashion. At 0924 star-shells from the *Belfast* lit up the *Scharnhorst* in the predawn Arctic gloom, and in only two minutes one of HMS *Norfolk*'s 8-inch shells demolished the forward fire-control director and its radar antenna. The startled *Scharnhorst* sheered off, and in the heavy seas she soon pulled away from the three cruisers. Admiral Burnett was too wily to allow his cruisers to be drawn away from the convoy, and confidently forecast that the enemy would be back. Within three hours his prediction was proved correct when the *Scharnhorst* was sighted again, coming up from the south. This time she made a more determined effort to push past the cruisers, and the range came down to 11,000 yards as her 11-inch shells bracketed them with accurate salvoes. The *Norfolk* was hit several times but the delay distracted the Germans' attention, and during the mêlée the *Duke of York* approached to within 12,000 yards without being seen.

There were four destroyers with the cruisers, the *Matchless*, *Musketeer*, *Opportune* and *Virago*, and they had already launched a torpedo attack to take the pressure off. The heavy seas made it very difficult to overhaul the *Scharnhorst*, and although all four destroyers got close enough to fire their puny 4.7-inch and 4-inch guns at the battlecruiser the range was too great for an effective torpedo attack.

The British battleship had plenty of time to maneuver and bring the maximum number of guns to bear, and at 0450 the first starshell burst over the *Scharnhorst*, followed immediately by salvoes of 14-inch and 6-inch shells. Once again the *Scharnhorst* tried to break away, but this time her opponent was able to keep up, for the heavy seas evened out any nominal differences between the two ships' top speeds. The cruisers were left behind as the big ships traded punches at a range of 17,000–20,000 yards.

A 14-inch hit damaged one of the *Scharnhorst*'s propeller shafts, and Admiral Fraser signalled to his four destroyers to attack with torpedoes.

It has already been mentioned that the weather was too rough for the German destroyers, and so bad that even 10,000-ton cruisers were unable to maintain full speed. The *Saumarez*, *Savage*, *Scorpion* and *Stord* (Norwegian Navy) displaced only 2000 tons fully loaded, and their frail hulls whipped and shuddered as they plunged through the waves and buried themselves in clouds of spray. The *Saumarez* and the *Savage* slowly drew away from the *Duke of York* and crept up on their quarry. The *Scorpion* and *Stord* worked their way on to the starboard quarter, leaving the other pair of destroyers to draw fire on the port side. The *Saumarez* and *Savage* came under heavy fire, but the *Scorpion* and *Stord* managed to approach to within 3000 yards, virtually point-blank for a torpedo attack. At least one of the *Scorpion*'s torpedoes hit, and the *Scharnhorst* turned away, straight into the arms of the other two destroyers. Once again shuddering underwater explosions told that three torpedoes had hit. The destroyers had done their job, and they eased down thankfully as the *Duke of York* took over the work of finishing the battle. The range was now only 10,400 yards and the cruisers were joining in, firing at the dull smoky glow that was all that anyone could make out in the murk. It was all over by 1945, when the cruisers closed in to find only 36 men out of the 2000 who had been aboard at Alten Fjord only a day before.

The Battle of the North Cape was the last major action in European waters and it marked the end of the Germany Navy's attempt to dominate the Atlantic. Undoubtedly the contribution of the destroyers in the battle was a most important part of the victory, for if they had not slowed the *Scharnhorst* down she could have eluded the Home Fleet and possibly have returned safely to base.

Above: The French destroyer *Le Fantasque* in 1940.
Right: HMS *Nepal* approaches HMS *Queen Elizabeth* as her seamen
prepare to fire a line across. The destroyer was first named *Norseman*
but was damaged by German bombs while building.
Below: Destroyers in service on the Arctic convoys were given special
equipment to combat the intense cold. HMS *Musketeer* and others had
steam-heated gun mountings and asbestos insulation for their
bulkheads.

The Italian destroyer *Folgore* was sunk by the guns of Royal Navy
cruisers and destroyers in December 1942.
Below: French and British warships at Alexandria in the early stages
of the war.

THE MALTA CONVOYS

Destroyers played an important part in Mediterranean naval operations partly because of the shorter distances but above all because the British destroyers were often the only vessels capable of matching the Italian warships' high speed.

The very first action of the Mediterranean, the action off Calabria on 9 July 1940, set a pattern which was to become familiar in the next three years. The Italian Fleet was sighted by the British cruisers at long range, and although a gunnery duel started, the Italians broke off when the flagship *Giulio Cesare* was hit by HMS *Warspite* at nearly 25,000 yards. Cunningham's destroyers, three flotillas totalling 14 boats, raced after the fleeing Italians but failed to make contact. The Italian destroyers did their work well, laying dense smoke-screens and engaging with gunfire, and by the time the British flotillas pushed past and penetrated the smoke-screens the Italian battleships were hull down on the horizon, heading for home.

The next action, off Cape Spartivento four months later, was even more disappointing, and the destroyers could not even get into action, but in March 1941 the third of these 'stern-chase' engagements turned into the decisive battle which Cunningham hankered after, the Battle of Cape Matapan.

The fortunes of war change very rapidly, and the triumph of Matapan was quickly followed by the Royal Navy's most gruelling test of the entire war, the Battle for Crete. Following rough handling of the Italian invaders by the Greek Army and its British allies, Hitler decided to retrieve Mussolini's fortunes by sending German troops into Yugoslavia on 6 April 1941. Within two weeks the British and Greek forces were overwhelmed and forced to withdraw to Crete. There they were virtually devoid of any air cover as the RAF had been pulled back to Egypt, and the defense of the island was left to the Mediterranean Fleet. The Royal Navy had two tasks: first, to prevent a seaborne invasion, and second, to cover the evacua-

tion of as many of the garrison as possible. It succeeded in both of these aims, but at a terrible cost in lives and ships.

On 20 May 1941 the Luftwaffe began to attack the ships patrolling north of Crete in conjunction with landings of gliders and paratroops on the island. Next day the destroyer *Juno* was sunk southeast of Crete when a bomb from an Italian high-level bomber detonated her magazine; she sank in two minutes. That night Rear-Admiral Glennie, with the cruisers *Dido*, *Orion* and *Ajax* and the destroyers *Janus*, *Kimberley*, *Hasty* and *Hereward* found a convoy of light craft, including commandeered Greek fishing boats, crowded with German invasion troops. Here at last was a tangible enemy, and the cruisers and destroyers ran amok, firing indiscriminately at anything they could see. When they had finished two and one-half hours later the invasion convoy had ceased to exist, and an estimated 4000 German troops had been killed or drowned. A seaborne invasion of Crete was not possible so long as the sea passage was disputed.

Next day the air attacks began again with renewed ferocity. The destroyers were particularly vulnerable when unsupported by larger ships for their antiaircraft armament was painfully weak. First to go was the *Greyhound*, and although the cruisers, *Gloucester* and *Fiji* tried to protect her, they were very low on antiaircraft ammunition; as soon as their defensive fire slackened the Stukas closed in and sank them as well. The destroyers patrolled north of the island on the lookout for invasion forces, but in fact the Germans and Italians had given up trying to run another convoy. Under cover of darkness destroyers found time to evacuate the King of Greece and the British envoy to Greece, another of the responsibilities which tended to be given to destroyers.

On the morning of 23 May the already famous 5th Flotilla under Captain Lord Louis Mounbatten found itself without

heavy support as the big ships had been prematurely withdrawn because it was feared that they were low on ammunition. It was about 0800, and the *Kelly* was leading the *Kashmir*, *Kipling*, *Kelvin* and *Jackal* back to Alexandria after attacking a force of troop-carrying caiques. Suddenly the drone of aero-engines heralded the arrival of the dreaded Stukas, two dozen of them. The *Kashmir* was hit and sank very quickly, for the flimsy hull of a destroyer was easily ruptured by the explosion of a heavy bomb. Then the *Kelly*, making 30 knots was hit as she put her helm hard over. She lurched to port, and still moving fast, slid over and lay bottom up for half an hour before disappearing.

The dazed survivors, covered in oil fuel, had to endure machine-gunning until the Stukas ran low on fuel and returned to base. The *Kelvin* and *Jackal* were ordered to make their escape to avoid further losses, but the *Kipling* bravely stayed behind for three hours, and managed to rescue 279 survivors. The risks she ran were terrible, but abandoning flotilla-mates was not part of the destroyer tradition. On the way back to Alexandria the *Kipling* had another 80 bombs dropped at her, and when still 70 miles from home she suffered the ultimate indignity; she ran out of fuel and had to be towed into Alexandria.

Once the German paratroops gained a sizeable bridgehead in Crete the island was doomed, and the call went out for the Navy to make an even greater effort than it had already, by evacuating the 32,000 men of the garrison. It was another Dunkirk but under much greater difficulties.

Destroyers and the fast minelayer *Abdiel* had already been running in with urgently needed ammunition and stores as even the fastest merchantmen found the trip suicidal. The problem with Crete was that the only good port for offloading stores or embarking was on the north side, the side most exposed to German air attack. On the night of 28–29 May Rear-Admiral Rawlings took the cruisers *Orion*, *Ajax* and *Dido* and six destroyers into Heraklion in an attempt to evacuate the defenders.

At first everything went well, and by 0320 the 4000 troops were safely embarked. Then the *Imperial*'s steering gear jammed, probably as a result of near-misses during the daylight passage to Crete. Admiral Rawlings dared not allow his force to be caught so close to the Luftwaffe's airfields at daybreak and so he ordered the *Hotspur* to take off her troops and sink her. With 900 men on board the *Hotspur* rejoined an hour later, but it was too late, and the sun was up when the eight warships headed southwards through the Kaso Strait at the eastern end of Crete. Soon they were picked up by Axis reconnaissance aircraft, and the bombing began at 0600. The *Hereward* was hit, but there was no question of turning back to help her; she drifted inshore before sinking, so fortunately the larger part of her crew and the soldiers she had embarked survived to become prisoners of war. The *Decoy* was also hit but managed to limp along at reduced speed. The *Dido* and *Orion* were hit by bombs, and a second attack two hours later killed or wounded over 500 troops packed in the *Orion*'s forward mess-decks.

While this was going on another four destroyers had managed to get 700 troops out of the tiny harbour of Sphakia on the southeast coast virtually without loss. The reason was that,

unlike Admiral Rawlings' force, the air cover planned had been in the right place at the right time. Encouraged, Cunningham decided to continue the evacuation, and the following night the cruisers *Phoebe*, *Perth* and *Calcutta*, the fast transport *Glengyle* and three destroyers rescued a further 6000 men from Sphakia without losing a ship. The destroyers made one last effort on the night of 31 May–1 June and saved 4000 men, bringing the total to over 18,000 landed safely in Egypt.

The fall of Crete left the British in a precarious position, with all the gains since July 1940 wiped out. Their only forward base, the island of Malta, was cut off and liable to be bombed or starved into submission. The defeat of the Eighth Army in Libya meant that the Italian Navy could run supply convoys into Benghazi and Tripoli out of reach of the surface and air forces. Malta was now unusable by surface forces and its airfields were only barely usable by its defending fighters. To add to the Navy's burdens, the fortress of Tobruk and the Eighth Army's advance bases on the Libyan frontier had to be supplied by sending ships along 'Bomb Alley', a route dotted with wrecks.

The need to keep Malta supplied required far greater exertions. As early as May 1941 the Admiralty had increased the number of submarines in the Mediterranean, first by ordering a flotilla based on Gibraltar to operate against Italian shipping in the Tyrrhenian Sea and then by allocating some of the newly constructed submarines to the flotilla based on Malta. Throughout the summer of 1941 these submarines played havoc with the Italian supply convoys, backed up by air attacks. In September two aircraft carriers, the *Ark Royal* and *Furious* ferried 49 Hurricane fighters as a prelude to flying in twin-engined bombers to reestablish a strike force on the island. The success of these moves led to the reestablishment of a surface strike force at Malta in October 1941.

Known as Force K, it comprised the light cruisers *Aurora* and *Penelope* and the destroyers *Lance* and *Lively*, under the command of Captain W G Agnew RN.

Force K had only one brief, to deny the Axis forces the sea route between Italy and North Africa, and it quickly showed how vulnerable that route was. On 8 November a reconnaissance aircraft reported a convoy, 40 miles east of Cape Spartivento, seven merchant ships escorted by six destroyers, with a support force of two heavy cruisers and four destroyers. Ignoring these odds Agnew took his two cruisers and two destroyers in at first light next day and annihilated the convoy. All the merchant ships were sunk as well as the destroyer *Fulmine*, without loss, and the *Libeccio* was later torpedoed by the submarine *Upholder* while trying to rescue survivors; the support force apparently took no action to avoid the catastrophe.

Below: Throughout his long life Lord Mountbatten always retained a special regard for HMS *Kelly*, the flotilla leader which he captained. She was sunk by a German dive bomber during the Battle of Crete in May 1941.
Right: Three Italian torpedo boats of two world wars: (left to right) *Tilfone* (1942), *Antonio Mosto* (1915) and *Augusto Riboty* (1917).

A week later the same four ships achieved another 100 percent success by wiping out a special convoy of two ships, the *Maritza* and *Procida*, carrying aviation gasoline urgently needed by the Luftwaffe in North Africa. The convoy was sighted 100 miles west of Crete, and despite a valiant defense by the two escorting torpedo boats, Force K sank the gasoline carriers with ease. On 29 November further reinforcements arrived at Malta, Force B under Rear-Admiral Rawlings, comprising the cruisers *Ajax* and *Neptune* and two more destroyers. Malta was an ulcer which threatened to drain the Axis strength in the Mediterranean, and for the first time the German command in North Africa began to talk of the possibility of defeat if Malta was not subdued. As if to underline this gloom, on 1 December Force K attacked and sank a supply ship and a tanker bound for Libya, as well as its escorting destroyer, the *Alvise da Mosto*.

On 13 December another action occurred, one of the most brilliant destroyer actions of World War II. This time there was no premeditation, for the *Sikh*, *Legion* and *Maori* and the Netherlands Navy's *Isaac Sweers* were merely en route from Gibraltar to Alexandria as reinforcements for Cunningham's

Top: Although suitable for the Mediterranean, French destroyers like *Le Fantasque* were unable to cope with severe Atlantic conditions.
Above: A massive concentration of antiaircraft fire protects the invasion fleet during Operation Torch against North Africa, November 1942.

14th Flotilla. So desperate had the fuel situation become in North Africa that the light cruisers *Alberico da Barbiano* and *Alberto di Guissano* had taken on a deck cargo of cased gasoline at Palermo, destined for Tripoli. When the sighting was made by a Wellington bomber from Malta it was intended that land-based torpedo-bombers and Force K would intercept, and the *Sikh* and her division were only meant to act in support, but at the last moment Force K was ordered to remain in Malta. Commander Stokes in HMS *Sikh* received fresh orders too late to reach the interception point, and to his chagrin he saw the two cruisers disappearing behind the high cliffs of Cape Bon. Stokes maintained course with little hope of catching the Italians, but suddenly he realized that the two cruisers had reversed their course and that he had an opportunity denied to most destroyer commanders for a set-piece attack against major warships.

What had happened was that the Italian squadron had been attacked by the RAF bombers without success, but Admiral Toscano expected to be attacked in much greater strength at daylight and had decided to turn back. Stokes led his destroyers close inshore so that they were hidden by the land behind them, with the Italians silhouetted against the skyline. At 0225 the *Sikh* fired a salvo of four torpedoes and saw the leading cruiser, the *Alberico da Barbiano* burst into flame as three of the 'fish' hit amidships. The *Legion* hit the *Alberto di Guissano* with only one torpedo, but she too burst into flame as gasoline drums on her decks burst and scattered flaming fuel everywhere. The *Maori* and *Isaac Sweers* pumped shells into the two hapless cruisers as they raced past. Only the second cruiser had time to fire three wild salvoes with her 6-inch guns, and seeing that their victims were beyond hope the four destroyers disappeared as quickly as they had arrived. The torpedo boat *Circe* picked up survivors, but a large number of lives were lost including the unlucky Admiral Toscano. His superiors at *Supermarina*, the Italian Naval HQ, had warned him of the presence of the four enemy destroyers but had considered that four destroyers would not dare to tackle two cruisers; he would have done better to take his chances with the RAF at daybreak, for British land-based bombers had a dismal record of failure against Axis warships.

In January 1941 the Eighth Army's fortunes improved, and with the airfields in Cyrenaica back in British hands Admiral Cunningham felt more optimistic about the Navy's chances of running a convoy through to Malta. In March he asked Admiral Vian to escort a small convoy of fast merchantmen from Alexandria to Malta.

It was a desperate mission for Malta was nearly on its knees, but Cunningham pointed out to Vian that the Italians had never yet attacked through a smoke screen.

The Second Battle of Sirte was one of the most dashing exploits in Vian's career. It showed that even without a battle-fleet behind them the Royal Navy's light forces were able to force the Italians to treat them with respect. The 'Fighting Fifteenth,' otherwise known as Vian's 15th Cruiser Squadron, left Alexandria early on the morning of 20 March 1942 with 15 destroyers escorting the fast transports *Breconshire*, *Clan Campbell*, *Pampas* and *Talabot*. Two days later Vian was told the unwelcome news that Italian heavy units had left Taranto. Later the cruiser *Penelope* and the destroyer *Legion* joined the convoy bringing the total number of cruisers up to five, including the elderly antiaircraft cruiser *Carlisle* which was not equipped for surface action. Throughout the morning Italian bombers made desultory attacks with torpedoes and bombs, but with no result. The midday meal was eaten at Action Stations, sandwiches and mugs of tea, when a float plane suddenly dropped a string of red flares ahead of the convoy. A float plane could only have come from a cruiser or a battleship and the markers were intended to guide an enemy squadron.

Above: Heavy seas crash over the bow of a destroyer.
Below: HMS *Kipling* and *Kimberley* of the 5th Flotilla. Eleven out of the 16 'J' and 'K' Class destroyers in the Mediterranean were lost.

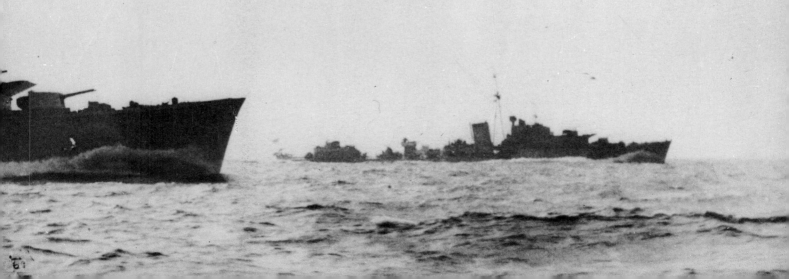

At 1410 the cruiser *Euryalus* reported smoke on the horizon and seven minutes later the masts and funnels of three big ships came into view. Vian signalled to the *Carlisle* and the six small 'Hunt' Class destroyers (which had no torpedo-tubes) to stay with the convoy and steer south towards Sirte to keep clear, while his flagship the *Cleopatra*, the *Dido*, *Euryalus* and *Penelope* and the fleet destroyers prepared to fight a surface action. 'Make smoke' was the order, and soon clouds of black funnel smoke and choking white clouds from the chemical smoke-floats mixed to form a screen between the Italian Fleet and the convoy. At 1436 two heavy cruisers and a light cruiser, afterwards identified as the *Gorizia*, *Trento* and *Giovanni delle Bande Nere*, opened fire on the 15th Cruiser Squadron at a range of 27,000 yards, but their shells fell short. The British cruisers were also out-ranged, but at a combined approach speed of 50 knots it was only a matter of minutes before the 5.25-inch guns of the *Cleopatra*, *Dido* and *Euryalus* were firing back. The rising wind made shell-spotting almost impossible for both sides and no hits were scored. After an hour the Italian cruisers sheered off to the north but no sooner had Vian's cruisers regained contact with the convoy than the alarm bells sounded again. The destroyer *Zulu* had sighted the enemy again, this time in two groups, the cruisers in one and the battleship *Littorio* 15 miles away with four destroyers.

For two hours the British cruisers and the destroyers played a lethal game with the Italians, daring them to come through the smoke-screen to face a torpedo attack. When the Italians tried to work their way around the westward end of the smoke-screen Vian used his destroyers to push them back. Hits were scored on both sides, but no serious damage was done as the ships weaved in and out of the smoke-screen in clouds of spray. Captain Poland and the 14th Flotilla made a determined torpedo attack on the enemy and forced him to withdraw. All this time sporadic bombing was taking place, an added distraction. It was 1820 before the Italians finally gave up and withdrew for the last time leaving the British to cope with what was now a mounting storm. In fact both sides suffered considerably more damage from the storm than from the gunfire; the *Littorio* returned to harbor with thousands of tons of water aboard and the destroyers *Lanciere* and *Scirocco* foundered that night. Vian's cruisers had to reduce speed to 18 knots and later to 15 knots; even then the destroyers fell behind and the *Zulu* had her forecastle stove in by a heavy sea.

Below: American destroyers began to operate in the Mediterranean with the Torch landings in November 1942. Seen here is USS *Swanson* (DD.443).

The last great Malta convoy was Operation Pedestal in August 1942 which called for the support of two battleships, three fleet carriers, seven cruisers and 20 destroyers to get only 14 fast cargo ships through. In a four-day battle nine merchantmen, a carrier and two cruisers were sunk, and a carrier and two cruisers were badly damaged. But Malta was saved particularly by the tanker *Ohio*, whose cargo of aviation gasoline was the most vital of all, for it was needed to keep the Spitfires and Hurricanes flying. The *Ohio* was crippled and had been on fire, but the destroyers *Penn* and *Ledbury* lashed themselves alongside to keep her afloat long enough to crawl into Bighi Bay. Although she sank at her moorings her cargo was intact, and it enabled Malta's aircraft to begin strikes against Rommel's supply convoys once more.

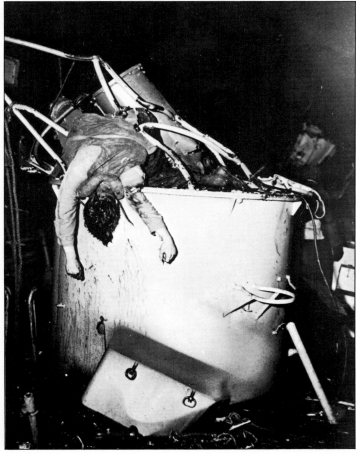

Top left: Italian destroyers suffered heavily at the hands of the Royal Navy. The *Turbine* was one of the casualties.
Left: A US destroyer lays a chemical smoke screen off the Salerno invasion beach. Aircraft identification silhouettes are painted on the rail.
Above: A dead US Coast Guardsman on the USS *Menges* (DE.320). The *Menges* was torpedoed by *U.371* in the western Mediterranean in 1944.

WAR IN THE PACIFIC

It was a destroyer of the US Pacific Fleet which had the first brush with the Japanese in World War II. The four-stacker *Ward* was on routine patrol off Pearl Harbor and in the early morning of 7 December she was heading for home after an uneventful two days. At 0357 she was warned by a minesweeper that something resembling the periscope of a submarine had been sighted. A sonar search revealed nothing, but about two and a half hours after the report the *Ward*'s lookouts spotted a small submarine trailing the target ship *Antares* on her way to the main entrance.

The old destroyer's crew was efficient, and the second 4-inch shell was seen to hit at a distance of less than a hundred yards. A pattern of depth-charges completed the destruction of the mystery submarine, which was in fact one of a force of midgets which had been launched from Japanese fleet submarines some distance away. The idea was that the attack was to coincide with the air strike which was already winging its way from Admiral Nagumo's carriers, and to profit by the resulting confusion in the anchorage. The subsequent failure to take note of the *Ward*'s timely action was just one more of the oversights and miscalculations which contributed to the disaster of Pearl Harbor.

After the Pearl Harbor raid destroyers were soon fighting in the East Indies. The US Asiatic Fleet had only 13 destroyers, all well past their prime, to defend the Philippines. When their base at Cavite was put out of action by Japanese bombers three days after Pearl Harbor, the Commander in Chief, Admiral Thomas C Hart had even less chance of protecting such an enormous area. Hart was ordered to get his destroyers to the Dutch East Indies, where in conjunction with Australian, British and Dutch warships, there might be some hope of defending the so-called 'Malay Barrier.'

Below: The Japanese captured USS *Stewart* at Surabaya in March 1942. They converted her to a fast fuel carrier, radically altering her appearance.

On 20 January 1942 the cruisers *Boise* and *Marblehead* and six destroyers of DesDiv 59 were ordered to attack a Japanese force of transports heading for Balikpapan in eastern Borneo. The cruiser *Boise* damaged herself by hitting a pinnacle of rock and had to return to base escorted by a destroyer. Then the *Marblehead* developed machinery trouble and returned taking another destroyer as escort. This left only the elderly *John D Ford*, *Parrott*, *Paul Jones* and *Pope* to deal with an amphibious force escorted by the light cruiser *Naka* and 12 destroyers. But fortune favors the bold, and Commander Talbot's tiny force reached Balikpapan undetected; the Dutch had set the oil refinery on fire and huge clouds of smoke shrouded the anchorage. It was ideal for a destroyer attack, with the transports at anchor in the harbor silhouetted against the glow of fires ashore.

The destroyers raced in aiming their first torpedoes at a line of transports outside the harbor. The *Parrott* fired three torpedoes but obtained no hit, and then launched another salvo of five,

but it also missed. Two more torpedoes fired by the *John D Ford* and *Paul Jones* also missed, although the range was down to 1000 yards.

The Japanese were now alert to the fact that an attack was in progress and the anchorage soon bustled with activity as alarm bells sounded and guns fired. Fortunately for the Americans the Japanese destroyers seem to have been ordered to start a submarine hunt and the ships remained undetected for a while longer. During a second attack three of the *Parrott's* 'fish' behaved properly, and this time a transport blew up. The column of destroyers left a trail of destruction as they ran southwards sinking another transport and a patrol craft totalling 23,000 tons of shipping. When they had no torpedoes left they used their 4-inch guns to sink another transport before leaving the scene. The confusion and destruction they had caused was out of all proportion to their relative strength for all four were 'four-stackers' built in World War I, and officially regarded as unfit for front-line service.

It was the only success scored by ABDA. The Japanese continued their inexorable drive on the East Indies, investing Singapore in the west and reaching as far as Rabaul in the east. With the flanks in enemy hands the center was soon untenable; Surabaya on the north side of Java was threatened, and Tjilatjap on the south side was the only other suitable base. A holding action was needed, and so the Dutch Admiral Karel Doorman was given command of a Combined Allied Striking Force, comprising the US cruisers *Houston* and *Marblehead*, the Dutch cruisers *de Ruyter* (flagship) and *Tromp*, the US destroyers *Barker*, *Bulmer*, *John D Edwards* and *Stewart* and the Dutch destroyers *Banckert*, *Piet Hein* and *Van Ghent*. To avoid the risk of air attack Doorman proposed a night attack on the Japanese invasion forces in the Makassar Strait but, to be in position by nightfall the task force had to cross the Java Sea in daylight.

Inevitably the Combined Striking Force was sighted by Japanese aircraft and a force of bombers attacked in the morning of 4 February. The cruisers were the main target and when both the *Houston* and *Marblehead* were badly hit Admiral Doorman ordered a return to Tjilatjap. With reinforcements from Surabaya, the British cruiser *Exeter*, the Australian *Hobart*, the Dutch *Java* and three more Dutch and US destroyers, Doorman was ordered to launch another strike to protect Palembang, the capital of Sumatra. This raid on 15 February suffered six hours of bombing and again Doorman had to order his ships to retire; as the British had learned in the Mediterranean, naval operations could not be mounted without air cover. The surrender of Singapore, announced the same day, marked the beginning of the end. Admiral Hart was recalled to the United States. His successor was the Dutch Admiral Conrad Helfrich.

Attrition was taking its toll of ABDA's destroyers; the Dutch

Above: The Japanese destroyer *Hayanami* at high speed. On the measured mile at Kyogasaki in 1943 she attained a speed of 35.15 knots.

Above: USS *Nicholas* (DD.449). Her armament includes depth charges, torpedoes and 5-inch guns.

Van Ghent and *Kortenaer* both ran aground, while the USS *Peary* was sunk in a devastating Japanese bombing raid on Darwin in North Australia. The *Edsall* was damaged by a premature explosion of one of her depth-charges and the *Whipple* collided with the cruiser *de Ruyter*. The third attempt to halt the Japanese, a raid in the Badoeng Strait on 19 February, at last produced some results.

Some damage was caused to Japanese destroyers but in return the Dutch destroyer *Piet Hein* was sunk and the USS *Stewart* and the cruiser *Tromp* were disabled. The US destroyers were beginning to suffer from wear and tear as well as battle damage; operating so far from a main base meant that their tender, the *Black Hawk*, was running out of spares. Even under

ideal conditions a squadron of 'cans' needed constant nursing, and these destroyers had been afloat for a quarter of a century. By 20 February the ABDA force was reduced to five cruisers and nine destroyers, including three British, which had escaped from Singapore.

On 27 February Doorman's weary forces finally ran into the heavy ships which had been supporting the Japanese invasion, and the last round began. They were part of Admiral Kondo's Southern Striking Force, the heavy cruisers *Haguro* and *Nachi* and two groups of seven destroyers each, led by two outstanding Japanese destroyer leaders, Rear-Admirals Tanaka and Nishimura. Although on paper they did not have a big margin of strength over the ABDA Striking Force the Japanese had the priceless advantage of air cover, and their modern destroyers had the deadly 'Long Lance' 24-inch torpedo.

When the Japanese ships were sighted just after 1600 the the Allied force was steaming north, with the three British destroyers spread out in line abreast as a screen ahead of the line of cruisers, and the Dutch and American destroyers steaming in line ahead, parallel and on the port quarter. As the Japanese were steaming roughly southwest across their bows, this disposition meant that the bulk of Doorman's destroyers were on the disengaged side. It was the worst place to be, too far away to fire torpedoes, and as inter-Allied communications at this early stage of the war were poor, the destroyers were relying on garbled orders. At 1616 the Japanese opened fire from about 28,000 yards, bracketing the main column with accurate salvoes, and the cruiser *Jintsu* closed in to 18,000 yards to fire at the three destroyers leading the line. Doorman ordered his line to wheel to the west to avoid having his 'T' crossed, and as a result the destroyers were now level with the flagship *de Ruyter*.

The first casualty was the heavy cruiser HMS *Exeter*, which suffered a severe explosion on board. While the line was weaving to avoid her as she slowed down, a torpedo hit the *Kortenaer*. As a column of steam and smoke billowed up she seemed to pause for a moment, then turned turtle and broke in two. There was no time to look for survivors and the other destroyers hurried on, jockeying desperately for a position from which they could attack with torpedoes. The British destroyers tried to drive off the *Jintsu* but *Electra* was hit by a salvo of shells which left her sinking. The other two fell back to give assistance to the crippled *Exeter*, but the American destroyers were now in a position to attack, and in spite of a last-minute cancellation of the order, they carried out an attempt. Unfortunately the range was 10,000 yards, for anything closer would have been suicidal and all the torpedoes missed.

The cruisers had now disappeared, and the four destroyers tried to catch up. They eventually returned to Surabaya to refuel leaving Doorman and his cruisers to sail on to a further disastrous night action. Harassed by torpedo attacks in the light of flares dropped by Japanese float planes, the cruisers steamed on. At 2125 the *Jupiter* was suddenly blown up, and as no Japanese ships could be seen it was assumed that she had been mined, but it was just an example of the staggering range of the 'Long Lance' torpedo. By midnight the ABDA force was all but annihilated, with the *de Ruyter* and *Java* sunk and the *Houston* and *Exeter* badly damaged. The three surviving cruisers and two destroyers made their way back to Surabaya with nothing to show for their sacrifice. There was now nothing to

Above: USS *Helm*'s whaler picks up survivors from the oiler *Neosho* during the Battle of the Coral Sea.

stop the Japanese from capturing the entire East Indies. The following evening the cruisers *Houston* and *Perth* were sunk while trying to escape southwards through the Sunda Strait. On the morning of 1 March the *Exeter* and the destroyers HMS *Encounter* and USS *Pope* were trapped by the *Haguro* and *Nachi* in the Java Sea supported by two heavy cruisers.

The *Exeter* went down fighting, and when it was hopeless she ordered the two destroyers to make their escape while there was still time. The *Encounter* was hit by shellfire just after a destroyer torpedo finished off the *Exeter*, but the *Pope* managed to dodge behind a rain squall which hid her from the Japanese ships. With a faint chance of survival the old destroyer hurried away, making for the coast of Borneo, but suddenly the rain squall blew over, leaving her exposed once again. There were no ships in sight but a float plane from one of the cruisers spotted her

Below: USS *Conway*'s stern dips low in the water as she surges forward under full power.

Above: USS *Trippe* (DD.403) underwent a refit in 1943. Half her torpedo tubes were removed to reduce weight above the waterline.

and within half an hour six dive bombers from the carrier *Ryujo* were on the scene. Incredibly, the *Pope* survived 13 attacks, and the carriers had to send a second group of bombers to finish her off.

On 7 August 1942, the US Marines landed on Guadalcanal in the Solomon Islands and seized an airstrip which had just been completed. They were not to know, as they triumphantly christened it Henderson Field, that they were witnessing the start of the most bitterly contested naval action of the entire Pacific War. Operation Watchtower had been launched to forestall the Japanese attempt to establish a foothold in the Solomons as a prelude to an attack on Australia. The Battle of the Coral Sea had checkmated an attempt to do it by seapower alone, but this time the Japanese intended to use all three services. The Americans were equally determined to stop them, for whoever possessed the Solomons chain held the key to the southwestern Pacific.

Below: The gallant carrier USS *Yorktown* lies stricken in the water during the Battle of Midway. A *Porter* Class destroyer stands by to give help.

The first day of the landings went reasonably well, with no opposition from the Japanese Navy, although heavy air attacks were mounted the next day. Not until the night of 8 August was it apparent what sort of nightmare was unfolding. USAAF bombers and a submarine reported seeing a force of Japanese warships leaving Rabaul. A series of delays prevented the reports from being dealt with, and the results were tragic. The force comprised five heavy and two light cruisers under Admiral Mikawa, and it was steaming at high speed towards the 'Slot,' otherwise known as Savo Sound, between Guadalcanal and the northern islands of the Solomons chain. Mikawa's cruisers were going to drive their way through the American and Australian warships to clear a path for six transports carrying reinforcements for the defenders of Guadalcanal.

The first mistake occurred on the morning of 9 August when Australian aircraft twice sighted Mikawa off Bougainville but delayed reporting it until late in the afternoon. The message had to go via Brisbane before it reached Admiral Victor Crutch-ley RN, whose three cruisers and two destroyers were on patrol in Savo Sound, and via Pearl Harbor before it reached Admiral Turner USN, in command at Guadalcanal. It was over eight hours before either flag officer received the report of the first sighting. The report included an erroneous sighting of 'seaplane tenders,' which led Admiral Turner to assume that an air attack rather than a gun and torpedo attack was most likely and once this idea had taken hold, other incorrect assumptions followed. Aerial reconnaissance might have cleared up the misunderstanding, but the US carriers had been withdrawn the night before to refuel, and bad weather had grounded the land-based search aircraft. At midnight the old submarine *S.38*, the same one which had first seen Mikawa's departure from Rabaul, torpedoed one of the six transports following the Japanese cruiser force. The remaining five turned back to Rabaul, but Mikawa's ships were now only 35 miles from Savo Island, still unsuspected.

The destroyer *Ralph Talbot* raised the alarm when one of the

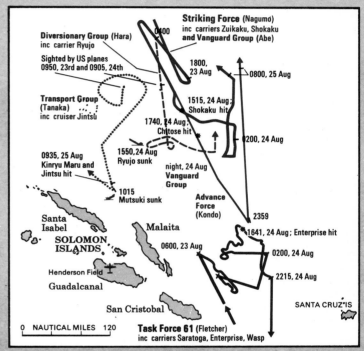

The Battle of Savo Island, 8 August 1942.   The Battle of the Eastern Solomons, 24 August 1942.

Top: The carrier USS *Hornet* was crippled by Japanese dive bombers at the Battle of Santa Cruz. To prevent the possibility of her capture by the enemy the destroyer USS *Mustin* put six torpedoes into her. However they failed to sink her and she was eventually sent to the bottom by Japanese torpedoes.

Above: The view through the periscope of USS *Nautilus* (SS.168) shows the Japanese destroyer *Yamakaze* slipping beneath the waves.

Japanese cruisers' float planes flew overhead, but bad radio reception prevented the call from getting through; her sister *Blue* picked it up and also made radar contact, but she also failed to make contact with Admiral Turner's flagship. In the sultry night, with changing visibility and rain squalls, the Japanese cruisers even managed to pass the *Blue* and *Ralph Talbot* without being detected. Both 'cans' were steaming away from the Japanese cruisers, and the lookouts were gazing ahead only, relying on the SC radar to give all-round surveillance. They were not to know that the mass of Savo Island nearby was producing a false echo which masked the echoes from the ships slipping past little more than 500 yards from the *Blue*. The next destroyer was the *Jarvis*, which had been torpedoed by a wave of torpedo bombers the day before; even if she had sighted the line of cruisers steaming at 25 knots her radio had been put out of action and there was no way in which to pass on a warning.

At 0143 the destroyer *Patterson* radioed an alarm, but it was too late. The float planes overhead dropped parachute flares to illuminate the Allied ships and a hail of gunfire and torpedoes was unleashed. The Australian cruiser *Canberra* was hit by 8-inch shells and then two torpedoes hit her on the starboard side.

She was soon on fire and completely disabled, but the *Patterson* was able to make some sort of reply. The *Bagley*, on the *Canberra*'s starboard bow, managed to get off a salvo of torpedoes, but too late. At 0147 a torpedo blew off the heavy cruiser *Chicago*'s bow, and she sheered off to the west away from the battle. The Japanese cruisers now moved north, splitting into

two groups, and between Savo and Florida Island they fell in with the Northern Force, the heavy cruisers *Astoria*, *Quincy* and *Vincennes* with two destroyers. Like the Southern Force, which no longer existed, Captain Riefkohl's ships had been at action stations for up to 36 hours, and they had been allowed to stand down to the second state of readiness, with half the crew on watch and the other half turned in. The gun flashes to the south had been mistaken for the *Chicago* firing at aircraft, understandable in the light of the general assumption that an air attack was likely, and the *Chicago* had not sent any warning about surface ships. The three cruisers were in line ahead on a 'box patrol' at 10 knots, and were just turning on the northwest leg of the 'box' when they were sighted by Mikawa's flagship *Chokai*. The five American ships were in the worst possible position caught between the two Japanese columns.

The cruisers *Chokai* and *Aoba* opened fire quickly and scored hits on the *Quincy* before turning to the *Astoria* and *Vincennes*. The two destroyers were ignored, for the cruisers were after their own kind. In any case the *Helm* and *Wilson* were so confused that they achieved nothing apart from firing a few 5-inch shells. The *Ralph Talbot*, whose sighting of the float plane three hours earlier had failed to get through, was now punished by the light cruiser *Yubari* on the way out again. None of her torpedoes hit, and in return she was hit by several 140-mm shells. All power was lost, but before she could be sunk she was hidden by a rain squall, and managed to extinguish her fires and limp into Tulagi.

It was left to the destroyers to pick up the pieces. First there was the blazing hulk of the *Canberra*, and the *Patterson* risked

Below: *Akebono* and *Ushio* maneuver in line ahead.

exploding ammunition to go alongside and fight the fires. The *Blue* also came alongside and took off nearly 700 Australian survivors, and at 0800 the wreck was torpedoed by the *Ellett*.

The *Bagley* and *Helm* had already performed the same melancholy duty for the *Quincy* and *Vincennes* which had capsized about an hour after the action. The *Bagley* also rescued survivors of the *Astoria* and put a large firefighting party back on board to try and save her. With the *Wilson* she stood by all night until relieved by the *Buchanan*, but the efforts of all three destroyers were not enough and the crippled cruiser sank at midday. With four cruisers sunk and over 2000 men dead and injured, the Battle of Savo Island was a disaster for the Allies, and it showed that the lesson of Jutland had not been learned; one side had practiced night-fighting and the other side had not. The only crumbs of comfort were that Admiral Mikawa had failed to sink the transports lying off Lunga Point, and that on the way home the heavy cruiser *Kako* was torpedoed and sunk by the US submarine *S.44*. The men who lived through that night of destruction gave Savo Sound a new name to commemorate the ships which sank, Ironbottom Sound.

The Japanese Commander-in-Chief, Admiral Isoroku Yamamoto, was disappointed at the result of Savo Island battle, for the brilliant success of Mikawa in rolling up the Allied patrol line had not been followed by the destruction of the invasion force. During the inevitable lull which followed, the Japanese at Rabaul had been able to reinforce their garrisons on Guadalcanal and Tulagi. The ships which covered these supply runs also bombarded the Marines' positions ashore and threatened their supply lines. The chance was taken to build up a strong force for the task of expelling the Americans from the Solomons, with reinforcements from Truk and elsewhere. An Occupation Force of four transports with a close escort of four old destroyers and a cruiser was supported by a Mobile Force composed of the carriers *Ryujo*, *Shokaku* and *Zuikaku*, the seaplane carrier *Chitose*, three battleships, 11 cruisers and 23 destroyers. Against this the Allies had three carriers, the *Saratoga*, *Enterprise* and

Wasp, with one battleship, seven cruisers and 18 destroyers, split into three task forces.

The Battle of the Eastern Solomons on 24 August was another carrier battle in which the destroyers had little to do but act as handmaidens to the carriers. It was indecisive, as the American carriers' planes sank the carrier *Ryujo* in exchange for serious damage to the *Enterprise*. An interesting feature of the Japanese side of the operation was the use of four old destroyers of the *Mutsuki* Class, built in 1923–27, as fast transports. Their top sea speed was about 30 knots, and so they could keep up with a naval force unlike any ex-mercantile transport, and this made them useful for the high-speed runs from Rabaul to the Solomons. These runs were made with such monotony from August 1942 onwards that they were known to the Allies as the 'Tokyo Express.' On the morning of 25 August the *Mutsuki* was standing by the damaged transport *Kinryu Maru* when Army B-17s from Espiritu Santo scored a hit on her with bombs, which sank her. She was the first victim of USAAF medium-level bombs, and when Commander Hatano of the *Mutsuki* was rescued by the destroyer *Yayoi* it was reported that he said with a wry smile that it only proved that even the B-17s made a hit once in a while.

Japanese submarines were also present in the Solomons in growing numbers, and in the weeks after the Battle of the Eastern Solomons they showed how they could influence the campaign. On 31 August the carrier *Saratoga* was hit twice by torpedoes from *I.26*; although she was in the care of seven destroyers the force was zigzagging at only 13 knots to conserve the cans' fuel. The 'Sara' had been hazarded in a misguided attempt to provide cover for the fast convoys bringing supplies to Guadalcanal and Tulagi, and it was the same misuse of a fleet carrier which had caused the loss of HMS *Courageous* in September 1939. The American carrier was luckier, for she survived, but two weeks later on 14 September, three torpedoes from *I.19* ripped into the starboard side of the *Wasp*. This time the carrier was fatally damaged, and as her aviation gasoline burned it set off explosions of torpedoes and bombs, which made the job of the damage-control parties almost impossible. A sister of the *I.19*, the *I.15* was on station seven miles away, and she fired a spread of six torpedoes, one of which hit the battleship *North Carolina* abreast of A 16-inch gun turret, while a second ran on

Below: Destroyers of DesRon 12 make 'S'-turns in Ironbottom Sound to honor the dead. Savo Island is in the background.

much further and hit the destroyer *O'Brien*. She had one of the most remarkable escapes of any destroyer in history for the 21-inch torpedo hit her right on the bow and blew it off in a tremendous explosion, but without sinking her or causing any casualties. The *I.15* nearly got the carrier *Hornet* as well, and the lookouts on the bridge of the escorting destroyer *Mustin* were horrified to see a torpedo track passing under their own keel. Fortunately it was this torpedo which hit the *North Carolina*, as a hit on the carrier could have been the knockout blow for the Solomons campaign.

By mid-afternoon the *Wasp* was beyond hope and the fire-fighting parties were forced to abandon ship; when a violent explosion blew out the midships elevator 20 minutes later Rear-Admiral Scott ordered everybody off. The carrier lay burning for another two hours, with continuing explosions tearing her hull apart. Admiral Scott hoped to get firefighting parties aboard later, but at 1745 Rear-Admiral Noyes ordered the scuttling of his former flagship. The destroyer *Lansdowne* had the melancholy job of sinking the *Wasp* with four torpedoes. The *O'Brien* managed to limp to Noumea for emergency repairs, but an estimate of her seaworthiness by repair staff of the destroyer tender based there proved to be over-optimistic, and on 19 October her badly strained hull broke up off Samoa, one of the rare examples of structural failure in destroyers.

The 'Tokyo Express' was still running and it became one of the outstanding achievements of the Imperial Japanese Navy. Without the benefit of radar, the Japanese had still achieved a proficiency in night-fighting shown to overwhelming advantage off Savo Island. After the first battle Admiral Mikawa sent Rear-Admiral Raizo Tanaka and his 2nd Destroyer Flotilla to run 900 troops to Guadalcanal, and the success of this operation led to further attempts. On most evenings, just before nightfall, a force of destroyers or other small warships would leave Rabaul and dash down the 'Slot' between New Georgia and Santa Isabel, arriving off Guadalcanal about midnight. The troops and supplies were landed at Cape Esperance or Tassafaronga, and then

Above: The repair ship *Prometheus* services the battleship USS *South Dakota* and two destroyers damaged in a collision.

the 'Tokyo Express' headed southeast to bombard Henderson Field, and then about one and one-half hours after arrival, they were homeward bound. At daybreak the sweating and cursing Marine Corps would fill in the holes in the airstrip to allow the defending fighters to take off, but once night fell the Japanese Navy was once again in command.

It was 'Tenacious Tanaka' (his nickname was bestowed by his reluctant Marine Corps admirers) who was leading the transports in the light cruiser *Jintsu* in the Battle of the Eastern Solomons on 24 August. When his flagship was damaged by a bomb he transferred to the destroyer *Kagero*. On the night of 4–5 September Tanaka's destroyers sank the flush-deckers *Gregory* and *Little* off Lunga Point with gunfire before escaping. The Japanese did not have it all their own way, and on the night of 11–12 October an attempt to repeat the success of Savo Island by bringing heavier forces down the 'Slot' brought on the disastrous Battle of Cape Esperance. This time the Americans were waiting; Admiral Scott's Task Force 64 was plotting Admiral Aritomo Goto's path on radar.

The Americans had learned by their mistakes, and although their estimate of Goto's force underestimated its strength the sighting reports were passed rapidly to Admiral Scott's Task Force 'Sugar' guarding the approach to Ironbottom Sound.

The battle which followed was confused to say the least. Admiral Scott had the tactical advantage over Goto's cruisers, and managed to cross his T. The four cruisers went into action as planned but three of their four destroyers got out of station and found themselves between the two opposing battle-lines. As a result Admiral Scott ordered a ceasefire to avoid what he thought was an attack on his own forces, but Admiral Goto was equally confused, and thought that he too was being fired on by his own side. But it was American gunfire which hit the flagship

Aoba and mortally wounded it and Admiral Goto. The destroyer *Duncan* had been hit, possibly by an American shell but Lieutenant-Commander Taylor continued an attack which he was making on the heavy cruiser *Furutaka*. Just as she fired two torpedoes she was hit by another American salvo which crippled her, and she sheered off in flames, nearly out of control. The USS *Farenholt* was also hit by her own side, but she survived a shell in the forward fire-room and crawled out of range.

The Japanese destroyer *Fubuki* came within a mile of the heavy cruiser *San Francisco*, a range at which the 8-inch shells sank her in minutes. The cause of her loss was a turn by the heavy cruiser *Furutaka*, and she too ran into the American cruisers' concentration fire. Although soon ablaze from end to end she stayed afloat for about another hour. Next day two more Japanese destroyers, the *Murakumo* and *Natsagumo* were sunk by Henderson Field's dive-bombers, making the Japanese losses for the battle three destroyers and a heavy cruiser sunk, and two more cruisers damaged, at a cost of one US destroyer sunk and one destroyer and two cruisers damaged.

The Japanese were so galled by the air strikes of the Marine Corps pilots from Henderson Field that only a day later they sent the fast battleships *Haruna* and *Kongo* to shell the airstrip. This caused so much disruption that the following night, 14–15 October, Tanaka's destroyers ran a convoy of five transports into Tassafaronga, bringing 4500 fresh troops and large quantities of ammunition and food for the defenders. The previous night nearly a thousand 14-inch shells had landed on Henderson Field; this time the airstrip was pitted with hits from nearly as many 8-inch shells. However, the invaders were holding their own against furious attacks, and the vital airfield remained in the Marines' tenacious grip. The strain was almost intolerable, with air attacks by day and bombardments by night. Another attempt to loosen the US Navy's grip resulted in the Battle of the Santa Cruz Islands on 26 October in which the opposing carrier air groups did most of the fighting, and the destroyers could do little but watch. The major casualty was the USS *Hornet* which was set on fire by four bombers early in the battle.

During the first two weeks of November Tanaka's destroyers continued to run the 'Tokyo Express,' with over 60 missions. The Americans were also exerting every effort to bring in convoys, and the respective covering forces clashed in the action known as the Battle of Guadalcanal. For the superstitious the date, Friday 13 November, was a bad omen, and so it turned out. It was the Japanese who arrived first, Vice-Admiral Hiroaki Abe's Striking Force of two battleships, a cruiser and 16 destroyers were sent, all to get Tanaka's 12 destroyers and 11,000 men through.

Against this the Americans could only put Rear-Admiral Daniel J Callaghan's Task Group 67.4, five cruisers and eight destroyers, although the battleships *South Dakota* and *Washington* and the carrier *Enterprise* were a day's steaming away. It was a savage mêlée, and lack of radio-discipline completely cancelled out the American Squadron's advantage of radar. The TBS net was jammed with calls for ranges, bearings, tactical orders, anything which would avert the catastrophe which was fast approaching.

The cruiser *Atlanta* opened fire with her 5-inch guns at 1600 yards, but in return a hurricane of fire swept her as the disciplined Japanese gun-crews swung into their night-fighting drill. A shell on the bridge killed Admiral Norman Scott and all but one of his staff, and soon after she was stopped by torpedo-hits. The destroyers were equally bewildered by the sudden loss of cohesion, and found themselves in a welter of ships charging about firing at one another. The *Barton* had to go hard astern to avoid colliding with her target, but as she did so a brace of torpedoes hit her and broke her in half. The *Cushing*, *Laffey*, *O'Bannon* and *Sterrett* found themselves taking on the battleship *Hiei*, and even fired their 5-inch guns at her. The *Cushing* was slowed down by hits from the *Hiei*'s secondary armament and when the battleship sheered off into the smoke-haze, Japanese destroyers came up to finish her with gunfire. The *Laffey* fired two torpedoes at the *Hiei* so close that the watchers on the bridge saw the two 'fish' bounce out of the water after hitting the battleship's 'bulge' without exploding. Retribution was swift, and within seconds the *Laffey* was hit by 1400-pound shells and a torpedo, which left her shattered and killed nearly her entire crew. For his determined bravery Lieutenant-Commander W E Hank was awarded the Navy Cross posthumously.

The *Sterrett* and *O'Bannon* found themselves on the opposite side of the *Hiei* and probably benefited from the distraction offered by the *Cushing* and *Laffey*'s destruction. At one moment the *O'Bannon* found herself so close to the *Hiei* that, just like the *Spitfire* and the *Nassau* at Jutland, the 14-inch guns could not depress low enough to hit the destroyer. The *Sterrett* was roughly handled by two of the *Hiei*'s escorting destroyers, but she also lived to tell the tale. The *Monssen* also ran into a group of destroyers with the *Hiei*, but she did not escape. She was overwhelmed by gunfire and set ablaze from end to end; some 130 men died in the inferno, although three heroic crewmen reboarded her and rescued some of the wounded. Other destroyers were damaged in the witches' sabbath that night, but the worst was over for them. Admiral Callaghan, whose confusing and contradictory orders had been a prime cause of the carnage, was killed on the bridge of his flagship, the heavy cruiser *San Francisco*, by gunfire from the *Kirishima*. The *Hiei* was hit by 8-inch shells from the American cruisers, and was seen to make a half-circle turn and stagger north along the east side of Savo

Below: USS *O'Bannon* in 1942. She distinguished herself in the Battle of Guadalcanal in November 1942 when she took part in a destroyer attack on the battleship *Hiei*.

Above: The forward torpedo tubes and a 20-mm antiaircraft gun of USS *Jouett* (DD.396).

Island. At about 1100 next morning the battered cruiser squadron ran into the Japanese submarine *I.26*'s patrol area, and in spite of a depth-charge attack by the *Sterrett* her torpedoes hit the antiaircraft cruiser *Juneau*. The magazines must have been detonated and the ship blew up with the loss of all but 10 of her 700-strong crew.

The second act of the drama unfolded the following night when the American reinforcements had arrived. Four destroyers, the *Benham*, *Gwin*, *Preston* and *Walke* were escorting the battleships *South Dakota* and *Washington* which were positioned off Savo Island to intercept Vice-Admiral Kondo's Bombardment Group, the *Kirishima*, four cruisers and nine destroyers. Other targets were the remnants of the latest 'Tokyo Express,' which had been badly mauled that day by the aircraft of the carrier *Enterprise*, but Kondo's force was the more important.

With the radar coverage provided by his flagship *Washington*, Rear-Admiral Willis A Lee picked up Kondo's ships at a range of 16,000 yards, but once again Japanese eyesight and the superb night-glasses provided to their lookouts gave them the first sighting. The *Preston* was hit just after 2322 and 20 minutes later she was sinking from repeated hits. The *Walke* tried to launch torpedoes but was also hit by shells and then torpedoed. She sank a few minutes after the *Preston* and, almost immediately afterwards, the *Benham* was hit by a torpedo. She was later rescued by the *Gwin*, and the two ships began the long crawl back to Espiritu Santo, but the *Benham*'s bulkheads collapsed under the strain some 12 hours later, and she had to be scuttled.

The two battleships had joined in the firing, but the *South Dakota* was soon in trouble when an electrical failure blacked out the ship, including her radar 'eyes.' She blundered past the burning destroyers and nearly got sunk by approaching too close to the Japanese battle-line. But the *Washington*'s salvoes caused great destruction against the *Kirishima* and probably helped to distract her attention from the lumbering *South Dakota*. The *Kirishima* sank later, and Admiral Kondo withdrew to avoid further losses. This still left Tanaka's transports, but these were caught just at the moment that they arrived at Tassafaronga and the destroyer *Meade* was able to inflict heavy losses on the four helpless targets.

Guadalcanal was the US Navy destroyer's equivalent of Jutland, a muddled series of actions in which they covered themselves with glory. There was the same blend of muddle and heroism, with faulty communication causing heavy losses, but also a devotion to duty which went a long way to snatch victory out of defeat. There was another parallel with Jutland, for although the Japanese could boast that they had sunk a lot of USN ships they had finally lost the initiative and were never to regain it.

Tanaka was to have one more success, in the Battle of Tassafaronga on the night of 30 November–1 December 1942. His eight destroyers and fast transports were jumped by Rear-Admiral Carleton H Wright's Task Force 67, but once again Japanese tactics were superior. The US destroyers' torpedoes all missed, whereas four US cruisers were torpedoed, and one later sank. But the 'Tokyo Express' was running out of steam, and the Japanese High Command had come to realize belatedly that they would never expel the Americans from the Solomons. The last runs of the 'Tokyo Express' were made in reverse, evacuating the garrison that had been kept supplied at such a high cost in lives, ships and aircraft. On the night of 1–2 February 1943 a week-long operation started, the lifting of 12,000 soldiers for the loss of only one destroyer. Although Tanaka was no longer in charge it was a fitting tribute to a remarkable destroyer man and the skill of his crews.

VICTORY OVER JAPAN

The island-by-island campaign to occupy the rest of the Solomons chain after the Marines' hold on Guadalcanal was established was a land, sea and air campaign, but inevitably the destroyers played an essential role, for their speed and torpedo armament made them tough opponents for the Japanese. The battles could be taken as a destroyer's roll of honour, Kula Gulf, Kolombangara, Vella Gulf, Vella Lavella, Empress Augusta Bay and Cape St George, but in addition there were scores of other actions through 1943 in which destroyers fought hard and often.

The first of the new men to rise to prominence was Rear-Admiral W I 'Pug' Ainsworth, who was appointed Commander Destroyers, Pacific (ComDesPac) in June 1942. He had a distinguished career as a destroyer captain, and had been in command of a destroyer squadron in the Atlantic in 1941. Admiral Halsey appointed him to command Task Force 67 after the force had been roughly handled by Tanaka's destroyers in the Battle of Tassafaronga. He showed his mettle by leading a destroyer raid on Munda, at the northwest end of New Georgia, on the night of 4–5 January 1943. For the first time the Americans got the better of the exchange, and it showed that a new spirit of confidence had been generated. In his report Ainsworth said, 'The night bombardment of Munda is . . . the first naval action in which our Navy has coordinated surface, submarine and aircraft units in a night bombardment. As an initial venture in this field of operation, this action may be taken as our first lesson in night amphibious warfare.'

Another exploit of Ainsworth's destroyers was the laying of a minefield right in the path of the 'Tokyo Express' route between Arundel and Kolombangara. The minelayers were three old flush-deckers, the *Breese*, *Gamble* and *Preble*, which had been converted in the 1930s to 'three-stackers' with mine-rails for laying 80 mines. On the night of 6–7 May 1943 the three old destroyers, with the new *Fletcher* Class *Radford* using her radar to act as a guide, laid 250 mines in the middle of Blackett Strait. Admiral Ainsworth covered the operation with three

light cruisers and three fleet destroyers. The whole escapade was accomplished without loss, although a Japanese float plane spotted the force as it withdrew. The risks were justified sooner than anticipated, for the next morning four enemy destroyers ran straight into the minefield. In quick succession the *Oyashio*, *Kagero* and *Kurashio* were hit, and only the *Michishio* escaped. Packed with survivors, she was strafed by US aircraft from Guadalcanal which had been called up by one of the Australian coast-watchers. Five days later Admiral Ainsworth's force attempted a similar coup, but a series of mishaps gave away the position of the minefield prematurely, so that the Japanese minesweepers were able to deal with it quickly.

Ainsworth's Task Group 36 met the Japanese headlong in the Battle of Kula Gulf on the night of 5–6 July. Once again it was a confused battle in typical Solomons conditions, a moonless and humid night with visibility up to two miles but liable to be reduced by sudden rain squalls. The Japanese force was a group of 10 destroyers under Rear-Admiral Teruo Akiyama, running supplies to Vila-Stanmore, whereas the Americans had the cruisers *Honolulu*, *Helena* and *St Louis* and DesRon 21, the destroyers *Nicholas*, *Jenkins*, *O'Bannon* and *Radford*. Although the Japanese were outnumbered, four of their destroyers were of a new and powerful type known as the *Akizuki* Class, and one of these, the flagship *Niizuki* had the new Type 22 radar set. As all 10 also had the 24-inch 'Long Lance' torpedoes with reloads the American advantage of fire-power was not as great as it looked on paper.

Although the Japanese lookouts saw the American column at a range of about 7000 yards American gunnery was good, and the first salvo of 6-inch shells from the cruisers crippled Akiyama's flagship *Niizuki*. The *Suzukaze* and *Tanikaze* were hit by apparently 'dud' torpedoes, and when their own torpedoes

Below: The Japanese destroyer *Sagiri* in 1931, shortly after being modernized.

missed they turned away behind their smoke-screen to reload. This time one of the salvoes ran straight, and the three 'Long Lances' which ripped into the cruiser *Helena* broke her back. So furious was the action by this time that the Admiral and his captains failed to notice what had happened, and did not know until the stricken ship failed to answer her call-sign. Ainsworth kept his formation under control and achieved a crossing of the enemy's T, but once again the torpedoes failed dismally and the *Hatsayuki* was hit by three 'duds.' In this first phase the American tactics had been sound but the enormous advantage conferred by the 'Long Lance' got the Japanese out of trouble.

In the second phase the US destroyers made contact once more and inflicted damage on two enemy ships. The *Nagatsuki* was so badly damaged that she later had to be beached near Vila where she was destroyed by bombing. The *Nicholas* and *Radford* were in the middle of rescuing survivors of the *Helena* when they sighted the *Amagiri* which was on a similar errand of mercy for the *Niizuki* survivors. Having chased her off the two destroyers returned to the job of rescue, only to be interrupted again by the *Mochizuki*. Lieutenant Commander Hill took the *Nicholas* off at full speed followed by the *Radford*, leaving their boats to continue picking up survivors. The *Mochizuki* having been chased away, they returned and picked up their boats before rejoining Admiral Ainsworth.

The results of the battle were disappointing, but they showed that the Japanese could no longer count on getting the first blow in. The loss of the *Helena* was hardly offset by the sinking of the *Niizuki*, but the loss of Admiral Akiyama was another blow to Japanese morale. Unfortunately the Battle of Kolombangara a week later showed the dangers of using cruisers against the Japanese destroyers. Once again ships were hit at ranges previously thought impossible for torpedo attack, and

Above: In a night action a destroyer's 5-inch 38 caliber guns give a dramatic flash.

the cruisers *Leander* (New Zealand), *Honolulu* (Ainsworth's flagship) and *St Louis* were hit. The Japanese light cruiser *Jintsu* was destroyed, killing Admiral Izaki and nearly 500 of her crew, and the attempt to get supplies through to the defenders of Vila – Stanmore was frustrated this time. The *Gwin*, the only destroyer which had survived the battleship action at Guadalcanal, was hit by a single torpedo toward the end of the action. With the help of her squadron-mate, *Ralph Talbot*, she was still afloat nearly seven hours later but desperately wounded. US aircraft from airfields in the Russell Islands provided cover against marauding Japanese bombers while the destroyermen labored to save what was now only a smouldering hulk. At about 0900 the commander of DesDiv 23, Commander Higgins, decided that nothing further could be done, and ordered her to be scuttled.

The second name to rise to fame in the Solomons was that of Commander Frederick Moosbrugger, who had been given command of DesDiv 12 at Tulagi. When Munda fell at the beginning of August 1943 he was given the job of intercepting another 'Tokyo Express' run in Gizo Strait supported by fighter cover and PT-Boats. Flying his flag in the *Dunlap*, he had the *Craven* and *Maury* under him as well as DesDiv 15, the destroyers *Lang*, *Stack* and *Sterrett*. On the night of 5–6 August the two divisions steamed north of Vella Gulf, between Vella Lavella and Kolombangara. First contact was obtained by the *Dunlap* on radar at 2333 and only minutes later Moosbrugger gave the order via TBS (the Talk Between Ships short range radio net). 'Stand by to fire torpedoes.' The range came down to 1000 yards and for once the

Above: A *Fletcher* Class destroyer heads towards Japan in 1945.

Japanese seem to have been taken completely by surprise. Within minutes the *Kawakaze* sank after four torpedo-hits from the *Stack*. The *Arashi* and *Hagikaze* blew up leaving only the *Shigure* to make her escape at high speed back to Bougainville. This was the Battle of Vella Gulf and it was unusual in that the US Navy suffered no losses at all. But this was not accidental, for Moosbrugger had insisted that his destroyers did not use the unreliable magnetic exploder on their torpedoes' warheads; instead the old and trusted 'contact' setting was used. Another improvement was the fitting of flash-guards to the lips of the torpedo-tubes to reduce the risk of the flash of the cordite impulse-charge being seen by Japanese lookouts as the torpedoes were fired.

The upshot of all these confused and deadly night actions was the cancelling of the 'Tokyo Express' on the orders of the new Japanese Commander in Chief, Admiral Koga. This meant that the outlying garrisons had to be ferried back to Bougainville in landing barges, and so a tempting 'soft-skinned' target was presented to the commander of DesDiv 12 and his fellow destroyer commanders. Between 9 August and 4 October the destroyer squadrons sank some 40 landing barges and escorting gunboats and other light craft. The carnage forced Admiral Koga to reform the 'Tokyo Express,' and this quickly brought on another action, the Battle of Vella Lavella, on the night of 6–7 October. This time honors were more even, for three US destroyers took on six Japanese and each side lost one ship to torpedoes. Unfortunately the *O'Bannon* damaged herself by ramming the sinking *Chevalier* in the confusion, but the *Selfridge* managed to limp home after taking a torpedo-hit.

Captain Arleigh A Burke rose to prominence as a result of his leadership of DesRon 23 in the Battle of Empress Augusta Bay on the night of 2 November 1943. The Japanese had despatched the heavy cruisers *Myoko* and *Haguro*, the light cruisers *Sendai* and *Agano* and six destroyers to cover a force of five fast transports heading for Cape Torokina. The American Admiral Merrill was flying his flag in the light cruiser *Montpelier*, with her sisters *Cleveland*, *Columbia* and *Denver* and eight destroyers of Burke's DesDiv 45 and Commander B L Austin's DesDiv 46. It is interesting to note that Merrill's answer to the menace of the 'Long Lance' was to allow his destroyers to attack with torpedoes first to force the Japanese to keep their distance, and then use radar-assisted long-range gunfire to keep the advantage on his side. Unfortunately a turnaway by the Japanese squadron meant that DesDiv 45's torpedoes all missed. As soon as Admiral Merrill realized that the Japanese had spotted his cruisers he countermanded his original plan and ordered the cruisers to open fire. The cruiser *Sendai* reeled under the impact of a number of 6-inch shell hits and in the confusion the destroyers *Samidare* and *Shiratsuya* collided with one another.

The Americans also had their problems. The destroyer *Foote* lost station, was hit in the stern by a Japanese torpedo, and then narrowly escaped being run down by the cruiser *Cleveland*. The *Spence* and *Thatcher* swung together with a crash and sparks flew as the two steel hulls ground side by side at 30 knots. The mishap caused no serious damage to either destroyer but at that moment the enemy heavy cruisers *Haguro* and *Myoko* appeared only 4000 yards away and in the excitement it was assumed that they were American so no torpedoes were fired. The mistake was understandable and shortly afterwards there was classic exchange between Austin and Burke over the TBS:

Austin: 'We've just had another close miss. Hope you are not shooting at us.'

Burke: 'Sorry but you'll have to excuse the next four salvoes. They're already on their way.'

This misunderstanding had no ill-effects, and when one of Austin's destroyers, the *Spence*, found that she had too little ammunition to finish off the disabled *Hatsukaze*, Burke's division was called up to complete the task. The destroyers were straining on the leash to pursue the Japanese, but Admiral Merrill wisely ordered them to fall back on his cruisers once more, with the result that they escaped damage from a determined air attack next morning.

Arleigh Burke was soon christened '31-knot Burke' and the 'cans' of Destroyer Squadron 23 were known as the 'Little Beavers' from their unofficial insignia. The flagship was the *Fletcher* Class *Charles Ausburne*, which won 11 Battle Stars in three years. Burke's nickname was won in November 1943, when DesRon 23 was refuelling at Hathorn Sound in Kula Gulf. Orders came through to steam at top speed to intercept a Japanese convoy evacuating air force personnel, and the *Charles Ausburne* confirmed that she and her three squadron-mates would make the arranged rendezvous by a specified time. Back at Admiral Halsey's head-quarters the operations officer worked out the average speed needed for the run as 31 knots and remembered that Burke had recently insisted that his squadron could only make a maximum formation speed of 30 knots. Admiral Halsey's next order to Burke read:

'Thirty-one knot Burke get athwart the Buka-Rabaul evacuation line about 35 miles west of Buka X. If no enemy contacts by 0300 . . . 25th . . . come south to refuel same place X. If enemy contacted you know what to do.'

The result was the Battle of Cape St George, fought in the early hours of 25 November 1943 between the *Charles Ausburne*, *Dyson*, *Claxton*, *Converse* and *Spence* and the Japanese *Onami*, *Makinami*, *Amagiri*, *Yugiri* and *Uzuki*. In Burke's own words the moonless night was ideal 'for a nice quiet torpedo attack,' and so it proved. The first attack hit two Japanese destroyers, the *Onami* and *Makinami*, and then the American destroyers settled down to a long stern chase as the remaining three enemy destroyers fled to the north. Such was Burke's instinct for destroyer tactics that after 15 minutes he suddenly ordered his squadron to swing to starboard to avoid a possible torpedo attack. As the five destroyers swung back on to their original course three Long Lances exploded astern, detonated either at the end of their run or by running into the wakes of DesRon 23. Under such circumstances it is hardly surprising that the 'Little Beavers' came to regard themselves as a lucky formation, and they responded by adding the *Yugiri* to their night's score.

The struggle for the Solomons was over and the destroyers had contributed greatly toward that achievement. From the first days of trial and error, when the Japanese destroyers and cruisers held the whip hand, destroyers had done all the hardest fighting. Their losses had been heavy but gradually they had

Top right: Antiaircraft armament became increasingly important as the war drew to a close and the Japanese began to employ kamikaze tactics. Seen here is USS *O'Bannon*'s after 20-mm battery.
Center right: USS *Shannon* (DM.25) seen here off Okinawa in 1945.
Below right: USS *Ellyson* was converted to a fast minesweeper (DMS.19).

learned to beat the Japanese at their own game, and had become more cunning and resourceful. As one anonymous destroyer-man said, 'in the Solomons everyone felt they were living on borrowed time.'

The American advance across the Central Pacific was comparatively uneventful for the destroyer forces but they came to the fore with the return to the Philippines. The Battle of Leyte Gulf is only a convenient name for a series of four big battles which took place over a period of four days. Together they amount to the greatest sea battle in history and, for the only time in the Pacific, all warship-types played the role for which they had been designed: battleships fought battleships while destroyers attacked with torpedoes and defended their own fleets. It opened with a landing in Leyte Gulf on 20 October 1944, but three days previously the Japanese had initiated their Sho or 'Victory Plan' when they learned that demolition teams and battalions of Rangers had reconnoitered the Leyte beaches. Under the Sho Plan there were four fleets:
1. The Main Body under Vice-Admiral Ozawa, composed of four carriers, two battleship/carrier hybrids, three cruisers and eight destroyers, coming from the Inland Sea.
2. Force A under Vice-Admiral Kurita, composed of five battleships, 12 cruisers and 15 destroyers, coming from Borneo.
3 & 4 Force C, which was in two parts, the Van Squadron under Vice-Admiral Nishimura with two battleships, one cruiser and four destroyers, and the Rear Squadron under Vice-Admiral Shima. This last body included three cruisers and four destroyers, and although both sailed from Borneo they were under separate command.

To the Americans they were known merely by the areas in which they were first spotted, so that the Main Body was labelled the 'Northern Force,' Force A became the 'Center Force' and the two squadrons of Force C became the 'Southern Force.'

Admiral Ozawa and the Northern Force were merely a decoy to lure Halsey's Fast Carrier Task Force away from the invasion area, which in turn would allow Kurita to unite his Center Force with Shima's Southern Force to sweep into Leyte Gulf and destroy the invasion fleet. The Center Force was to reach Leyte

Gulf by passing through the San Bernardino Strait between Luzon and Samar and the Southern Force would pass through Surigao Strait between Leyte and Mindanao. Things went wrong on both sides. At first the departure of Ozawa's Northern Force was undetected and so it did not function as a decoy as early as had been hoped. Then Kurita lost three heavy cruisers in an ambush by US submarines off Palawan on 23 October. Next day carrier planes attacked the Center Force and sank the giant battleship *Musashi*, and a temporary turnabout by Kurita was mistaken for a complete withdrawal. As Ozawa's Northern Force had now been located a jubilant Halsey decided that it was the main Japanese striking force and set off in pursuit. At 1512 on 24 October he signalled his intention of forming a new task force of battleships and carriers to guard the exit of the San Bernardino Strait. Although nothing was done about it, the Seventh Fleet, which had the responsibility of guarding the invasion fleet assumed that the task force had been formed and that the exit was guarded. The other exit, Surigao Strait, was guarded by Admiral Jesse Oldendorf's six old battleships and eight cruisers with 20 destroyers in attendance, but the failure to watch the San Bernardino Strait put the entire invasion armada at the mercy of Admiral Kurita's powerful force.

Oldendorf had been warned at midday to expect a night engagement and he had laid a cunning trap. He sent 30 PT Boats forward to give early warning of Nishimura's approach. Further in he put the destroyers of DesRon 54, the *McDermot* and *Monssen* on the right flank and the *Remey*, *Melvin* and *McGowan* on the left flank. Tucked away close to the coastline of Leyte was the third line of defense, the *Hutchins*, *Bache*, *Dale*, *Arunta* (Australian), *Beale* and *Killen* of DesRon 24. The final element of the trap was a double line of five cruisers and six battleships, with the remaining nine destroyers of DesRon 56 in the center. The Strait is 12 miles wide at this point, and so the cruisers were used to extend the patrol line in case the Japanese tried to slip past. Although nothing much was expected of the PT Boats, they were stationed as far down the Strait as possible so that their surface-warning radar sets could give accurate coverage.

The PT Boats made contact at 2230 and although they did

Above left: Smoke laying was an important destroyer task. Here a *Fletcher* Class unit hides a battleship at the Battle of Leyte Gulf, 1944.
Below left: US escort carriers and destroyers under heavy Japanese fire at San Bernadino Strait.
Below: USS *Johnston* (DD.557) being commissioned at Seattle in October 1943.

Above: Destroyers of DesRon 23 on maneuvers in the Solomon Islands 1943–44.

their best, the Japanese brushed them aside and steamed on. DesRon 54 did not catch sight of them until 0300 but their first torpedo attacks had no effect either, and they had to retire at high speed, zigzagging and making smoke. But three out of the 47 fired hit, two against the battleship *Fuso*'s side and one against the destroyer *Michishio*. It must have been a majestic sight, four destroyers leading the flagship *Yamashiro*, the *Fuso* and the cruiser *Mogami* at one-kilometer intervals, weaving to dodge the torpedoes and trying to pick off the attacking destroyers in the glare of searchlights.

At 0349 the *Fuso* finally blew up, and the two halves of the battleship drifted crazily down the Strait for some time before sinking. But Nishimura ploughed on doggedly, and his flagship seemed to be impervious to the hail of torpedoes and shells fired at her by DesRon 24. Another destroyer, the *Yamagumo* had been sunk, but still the Japanese advanced. One of DesRon 24's destroyers, the *Killen* is credited with a killing torpedo-hit on *Yamashiro*, for her skipper Commander Corey, decided to order a depth-setting of 22 feet on the torpedoes to inflict maximum damage. The salvo ran straight, but the blazing battleship still careered on towards Oldendorf's waiting battleships. Although the plan was to finish off the Japanese by gunfire some of the destroyers of DesRon 56, held in reserve between the battleships and the cruisers, took a hand in the action. One of their torpedoes hit the destroyer *Asagumo* but the *Albert W Grant* was hit by 6-inch shells from her own side before she could get out of range. In all she was hit by seven Japanese 4.7-inch shells and 11 US 6-inch, and suffered heavy casualties.

It was left to the battleships to administer the *coup de grâce* to the *Yamashiro*, and the tortured battleship finally capsized at 0419. The cruiser *Mogami* and the destroyer *Shigure* fled at high speed, and when Admiral Shima learned of the disaster he withdrew. Air attacks and PT Boats accounted for the cruisers *Abukuma*, *Nachi* and *Mogami* and two of his destroyers, with the result that only three destroyers out of the whole Southern Force survived the Battle of Surigao Strait. The victors emerged almost without a scratch, apart from the sorely tried *Grant*, and even she lived to fight another day.

As Admiral Oldendorf's ships finished their work the news came through of desperate fighting off Samar. Not until 0645 had anyone been able to ascertain the unwelcome news that no

Above: USS *Drayton* (DD.366) sported an unusual camouflage which led to her nickname of 'The Blue Beetle.'
Below: USS *Heerman* (DD.532) laying smoke off Samar, October 1944.

ships were guarding the San Bernardino Strait. In another ten minutes Rear-Admiral Sprague's escort carriers learned the awful truth, as 18-inch shells from the giant battleship *Yamato* began to fall around them, Kurita's Center Force had got within 17 miles of the escort carriers which were providing air cover for the massive fleet of transports and landing craft in Leyte Gulf. The six 'jeep carriers' were escorted by only three destroyers and four DEs, the *Hoel*, *Heermann*, *Johnston*, *Dennis*, *John C Butler*, *Raymond* and *Samuel B Roberts*, and they were all that stood between Kurita and a slaughter of the defenseless transports. The alarm had been sounded and reinforcements were on the way, but they were too far away to be of any immediate help. The DEs were not designed to fight anything but submarines, but fortunately most of the earlier vessels of this type had been completed with a set of triple torpedo-tubes, which gave them some limited offensive capability. In speed and maneuverability, however, they were not in the same class as destroyers, and would not be able to look after themselves so well. As for the escort carriers, their small hulls were built to

128

mercantile standards and they were even slower than the DEs, to say nothing of their stores of highly inflammable aviation gasoline.

The *Johnston* under Commander Ernest E Evans found the heavy cruiser *Kumano* within range and rushed to the attack. She launched a salvo of torpedoes but staggered in the water as a salvo hit her. With her speed severely reduced she continued to fire at her opponents, which included the battleship *Kongo*.

She gamely followed the *Hoel* and *Heermann* as they obeyed Admiral Sprague's call for a torpedo attack, but by 0830 her speed was down to 15 knots and only two 5-inch guns were

Below: USS *Hazelwood* (DD.531) attends an *Essex* Class carrier.

firing. The *Johnston* clung to life grimly but the Japanese shells were reducing her to a shambles. Only one shaft was turning, the gyro-compass had been knocked out, and the ship was so helpless that she could not take avoiding action when the *Heermann* collided with her. The *Hoel* (Commander Leon Kintberger) suffered a similar fate, being hit by two of the *Kongo*'s 14-inch shells while racing in to fire her torpedoes. She tried to get clear but found enemy battleships to port and cruisers to starboard. An hour later the destroyer was still afloat after being battered by 40 hits, but when she sank shortly afterward 253 officers and men died. The attack was not in vain as one torpedo hit the 8-inch gunned cruiser *Kumano* and ultimately influenced the outcome of the battle.

Above: The light cruiser USS *Birmingham* and a *Fletcher* Class destroyer near the crippled carrier USS *Princeton*.
Right: A Gunners Mate cleans the after 5-inch gun of USS *Brown* (DD.546) following a night air action off Formosa, October 1944.

Sprague used the code 'men' to signify escort carriers and 'small boys' for his destroyers and destroyer escorts, which accounts for his next signal:
'Small boys on my starboard quarter interpose with smoke between men and enemy cruisers.'

The DEs began to lay a smoke-screen but three of them were ordered to make a torpedo attack as soon as the three destroyers had finished theirs. The *Samuel B Roberts* was soon hit, but not

Main picture: Modern destroyers and frigates on NATO maneuvers. Foreground to back: The Danish frigate *Peder Skram* (F.352); the US guided missile destroyer *Coontz* (DDG.40); the Norwegian frigate *Trondheim* (F.302); the Dutch frigate *Isaac Sweers* (F.814); the Canadian helicopter destroyer *Huron* (DDH.281); the Portuguese destroyer *Almirante Megalhaes Correa* (F.474); HMS *Norfolk* (D.21) and the German destroyer *Bayern* (D.138).

Inset left: The USS *Roper* (DD.147) seen here on convoy in 1942 was one of five *Wickes* Class ships converted to fast transports.

Inset right: Checking the 21-inch quintuple torpedo tubes aboard the USS *O'Bannon* in the Pacific in 1943.

132

before her salvo of three 'fish' had been fired. Soon her forward 5-inch guns were knocked out, half her armament, but the after gun continued to fire for an hour. Over 300 rounds were fired and even the starshell and practice rounds were fired when nothing else was left. Even though the air-blast had failed, making the gun dangerous to load, the gun-crew continued to load by hand until the heat of the breech 'cooked off' a cordite-charge and wrecked the gun-house.

The *Dennis* was damaged during her torpedo attack, but the *Raymond* escaped, like the *Heermann* before her, with only slight damage. The *John C Butler* was ordered to continue laying the smoke-screen, and the *Dennis* thankfully took cover behind it with the carriers. The carrier *Fanshaw Bay* was hit by four 8-inch shells but they did not stop her. The *Gambier Bay*, however, was hit and set on fire, and had to be abandoned. But the carriers were to undergo a further ordeal, for what Kurita's guns could not achieve, land-based aircraft from Luzon could. At about 2300 the *Saint Lô* and the *Kitkun Bay* were hit by aircraft diving onto their flight decks, a foretaste of the kamikaze attacks to come. The *Kitkun Bay* survived the initial blast

of two Zeroes but later her avgas exploded and tore her flimsy hull apart.

Sprague's small force had been nearly annihilated, but the Japanese never got through to the invasion fleet off Leyte. If there is a chapter in destroyer-operations to match the heroism of Guadalcanal it must surely be the Battle of Samar. With the fate of the entire Philippines campaign depending on them, the seven small ships never flinched.

On the first day of April 1945 a huge invasion force prepared to capture the island of Okinawa in the East China Sea. It was the last step before the invasion of the Japanese Home Islands; possession of the precipitous volcanic island and the rest of the Ryukyu group was vital. Yet, as the bombarding ships 'softened up' the defenders there was an ominous silence.

For Operation Iceberg the US Navy had mustered over 1500 ships, including 40 aircraft carriers and 18 battleships. Most of these were allocated to Admiral Turner's Task Force 51, the Okinawa Expeditionary Force: 10 battleships, 18 escort carriers, eight heavy cruisers, 82 destroyers and 54 destroyer escorts.

The majority of destroyers and DEs were to screen the invasion area, either by patrolling or maintaining a 'picket line' to give early radar warning of the approach of Japanese aircraft. The threat from kamikazes was known, and it was expected that the Japanese would spare no effort to destroy ships.

The 'radar picket' was an innovation suggested by previous experience, and its purpose was to give early warning of raids by aircraft or surface warships, and in addition to provide fighter-direction. Distant radar pickets were stationed 40–70 miles away from the transport area but there was also a close picket line only 20–25 miles out. There were also destroyers and DEs assigned to radar picket stations in the outer and inner anti-submarine screens. The distant picket line was composed of groups each of which had one Fighter-Director (FD) destroyer and two Landing Craft, Support (LCS) equipped with radar to extend the radar range. The FD destroyers could control any aircraft of the Combat Air Patrol (CAP) assigned to them by the central fighter-direction unit to deal with hostile aircraft in their areas. The force was known as Task Flotilla 5, and it was commanded by Commodore Moosbrugger.

Although the defenders of Okinawa fought tenaciously from the warren of caves and pillboxes on the island, the land fighting was matched by the ferocity of the sea battle. It was soon realized that the main weight of Japanese air attack was falling on the picket line, and that one destroyer to each picket station was not enough. Yet the DEs did not carry enough antiaircraft guns to stand up to continuous air attack. The picket groups were strengthened and eventually comprised three or more destroyers and four LCSs and strenuous efforts were made to keep a CAP over as many stations as possible. As radar stations were established ashore the 16 floating stations were reduced, and after six weeks only five were in use. Another problem was the small number of FD destroyers available and, as ships were damaged or sunk, it became necessary to equip fresh ships as rapidly as possible.

The onslaught on the destroyers began on 6 April, when the *Bush* and *Colhoun* were sunk by kamikaze aircraft. Seven more destroyers and a DE were badly damaged in attacks of an intensity never seen before. The *Colhoun* was hit by no fewer than four kamikazes, but stayed afloat for more than seven hours. The problem of dealing with kamikazes was the human guidance system, which made them in effect operational air-to-surface

guided missiles. Once the aircraft had been steered into its final dive the target ship had to destroy it by literally shooting it apart. This the 40mm Bofors antiaircraft gun could not do as it did not fire proximity-fused (VT) ammunition; nor did the five-inch dual-purpose gun fire fast enough to do the job. It was found that the best tactic for destroyers was not to weave and zigzag, as they normally did under air attack, but to remain steady to maintain a good gun-platform as long as possible to give the AA guns the best chance. Destroyers are such lively craft that the motion and vibration of being thrown about at high speed was too much for their fire-control, whereas larger warships could cope with evasive maneuvers with no loss of accuracy.

But all this was academic, for the immediate problem of the destroyers was to survive the 'divine wind' which was striking them down in ever-increasing numbers. Added to the obsolescent aircraft was the Ohka or 'Baka' bomb, a small piloted rocket

Left: Launched in December 1943, USS *O'Brien* (DD.725) had twin five-inch gun mountings and heavy antiaircraft defenses.
Below: The destroyer-minelayer USS *Aaron Ward* (DM.34) still floats after being hit by no less than five kamikazes off Kerama Retto in May 1945.

bomb which achieved a diving speed of 535mph. The attacks continued right through to the end of July and, in all, 13 destroyers and DEs were sunk off Okinawa and another 88 damaged. In many instances the casualties were on a terrible scale – as many as a third of the entire complement; in others the loss of life was miraculously light. One of the worst cases was, ironically, not a kamikaze attack. On 18 May the *Longshaw* was on the fifth day of a gruelling routine of fire-support off the beaches when she ran aground on a reef. Japanese shore-batteries ranged on her and began to demolish her methodically until her superstructure was a mass of tangled steel. The captain gave the order to abandon ship, but the casualties continued to mount up. The wrecked destroyer resembled a slaughterhouse, with dead and wounded trapped in every corner. Thirteen officers and 73 enlisted men were killed and 90 wounded.

After the battle was over Moosbrugger paid tribute to his destroyers:

'The performance of the personnel of the screening and radar picket ships, both individually and collectively, was superb through the Okinawa campaign. Acts of heroism and unselfishness, fighting spirit, coolness under fire, unswerving determination, endurance and qualities of leadership and loyalty exceeded all previous conceptions set for the US Navy. The radar picket station groups took every blow that the Japs could inflict and absorbed terrific punishment in personnel casualties and material damage, . . .'

While the American destroyers were locked in their terrible struggle with the kamikazes four British destroyers of the East Indies Fleet fought what turned out to be the last classic destroyer action in history. On 9 May two submarines in the Malacca Strait sighted the heavy cruiser *Haguro*, a destroyer and two patrol craft heading northwest. The small Japanese force was carrying supplies to the Andaman Islands and Vice-Admiral H T C Walker detached escort carriers and the 26th Destroyer Flotilla under Captain Manly Power to search north of Sumatra for it. On the morning of 15 May an aircraft from HMS *Shah* signalled that she had sighted the *Haguro*, and at 2300 that night the flotilla leader HMS *Saumarez* picked up a radar contact at a distance of 34 miles. Captain Power planned his attack with care, ensuring that whichever way the *Haguro* turned she could be caught.

Even at this late stage the Japanese had not lost their boldness, and while the four destroyers were moving into position the cruiser suddenly reversed course. There was a brisk flurry of gunfire during which the *Saumarez* was hit several times. She and HMS *Verulam* fired their torpedoes, and when the *Haguro* turned away to avoid these she ran into the torpedoes from the *Venus* and *Virago*. The cruiser sank just before 0200 on 16 May, about 45 miles southwest of Penang, but her escorting destroyer the *Hamakaze*, escaped and was able to pick up survivors when the 26th Flotilla had left the scene. Although only a minor action it was appropriate that British destroyers should finish

Above: USS *Edwards* (DD.619) of the *Bristol* Class on a shakedown cruise in the Caribbean in 1942.
Left: USS *Trippe* (DD.403) survived World War II only to be used as a target during the atom bomb tests at Bikini Atoll in 1946.
Below: Two *Allen M Sumner* Class destroyers in the Mindanao Sea off the Philippines in January 1945.

their long and distinguished war career with a text-book operation.

It is difficult to establish the last action fought by destroyers but in the European Theater it was probably between German destroyers or torpedo boats and Soviet aircraft as the *Kriegsmarine* struggled to evacuate Eastern Prussia in the face of the Russian advance. On 5 May 1945 the *Hans Lody*, *Friedrich Ihn*, *Thoedor Riedel*, *Z.25*, *T.17*, *T.19*, *T.28* and *T.35* fought off attacks by Soviet motor torpedo boats to escort a convoy with 45,000 refugees to Copenhagen. It was the *Kriegsmarine*'s swansong, and as at Dunkirk and Guadalcanal, destroyers bore the brunt. In the Pacific, the situation was similar but on a much larger scale as US carrier aircraft wiped out the remnants of the Imperial Japanese Navy in each and every anchorage. The last amphibious landing was in Borneo, and on 30 June, just six weeks before the surrender, US destroyers fired 18,820 rounds of 5-inch ammunition at Balikpapan. It was appropriate that they should be at the scene of DesDiv 59's heroic action in January 1942.

Below: Destroyers of the British Home Fleet on patrol in the North Sea, probably shortly before the outbreak of World War II.

Cruisers

Previous page: The British light cruiser *Cardiff* leads the ships of the German High Seas Fleet (not shown) into the Firth of Forth in November 1918 after the German surrender.
Page 137: The heavy cruiser USS *Chester* (CA.27) seen in May 1945.
Below: The USS *Atlanta* at speed. The *Atlanta* served off Guadalcanal.

EYES OF THE FLEET

The cruiser has fought in many famous naval battles and yet few people could give an accurate description of her function as a warship. Even naval historians have difficulty in defining just what a cruiser does.

The word 'cruizing' was used in the eighteenth and early nineteenth century to describe independent operations by a single ship, unattached to any squadron. 'Cruizers' were usually frigates but often smaller sloops and brigs, and very rarely ships-of-the-line. The essential meaning of the word was a description of function, not a classification of a ship-type. These operations could be against privateers, or against an enemy's shipping, or they could be merely to provide a squadron with intelligence.

The term continued to be used when steam was introduced, but in the 1880s it came to be applied to a broader category of warships, smaller than the battleship and the big steam frigate. As their function was to operate independently they were correctly described as cruisers, but because they were sizeable warships, they came to be thought of as a separate category. By 1889 the last of the Royal Navy's big steam frigates had been rerated as cruisers on the Navy List and a new category of warship was created.

As a cruiser's main task was to catch commerce-raiding warships and to prey on enemy shipping, speed was important. The engines of the day were cumbersome, and it was necessary to carry masts and yards as well, to save coal on long passages. This in turn limited the amount of armor which could be applied. In the 1870s and early 1880s the British and Russians both tried

to produce classes of 'belted' cruiser, but the weight of wrought-iron armor was so great that the narrow armored belt was submerged when the ships were at their load draught. Thereafter designers restricted themselves to providing an arched steel deck, which protected the machinery and magazines from shell fire.

As early as 1871 the British industrialist, Sir William Armstrong, realized that guns and shells would defeat side armor. Since armor could not produce invulnerability, weight could be devoted to armoring the bows, while watertight compartments could limit flooding elsewhere. In 1879 Armstrong's shipyard received orders for gunboats from Chile and China. In this trio Armstrong's ideas were developed: two heavy guns and a partial deck over the machinery; boilers and magazines below the water line.

The next stage was a Chilean cruiser, the *Esmeralda*, a ship which made Armstrong's fortune, led to an increase in the speeds of warships and ultimately caused sails to be abandoned. The *Esmeralda* had a complete deck instead of the earlier partial deck, and as she also carried two single 10-inch guns she created a tremendous impression of fighting power on a modest displacement.

The *Esmeralda* proved to be a poor seaboat, with freeboard sacrificed in favor of gunpower. Nor was the armor as thick or the endurance as great as claimed. However, for small navies prestige and reputation counted for at least as much as actual capabilities.

The French broke away from the 'protective deck' concept in 1888, when they designed the *Dupuy de Lôme*. The designer Emile Bertin was able to armor the whole length of water line with a narrow belt. A protective deck was also provided, to stop shells which plunged over the top of the belt, and below it was

Above: A *San Francisco* Class heavy cruiser alongside a repair ship in the Pacific during World War II.
Left: The French light cruiser *Gloire* seen in 1943 in an unusual camouflage scheme applied during a refit in the United States.

another partial thin deck to catch any splinters penetrating the main deck. Coal stowed between these decks provided further protection, while the watertight compartments were filled with cellulose, which was meant to swell and fill any holes made by shell-hits. The *Dupuy de Lôme* caused a great sensation when she appeared in 1893, and inspired the French Navy to build a new series of fast commerce-raiding cruisers.

The next step was to concentrate the armor over more important areas. The result was that a new type of cruiser appeared: the 'armored' as opposed to the 'protected' cruiser. Predictably it was Armstrong's yard which seized the opportunity when building a new *Esmeralda* for Chile. Unlike previous cruisers she had a narrow water-line belt of 6-inch armor in addition to her protective deck, and carried single 8-inch quick-firing guns on the forecastle and stern. She was hailed as the most powerful warship in the world, and it was claimed that her two 8-inch and sixteen 6-inch guns delivered a greater weight of shells per minute than the most powerful battleship afloat.

The *Esmeralda* came close to the French idea of a commerce-raiding cruiser, but the next Armstrong cruisers were definitely more powerful. The Chileans ordered the *O'Higgins* in 1896 before the *Esmeralda* had started her trials. She was given four single 8-inch guns and a heavy secondary battery of 6-inch and 4.7-inch guns. Her vitals were protected by a 5–7 inch belt.

The *O'Higgins* proved to be what Armstrong's customers wanted and Japan ordered the *Asama* and *Tokiwa* shortly afterwards, followed by the similar *Idzumo* and *Iwate* in 1898. These four were to form the backbone of the Imperial Japanese Fleet during the war against Russia and their outstanding performance did much to foster inflated ideas of the armored cruiser's worth.

The heroic work done by the eight modern armored cruisers at Tsushima might have guaranteed the type a long lease of life, but already events were in train which would reduce them to obsolescence. In 1904 Admiral Fisher became the Royal Navy's First Sea Lord and immediately set up a Committee on Designs to give effect to his ideas for new ships. The most revolutionary was his battleship *Dreadnought*. The secret of *Dreadnought*'s high speed of 21 knots was the adoption of the relatively untried Parsons turbine, and Fisher decided to produce a *Dreadnought*-equivalent of the armored cruiser, to fulfill the same role as the older type. This new armored cruiser was to have 12-inch guns, to enable her to fight battleships on more equal terms. Naturally 25 knots could not be achieved on the same displacement as *Dreadnought* without some sacrifice. One twin 12-inch gun mounting had to go and armor was restricted to the same 6-inch armor belt as the existing cruisers. Fisher claimed that the ships' speed would enable them to 'keep out of trouble.'

The new ships certainly fulfilled their designers' requirements when they made 25.5 knots on trials. They virtually killed off the old armored cruiser and for a while there was even talk of the smaller cruiser disappearing. The principal roles envisioned for them were to scout ahead of the battle fleet, to run down and destroy enemy armored cruisers on the trade routes and to finish off crippled battleships in a fleet action. The value of 12-inch guns in the last two roles was questionable, but for the scouting role it was claimed that 12-inch guns would enable these ships to push a reconnaissance past a screen of cruisers, and get within gun-range of the enemy battle line.

The term 'dreadnought armored cruiser' was too cumbersome to last and in 1913 the term 'battlecruiser' was coined. It was, with hindsight, an unfortunate choice, for it suggested a ship of capital rank, whereas a look at the design of *Invincible* reveals that she was no more than a turbine-driven cruiser, armed with four twin 12-inch gun turrets. It was not foreseen that the battlecruisers would be mistaken for fast battleships, which they most definitely could not be. This confusion of title and function was to have tragic consequences.

The glamor of the *Dreadnought* and the *Invincible* Class focused attention on major warships but the traditional cruiser was still important. The protected cruiser had been divided into three types: 1st, 2nd and 3rd Class, ranging from ships as powerful as armored cruisers down to vessels little better than gunboats. The term 'scout' came into vogue at the turn of the century for the latest 3rd Class cruisers and for a while the Royal Navy built no other cruisers.

Other navies showed a declining interest in smaller cruisers, preferring to build very big armored cruisers. The knowledge that Germany was continuing to build small cruisers was sufficient warning to the British that they must stay in the game. In 1908 work began on a new design, despite Fisher's dislike of cruisers, and the first of the class was ready at the end of 1910. The *Bristol* Class ships were a great improvement over the scouts, being bigger and sturdier. With experience gained from the scout *Amethyst*, the *Bristol* Class ships were driven by steam turbines at 25 knots. This equalled the speed of the scouts. The extra 1000 tons of weight were used to provide an armored deck and two 6-inch guns, in addition to ten 4-inch guns.

On paper contemporary German cruisers were superior, with a small patch of splinter-proof side armor over the machinery and boilers and a two-knot advantage. Maximum speed, however, was achieved by overload and in practice they were only good for 25 knots. Although it was widely believed that the German 4.1-inch gun could outrange the British 6-inch gun, and that the lighter shell allowed a higher rate of fire, time was to show this was fallacious. In practice the heavier British gun could not only outrange the 4.1-inch and inflict more damage, but could also shoot more accurately at extreme range.

Both sides continued to build small cruisers, but the Germans clung to the idea of a large number of light guns while the British moved on to a much heavier armament. The next class after the *Bristol*, were very similar but dropped the 4-inch guns and had a uniform armament of eight 6-inch, as well as a longer forecastle for seaworthiness. In the next design the forecastle was extended two-thirds of the length of the ship, allowing five of the eight 6-inch guns to be mounted at maximum height. In this *Chatham* Class the British finally achieved the sort of cruiser they wanted, with sufficient endurance to hunt down commerce-raiders yet with sufficient speed and armament to serve as fleet scouts.

The United States Navy had not followed a very coherent policy of cruiser-building. Going back as far as the War of Independence, individual American warships had achieved great fame as commerce-raiders, and there was a natural tendency to think in terms of fast cruisers for this single purpose. There was also the problem of severe financial stringency. Even when the threat of war with Spain caused money to be spent, it tended to be spent on capital ships, rather than cruisers. The Americans had no vast seaborne trade to protect and so there was no compulsion to build anything like the standard 2nd Class cruisers which British shipyards turned out in large numbers in the 1890s.

The French stopped building small cruisers in the mid-1890s, having convinced themselves that the whole *raison d'etre* of a navy was to operate against commerce rather than fight an enemy fleet. Developments of the *Dupuy de Lôme* were built in considerable numbers, but in spite of their imposing appearance they were not good steamers and not particularly well protected.

The Japanese were closely associated with the British, and so they tended to follow Royal Navy ideas. As their armored cruisers had behaved so well at Tsushima they decided to go ahead with plans for building improved types. The war with Russia accelerated the plans, for the Japanese Diet wanted to ensure that the Navy would not be too weakened by war losses to deter any other aggressors. Armored cruisers could be built faster than battleships and so the keel of the first ship, the *Tsukuba* was laid in January 1905. She and her sister *Ikoma* were built at Kure. They were the most heavily armed cruisers of their day with 12-inch guns in two twin turrets, a dozen 6-inch and another dozen 4.7-inch. Although not as fast as some foreign armored cruisers, 20.5 knots gave them a good margin over contemporary battleships.

The British, having created the successful 'Town' Class,

decided that a new class of smaller cruiser was needed to work with destroyers. In 1912 the decision was made to produce a new intermediate type, more powerful than the scouts, five knots faster and carrying two 6-inch guns. The *Chatham* and *Birmingham* Classes had introduced a small strip of water-line armor, intended to keep destroyer-sized shells from penetrating boiler-rooms and machinery spaces. This feature was incorporated into the new cruisers in a much improved form.

Normally armor plates were bolted to the hull, which had to be strengthened to take this additional 'skin' but in the new cruisers it was decided to build the hull with a longitudinal strake of high-tensile steel in addition to the normal 1-inch side plating. In effect this made the armor part of the hull and provided sufficient structural strength to allow the rest of the hull to be lighter. Weight was also saved by using destroyer-type fast-running turbines and boilers and by providing oil fuel. Previously coal had been used in all cruisers, but oil has greater thermal efficiency and so the weight saved could be used for higher speed.

The British also established a precedent by abolishing the cumbersome system of grading cruisers into scouts, 1st, 2nd and 3rd class, protected and armored, etc. Instead the armored cruisers and big deck-protected cruisers were lumped together as 'cruisers,' while all the old protected cruisers, the scouts, 'Towns' and the new *Arethusa* Class became 'light cruisers.' Exactly where the dividing line came was not laid down, but there was a general consensus that light cruisers had guns up to 6-inch caliber, whereas the bigger ships had guns of higher caliber. Significantly the hybrid battlecruisers were no longer

included in the cruiser-category, all navies having come to accept them as capital ships ranking just below battleships.

When war broke out in August 1914 the 360-odd cruisers in the world were a collection of ancient and modern. The Royal Navy led the world with 114 of all sizes. Battleships being so prestigious it was inevitable that much of the fighting would have to be done by smaller units, and this provided the cruiser with its rationale. The cruiser was still the largest warship which could be built in reasonable numbers, and she would therefore be called on to perform the widest variety of tasks.

Above: the USS *St Louis* rigged for coaling in 1918.
Below: The armored cruiser *Saratoga* seen circa 1911 while flagship US Asiatic Fleet.

The last of Scharnhorst and Gneisenau

W.L. Wyllie

The opening weeks of World War I seemed to confirm prewar notions about how navies would function. There were a number of German cruisers in the Far East and a small Austro-Hungarian squadron. The German ships were the modern armored cruisers *Scharnhorst* and *Gneisenau* and the light cruisers *Emden*, *Dresden*, *Leipzig* and *Nürnberg* under the command of Vice-Admiral Maximilian von Spee, flying his flag in the *Scharnhorst*.

A month before the outbreak of war von Spee took his squadron to the South Pacific, leaving Fregatten-Kapitän von Müller in the *Emden* at Tsingtao, the German base on the southern coast of China. As soon as the news of impending war was received von Müller put to sea ready to harass enemy shipping in the Far East. In the meantime the base prepared colliers and supply ships to replenish the main squadron in the South Pacific.

Von Spee chose to take his ships to the coast of South America, close to neutral harbors where he could continue to get coal, and well out of the way of the powerful Japanese Navy. However he decided that it was still worth sending one cruiser into the Indian Ocean to cause disruption. The *Emden* had joined the squadron on 12 August and as the fastest ship was ideal for the task. So two days later she left the squadron and headed for the Palau Islands accompanied by a collier.

From the Palaus the *Emden* went south and then west, taking care to hide her true destination as far as possible. When she reached the Lombok Strait von Müller decided that it was time to adopt a disguise, and soon the ship sported a fourth funnel made of wood and canvas. The result was that she reached the

Bay of Bengal unrecognized by the British, French and Japanese warships hunting for her.

The first capture was made on 10 September, a Greek collier which was pressed into service to serve the *Emden*'s needs. During the following week another five ships were captured; four were sunk and the fifth was used to transport the prisoners. Despite this the Allies did not know the *Emden* was in the area until a neutral Italian merchantman reported that she had been stopped and searched. The news was sufficient to bring trade to a standstill.

The cause of all this havoc was no longer in the area, having slipped away to look for targets off Rangoon before doubling back. On 22 September she stood about two miles offshore and bombarded the oil storage tanks at Madras. Two were set ablaze, three more were damaged and random shots fell in the city and damaged shipping in the harbor. It was a blow to British prestige and all shipping came to a halt only a day after it had restarted.

The culprit disappeared from the scene in as mysterious a fashion as she had arrived and then twisted the British lion's tail again by calling at Diego Garcia. The people on this tiny island had not heard of the outbreak of war, and so they welcomed the *Emden* and permitted the crew to relax ashore and carry out minor repairs. Still the *Emden*'s luck held and she sank four more ships off Ceylon. Von Müller next planned a raid on Penang on the west coast of Malaya, where he expected to find a large number of merchantmen.

With her dummy funnel rigged the *Emden* was approaching Penang just after 0300 on 29 October when her lookouts made out

A dramatic view of the Battle of the Falkland Islands. The *Scharnhorst* succumbs to the British fire while the *Gneisenau* tries to fight on.

148

a string of lights to starboard. They belonged to the Russian light cruiser *Jemtchug*, but the Russian lookouts failed to see the strange cruiser gliding closer and closer. At a range of only 300 yards the *Emden* fired a torpedo from her starboard submerged tube; it ran true and detonated below the *Jemtchug*'s after funnel. The Russians gamely tried to reply and one gun actually returned the fire, but the *Emden*'s broadsides completed the devastation. A second torpedo finished the Russian ship off and when the smoke cleared only the *Jemtchug*'s mast was visible above water.

Von Müller now turned northwards, deciding that it was time to get clear. Still he could not resist the temptation to stop a British merchantman before leaving, but while his prize crew was boarding the lookouts sighted a strange warship. It was the French destroyer *Mousquet*, determined to try to stop the *Emden*. Although hopelessly outclassed the little destroyer put up a brave fight before she was overwhelmed.

Now the odds were shortening, for the British and Japanese were determined to catch the *Emden* and had 15 cruisers available. Von Müller decided to destroy the cable station in the

Cocos-Keeling Islands in the southwestern Pacific. As well as interrupting communications between Australia and Great Britain, he intended to decoy some of the Allied cruisers away from the Indian Ocean. It was apparently his intention to elude his pursuers and slip back into the crowded shipping routes, but this time his luck was out. Although the *Emden*'s radio was tuned to the same frequency as the station at Port Refuge to jam any transmissions, the British operator managed to transmit 'Unidentified ship off entrance' before the landing party started to wreck the installation. Shortly afterward the *Emden* picked up a transmission from an unknown warship but as she was estimated to be 250 miles away there seemed to be no need to worry.

However the message had been picked up by a force of Allied cruisers escorting a troop-ship convoy, and the Australian *Sydney* had been detached to investigate. She was only 52 miles away and her smoke was sighted at about 0900 hours, three hours after the *Emden*'s arrival. The Germans were in the worst possible position, taken by surprise with 46 officers and men ashore at the cable station. In his report Captain Glossop of the *Sydney* noted that the *Emden* replied to his fire at 10,000 yards, but as his own 6-inch guns had no difficulty in shooting at 14,000 yards this was easily dealt with. Even more important was the protection given by the narrow strip of waterline armor which entirely defeated the *Emden*'s 4.1-inch shells at 8000 yards. It was also noted that the German shell seldom burst whereas the *Sydney*'s caused terrible damage. By 1045 *Emden*'s fire was becoming feebler as casualties and damage mounted. With two funnels demolished and the foremast blown over the side she was rapidly being reduced to a wreck and von Müller decided to run her ashore on North Keeling Island. After a brief respite, when the *Sydney* turned away to catch the escaping collier, the attack started again. Von Müller wished to surrender, but all signal books had been destroyed and it was impossible to reply. After a

further five minutes of slaughter someone finally found a white flag and the *Emden*'s ordeal was over. She had lost 134 killed and 65 wounded, against three killed and 13 wounded in the *Sydney*.

The cruise of the *Emden* has never been equalled as an example of cruiser warfare, not only for her success in travelling 30,000 miles and sinking 70,000 tons of shipping, but also for the chivalry and ingenuity of Karl von Müller. By her exploits she disrupted important shipping and tied down a large number of enemy warships.

The fate of the rest of the Far East Squadron was even more dramatic. Von Spee took his ships to Chilean waters where on 1 November he encountered a British squadron under Rear-Admiral Cradock. The British squadron included two elderly armored cruisers, the *Good Hope* and the *Monmouth*, a modern light cruiser HMS *Glasgow* and an armed merchant cruiser, the ex-liner *Otranto*. Six years earlier the *Good Hope* had been the crack gunnery ship of the Channel Fleet, but now she and the *Monmouth* were manned for the most part by reservists and were ill-fitted to face the *Scharnhorst* and *Gneisenau*. The British flagship had two single 9.2-inch guns and sixteen 6-inch and the *Monmouth* had fourteen 6-inch; the two German ships were each armed with eight 8.3-inch (21cm) and six 5.9-inch (15cm) guns.

If Cradock seems rash in his anxiety to court destruction, one must remember certain points. First, the cruise of the *Emden* had shown what havoc could ensue from a well-handled commerce-raiding cruiser. Second, another cruiser-admiral, Troubridge, had just been severely censured for failing to risk his ship in battle against what he judged to be a superior force. With this in mind Cradock lodged a letter with the British Consul at Valparaiso saying that he did not intend to be accused of any dereliction of duty. A third, and even more valid argument, was the

The USS *Columbia* seen in Hampton Roads in December 1916. The *Columbia* became known for her high coal consumption.

150

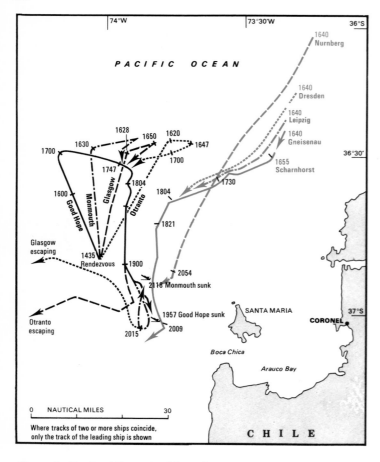

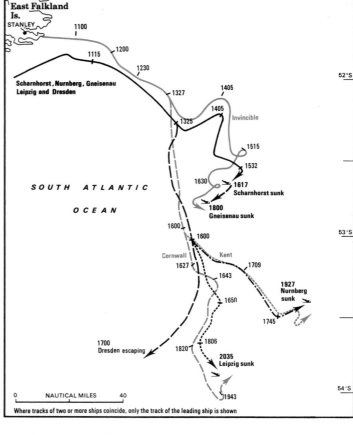

Above the Battle of Coronel, 1 November 1914.
Above right: The Battle of the Falkland Islands.

possibility of inflicting damage on von Spee's ships. At such a distance from a main base all but the slightest damage would seriously impair a raider's efficiency.

The Battle of Coronel was a one-sided affair. Cradock's ships were silhouetted against the setting sun while von Spee's were difficult to pick out in the fading light, making it impossible to equalize the disparity in gunpower. Cradock ordered the slow *Otranto* to stay clear of the battle and gave the captain of the speedy light cruiser *Glasgow* discretion to get clear if the squadron was overwhelmed. In the grim knowledge that they could not escape, the two British armored cruisers turned to face the five enemy cruisers. The action began at 1900 as the sun set. An hour later both ships were helpless wrecks, and they sank with the loss of all hands. The *Glasgow* escaped with little more than splinter damage, for von Spee's ships had concentrated their fire on the *Good Hope* and *Monmouth*.

Cradock was attacked posthumously for not falling back on the *Canopus*, a slow but powerful old battleship which was in support, but if von Spee's squadron had disappeared Cradock would have been bitterly criticized for not bringing him to action. Although von Spee's ships had suffered no damage they had used a lot of ammunition and this could not be replaced.

Von Spee now decided to attack the tiny British coaling station in the Falkland Islands, on the other side of the continent. The decision was a fatal mistake, but in the world of 1914, as in 1982, such gestures counted for a lot and von Spee may also have thought that it was the least expected of all the moves open to him. However the British knew that they had blocked his escape route to the Panama Canal with a powerful Anglo-Japanese squadron, had covered a move back to the central Pacific with another squadron and had sufficient ships in the South Atlantic to prevent a raid on the River Plate shipping.

Not content with this massive concentration the Admiralty

released two battlecruisers from the Grand Fleet, the *Invincible* and *Inflexible*, to be sent to the Falklands to reinforce the cruisers. Correctly divining that von Spee would want to break into the Atlantic for an eventual return to Germany, but also guessing that he would avoid the Panama Canal because it would give away his whereabouts, the British were taking no chances. The *Canopus* was ordered to put herself aground on the mud flats to act as a gun battery in defense of Port Stanley.

The battlecruisers sailed on 11 November, only 10 days after Coronel. They met a cruiser force led by Admiral Stoddart off the coast of Brazil and reached Port Stanley on the night of 7 December. They were just in time, for at 0800 next morning, while the ships were still taking on coal, lookouts reported that von Spee's ships were in sight. It was an anxious moment for the British admiral, Sturdee, for if von Spee had maintained speed he might have been able to engage the British ships one by one as they came out of the harbor. However the German lookouts spotted the gaunt outline of four tripod masts through the murk. This could only mean dreadnoughts, either battleships or battlecruisers, and von Spee knew that he was doomed.

The *Canopus* fired a few shots to discourage an approach to the harbor, and the two leading German ships immediately turned back with their terrible news. The British armored cruisers already had steam up and they weighed anchor as fast as they could but it was 1000 before the two battlecruisers could get clear. Von Spee's ships had about 15 miles' start but they had not docked for some time and their hulls were foul with marine growths. The British settled down to a long stern chase, content to spend the rest of the morning overhauling their prey.

Just before 1300 the *Leipzig* began to drop behind and the *Inflexible* opened fire on her at 16,000 yards. To try to save his smaller ships von Spee turned back with *Scharnhorst* and *Gneisenau*, giving his light cruisers orders to scatter. With a speed advantage of several knots as well as a massive preponderance of gunpower, the two battlecruisers managed to prevent the armored cruisers from closing and contented themselves with firing at very long range. The result was a long drawn out battering for the *Scharnhorst* before she sank at 1617 while the *Gneisenau* lasted until 1800 hours. Only 200 survivors were picked up.

The light cruisers had been left to Stoddart; the *Kent* went after the *Nürnberg* while the *Cornwall* and *Glasgow* chased the *Leipzig*, omitting in the confusion to mark the *Dresden*. The 14-year old *Kent* exerted herself to catch the *Nürnberg*, although her claimed feat of reaching 25 knots was an exaggeration, while the *Glasgow* and *Cornwall* had less trouble catching the *Leipzig*. By nightfall von Spee's squadron was no more, with only the *Dresden* surviving to hide among the islands of Tierra del Fuego. The *Bristol* and an armed merchant cruiser rounded up all the German colliers as well to make the victory complete. The *Dresden* was caught three months later by the *Kent* and *Glasgow*. Seeing that escape was impossible her captain scuttled her to avoid capture.

Two more cruisers had been at large, the *Königsberg* and *Karlsruhe*, but in November 1914 the *Karlsruhe* sank after a boiler explosion, 200 miles east of Trinidad. The *Königsberg* was swiftly trapped in her lair in the Rufiji River in East Africa by the cruiser *Chatham*. Her career as a raider had been brief but eventful; on 20 September she had caught the smaller cruiser HMS *Pegasus* lying at Zanzibar with her boiler-fires drawn and had sunk her as easily as the *Emden* had sunk the *Jemtchug* at Penang. She was not finally destroyed until July 1915, by special shallow-draught river monitors sent out from England.

Below: The *Gneisenau* (shown here) and her sister the *Scharnhorst* were built in 1904–08. Their design benefitted from analysis of the Tsushima battle.

Above: SMS *Berlin* was completed in 1905 and was converted to serve
as a minelayer in the early part of the war.
Top: The armored cruiser HMS *Bacchante* at Mudros in 1915. The
monitor *M.23* moves slowly past.
Below: HMS *Aurora* of the *Arethusa* Class. The *Arethusa* Class
displaced 3530 tons and carried two 6-inch and six 4-inch guns at a
maximum speed of around 29 knots.

IN THE NORTH SEA

While German and Allied cruisers were chasing one another around the trade routes their sisters were in action closer to home. By an exasperating series of errors the British Mediterranean Fleet let the German battlecruiser *Goeben* slip through their fingers after having her literally in their sights. Rear-Admiral Troubridge, commanding a squadron of four modern armored cruisers, refused to engage the *Goeben* and the light cruiser *Breslau* on the grounds that his orders prohibited engaging a superior force. Not even the skilful pursuit by the light cruisers *Gloucester* and *Dublin* could offset the disgust felt by the Royal Navy for such a paltry excuse and Troubridge's career was ruined. In the light of what happened at the Falklands four months later it is ludicrous to suppose that the *Goeben* and *Breslau* could have picked off the *Defence, Warrior, Duke of Edinburgh* and *Black Prince*, the two light cruisers and 10 destroyers at will.

The *Goeben* and *Breslau* reached Constantinople in due course and their arrival convinced Turkey that the time was ripe to enter the war on Germany's side. The two ships became *Yavus Sultan Selim* and *Midilli* respectively on 16 August, but continued to be effectively under German control. On 27 October they sortied from the Bosphorus to attack Russian ships and thus dragged Turkey into war with Russia as well. The Russian Black Sea Fleet was relatively weak but it was handled energetically and cruisers on both sides fought in a number of skirmishes.

In the North Sea events moved equally swiftly. A cruiser, the scout HMS *Amphion*, became the first naval casualty of the war only 13 hours after the outbreak while leading a flotilla of destroyers from Harwich to intercept a mysterious steamer seen 'throwing things overboard.' After sinking the auxiliary minelayer SMS *Königin Luise*, she ran into the minefield laid the previous day. The explosion blew away the *Amphion*'s forecastle and when a second mine set off the magazine she sank rapidly.

On 28 August the British took the initiative and sent a powerful force into the Heligoland Bight to test the German defenses. The spearhead was the scout *Fearless* and the new 'light armored cruiser' *Arethusa* with 32 destroyers. As intended the German light forces came out to protect their torpedo boats, and soon the *Stettin* and *Frauenlob* were hotly engaging the British forces. The *Arethusa* was having trouble with her 4-inch guns, which were of a new type, and after receiving 35 hits was reduced to one 6-inch gun. At 1030, when the sweep should have been over, she was still trying to get her guns working and carrying out minor machinery repairs. The German light cruiser *Strassburg* loomed out of the mist and for a while it looked as if the *Arethusa* might be sunk, but in the nick of time four 'Town' Class cruisers under Commodore Goodenough arrived and drove off the attackers. However, further German reinforcements were hurrying out and once again the tide of battle swung against the British. Fortunately for them, a destroyer put a torpedo into the light cruiser *Mainz* and then five battlecruisers under Vice-Admiral Beatty arrived. Their impact on the action was swift and decisive, the *Köln* and *Ariadne* being sunk in short order and the *Frauenlob*, *Strassburg* and *Stettin* damaged.

The British forces prudently withdrew at this juncture, having taken enough risks for one day. They had inflicted heavy casualties and suffered comparatively lightly in return and the effect on German morale was far-reaching. The Kaiser immediately forbade any sorties which might lead to losses and the Naval Staff was forced to agree to a defensive policy. The result was that British light forces gained the ascendancy in the North Sea.

A Harwich Force, comprising light cruisers and destroyers under Commodore Tyrwhitt, was stationed to guard against any attempt by the High Seas Fleet to enter the English Channel. From August 1914 a constant stream of soldiers and supplies passed across the Channel to France and the British knew how vulnerable this supply line was to surface attack. The Harwich Force was charged with the task of protecting it and Tyrwhitt interpreted this to mean that offense was the best form of defense. His forces were constantly on the move, in all weathers, and although the rate of attrition was high, throughout the four years of war German surface forces were only able to sink one empty transport in the Channel.

Action with light cruisers and destroyers could be a terrifying and hectic business and the outcome was largely a matter of luck. There was the constant risk of being torpedoed, the hidden menace of mines and the hazards of operating in close formation at high speed. Tyrwhitt's flagship, the *Arethusa*, came to grief in

February 1916 in a newly-laid minefield off Harwich and although the sturdy little cruiser did not sink, the tow parted in rough weather, allowing her to drift onto a shoal. Eventually she broke her back and had to be written off. Tyrwhitt transferred his broad pennant to the *Cleopatra* and was back in action almost immediately. In March 1916 four light cruisers and ten destroyers escorted a seaplane carrier in an attempt to bomb Zeppelin sheds at Tondern. The following night the captain of the *Cleopatra* sighted a ship steaming past on the port bow and realized from the sparks billowing out of her funnels that she was a coal-burner and therefore German. Increasing speed the cruiser turned to starboard and suddenly two destroyers appeared across her bows. The *Cleopatra* rammed the second destroyer, the *G.194*, cutting her in two while the *Undaunted* opened fire with her guns. No survivors from the German destroyer were found.

The *Arethusa* Class proved ideal for close-range action of this kind. Their only weak point was the mixed armament and this was altered in succeeding classes. First the 4-inch guns were replaced by 6-inch and extra torpedo tubes, and then as the design was expanded more 6-inch guns were carried. By 1916 the latest variant, the *Centaur*, carried five 5-inch and eight 21-inch torpedo tubes, earning the nickname of 'Tyrwhitt's Dread-

noughts.' The Germans had been following the British trend toward more guns and their last prewar light cruisers, the *Frankfurt* and *Wiesbaden* were given a uniform armament of 5.9-inch guns. Wartime shortages meant that only six more of the class were completed.

The High Seas Fleet received four more cruisers during the war. Two Russian cruisers building at Danzig became SMS *Pillau* and SMS *Elbing* and four sets of steam turbines for a Russian battlecruiser were installed in two specially built minelayers. These were the *Brummer* and *Bremse*.

The Battle of the Dogger Bank, fought on 23 January 1915, showed that even a big modern armored cruiser like the German *Blücher* had no hope of standing up to capital ships' guns. The British light cruisers played their part in scouting for the battle-cruisers, with the *Aurora* making the first sighting report and the *Arethusa* helping to finish off the badly damaged *Blücher*. It was a classic example of how light cruisers could stiffen a destroyer attack, for the *Blücher* had crippled the leading British destroyer when the *Arethusa* arrived with the rest of the Harwich Force destroyers to cover the final torpedo attack which sank the German cruiser.

The Battle of Jutland on 31 May 1916 saw cruisers functioning just as they had been intended to, scouting for the battle fleet and

Top right: *Calliope* and her sister ship *Champion* were the first British light cruisers to have only two funnels.
Right: HMS *Birmingham* seen with baffles fitted to the funnels in the hope of confusing enemy range takers.
Below: SMS *Dresden* belonged to the last class of German light cruisers built during World War I. Of the 10 ships planned only the *Dresden* and *Köln* were completed.

leading destroyers in attacks. There were no fewer than 45 cruisers of all kinds involved, 34 of them British. All three types were present on the British side, the armored cruisers acting as a heavy scouting wing of the Grand Fleet, the light cruisers and even four scouts attached to the battle squadrons. The Germans on the other hand had only light cruisers with the High Seas Fleet, some of them quite elderly.

Inevitably the first sighting was made by cruisers. A Danish ship blowing off steam in a position between the outer wing of each fleet attracted the attention of the German cruiser *Elbing* and the British *Galatea*. After months of fruitless sorties there was a noticeable exhilaration when the signal 'Enemy in Sight' was hoisted to the cruisers' mast heads. The only full-scale fleet action of the war was about to begin.

First blood went to the *Elbing*, with a hit below the *Galatea*'s bridge, but it failed to explode and Commodore Alexander-

Sinclair's flagship turned away to try to entice the 2nd Scouting Group northward. His aim was to lead the whole enemy fleet north, allowing Beatty and the battlecruisers to get between it and its bases. However by doing this Alexander-Sinclair was failing in his first duty, that of forcing his way past the German cruisers to find out what force they were screening. Until that information was available Beatty could form no battle plan and the Commander in Chief, Admiral Jellicoe, could not coordinate movements with his subordinate. So for the moment Beatty could only try to engage the 2nd Scouting Group, in ignorance of the fact that Vice-Admiral Hipper and his battlecruisers were coming up in support. The German scouting was more methodical, although the *Elbing* reported the British light cruisers as battlecruisers, and a further report from her about recognition signals was misinterpreted as a sighting of 24 or 26 battleships! Thus Hipper received muddling information at the outset of the battle, and had no knowledge of the whereabouts of either Beatty or Jellicoe.

At 1529 *Galatea* caught sight of five columns of heavy smoke behind the pursuing German light cruisers, and interpreting them correctly as major warships steaming at maximum speed, signalled the course and bearing to Beatty. At 1548 the first shots were fired and it was time for the light cruisers to draw clear. In the first phase the *Indefatigable* blew up under heavy fire from the *von der Tann*, and Beatty ordered the light cruiser *Champion* and her destroyer flotilla to make a torpedo attack to relieve the pressure. In the meantime the battle was swinging back in Beatty's favor, as his four powerful fast battleships of the *Queen Elizabeth* Class had come up in support. Despite the loss of a second battlecruiser, HMS *Queen Mary*, the British salvoes were scoring more and more hits. On his own initiative Commodore

Left: The approach to the Battle of Jutland.
Below: Although the *Birmingham* suffered extensive damage at Jutland there were no casualties among the crew.

Heinrich in the light cruiser *Regensburg* ordered his destroyers and torpedo boats to attack Beatty's line and take the pressure off Hipper.

In contrast to the 1st Light Cruiser Squadron's misguided attempt at trailing its coat the 2nd Light Cruiser Squadron under Commodore Goodenough showed how light cruisers were meant to perform their job. Regardless of the danger, Goodenough pressed on southward until at 1633 he succeeded in closing to within 13,000 yards of the main body of the High Seas Fleet under Vice-Admiral Scheer, 22 battleships and their attendant destroyers. Because Goodenough kept his ships bows on they were mistaken at first for friendly ships, but as soon as they turned away their unmistakable four funnels gave them away and the German battleships opened fire. However, the four cruisers weaved their way through the 200-feet high splashes to safety, all the while sending out the vital signal, 'Have sighted enemy battle fleet, bearing southeast. Enemy's course north. My position 56 degrees 34 seconds north, 6 degrees 20 minutes east.'

Goodenough was only two miles ahead of the *Lion*, Beatty's flagship, when he made his momentous sighting, and so it was only a matter of minutes before the admiral could see for himself. Secure in the knowledge that his own Commander in Chief was in support, Beatty turned away and headed northwest, with Scheer and Hipper in pursuit. The Grand Fleet was disposed in cruising order with the 4th Light Cruiser Squadron and the destroyers forming an antisubmarine screen while the armored cruisers of the 1st and 2nd Cruiser Squadrons were eight miles ahead as a scouting screen. In addition Jellicoe had pushed his 3rd Battlecruiser Squadron under Rear-Admiral Hood 20 miles ahead to provide a rapid reinforcement for Beatty as soon as contact was made. With Hood were seven light cruisers. It must be remembered that without aerial reconnaissance scouting was the hardest job of all and visual contact was essential.

Precise news was just what Jellicoe did not get, for apart from Goodenough, none of the subordinate commanders seems to have understood the need to signal precise bearings and courses of any ships sighted. Captains tended to rely too much on the senior officer present to make all situations reports, a weakness which was compounded when the *Lion*'s radio equipment was shot away leaving Beatty unable to pass signals. After several attempts at getting coherent reports out of the battlecruisers Goodenough's detailed information came as a refreshing change. At 1630 Beatty's and Jellicoe's cruisers made contact at last, the *Falmouth* of Beatty's 3rd Light Cruiser Squadron and the armored cruiser *Black Prince* of Jellicoe's 1st Cruiser Squadron. Once again the reports were couched in terms which were unhelpful. Even the reliable Goodenough fell into a common trap when at 1750 he gave a bearing which was a 180 degree reciprocal of the correct one; in the heat of battle such confusion happens but some of the reports of the other commanders were consistently inadequate. All the time visibility was decreasing, with funnel-smoke adding to the gloom.

The final deployment and engagement between the two fleets are too well known to be described here, but in the preliminary stages of Jellicoe's masterly resolution of the confused situation an important cruiser engagement occurred. As we have seen, Admiral Hood's three battlecruisers had pushed ahead of the Grand Fleet to improve the liklihood of bringing the High Seas Fleet to action. This was the sort of work the battlecruisers were suited for and Hood thought more like a cruiser admiral than a battle-fleet commander. With the light cruisers *Canterbury* and *Chester* scouting ahead he was hoping to meet Beatty's battlecruisers but because of a dead-reckoning error made by the *Lion* he was much closer to Hipper's ships.

The *Chester* heard gunfire to the southwest and when investigating she ran into Boedicker's 2nd Scouting Group of four light cruisers at a range of little more than three miles. The *Chester* was immediately deluged by a rain of shells without making an effective reply. Showers of shell splinters scythed down her gun crews, although luckily nothing vital was hit and she was able to claw her way clear. Her agony had been exacerbated because

she had been designed for the Greek Navy with a new type of 5.5-inch gun, whose shield did not extend all the way down to the deck as in the Royal Navy's 6-inch. As a result splinters had swept under the shields and three-quarters of the wounds reported were below the knee.

The German cruisers were quickly punished when Hood's battlecruisers came storming out of the mist. The *Wiesbaden* was crippled by 12-inch shells, while the *Pillau* had four boilers put out of action and a fire started in her stokeholds. The survivors of the 2nd Scouting Group fled. Understandably Boedicker concluded that he had run into the main British Fleet and so did Commodore Heinrich, who launched his torpedo boats in an attack. A wild *mêlée* resulted, but again the attack failed and the Germans fell back to regroup.

A second cruiser epic was now about to unfold. The disabled *Wiesbaden* lay between the opposing lines of ships and she was fired on in turn by the British ships as they passed. Still she refused to surrender and her guns fired intermittently. Then Rear-Admiral Arbuthnot's 1st Cruiser Squadron came into view, crossing the bows of the *Lion* in its haste to get at the *Wiesbaden*. Once again the treacherous visibility allowed ships to get surprisingly close and while the cruisers were briskly pouring 9.2-inch shells into the blazing hulk they were surprised by the German battlecruisers and the 3rd Battle Squadron. The *Warrior* was quickly set on fire, but the fate of the *Defence* was the same as the *Indefatigable* and *Queen Mary*; a giant explosion and only a pall of smoke to mark her grave. The *Warrior* might have followed her flagship but for the battleship *Warspite*, whose helm jammed as she was maneuvering to take up her position astern of the main fleet. Tempted by a brand new battleship rather than a mere cruiser the German ships shifted target and the *Warrior* gratefully limped away.

With the main fleets in action the cruisers could go back to maintaining a watch, but once the German Fleet had finally disengaged, the light forces had to maintain contact once more and provide information. The resulting night action was, if anything, more savage than the day fighting. However, before night fell the *Wiesbaden* scored a final success by torpedoing the British dreadnought *Marlborough* in the engine-room. As the *Wiesbaden* sank with all hands later that night, we will never

Below: Chart of the night action at Jutland showing where the cruisers *Frauenlob*, *Elbing* and *Black Prince* sank.

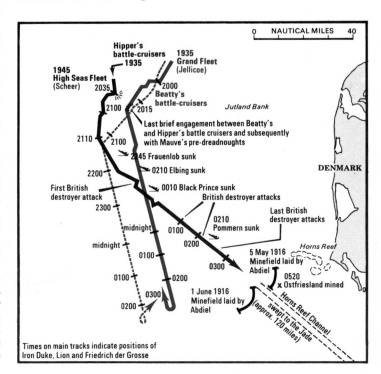

know what heroism it took to get that torpedo tube trained and fired.

In the fading twilight the light cruisers *Castor*, *Calliope*, *Comus* and *Constance* skirmished with the German 3rd Squadron of battleships, but their message to Jellicoe failed to give any details. At 2010 the 3rd Light Cruiser Squadron engaged the 4th Scouting Group and hit the *München*, but soon lost contact without giving any range, course or bearing to the Commander in Chief. The most tantalizing chance of all was presented to the *Caroline* and *Royalist* when at 2045 they sighted three battleships of the German 1st Squadron; just as they turned to attack with torpedoes Vice-Admiral Jerram of the British 2nd Battle Squadron convinced himself that they were British ships and countermanded the attack. The German and British battleships parted without firing a shot.

The situation at the end of this daylight phase was that the two fleets were out of touch but proceeding roughly southward on parallel courses. The British were steaming slightly faster to ensure that they would be between the Germans and their bases at daylight, and had left their light cruisers and destroyers astern to guard against any German attempt to force their way around behind the fleet. Jellicoe was very wary of fighting a night action, for he rightly felt that the risks of friendly ships being attacked far outweighed any possible gain. Given the scattered forces and the primitive communications available in 1916 it was a reasonable conclusion, but the Germans had reached a different one. They had assiduously practiced night fighting and in any case dared not face the Grand Fleet in the morning. It was desperation as much as confidence in his fleet's skill that decided Scheer to risk crossing astern of Jellicoe's main fleet.

He was also aided by luck. At about 2130 the *Lion*, whose signal books had been destroyed in the battle, asked her consort *Princess Royal* to provide the night challenge and reply. This was passed by flashing lamp 'in clear' and was seen by light cruisers of the 2nd and 4th Scouting Groups. Before they turned away they had intercepted the correct challenge, although they had not had time to observe the reply.

Throughout the night engagements which followed British ships held their fire for a fatal few seconds because they were challenged correctly. The first ship to suffer was the light cruiser *Castor*, which was roughly handled by the *Hamburg* and *Elbing* when she mistook them for friendly ships.

Characteristically Goodenough's 2nd Light Cruiser Squadron avoided confusion by correctly interpreting the significance of the gun-flashes of the *Castor* engagement, and they were ready when they met the 4th Scouting Group. The distance came down steadily to 800 yards before the Germans gave their own challenge. Immediately the *Dublin* opened fire and she and the *Southampton* switched on their searchlights. A murderous fight ensued, with both sides firing rapidly and shells bursting everywhere. Shell splinters caused terrible casualties on the *Southampton*'s open deck and both she and the *Dublin* were soon ablaze. The *Nottingham* and *Birmingham* kept their searchlights switched off and pumped shells into the German cruisers without suffering any casualties. So great was the uproar that when a torpedo from the *Southampton* hit the *Frauenlob* nobody on the bridge heard the explosion. Then as if by a miracle the searchlights went out and the firing stopped. The *Frauenlob* broke in two and sank and the rest of her squadron vanished into the night.

The *Southampton* had suffered grievously from splinter damage, with 35 killed and 55 wounded, and her upperworks were riddled with holes. She had been hit 18 times but damage to hull and machinery was superficial. Her sister *Dublin* was hit 13 times but had much lighter casualties. However, with her navigating officer dead and all charts destroyed she lost contact with her squadron during the night.

When the German battleships crashed through the destroyer screen similar scenes were repeated. The armored cruiser *Black Prince*, suddenly blundered into the German battle line and blew up after battleship after battleship had riddled her at point-blank range. In the confusion caused by British destroyers' attacks the light cruiser *Elbing* tried to dodge through the German battle line and failed; she was run down by the battleship *Posen*. The *Rostock* nearly succeeded in the same maneuver, but took a torpedo hit as she slid through between two battleships; she too had to be abandoned.

Jutland (or Skagerrak to the Germans) was tactically indecisive but cruisers on both sides showed that they were much tougher than anyone had claimed. On the other hand, the original British battlecruisers showed only too clearly that they had been cast in the wrong role. Like the *Defence*, on whose design they had been based, the *Invincible* and *Indefatigable* could not hope to engage battleships in a slugging match. On the other hand ships like the *Chester*, *Southampton* and *Wiesbaden* survived very heavy attack. Time and again the light cruisers provided the extra muscle which destroyers lacked, at the same time being small enough to be risked and tough enough to take punishment. Of all the ship types which were tested at Jutland the light cruiser emerged as the most satisfactory, and it is significant that only three were sunk by torpedoes and gunfire, the *Wiesbaden*, *Frauenlob* and *Rostock*.

Above left: The German light cruiser *Pillau* was heavily damaged at Jutland. At the end of the war she was handed over to the Italians as part of the reparations settlement. As the *Bari* she was sunk by Allied air attack in 1943.
Below: The German cruiser *Köln* seen making heavy smoke during her trials in 1917. Especially later in World War I the quality of coal available to the German Navy often made this problem unavoidable.

LESSONS OF JUTLAND

Jutland clearly confirmed the value of the light cruiser as a fleet scout and as stiffener for destroyer attacks. Nothing could be done for the moment about the vulnerability of gun crews to shrapnel and shell splinters, for the 'Town', *Arethusa* and 'C' Classes were all too small for turret mountings, but note was taken for the future. What did improve was fire control and communications.

In June 1917 a platform was installed on the forecastle of HMS *Yarmouth* to test the theory that a Sopwith Pup fighter could be flown from a 20-foot runway. If this proved feasible cruisers could not only launch aircraft to deal with the Zeppelin nuisance but also to investigate suspicious ships. The device was so successful that the Zeppelin threat rapidly disappeared and cruisers found their aircraft more and more useful in the reconnaissance role.

The first flight from a ship had, by coincidence, also taken place from a light cruiser. On 14 November 1910 Eugene B Ely took off from the forecastle of the American scout cruiser USS *Birmingham* in Chesapeake Bay. Ely's epoch-making landing on a ship was also made on a cruiser, the big armored cruiser *Pennsylvania*, two months later. In October 1915 a prototype

catapult was installed on the quarterdeck of the armored cruiser *North Carolina* and in 1917 production models were installed in the *Seattle* and *Huntingdon*. However, they were removed as soon as the US Navy went to war, on the grounds that they would interfere with gunnery.

The German Navy reduced most of its armored cruisers to reserve in 1915–16 to ease the manpower shortage, but in 1917 plans were drawn up to convert the *Roon* to operate seaplanes. The project was dropped but a similar conversion was provided for the light cruiser *Stuttgart*, allowing her to operate three floatplanes.

As mentioned, the Royal Navy made a minimum of alterations to its standard light cruiser design, and from the *Caroline* Class developed a series of 'stretched' variants. There were other cruisers built to meet real or imagined wartime requirements. The most unusual of these were three 'large light cruisers' or small battlecruisers ordered by Lord Fisher in 1915. The original battlecruisers were not all they were claimed to be, but these can only be described as grotesque aberrations. The *Glorious* and *Courageous*, both with 18,000-ton hulls, were given

Above: Gunnery drill aboard the American cruiser *Chester* (CL.1).
The picture shows the forward 5-inch gun and range-finder and in the
foreground a 3-inch gun.
Below: The Japanese *Tenryu* was structurally a very similar design to
the British *Calliope* and *Caledon* Classes but had 5.5-inch guns and
more powerful machinery.

Above: In an effort to accomodate scouting aircraft some British 'C'
and 'D' Class ships were built with a combined bridge and hangar.
This experiment was not a success.

four 15-inch guns in two turrets, a speed of 31 knots and the same
scale of armoring as the *Arethusa*. A third vessel of this type,
HMS *Furious*, was to have two single 18-inch guns.

The *Furious* was appropriated for conversion into the Royal
Navy's first proper aircraft carrier, but the *Courageous* and
Glorious joined the Fleet at the end of 1916. The *Courageous*
served for a while as a minelayer but when a raid into the
Heligoland Bight was planned in late 1917 both were chosen to
stiffen the light cruisers and destroyers.

The British force comprised the 1st Cruiser Squadron
(*Courageous* and *Glorious*), 1st and 6th Light Cruiser Squadrons
(eight ships) with four battlecruisers in support. The intention
was to attack the German minesweeping forces keeping channels
clear for U-Boats returning from patrol. The British hoped to
repeat their success of August 1914, rolling up the patrol line and
inflicting casualties on supporting forces if they intervened.

The action began at 0730 on 17 November 1917. Four German
light cruisers under Rear-Admiral von Reuter laid heavy smoke-
screens while he ordered his forces to fall back but the British
ships pressed on through the smokescreens, firing at indistinct
targets and hoping that the Germans would lead them through
the swept channels in the minefields. Von Reuter was hoping to
lure the British into a trap, between his light cruisers and two
supporting battleships. These eventually came into action at
about 0950 at extreme range.

Rear-Admiral Alexander-Sinclair, flying his flag in the *Cardiff*,
ordered his ships to turn about and retire with covering fire from
the battlecruiser *Repulse*. As an action it was a disappointment
to the British, who missed their last opportunity of bringing
major German warships to battle. Despite the heavy fire, both
sides' light cruisers came off lightly; the British ships were
straddled repeatedly but suffered only seven hits while the
Germans took five. The worst damage was suffered by the
Königsberg, which took considerable damage from a 15-inch shell
from HMS *Repulse*. For the British there had been problems of
visibility, added to the dangers of the very large minefields in the
Heligoland Bight, which reduced the freedom of movement.
What the action demonstrated was the uselessness of Fisher's
'large light cruisers' for their 15-inch guns fired so slowly that
they could not get ranging salvoes to group around a fast-
moving cruiser.

Another class of cruisers started in 1916 was known as the
'Improved *Birmingham*' type or *Hawkins* Class. They were
intended to operate on the trade routes with heavy armament,
seven single 7.5-inch guns, and a speed of 30 knots. In March
1918, in response to a panic about ultra-fast light cruisers
believed to be building in Germany, three more light cruisers
were ordered, the *Emerald* Class, with 90 feet more length and
8.5 feet more beam to allow space for double the horsepower of
the 'C' and 'D' Classes. The designed speed was 33 knots, although
on a displacement of 7600 tons they had the puny armament of
seven single 6-inch guns in shields.

This demand for higher speed was undoubtedly influenced by
the German minelaying cruisers *Brummer* and *Bremse*. Although
only capable of 28 knots at full load, British Intelligence credited
them with 35–36 knots, and it was felt that the Royal Navy should
have cruisers with some chance of catching them. The fact that
these two light cruisers successfully accomplished the destruction of a convoy in 1917 lent some point to the British fears.

The attack took place at daylight on the morning of 17 October
1917 and the victims were a dozen merchantmen (two British,
one Belgian, one Danish, five Norwegian and three Swedish),
escorted by two destroyers and two armed trawlers. In the misty
half-light the two cruisers, which looked similar to the British
Arethusa Class, managed to close to within 4000 yards before
being sighted by HMS *Strongbow*. The confusion caused the
destroyer to challenge twice but just as she realized her mistake
she was shattered by a salvo of 5.9-inch shells from the *Bremse*,
now closing to little more than a mile. With her radio destroyed
she could not warn her consort astern, the convoy or the distant
escorts and was left helpless and sinking.

The *Mary Rose* had been alerted by the flash and sound of
gunfire ahead but she too was smothered by accurate salvoes,
this time from the *Brummer*, and was hit almost as soon as she
challenged. She sank quickly and the cruisers turned to finish
off the *Strongbow* and the convoy at their leisure. Two hours
later 10 of the merchant ships had been sunk and some 40 neutral
seamen and 135 British were dead. It was a classic example of
cruisers used intelligently, and it was to remain uppermost in the
minds of the admirals who planned Hitler's new navy 15 years
later.

The dominance of the British light cruisers over their German
counterparts did not go unnoticed in the United States. In 1916,
as part of a massive augmentation of the US Navy, Congress
authorized the first of a dozen 'scout cruisers.' These were the
first modern light cruisers built for the US Navy in 12 years.

The class which resulted did not materialize until 1923–25 but even when first drawn up the design was so antiquated as to be quaint. On paper they outclassed all other cruisers, with a speed of 35 knots, but the eight 6-inch guns were disposed in old fashioned double-storeyed casemates on the broadside. Nor was the torpedo armament impressive; at a time when the British were planning to give the 'D' Class four triple 21-inch mountings, the American cruisers had only two twin sets. Before the *Omaha* was laid down in 1918 the Bureau of Ships bowed to criticism by adding two twin 6-inch gun mountings and two triple torpedo tubes. However the guns were only in light splinterproof shields and the rise of displacement could only be limited by reducing the armor to a small patch at the water line over the machinery spaces. Thus at a designed displacement of 7500 tons they were more poorly protected and slower than originally planned. The most impressive feature of the *Omaha* Class was their speed. With 90,000 shaft horsepower they all made 33–34 knots on trials but this was achieved at light displacement; at load draught they displaced over 9000 tons, making such speeds impossible.

The *Omaha* design naturally provoked a Japanese reply. Only two cruisers had been built during the war, the 3500-ton *Tatsuta* and *Tenryu*, but in 1918–19 five of an expanded type, the *Kuma* Class, were laid down. They had seven 5.5-inch guns and displaced 5500 tons. They and the six very similar *Natori* Class had the same installed power as the *Omaha* Class but being lighter ships they found it easier to reach their designed speed of 33 knots.

The *Tatsuta* and *Tenryu* had been intended principally as destroyer-leaders. In contrast the next class was designated as 'scouts' and was intended to displace 7200 tons. News of the US *Omaha* Class forced a change of mind and new plans were drawn up for eight 5500-tonners. The idea was to match the eight-gunned *Omaha* with seven 5.5-inch guns disposed more sensibly to give a heavier broadside but the Americans' decision to upgun the *Omaha* with twin center-line guns nullified this advantage. The next step was to be much more ingenious and will be covered in the next chapter.

The experiences of the war, particularly in the North Sea, had done much to restore the cruiser's reputation. Appropriately enough, a cruiser played a dramatic role in the last act of the

Above: The Japanese light cruiser *Sendai* seen with an aircraft catapult fitted aft. The *Sendai* entered service in 1925 and was sunk in November 1943 at Empress Augusta Bay.

naval war. When on 21 November 1918 the German High Seas Fleet steamed across the North Sea to surrender to the Allies, it was a small light cruiser HMS *Cardiff* which led the mighty dreadnoughts into the Firth of Forth. It was meant to humiliate the Germans but the gesture inadvertently paid a well-deserved compliment to the enormous burden shouldered by cruisers in the war.

Below: The USS *Birmingham* seen in Brest in October 1918. The *Birmingham* had served on escort duty in the Atlantic.

TREATY LIMITATI IMPOSED

The cruiser had started the war under something of a cloud but it finished the war with a greatly enhanced reputation, whereas the battlecruiser was now rightly regarded with suspicion. The battleship, moreover, was costly and more vulnerable to torpedoes and mines than had been thought. After the Armistice many navies looked to cruisers with renewed interest as the most cost-effective fighting ships.

The US Navy began to plan in 1919 for an entirely new strategy. Hitherto it was the eastern seaboard that had to be safeguarded against an ill-defined but sincerely felt threat from Great Britain, but from 1919 the expanding Japanese Empire was a much more certain threat in the Pacific. The *Omaha* Class were patently unsuited to long-range operations in the Pacific and new designs were needed, with more endurance and gunpower. The Bureau of Ordnance was investigating a new 8-inch gun and if this was to be adopted it would need a heavier mounting, and therefore a much bigger ship than the 7000-ton *Omaha*.

The Bureau of Construction and Repair began work on two parallel series of cruiser designs in 1919. The main weakness of these designs was the requirement for excessive speed, for it meant unarmored gun mountings and at best a meager scale of protection. This was to be a recurring theme in discussions on cruisers: high speed in a seaway and large fuel stowage inevitably meant a bigger and more expensive cruiser, with a big crew and higher operating costs.

The Japanese were keeping a wary eye on the Americans and as early as 1918 had drafted rough designs for an 8000-ton scout cruiser, armed with five or six twin 5.5-inch or four twin 8-inch, and a speed of 35.5 knots. The design was at such an undefined stage that although the Cabinet Council authorized the building of one per year for four years, the Navy asked for them to be deferred. The American decision in 1920 to increase the *Omaha*'s armament to 12 guns was one reason and the visit of HMS

Hawkins to Japan was another. The Japanese were very impressed by the British cruiser, particularly because of her weight of broadside. The 5500-ton *Kuma*'s broadside of six 5.5-inch delivered 228kg of shells against 544kg from the *Hawkins*.

The upshot was that the Japanese decided to adopt the 8-inch gun, drawing up plans for a 7500-ton ship armed with three twin mountings and capable of 35 knots. To save weight they adopted the same solution as in the British *Arethusa*; the armor protection worked longitudinally as part of the hull. A further innovation was to keep the longitudinal strength-members continuous, even if it resulted in an undulating deck-line.

In July 1921 the US President invited the Japanese, British, French and Italians to discuss ways of limiting their naval strength to avoid the sort of costly arms race which had led to

Above: The *Trenton* (CL.11) seen in the early 1930s.
Above left: The *Raleigh* is overshadowed by the dirigible *Los Angeles* and a blimp during maneuvers in 1930.
Top: The *Richmond* (CL.9) near the end of her long career, seen in Gatun Lake, Panama Canal in October 1945.
Below: The *Richmond* works up to full speed during builders' trials in May 1923. The uncluttered trials rig can be compared with the additional equipment found necessary in World War II as shown in the 1945 picture at top.

war in 1914. The major provisions of the resulting Washington Treaty were concerned with battleships, but the American delegation skilfully fought for the right to build the big 8-inch gunned cruisers that they had planned. The treaty created two classes of cruiser, 'heavy' cruisers of no more than 10,000 tons and 8-inch guns, and 'light' cruisers armed with lighter guns. Although numbers of heavy cruisers were fixed in the same ratio as capital ships, light cruisers were not limited in number.

The Japanese were in the most difficult position of all. Since it was obvious that the United States was hostile to any renewal of the Anglo-Japanese Treaty, they were faced with the possibility of war with one or both navies, but without knowledge of the latest technical developments. The Japanese decided to embark on a course, not of slavish copying as so many people still believe, but of almost reckless, innovation.

Late in 1917 approval had been given for an experimental small cruiser, but work did not start until 1921, when the order was given for a cruiser displacing only 2890 tons, armed with six 5.5-inch guns, four torpedo tubes and with a speed of 35.5 knots. The published standard tonnage of the *Yubari* was 2890 tons, whereas the ship actually displaced 17 percent more. Puzzled Western naval intelligence departments wrestled unsuccessfully with the *Yubari*'s staggering figures.

Nonetheless the *Yubari* was an ingenious design. On trials she showed no sign of hull weakness and reached 34.8 knots on a displacement of 3309 tons, a loss of only 0.7 knots in spite of being overweight. Another improvement was to give her twin 61cm (24-inch) torpedo tubes instead of the 53cm (21-inch) tubes in earlier cruisers. The extra volume gave greater range and destructive power than any comparable torpedo.

Profiting by the experience gained the Technical Department went on to design a much bigger cruiser, capable of matching not only the American *Omaha* Class but also the British *Hawkins* Class. It was in its way as startling a design as the *Yubari*, with

six 20cm (7.4-inch) guns, 3-inch side armor and a speed of 34.5 knots, all on a standard displacement of 7100 tons. It was thus well within the limit eventually imposed by the Washington Treaty. The order was placed on 20 June 1922, only four months after the signature of the Treaty.

As in the *Yubari* armor was worked in longitudinally, without plating behind it. In spite of all precautions taken in supervising weights the displacement rose by nearly 1000 tons during construction, as a result of errors in the calculations. In practice the *Kako* worked out at 9540 tonnes and her sister *Furutaka* at 9544 tonnes in the 2/3 trials condition. Fortunately the designer had insisted on a good metacentric height to limit the angle of the heel if the ship should be partially flooded. This, combined with the fact that topweight had been kept down, meant that the ships did not suffer unduly from the increased displacement. On trials both ships were extremely fast, making their designed speed of 34.5 knots.

The first US Navy cruisers built after the treaty make an interesting contrast with the *Furutaka*. The designers decided

against trying to protect the ship against 8-inch shell fire, opting for protection against hits from 6-inch shell and destroyers' guns. What emerged was a ship displacing 9100 tons in standard condition, armed with ten 8-inch guns and capable of 32.5 knots. In comparison with the Japanese ships the *Salt Lake City* and *Pensacola* traded speed for gunpower and endurance, for they were designed to steam 10,000 miles at 15 knots. They also struck an unusual note in having the triple turrets superimposed above the twin turrets.

The British response was quite different. The war had confirmed the need for freeboard in rough weather operations, the gunnery experts favored four twin gun-mountings, and tactical considerations dictated a speed of 33 knots to match the Japanese and American ships. However, by July 1923 preliminary calculations showed that a ship with these characteristics might have as little as 820 tons of armor out of the total 10,000 tons.

Above left: The Japanese heavy cruiser *Kako*, sister ship of the *Furutaka*.
Below: The Italian heavy cruiser *Gorizia* runs her trials in 1931 without her 8-inch gun turret fitted.

The Director of Naval Construction proposed to abandon side armor altogether, only protecting the magazines and ammunition hoists against 8-inch shell fire out to 20,000 yards. However the Admiralty Board subsequently dropped its requirement for 33 knots and this allowed a further 400 tons of armor.

Seven ships were laid down in 1924–25, including two for the Royal Australian Navy. The five British ships were given county names in honor of the old *Kent* Class of 1901, while the Australian ships were named HMAS *Australia* and HMAS *Canberra*. When the first ship, HMS *Berwick* appeared at the end of 1927 she was not greeted with any enthusiasm. Her high freeboard and three funnels seemed more appropriate to an ocean liner, especially when compared with the sleek lines of the *Furutaka*.

In April 1922 the French Chamber of Deputies voted funds for the first cruisers built in more than 15 years. The three 7000-ton *Duguay Trouin* Class carried four twin 6.1-inch (155mm) gun-mountings and made 33 knots on trials, but at the cost of having virtually no protection. In 1924 funds were voted for two heavy cruisers. The *Duquesne* and *Tourville* were little more than 8-inch gunned versions of the light cruisers, with only 430 tons of armor and a speed of 33.75 knots.

It was left to the Italians to complete the Washington cycle. In 1925 two heavy cruisers were begun, the *Trento* and *Trieste*. In keeping with an Italian policy of building fast ships they were designed for 35 knots, but with only a shallow water-line belt and a partial deck. To make matters worse the Italians had developed the habit of running trials under unrealistic conditions, without ammunition or gun mountings installed. It meant that the sea speed in full load condition was much lower. The *Trento* made 35.6 knots on an eight-hour trial but could count on only 30 knots when fully loaded.

TREATY LIMITATI AVOIDED

Nobody was satisfied with the first generation of heavy cruisers produced after the Washington Treaty. All were a disappointment, either too big and costly or much heavier than intended. It was hardly surprising, therefore, to see a series of improved versions appearing very soon afterwards.

The Japanese followed the *Furutaka* with two very similar ships, *Aoba* and *Kinugasa*, but with several improvements. Three twin 8-inch turrets were fitted instead of the six singles, while the antiaircraft armament was increased. As the standard displacement rose by only 200 tons they had no difficulty in reaching 34 knots. Even so, like the *Furutaka* they were cramped, wet and lightly armored.

The US Navy did not like the *Salt Lake City* Class, regarding them as deficient in seaworthiness and overgunned at the expense of protection. The next ships, the six *Northamptons* were given a raised forecastle to improve seakeeping and had a more rational arrangement of guns. Three triple turrets saved weight and reduced the area to be protected, while the weight saved was used to provide hangars amidships for the floatplanes. The US Navy was the first to appreciate the vulnerability of aircraft to weather damage and other navies eventually followed its example.

The British also looked at their *Kent* design, being concerned to improve speed and protection and provide a floatplane and catapult. Not much could be done to the scale of protection but some detailed improvements were made. In other respects the four *London* Class looked very much the same as the *Kents*. Four more ships were planned, but they were given a different 8-inch turret and further minor improvements to protection. The *Dorsetshire* and *Norfolk* joined the Fleet in 1930 but the *Northumberland* and *Surrey* were suspended in 1928 and cancelled in 1930.

Impressed by the *Furutaka* design and conscious of the need to keep up numbers of cruisers, the Admiralty graded the 'Counties' as A Class ships and called for designs for a smaller B Class type, of 8000 tons and with six 8-inch guns. Only the *Exeter* and *York* were built, and they showed considerable improvements. The shorter hull could be given 3-inch water-line armor, and higher speed was also possible. There was some reduction in freeboard but not sufficient to reduce seaworthiness. However in spite of achieving all this on a standard displacement of 8390 tons (*Exeter*) the B Class were unfavorably compared with the Japanese ships. It was alleged that the *Furutaka* Class could match them in protection and speed on only 7100 tons, whereas in fact there was little real difference in tonnage, and the *Furutaka* carried some 300 tons less fuel.

The French had intended to build more of the *Duquesne* Class but instead recast the design to remedy some of the deficiencies. The weight of armor was increased in all four ships, partly by redesigning machinery. The last of the four, the *Dupleix*, had 1553 tons of armor, as against 430 tons in the *Duquesne*.

The Italians were particularly worried about the weaknesses of their *Trento* Class. The building of 15,000-ton cruisers was considered, but as this was forbidden by treaty a slower but better-armored version of the *Trento* was chosen. She was to have a sea speed of 32 knots, 200mm (7.9-inch) armor and eight 8-inch guns.

Even the most ingenious Italian ship designers could not reconcile such requirements on a standard displacement of 10,000 tons, and it was soon clear that the armor had to be thinned. Even so with 150mm (5.9-inch) armor amidships the standard displacement worked out at 11,500 tons. By concealing the fact that the new ships were 15 percent over the Treaty limit the Italian Navy established a new fashion for outright cheating. Four of the class, the *Fiume*, *Zara*, *Gorizia* and *Pola* were built followed by a third *Trento* type, named *Bolzano*.

Even with a 15 percent margin over the Treaty limit it was a remarkable achievement to combine such heavy armor with speed. All four reached their designed speed of 32 knots, *Zara* being the fastest at 35.2 knots on 10,776 tons without gun turrets on board. At standard displacement they were good for about 33 knots but sea speed in load condition fell to 29 knots.

The Japanese now found themselves outclassed by the new 10,000-ton cruisers. They conformed to their doctrine of building ships equal or superior to all contemporaries and expanded the *Kinugasa* design to enable two more twin 8-inch gun-mountings to be incorporated and another inch of side armor. However the design worked out at 10,940 tons at standard displacement; the 2/3 trial displacement was 12,374 tons and there was no margin of stability. Nonetheless the four *Ashigara* Class made a great impression.

The Naval Staff liked the *Ashigara* design, so for an improved design the constructors were forbidden to make any reduction in fighting qualities to comply with the Washington Treaty. As a result the four *Takao* Class displaced 11,350 tons in standard condition. The scale of armoring was generally as in the *Ashigara* but 5-inch plating was provided for the magazines.

The American answer to these eight powerful ships was the *San Francisco* Class. The forecastle was lengthened to improve seakeeping and the water-line armor extended to take in the forward 8-inch turrets. There was no attempt to match the Japanese ships' speed but they were capable of 32.75 knots and had good endurance. In many ways they were the most balanced of the later Washington cruisers and all seven gave sterling service in World War II.

The signatories to the original Washington Treaty were well aware that they had inadvertently committed themselves to building very costly ships. The British were particularly keen to get away from the 10,000-ton 8-inch gunned cruiser and at the London Naval Conference in 1930 they were able to have a new treaty accepted dividing cruisers into Type A, armed with guns of greater than 6.1-inch caliber (allowing for the French light cruisers) but not exceeding 8-inch, and Type B, with guns of 6.1-inch caliber or less. The treaty also laid down an age limit for

Far left: The Italian heavy cruiser *Zara* was armed with eight 8-inch and twelve 3.9-inch guns.
Top: The *Suffren* was one of the four French ships built incorporating improvements from the *Duquesne* Class but was still too lightly protected.
Below: The *Alberto di Guissano* and her sisters of the 'Condottieri' type made astonishing speeds of up to 42 knots on trials but could only make 30 knots fully loaded.

Above: The 'panzerschiff' Deutschland pictured in 1937. The
recognition marks used by neutral warships during the Spanish Civil
War can be seen on the forward turret.

the replacement of cruisers as well as tonnage totals for each
navy. France and Italy refused to accept tonnage limitations, a
hollow gesture since neither had the resources to outbuild
Britain, the United States and Japan.

Up to now the arguments over cruisers affected only the five
front-rank navies, with Britain, Japan and the United States all
very much concerned with what the other two were doing, and
France and Italy mainly watching one another. However almost
imperceptibly Germany had edged back into the cruiser game,
and her efforts were to cause much disruption and dissent.

Under the Treaty of Versailles Germany was permitted to
retain eight very elderly protected cruisers. New construction
was permitted to replace these cruisers in due course but they
were not to exceed 6000 tons. There was no question of heavy
cruisers, the only other large ships permitted being 10,000 ton
ships with 11-inch guns, intended as replacements for six pre-
dreadnought battleships.

Work started almost immediately on the design of a new light

cruiser intended for training and known first simply as Kreuzer
A but launched as the Emden. She showed little improvement
over the Köln Class built in 1915–18, with eight single guns of an
older pattern, four winged out amidships and four on the center
line forward and aft. Speed was only 29 knots and armoring was
on a light scale but she provided valuable experience after a
comparatively long gap in construction.

Under the 1925–26 Program three more-powerful light cruisers
were planned, named Königsberg, Karlsruhe and Köln. The
attempt to provide a balanced design on such a limited displacement was not successful; they crammed three triple 15cm
mountings and four triple torpedo tubes into the narrow hull.
Endurance was only 5200 miles at 19 knots, which made them
useless for operating on the high seas. At 6650 tons in standard
condition they were 10 percent overweight and they were poor
bargains in spite of the technical ingenuity of the design.

These faults were tackled in the next cruiser, the Leipzig. With
another 3 feet on the beam she was more weatherly, and the
machinery was also improved. However, armoring and endurance were still low and standard displacement rose to 6710
tons.

In 1929 work started on the first replacement for the old battle-

ships. The Versailles Treaty had been deliberately framed to prohibit anything but a coast defense ship. Pains had been taken to exclude anything resembling the old armored cruiser, fast enough to run away from battleships and powerful enough to sink any light cruiser. Yet this was exactly what the German designers strove to achieve. On a nominal standard displacement of 10,000 tons (actually 11,700 tons) they mounted two triple 11-inch (28cm) gun turrets and by adopting an all-diesel power plant they could provide a staggering 10,000 miles endurance. Although the speed was only 26 knots and the armor no thicker than the best-protected heavy cruisers, the overall combination seemed ideal for a commerce-raider.

The name chosen for the ship, *Deutschland*, epitomized her importance to the German nation. By evading the restrictions of what was regarded as a vicious attempt to shackle Germany forever, she had shown that German genius and will could still triumph. Nor were foreigners slow to realize her importance. Dubbed a 'pocket-battleship' by the British press, it was claimed that the only ships capable both of catching and destroying her were the British and Japanese battlecruisers.

Two more *panzerschiff* were built, the *Admiral Scheer* and *Admiral Graf Spee* but a further three were cancelled since their shortcomings had now become obvious to the German Navy if

Below: The British cruiser *Southampton* carried twelve 6-inch guns. She was sunk in the Mediterranean in 1941.

not to anyone else. To meet them the French accelerated design work on a proposed *croiseur de combat*, while the British, Italians and Americans began to plan for 30-knot battleships. The British were particularly worried and began to consider what tactics should be used to counter ships of the *Deutschland* type.

The newly renamed *Kriegsmarine* rapidly set about building a fleet and in 1933 a further light cruiser was authorized, followed by two heavy cruisers the next year. The light cruiser *Nürnberg* was an improvement on the *Leipzig* but the *Admiral Hipper* and *Blücher* were much more formidable ships. Taking even more liberties with the 10,000 ton limit than any other Navy, they displaced 13,900 tons and so had a reasonable scale of protection and heavy armament; four twin 8-inch guns and a heavy anti-aircraft battery. Unfortunately they failed in the most important area of propulsion. The high pressure steam plant was not reliable and the 6800-mile endurance was poor.

The French reply to the *panzerschiff* was impressive but expensive. The particulars of the *croiseur de combat* were modified until a 26,500-ton battlecruiser emerged instead, armed with two quadruple 13-inch (330mm) gun mountings, steaming at nearly 30 knots but protected only by 9-inch side armor.

A more cost-effective solution to the problem was the heavy cruiser *Algerie*, completed in 1934. A balanced design, she was the most impressive of all the European Treaty cruisers with good endurance, 8700 miles at 15 knots. She was the only European 8-inch cruiser to bear comparison with the designs produced in the United States and Japan.

In 1931, with a full quota of 12 heavy cruisers, the Imperial Japanese Navy turned to a new type of powerful light cruiser, well protected and carrying sufficient 6-inch guns to pose a serious threat to most 8-inch cruisers. The *Mogami* Class ships were designed with five triple 6.1-inch gun turrets disposed as in the *Takao* Class and with similar protection and speed. This was asking a lot of only 10,000 tons but it was hoped that weight could be saved by the extensive use of light alloy in the superstructure and electric welding. As far as the outside world was

concerned the new cruisers had a standard displacement of only 8500 tons.

This time the Japanese had overreached themselves, and the first two ships, *Mogami* and *Mikuma*, ran into severe problems on their trials in the summer of 1935. During firing trials the welded seams started to open from the shocks transmitted through the hull. Then difficulties were encountered in training the main gun turrets, and it was found that the weight of the turrets and training machinery was deforming the hull. To cap everything the heavy antiaircraft armament (four twin 5-inch guns) contributed to a massive excess of topweight, making the ships unstable.

The *Mikuma* and *Mogami* were hurriedly put into reserve while the design was reexamined. By removing the after pair of 5-inch AA guns and the two aircraft catapults it was possible to reduce topweight, but it also proved necessary to add external bulges to the hull to improve stability. By the time the alterations were finished the displacement had risen to 11,200 tons and speed was reduced from 37 to 35 knots.

The US Navy was quick to see the advantage of the big light cruiser, for in bad visibility or night actions the 6-inch guns could bring a greater volume of fire to bear. It was the old argument for smothering fire and without radar to assist long-range gunnery there was considerable validity in it. In January 1935 the first of the nine *Brooklyn* Class light cruisers was laid down, carrying fifteen 6-inch guns in the same disposition as the *Mogami*. They were similar to the *San Francisco* Class in looks but with the aircraft hangar built over the square stern. Four aircraft were usually embarked.

The Royal Navy was permitted to build 91,000 tons of cruisers, and this had resulted in a program for 14 light cruisers of 6500 tons, the *Leander* Class, armed with four twin 6-inch mountings and capable of steaming 12,000 miles. Ultimately the design worked out at 7100 tons, which meant building only nine ships, the balance being taken up with the six smaller *Arethusa* Class of 5250 tons with six 6-inch guns. Protection was slightly thinner but AA armament remained the same and they also had 12,000 miles endurance. They were a sound answer to a knotty problem, for in the long run numbers of cruisers were more important to the British than individual quality.

The news of the *Mogami* Class upset these calculations, however, and the Admiralty reluctantly decided to build two 9100-ton cruisers with twelve 6-inch guns. This meant that the *Leander*s were cut to eight and the *Arethusa*s to four. The design had triple 6-inch turrets replacing the twins for the first time, protection scaled up and hangars provided for the catapult floatplanes. Unlike the Americans and Japanese the designers felt that a fifth turret with its limited arcs of fire was hardly worth the weight. The two ships were launched as the *Southampton* and *Newcastle* in 1936.

The Washington and London Naval Treaties expired in 1936, and Japan had already given the required two years' notice of her withdrawal from their provisions. The treaty of 1936 was no more constructive than its predecessors. All limitations on numbers were scrapped but the signatories agreed to exchange information on their building programs. No more Type A cruisers were to be built until 1943 and a new limit of 8000 tons was imposed on Type B cruisers but there were 'escalator' clauses to permit the signatories to exceed the limits if any nation was increasing its strength in specific categories. For the British it meant that they could get on with the cruisers which they needed, rather than worrying about tonnage totals. At the end of 1934 another two of the *Southampton* type were laid down, followed by four in 1935.

The sands were running out fast and it was evident to all but the most starry-eyed pacifist that Europe would probably be at war within three or four years. The Admiralty ordered two enlarged *Southamptons* in 1936, armored to withstand 8-inch shell fire. Although nominally still 10,000 tons the *Belfast* and *Edinburgh* had an actual standard displacement of 10,550 tons and were among the most powerful cruisers afloat. The good characteristics of the *Southampton* Class were maintained within the 8000-ton limit in the 'Colony' or *Fiji* Class ordered in 1937. They retained the twelve 6-inch guns and had a more effective distribution of the armor, all for a slight decrease in speed.

There was also the problem of what to do with the old light cruisers from the previous war. The *Hawkins* Class was supposed to be scrapped to comply with the 1930 Treaty and the 'C' and 'D' Classes were now too small for front-line duties. In 1935 experimental modernization had been carried out on the *Coventry* and *Curlew*, with their 6-inch guns replaced by single 4-inch antiaircraft guns for use in the Mediterranean as AA escorts. They proved a great success, and in 1938–39 four were taken in hand for more modern rearmament. At the same time a new type of light cruiser was under consideration for the big rearmament program which was to begin in 1937.

It was decided from the outset that the new small cruisers should be antiaircraft ships. A new dual-purpose twin 5.25-inch gun was the obvious choice for the new ships. They were given five of these mountings, three forward superimposed over one another and another two aft, with close-range light guns amidships. The new ships became the *Dido* Class and 16 were ordered by 1939.

The French, like the British, were anxious to get away from the expensive heavy cruiser, and after the *Algerie*, built no more of the type. Instead they turned successfully to fast light cruisers of 6700 tons to match the Italians' speed. In 1931 the cruiser-minelayer *Emile Bertin* was laid down, with nine 6-inch guns on a displacement of less than 6000 tons. She was a great success, making an average of 36.73 knots for eight hours and nearly 40 knots maximum. This was ideal for a getaway after laying mines, but apart from some flimsy side plating and a thin deck she was unprotected and had little endurance. The next class was based on the *Emile Bertin* but without her faults. On a standard displacement of 7600 tons the *La Galissonière* Class had the same armament but nearly 20 percent less power to permit good protection. Even so, on trials they made 32.5 knots easily and in light condition reached 35 knots.

Looking back on the Washington Treaty and the subsequent international agreements it can be seen how vain were the hopes of statesmen that they could force navies to build only certain types of cruisers. The prevailing obsession became one of matching individual cruisers in other navies. Yet experience had always shown that matched opponents were unlikely to meet in battle. The antidote to such ships as the *Mogami* or the *Deutschland* was to concentrate a number of smaller ships. Ironically in 1939 all four *Mogamis* went into dock for reconstruction and when they emerged the triple 6.1-inch guns had been replaced by twin 8-inch – at a stroke the Japanese had added four heavy cruisers to their strength and the rationale for the *Brooklyn* and *Southampton* Classes had vanished.

On the other hand there can be no doubt that the attention paid to cruiser design in the 1920s and 1930s did much to further research into new ways of weight-saving and better machinery. However it had been expensive, and much creative effort had been devoted for little result. After nearly two decades most navies had finally accepted that smaller cruisers were a better bargain than big ones.

As well as their fifteen 6-inch guns the *Brooklyn* Class carried eight 5-inch. They could make 32 knots.

CONVOYS AND COMMERCE-RAID

The German Navy, for all its progress since 1933 and the Anglo-German Naval Treaty of 1935, was not well placed to fight the Royal Navy. The third heavy cruiser, the *Prinz Eugen*, was not yet ready and her later sisters *Lützow* and *Seydlitz* were a long way away from completion. The *Lützow* was sold to the Soviet Union in 1940, while neither the *Seydlitz* nor the light cruisers authorized under the 1938 and 1939 programs were ever completed.

As the main effort of the German surface fleet was to be against British trade it was essential that ships be at sea before any sort of blockade could be formed. On 21 August 1939 the *Admiral Graf Spee* left Germany for the North Atlantic, followed three days later by her sister *Deutschland* each accompanied by a supply ship carrying fuel and provisions. Neither ship was

spotted, although a few days after the outbreak of war the *Graf Spee* had a lucky escape from detection when her floatplane sighted the heavy cruiser *Cumberland* only 30 miles away. The *panzerschiff* was able to break away undetected but inevitably her presence in the South Atlantic was revealed when she began to sink isolated merchant ships. As soon as the reports were confirmed the British and French set up eight hunting groups, six of them including cruisers.

As reports of sinkings continued to come in from the South Atlantic the Admiralty sifted them to try to predict the next move. As always the temptation was to spread ships around but the Admiralty wisely ordered Commodore Harwood, commanding Force G, to keep his force concentrated. He chose to cover the focal area around the River Plate reasoning that the con-

NG

Above: As part of the Nazi-Soviet agreement of 1939 Hitler gave Stalin the incomplete heavy cruiser *Lützow* seen here leaving for Leningrad in 1940.
Top: The destroyer *Glowworm* falls to the guns of the *Hipper*.
Below: The light cruiser *Köln* lies at anchor in Kiel in 1936. The torpedo boat *Seeadler* passes by in the foreground.

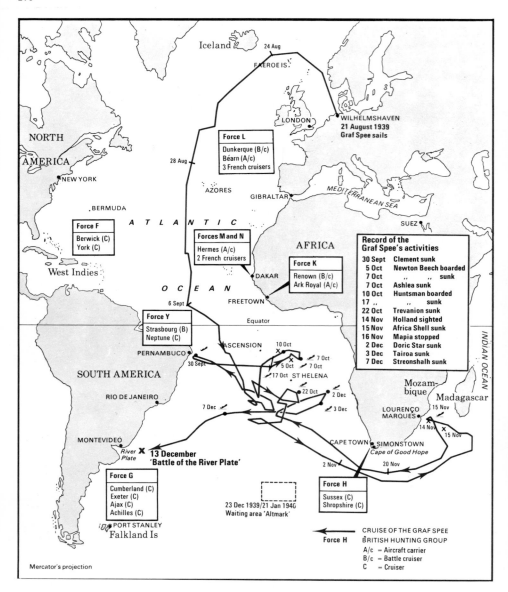

Iceland
24 Aug
FAEROE IS.

NORTH
AMERICA

LONDON

WILHELMSHAVEN
21 August 1939
Graf Spee sails

28 Aug

Force L
Dunkerque (B/c)
Béarn (A/c)
3 French cruisers

NEW YORK

AZORES

GIBRALTAR

MEDITERRANEAN SEA

SUEZ

BERMUDA

ATLANTIC

Force F
Berwick (C)
York (C)

Forces M and N
Hermes (A/c)
2 French cruisers

AFRICA

West Indies

OCEAN

DAKAR

Force K
Renown (B/c)
Ark Royal (A/c)

FREETOWN

6 Sept

Equator

Force Y
Strasbourg (B)
Neptune (C)

ASCENSION

10 Oct
7 Oct
5 Oct 7 Oct
17 Oct ST HELENA

PERNAMBUCO

30 Sept

22 Oct 2 Dec

SOUTH AMERICA

3 Dec

RIO DE JANEIRO

7 Dec

**Record of the
Graf Spee's activities**

30 Sept   Clement sunk
5 Oct   Newton Beech boarded
7 Oct   ,,   ,,   sunk
7 Oct   Ashlea sunk
10 Oct   Huntsman boarded
17 ,,   ,,   sunk
22 Oct   Trevanion sunk
14 Nov   Holland sighted
15 Nov   Africa Shell sunk
16 Nov   Mapia stopped
2 Dec   Doric Star sunk
3 Dec   Tairoa sunk
7 Dec   Streonshalh sunk

INDIAN
OCEAN

Mozam-
bique   Madagascar

15 Nov

LOURENÇO
MARQUES

14 Nov   15 Nov

MONTEVIDEO

River
Plate   **13 December
'Battle of the River Plate'**

CAPE TOWN   SIMONSTOWN
Cape of Good Hope

2 Nov   20 Nov

Force G
Cumberland (C)
Exeter (C)
Ajax (C)
Achilles (C)

23 Dec 1939/21 Jan 1940
Waiting area 'Altmark'

Force H
Sussex (C)
Shropshire (C)

PORT STANLEY
Falkland Is

Mercator's projection

CRUISE OF THE GRAF SPEE
Force H   BRITISH HUNTING GROUP
A/c = Aircraft carrier
B/c = Battle cruiser
C   = Cruiser

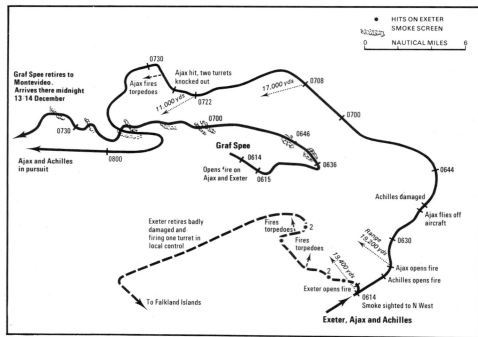

HITS ON EXETER
SMOKE SCREEN

0   6
NAUTICAL MILES

0730

**Graf Spee retires to
Montevideo.
Arrives there midnight
13-14 December**

Ajax fires
torpedoes

Ajax hit, two turrets
knocked out

0708

17,000 yds

11,000 yds   0722

0700

0730   0700

0646

Graf Spee

0614

**Ajax and Achilles
in pursuit**

0800

0636

Opens fire on
Ajax and Exeter

0615

0644

Achilles damaged

Ajax flies off
aircraft

Exeter retires badly
damaged and
firing one turret in
local control

Fires
torpedoes   2

Fires
torpedoes

Fires torpedoes

2

Range
19,200 yds

0630

Ajax opens fire
Achilles opens fire

19,400 yds

To Falkland Islands

Exeter opens fire   0614

Smoke sighted to N West

Exeter, Ajax and Achilles

Above: The British cruiser *Exeter* seen in January 1940.
Far left: The maps show the cruise of the *Graf Spee* and the Battle of the River Plate.
Left: The cruiser HMS *Kenya* in heavy seas.

centration of British shipping there would soon attract a commerce raider, and so it turned out. At 0608 on the morning of 13 December 1939 the *Graf Spee* was sighted.

Although on paper Harwood's cruisers were at a great disadvantage it was not going to be a one-sided affair. For a start his ships were experienced and in accordance with current Admiralty orders they had exercised for such an eventuality, with the *Exeter* playing the role of attacker only a few months earlier. The principle was to use speed to retain a tactical advantage and disperse the British cruisers. This had the advantage of denying the enemy the luxury of a single easy target and permitting each cruiser to spot the others' fall of shot at long range, a process known as 'flank marking.' Unfortunately the 8-inch gunned *Cumberland* had been detached to the Falkland Islands for repairs, leaving only the light cruisers *Ajax* and *Achilles* to support the *Exeter*.

The *Exeter* inevitably bore the brunt of the *Graf Spee*'s fire. She was soon heavily hit. After an hour only Y turret remained in action, the ship was listing 7–10 degrees to starboard and was 3 feet down by the bows. She might have been worse off had the *Ajax* and *Achilles* not repeatedly darted into range and then retreated under cover of smoke. These picador tactics forced the

Graf Spee to shift target several times to chase the light cruisers off before returning to its main target. In all, three 8-inch and seventeen 6-inch hits were scored on the German ship. It is interesting to note that the *Graf Spee*'s gunnery officer later commented that the devastating effect of the 8-inch shells clearly contradicted the belief that a *panzerschiff* could only be fought by a battleship. True, Harwood's three cruisers were badly battered, but the *Graf Spee* was in a bad position, damaged and far from home, with well over half of her ammunition expended.

The *Graf Spee* finally gave up and sought refuge in neutral Uruguayan waters. Every minute spent there increased the risk of more heavy units arriving to bottle her in Montevideo. In fact only the *Cumberland* arrived but adroit propaganda led the Germans to believe that the battlecruiser *Renown* and the carrier *Ark Royal* were only a few hours away. With shell-holes in her forecastle the *Graf Spee* dared not face the North Atlantic in winter without serious risk of flooding, while other damage would probably prove the last straw for her diesel motors. With all these problems Captain Langsdorff decided to scuttle his ship, a decision supported by Hitler, who could not bear the thought of a major German warship being sunk in battle. On the evening of 17 December, the *Graf Spee* moved just outside territorial waters and sent her crew away to a German steamer. Then, suddenly, she erupted in smoke and flame as the scuttling charges wrecked the ship.

The Battle of the River Plate gave a well-deserved fillip to

British morale in the middle of the Phony War and dispelled forever the myth of the pocket battleship. Even though the *Deutschland* had returned to Germany safely a month earlier, her haul of two ships totalling less than 7000 tons was meager. The German Navy recognized their shortcomings as well, and reclassified the two survivors as heavy cruisers in 1940. Hitler even insisted on changing *Deutschland*'s name to *Lützow* because her loss would damage German prestige!

The North Atlantic Theater

The German cruiser force was small enough in September 1939 but the Norwegian campaign in 1940 cut it to the bone. First to go was the new *Blücher*. She was steaming up Oslo Fjord ahead of the *Lützow* (the former *Deutschland*) and the *Emden* in the early hours of 9 April 1940, intent on occupying Oslo. Boldness had got the force two-thirds of the way up Oslo Fjord but when it reached the dangerous Drobak Narrows its luck ran out. The reservists manning the obsolescent 11-inch guns on the island fortress of Kaholm stood to their posts and opened fire as the *Blücher* entered the Narrows. The first salvo struck home and just over a minute later two torpedoes, fired from underwater tubes on Kaholm also hit. The *Blücher* was doomed and two hours later she capsized and sank.

On 10 April the light cruisers *Königsberg* and *Karlsruhe* were struck down, one by British dive bombers while lying off Bergen and the other by torpedoes from the submarine *Truant* off Kristiansand. The *Leipzig* had been badly damaged four months earlier by a British torpedo and the *Admiral Hipper* had been rammed by the British destroyer *Glowworm* on 8 April while heading for Norway. This left the *Kriegsmarine* with only the *Emden*, *Nürnberg* and *Köln* to support Hitler's projected 'Sealion' invasion of Britain after the fall of France.

The *Admiral Hipper* was repaired and sent out into the Atlantic at the end of 1940. As with other German warships her machinery was a constant headache, and her maximum speed was soon down to 25 knots. Had the British known this they might have turned it to advantage when on Christmas Eve 1940 the cruisers *Berwick*, *Bonaventure* and *Dunedin* met the *Hipper*. They were covering a convoy of troop ships bound for North Africa, and although she hit the *Berwick* twice the *Hipper* beat a hasty retreat.

On 22 May 1941 the heavy cruiser HMS *Suffolk* caught sight of two big ships close to the pack-ice in the Denmark Strait. She and the *Norfolk* had been stationed there to spot the battleship *Bismarck* and the heavy cruiser *Prinz Eugen* if they should try to break out into the Atlantic. Although the *Bismarck* fired ranging salvoes at the *Norfolk* the two cruisers managed to stay out of trouble, and the German Admiral Lutjens knew that other British ships would soon make contact. During the next day and the following night the *Suffolk*'s radar continued to track the German ships.

The two cruisers might have hoped that their risky pursuit was over when the British battlecruiser squadron came up at first light on the morning of 24 May. However, the *Hood* quickly blew up after a fire had started. The exact cause of the explosion will never be known, but it is known that the fire amidships was caused by the *Prinz Eugen*'s shells, not the *Bismarck*'s, another example of the unforeseen potency of 8-inch gunfire against capital ships.

During the subsequent chase the *Suffolk* and *Norfolk* hung on grimly. On the morning of 27 May, only three days after the destruction of HMS *Hood* they handed over their quarry to the battleships *King George V* and *Rodney* of the Home Fleet. Again a cruiser intervened with effect in a battleship action, for the first decisive hit was scored when HMS *Dorsetshire*'s 8-inch shells knocked out the *Bismarck*'s fire control.

Early in 1942 the battlecruisers *Scharnhorst* and *Gneisenau* and the *Prinz Eugen* made their audacious daylight run through the English Channel from Brest but it was a 'strategic withdrawal' from the Atlantic rather than a shift of any offensive significance. Thereafter German raiders might lurk in Norwegian Fjords and threaten convoys heading to north Russian ports but the danger to the Atlantic convoy system diminished.

The first few convoys to Murmansk were not molested, but PQ-13 ran into trouble in March 1942, when attacked by three large German destroyers. The cruiser HMS *Trinidad* had already done sterling work for the antiaircraft defense of the convoy and now her 6-inch shells smashed into the German leader *Z.26*. However when she attempted to fire a torpedo the intense cold froze the gyroscope so that the torpedo circled and plunged into the cruiser's own starboard boiler room. She managed to limp into Murmansk three days later. There she was repaired with a

Top: The German heavy cruiser *Admiral Hipper* on 2 July 1942. The
Hipper had been based at Trondheim but was sent north on that day
to form part of the threat to the ill-fated convoy PQ-17.
Above: The light cruiser *Karlsruhe* was refitted in 1939 to improve
stability by adding four feet to the beam.
Below: The heavy cruiser *Blücher* seen before the outbreak of war.
The *Blücher* was lost in Oslo Fjord in 1940.

massive metal patch and she was ready to return home to
England in May. However she came under heavy air attack, one
bomb blowing in the temporary patch while another set her on
fire forward. Although she was still steaming at 20 knots, with
her steering intact, the fire gained control and eventually the
Trinidad was abandoned.

On 30 April another valuable cruiser, the *Edinburgh*, was lost
while attached to a slow convoy. She fell victim to a torpedo from
U.456 being hit twice on the starboard side. Next day she was
attacked by three German destroyers. Although capable of only
8 knots and forced to steam in circles, the *Edinburgh* was game
to the end. When the *Hermann Schoemann* came dashing out of a
snowstorm it took only two salvoes from the *Edinburgh*'s single

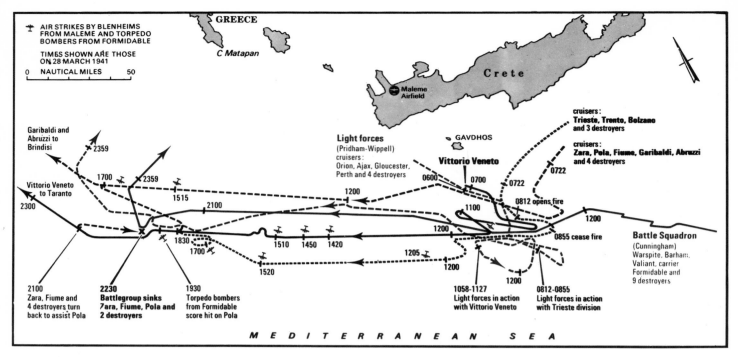

serviceable turret to cripple her. But the *Edinburgh* was hit by a third torpedo and she had to be abandoned.

The loss of these two cruisers forced a change in convoy tactics. From then on cruisers were kept away from the convoy, close enough to return if a surface attack developed but never close enough to provide the heavy AA defense which was so valuable in breaking up concentrated air attacks.

The disastrous story of convoy PQ-17 in July 1942 has been told many times. One cannot avoid comparing the actual fate of the scattered ships at the hands of U-Boats and bombers with the theoretical outcome of an attack by the *Tirpitz, Admiral Hipper* and *Admiral Scheer*. The commander of the covering force had four heavy cruisers and planned to use them as boldly as Harwood had at the River Plate. Nobody can tell whether such stratagems would have worked against a resolute attack, but the history of other cruiser actions shows that the *Kriegsmarine* was rarely able to match such tactics. As it was, only 11 of the original convoy of 37 reached a Soviet port.

The Battle of the Barents Sea at the end of 1942 shows what might actually have happened to PQ-17 if the local commanders had been left to work out the defense for themselves. On the morning of 31 December the convoy JW-51B was attacked. The close escort under Captain Sherbrooke comprised six destroyers and the distant escort under Rear-Admiral Burnett was made up of two 6-inch gunned cruisers, the *Sheffield* and the *Jamaica*. The German commander, Vice-Admiral Kummetz, hoped to bring the *Admiral Hipper* and three destroyers into action on the convoy's port quarter, forcing it to veer away to the southeast – right into the path of the *Lützow* and her destroyers. What in fact happened was that the destroyer HMS *Achates* laid a dense smoke screen while the other destroyers exchanged a desultory fire with the enemy at a range of about five miles. The visibility was poor, with snow squalls and patches of smoke making it necessary to fire by radar. Neither side was shooting well, the British destroyers' violent motion and constant icing up of gun-breeches made it all but impossible to fire steadily, but the much bigger *Admiral Hipper*'s shooting was equally erratic. However now the *Sheffield* and *Jamaica* were only 12 miles away, closing rapidly and totally undetected by Kummetz. Fortuitously a heavy snowstorm brought a temporary respite to Sherbrooke's destroyers and they escaped further punishment.

Although the defense had slowed the progress of the German plans they were working out as desired, for the British were being forced in the direction of the *Lützow*. However, because of the snowstorm, the *Lützow*'s captain, mindful of Hitler's instructions to take no risks, stood off to the east while the weather cleared.

The *Hipper* made contact again but wasted her fire on the *Achates*, still laying the smoke screen which hid the precious convoy. She had just shifted fire to another destroyer when a salvo of 6-inch shells from the *Sheffield* fell around her. The fourth salvo hit, and the startled *Hipper* hauled around in a circle to make her escape, but not before the British cruiser scored another two hits. Kummetz had strict orders about action with heavy units and withdrew to the west at top speed with the *Sheffield* and *Jamaica* in hot pursuit. Two luckless German destroyers, mistook the British for their own forces in the gloom, and closed in. The *Richard Beitzen* escaped but the *Friedrich Eckholdt* was destroyed.

The *Lützow* finally managed to make contact with the convoy but could only inflict splinter damage on one ship before the destroyers forced her away. With obvious relief her captain received orders from Kummetz to rejoin the flagship. There was one more brief exchange of fire before the German force retreated. Burnett had no intention of being lured away from the convoy, being content to have his two light cruisers put to flight a pair of ships armed with 8-inch and 11-inch guns.

The *Tirpitz* was never brought to action in the open sea but the battlecruiser *Scharnhorst* made one final attempt to destroy a Murmansk convoy almost exactly a year after the Barents Sea débâcle. Once again the convoy's cruiser escort saved the day, with the *Belfast*, *Sheffield* and *Norfolk* engaging the *Scharnhorst* without regard for the risk. An 8-inch shell from the *Norfolk* destroyed the battlecruiser's forward gunnery radar set, and all the time she was trying to work her way around the cruisers the Home Fleet was coming up in support. This time the covering force included the battleship *Duke of York*, whose 14-inch salvoes blasted the *Scharnhorst* and inflicted serious damage. It was left to the cruisers *Belfast* and *Jamaica* to finish her off with torpedoes.

The Mediterranean

Much was hoped for from the fast Italian cruisers but they got off to an inauspicious start. In July 1940 the *Bartolomeo Colleoni* and *Giovanni delle Bande Nere* were attacked by the Australian cruiser *Sydney* and five destroyers. Although the Italians had been credited with 37 knots their sea speed was only 30 knots, and so it came as something of a surprise to the *Sydney*'s captain

to find that he was overhauling the enemy. During the long-range gunnery duel which followed, the *Sydney*'s 6-inch salvoes hit and disabled the *Bartolomeo Colleoni* but her consort escaped.

The theory that armored 8-inch gun cruisers were a substitute for battleships was shown to be woefully wrong at the Battle of Cape Matapan on the night of 28 March 1941. The *Pola* had been hit by an aircraft torpedo earlier in the day. In the hope of towing her back to port, Admiral Iachino sent her two sisters to look for her after dark. By a series of coincidences the three ships were caught together by the British Commander in Chief, Admiral Cunningham, leading his force of three battleships. In the merciless glare of searchlights the *Fiume* and *Zara* were destroyed by 15-inch salvoes at less than 4000 yards. Then Cunningham's destroyers finished off the *Pola* and two destroyers. It was a victory which curbed any initiative the Italian Navy might have had, so that only two months later the British were left to complete the evacuation of Greece and Crete under only air attack rather than a combined air and sea assault.

In fact the air assault was deadly by itself. The evacuation of Crete cost the Royal Navy dear, particularly in cruisers. At first things seemed to go well, despite the crippling of the *York* by Italian explosive motor boats in Suda Bay, Crete. On the night of 21 May 1941 the *Dido*, *Ajax* and *Orion* and four destroyers wiped out an invasion convoy bound for Crete in commandeered fishing craft. However the next day Stuka dive-bombers sank the *Gloucester* and the *Fiji* after they had fired away all their 4-inch AA ammunition. Thereafter cruisers were warned not to allow their reserves of AA shells to fall below 40 percent.

The antiaircraft cruisers came into their own in the Mediterranean, where their lower endurance did not matter. Losses were particularly heavy, *Calypso*, *Cairo*, *Naiad*, *Bonaventure* and *Hermione* were torpedoed and *Coventry*, *Calcutta* and *Spartan* were sunk by air attack. In addition the *Carlisle* was so badly damaged that she was laid up at Alexandria and never repaired. In all 17 AA cruisers were lost.

The Italians were also suffering steady attrition from British aircraft and submarines. The old armored cruiser *San Giorgio* and the *Trieste* and *Muzio Attendolo* were sunk in port by bombing. The *Trento*, *Giovanni delle Bande Nere* and *Armando Diaz* were torpedoed by submarines and the *Gorizia*, *Bolzano*, *Taranto* (formerly the German *Strassburg*) and *Bari* (formerly the German *Pillau*) fell into German hands at the time of the Italian Armistice in September 1943. In addition, the *Alberto de Giussano* and *Alberico da Barbiano* were sunk in a night action by British and Dutch destroyers off Cape Bon. The disaster was compounded because the two cruisers were carrying an inflammable cargo of gasoline on deck, intended for the army in North Africa; both ships burst into flame immediately and sank with heavy loss of life. It transpired that the Italian Naval HQ had told Admiral Toscano of the presence of four Allied de-

Above: The British light cruiser *Ajax* served at the Battle of the River Plate and at Matapan.
Far left: Map of the Battle of Matapan.

stroyers, but it was considered that they would never dare attack two fast cruisers and their own destroyer escort.

Cruisers played their final part in the Mediterranean Campaign in 1944 when they supported the Allied landings at Anzio. As they had shown in the Torch landings in North Africa and were to show in Normandy, cruisers were ideal for providing fire support. Although lacking the range and power of battleships they drew less water and could be risked more readily. Their high speed also gave them a measure of immunity from enemy shore batteries. It was a pattern which was to be repeated 30 years later, during the Vietnam War.

Below: The burning wreck of the old *San Giorgio* seen in Tobruk harbor on 22 January 1941.

ACROSS THE PACIFIC

If the struggle between Fascism and Democracy began long before the outbreak of World War II the struggle between the United States and the Japanese Empire cast its shadow equally far ahead. Yet, although the invasion of China strained relations between the two countries, and in spite of attacks on British and American gunboats on the Yangtze and other incidents, the peace held until 7 December 1941.

Although the first cruisers in action were the USS *Honolulu* and *Raleigh*, attacked at Pearl Harbor, and the old Japanese armored cruiser *Idzumo* which sank the British gunboat *Peterel* at Shanghai, the first proper cruiser actions took place in the East Indies. A hurriedly organised American-British-Dutch-Australian (ABDA) Command was set up to defend the East Indies but it was at best a ramshackle arrangement, with too few ships, planes and men. The first losses were to air attack in the Makassar Strait on 4 February 1942. The Dutch *de Ruyter* escaped with only minor damage but the USS *Houston* had her after 8-inch turret destroyed and the *Marblehead* was hit in her steering gear.

Admiral Doorman, the Dutch naval commander, did his best

to fight back, and on 19 February his forces engaged the Japanese off Bali in the Battle of Badoeng Strait. He had the *de Ruyter* and *Java* with three destroyers in one group and the *Tromp* and four American destroyers in another. When the two forces made contact there were only three Japanese destroyers facing the *de Ruyter* and *Java* and their three destroyers. In the confused action which followed the Dutch *Piet Hein* was torpedoed without any loss to the Japanese. Then the second ABDA group arrived. Without even a common codebook the newcomers could not identify the recognition signals being flashed at them, and so made little contribution to the battle. The light cruiser *Tromp* was badly knocked about, while the three Japanese destroyers were all damaged.

Doorman was deprived of the *Tromp*, which returned to Australia for repairs, but by mid-February he had been reinforced by the British *Exeter*, repaired and modernized after the Battle of the River Plate, the *Dragon* and *Danae*, the Australian *Hobart* and *Perth* and the USS *Houston*, *Marblehead* and *Boise*. Against him were ranged a force of carriers, seaplane tenders and destroyers, as well as 11 heavy cruisers and four light cruisers. Only a few of these ships were concentrated for the Battle of the Java Sea on 27 February which nonetheless spelled the end of the ABDA force.

The Allied ships were completely out-fought and the result was never in doubt. The ships were outclassed and their crews were exhausted. The destruction began when the *Exeter* was set on fire by an 8-inch shell from the *Nachi* and minutes later the destroyer *Kortenaer* blew up from a torpedo hit. Doorman broke away, having failed to get at the invasion transports which had been his main target, but his force was in a sorry state. The *Exeter* managed to hold a straight course parallel to the southeast in company with four destroyers, while the other cruisers formed themselves into a second column about 10,000 yards away. But the Japanese were not going to let them go and by 1715 they were in range again, firing 8-inch salvoes and torpedoes. The *Exeter* was now making only five knots and she was the target chosen by the *Jintsu* and *Naka* and their destroyers. Only the bravery of two escorting destroyers saved her, and although the *Electra* was sunk the cruiser managed to limp back to Surabaya.

The rest of the force were not so fortunate. Later that night the *de Ruyter* was torpedoed by the *Nachi* and *Haguro*, sinking with Admiral Doorman and 344 officers and men on board. Four minutes later the *Java* also burst into flame after a torpedo hit, leaving only the *Houston* and *Perth* to make their way back to Batavia as best they could. Now it was *sauve qui peut* as all units tried to escape to Australia or Ceylon. The *Exeter* and *Encounter* were hunted down by the *Ashigara* and *Myoko* on 1 March, while

The *Omaha* Class light cruiser *Raleigh*, heavily damaged after the Pearl Harbor attack. The *Raleigh* was repaired and served mainly in the North Pacific until 1945.

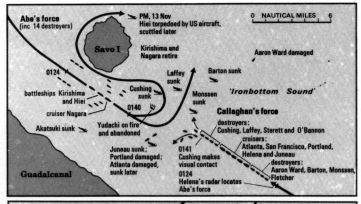

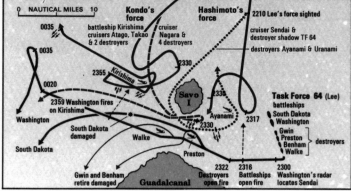

fire and then torpedoed her. Four minutes later the *Chicago* had her bow blown off by a torpedo. Moving north the Japanese now dealt with the USS *Quincy*, *Astoria* and *Vincennes* in turn. Surprise was complete and only the *Quincy* managed to retaliate, hitting the *Chokai* three times before sinking. The Japanese ships vanished as silently as they had arrived, leaving carnage behind them. Four heavy cruisers were sunk and one badly damaged in return for only slight damage to the flagship *Chokai*. The only comfort that the Allies could draw was Mikawa's failure to sink any of the transports lying off Lunga Point. The heavy cruiser *Kako* was also sunk by an American submarine during the run back to Rabaul.

The Japanese Navy continued to do its utmost to help the Army, running troops in under cover of darkness and bombarding Henderson Field at night. These fast runs down the island chain from Rabaul soon became known as the 'Tokyo Express' and under Rear-Admiral Tanaka they were conducted with audacity and skill. Without the benefit of radar the Japanese lookouts could still be relied on to make the first sighting and their designers' wisdom in providing the cruisers with torpedoes gave them a great advantage. Above all the attention paid by the Japanese to night fighting tactics gave them an edge in many of these actions.

In October 1942 the Americans decided to run a convoy of their own reinforcements into Guadalcanal, and this brought on a near disaster off Cape Esperance on the night of 11–12 October. The close escort for the convoy was Task Force 64 under Rear-Admiral Scott, with the heavy cruisers *San Francisco* and *Salt Lake City* and the light cruisers *Boise* and *Helena*, with five destroyers. The Americans fully expected the Japanese to try to stop the convoy but in fact its arrival had gone undetected. What the Japanese were intending was a night bombardment of Henderson Field by three heavy cruisers and two destroyers. As the Americans had foreknowledge of their time of arrival they were confident that they could get their revenge for Savo Island.

At 2235 Admiral Scott formed his force into line ahead, three destroyers leading the four cruisers and two more bringing up the rear. The Japanese Admiral Goto's force was also in line ahead but with a destroyer on either beam of the leading cruiser. Both sides made mistakes; Goto's lookouts sighted a burning floatplane but the Japanese commander did not interpret the information correctly, while the *Helena* picked up the Japanese force on her radar but failed to report the sighting for 15 minutes. The Americans had hoped to use their cruisers' floatplanes to drop flares as the Japanese had at Savo Island but their performance was disappointing. What information did reach the

the same day saw the end of the *Houston* and *Perth*. However they wrote a magnificent ending to the story of ABDA by charging the Japanese invasion transports lying in Bantam Bay. For a while confusion reigned and the Japanese destroyers fired at one another in their haste to fend off the two Allied cruisers. Although both ships paid the inevitable price, the transports had been damaged, although mainly by the Japanese shells and torpedoes.

So far all had gone in favor of the Japanese but the Battles of the Coral Sea and Midway brought their headlong advance under control. Cruisers played no special role in these two carrier battles but they demonstrated their efficiency as screening ships for the carriers, with ample speed to keep up with them and provide a heavy AA battery. At Midway the Japanese deployed seven cruisers while the Americans had eight (including two Australian ships). Only when the fighting shifted to the Solomon Islands in August 1942 did cruisers come into their own.

Guadalcanal and the Solomons generally were important because they were on the route of the Japanese advance. The Americans were alarmed by reports that Japanese engineers were building an airfield on Guadalcanal and so on 7 August the US Marines stormed ashore to seize it. The airfield, renamed as Henderson Field, was the key to the Solomons for, as long as it was in US hands, all Japanese forces could be attacked within a 250-mile radius. Equally, in Japanese hands it would make naval operations in support of the Marines all but impossible.

It was clear that the Japanese would spare no effort to dislodge the Americans. The day after the landings a force of five heavy and two light cruisers under Admiral Mikawa left Rabaul for Guadalcanal, intent on smashing their way through the Allied warships in Savo Sound to allow transports to land reinforcements on Guadalcanal. By a series of mischances, sightings of Mikawa's force were not relayed to Rear-Admiral Crutchley, commanding the force of Allied cruisers lying off Savo Island. Nor did two patrolling destroyers spot the Japanese cruisers gliding past in the dark.

When Mikawa attacked at 0143 his force had the Allied cruisers at their mercy. In the light of flares dropped by floatplanes they riddled the Australian *Canberra* with 8-inch shell-

flagship was garbled, so the tactical advantage was largely thrown away.

At 2346 the *Helena* opened fire on the flagship *Aoba* and the destroyer *Duncan* shot at the *Furutaka*. Admiral Goto was mortally wounded and the *Furutaka* was set on fire but the other cruiser, the *Kinugasa*, and the destroyer *Hatsuyuki* managed to obey Goto's last order to reverse course, and escaped serious damage. The Japanese were still very dangerous, and at midnight the *Kinugasa* surprised the *Salt Lake City* with uncomfortably accurate salvoes at 8000 yards. Then the *Boise* was hit four times and was only saved when the *Salt Lake City* steamed between her and the Japanese ships. The *Boise* was lucky to escape, for an 8-inch shell penetrated her forward turret while a 6-inch shell caused a bad explosion in her magazines.

Above: The heavy cruiser *Pensacola* carried ten 8-inch guns.
Far left: Both phases of the Naval Battle of Guadalcanal.

The *Furutaka* finally sank after many hits. The *Aoba*, however, survived an estimated 40 hits from 6-inch and 8-inch shells and was still making 30 knots at the end of the action, and the *Kinugasa* had only trifling damage. It had been a scrappy, inconclusive battle with both sides achieving their main objective of getting their troops safely ashore.

The next major action, the Battle of Guadalcanal on 13–14 November, did not go well for the Americans. On the first night

Below: The *Atlanta* Class antiaircraft cruiser *San Juan* carried eight twin 5-inch gun mountings.

Above: The heavy cruiser *Quincy* on 4 August 1942.
Far right: The *St Louis* leaves Tulagi anchorage in 1943.
Below: The *Minneapolis* sails out of Pearl Harbor.

the heavy cruisers *San Francisco* and *Portland*, the light cruiser *Helena* and the AA cruisers *Atlanta* and *Juneau* ran into a force which included the battleships *Hiei* and *Kirishima* and the light cruiser *Nagara*. Once again it was the *Helena*'s efficient radar which detected the enemy but she was positioned towards the rear of the column, a difficult position for it to function effectively. Again poor radio discipline overloaded the voice net with messages, with the result that Rear-Admiral Callaghan could make little sense of the reports.

The *mêlée* which ensued has been described as the most confused and horrifying naval action of the entire war. Callaghan's force did not know that it had charged right into the middle of the Japanese squadron until the *Atlanta* was illuminated by the searchlights of the *Hiei* and the destroyer *Akatsuki*. The battleship's 14-inch shells ripped into the flimsy superstructure, killing Admiral Scott. The *Atlanta* was then torpedoed, having managed to fire only one salvo. However the two Japanese ships were immediately fired on by the American destroyers and drew away; the *Akatsuki* was sunk shortly afterwards and the *Hiei*'s upperworks were set on fire. In the confusion the *San Francisco* started to fire on the *Atlanta* but soon realized her mistake. Only seconds later she herself was hit by 14-inch salvoes from the *Kirishima* and 5-inch fire from two destroyers. The *San Francisco*'s bridge was destroyed and Admiral Callaghan and his staff were killed.

The battle now degenerated into a sort of dogfight. Admiral Abe in the burning *Hiei* had lost control of his ships and the two American admirals were dead. Individual ships fired at whatever

targets they could see. In these conditions the Japanese were more likely to win, thanks to their superior training. The *Nagara* and the destroyers sank the destroyer *Barton*, crippled the *Portland* with a torpedo and set the AA cruiser *Juneau* on fire, before raking the *San Francisco* with gunfire. The *Helena* gave a good account of herself at first, using radar-controlled gunfire to drive off the *Amatsukaze* but she was then badly mauled by three more Japanese destroyers. When the firing died away at 0200 two Japanese destroyers and the *Hiei* were doomed (she would be sunk the next day by aircraft) but the Americans had lost two destroyers and an AA cruiser and had several badly damaged. The *San Francisco* and *Helena* survived but next day the battered *Juneau* was torpedoed by a Japanese submarine and two more destroyers had to be abandoned.

Another battle was fought the following night between two US battleships and a Japanese force comprising the *Kirishima* and the cruisers *Sendai*, *Nagara*, *Atago* and *Takao*. Once again there was confusion but the Americans got the better of the exchange, and the *Kirishima* was sunk by 16-inch shellfire from the *Washington*. Aircraft from Henderson Field had also caught Admiral Mikawa's bombardment force at daybreak the day

before, sinking the *Kinugasa* and damaging the *Chokai*, *Maya* and *Isuzu*. The Japanese could not accept losses on this scale and when an air strike devastated a reinforcement convoy brought in by 'Tenacious Tanaka' on 14 November it was the beginning of the end. Although the 'Tokyo Express' continued to run there was no longer any hope of supporting the Army by bringing on a full-scale naval battle. From now on the Japanese would be in retreat.

There were to be other battles in the Solomons but they were fought around the 'Tokyo Express', which began to reverse the process by steadily evacuating the garrison from Guadalcanal. The Battle of Tassafaronga on the night of 30 November/1 December showed that even if the Americans ruled the sea by day the Japanese ruled at night. Four US cruisers, the *Minneapolis*, *New Orleans*, *Pensacola* and *Northampton* were torpedoed in quick succession by eight destroyers under Tanaka's command. Good damage control saved three of them but the *Northampton* caught fire and had to be abandoned.

Much of the Japanese success in these night actions depended on the long accurate running of the 24-inch 'Long Lance' torpedo. Eventually cruisers provided the solution, using their

6-inch and 8-inch guns with radar control to lay down barrage fire at maximum range. This technique was used successfully by Rear-Admiral Merrill in the Battle of Empress Augusta Bay in November 1943. The new light cruisers of the *Cleveland* Class were coming forward, armed with twelve 6-inch guns and equipped with the latest fire-control radar. The rapid fire of the 6-inch was better suited to this sort of action than the 8-inch, and so the new *Baltimore* Class ships were more usually allocated to the carrier task forces.

Once the United States and other Allied forces broke out of the Solomons cruisers were usually confined to the less glamorous roles of carrier escort and shore bombardment. As ever the cruiser could make up in numbers for the small amount of battleships and there was no diminution of their importance. The US Navy had started an enormous program of cruiser construction early in 1942 to supplement the 1940 'Two-Ocean Navy' program. Three basic types were in hand, the *Cleveland* Class light cruisers, the *Baltimore* Class heavy cruisers and also the *Atlanta* Class antiaircraft cruisers.

The 10,000-ton *Cleveland*s were a development of the prewar *Brooklyn*s, sacrificing the redundant fifth triple 6-inch turret for a heavier AA battery of six twin 5-inch guns. They set a record as the largest class of cruisers ever ordered. Even allowing for nine converted to light aircraft carriers 30 were completed between 1940 and the end of the war. The *Baltimore* Class resembled the *Cleveland*s in being flush-decked with two slim capped funnels but their designers were now free of the 10,000 ton limit and so they rose to 13,600 tons – proof that the original limit had been too small for a balanced design.

These two classes were a logical progression from previous US cruisers but the third class marked a radical departure. The *Atlanta* Class resembled the British *Dido* Class AA cruisers in being much smaller (6000 tons) than the standard 'fleet' cruiser. Although also intended to fulfil a fleet AA defense role with the massive armament of eight twin 5-inch dual-purpose gun mountings (three forward, two on the beam and three aft) their main role was to act as a type of destroyer-leader and fight the big Japanese 'Special Type' destroyers.

There is one more class of American cruisers to be mentioned. This is the somewhat freakish *Alaska* Class, displacing 29,000 tons and armed with nine 12-inch guns. Although loosely referred to as battlecruisers they bore no resemblance to the original type and were always rated by the US Navy as large cruisers (CB). The *Alaska* Class was built partly as a result of an erroneous intelligence assessment of Japanese intentions but mainly as a result of somewhat morbid fears that the 8-inch gun would not be adequate to protect the carriers from attack by enemy cruisers. A very fast long-range cruiser with guns ranging out to 21,000 yards made some sense, but what resulted was a very expensive ship of limited utility. Only two were

completed, the *Alaska* and *Guam* in 1944, and although they proved magnificent steamers they never justified the colossal effort which went in to building them.

Two more designs were prepared during the war, and although they were not completed until much later they show how far the cruiser could be taken. On a displacement of 17,000 tons the armament of the *Des Moines* Class remained as nine 8-inch guns but the extra weight was used to provide fully automatic loading for them. The Mark XVI 8-inch 55-caliber gun fired shells with wrapped charges at a range of 10 per minute, about four times as fast as earlier marks of 8-inch. Without doubt these ships were the most powerful cruisers ever designed (excepting the *Alaska* Class) capable of delivering a heavy volume of fire up to 14 miles away. The *Worcester* Class, at 14,700 tons, ran the *Des Moines* Class a close second but it was intended to be an expansion of the AA cruisers, using a new dual-purpose automatic 6-inch 47-caliber twin mounting in place of the 5-inch 38 caliber.

As the end of the war approached the vast American cruiser program began to slow down to release shipyard resources for landing craft. In 1944–45 35 cruisers of all types were cancelled for the US Navy now had as many as it could man. Even so several others were not completed until some time after the war was over.

The US Navy took the cruiser to its ultimate in 1941–45, producing ships of unparalleled fighting power. What characterized American cruisers was their uniformity of equipment and massive antiaircraft armaments. Although other classes of warships had their virtues it could be argued that the US Navy had more conspicuous success with its bigger cruiser designs than anyone else. Their Washington Treaty designs set them on the right road, and right through to 1945 there was little need to make more than minor improvements. The Japanese cruisers, by comparison, showed more ingenuity but caused their designers many headaches. Nothing like the disastrous story of the *Mogami* Class happened in the US Navy and apart from a premature abandonment of torpedo tubes the designs met wartime requirements.

Although the arguments against 8-inch guns had some validity, the arrival of radar on the scene finally justified the choice. With radar-controlled gunnery hits could be obtained at maximum range and therefore the extra range of the 8-inch gun was more likely to be decisive. However it was in their high endurance and mechanical reliability that American cruisers showed real superiority. As had been foreseen in 1919 the battleground was to be the Pacific and ships would have to steam immense distances. The dollars invested in machinery and boiler improvements were well spent.

Top right: Secondary armament of the *Northampton*.
Right: Blistered paint on the guns of the *Salt Lake City*.
Below: The heavy cruiser *Baltimore* seen in 1944.

MISSILES AND NUCLEAR POWER

Even if the battleship had not been ousted from her position as the premier type of warship by the aircraft carrier, running and manpower costs made her an anachronism. In the years after 1945 there was still a need for heavy gunpower, and this combined with lower running costs to keep the cruiser in favor.

As part of the search to find an answer to the Kamikaze attacks in 1944 the US Navy initiated the 'Bumblebee' program, to develop a guided weapon capable of destroying high-speed aircraft. After a decade of development the Terrier guided missile was ready. Terrier was a big weapon 27-feet long and weighing more than a 16-inch shell without its associated fire control and radar, so there was little point in trying to install it in small warships. The logical ship to take Terrier to sea was a big cruiser and in 1954 two *Baltimore* Class, the *Boston* and *Canberra*, were taken in hand for reconstruction. When they reappeared in 1955–56 they were the world's first guided-missile cruisers.

The profile was completely altered, the entire after superstructure and triple turret being replaced by platforms carrying two twin-arm launchers, two directors on tall pedestals and a big platform for new radars. Below decks the former shell rooms and magazines were replaced by mechanical stowage and loading gear for a total of 144 Terrier missiles. Two missiles could be

Far right, top: The after 6-inch and 3-inch turrets of HMS *Blake*.
Far right: The Soviet *Kara* Class guided missile cruiser, *CG.539*.
Above right: British officers inspect the wreck of the *Hipper*, destroyed by bombing of Kiel harbor.
Below: The cruiser *Savannah* seen in Algiers in 1943. Two Liberty ships burn in the background after an air attack.

launched every 30 seconds. Terrier was a beam-riding missile, homing on to hostile aircraft by following a radar beam generated by the fire-control director. The success of this conversion led to six of the *Cleveland* Class being converted in 1956–60. The next conversion was much more elaborate than anything previously envisioned. The cruisers *Albany*, *Chicago* and *Columbus* were earmarked. The hulls were stripped down to the weather deck and entirely new superstructures built up, comprising two lofty 'macks' or combined 'mast-and-stack' with a high narrow bridge. There were twin-arm Talos missile launchers forward and aft and Tartar missile launchers on either side of the bridge. This gave superb all-round coverage, with the 70-mile Talos for long-range defense and the Tartar to deal with targets which got through the outer screen.

All three saw considerable active service after completing their reconstructions in 1963–64. In 1972 the *Chicago* covered the minelaying operation off Haiphong. When North Vietnamese interceptors were picked up on radar moving towards the mine-laying aircraft, the cruiser's Talos missiles were able to shoot down one MiG at a range of 48 miles and turn the rest away. Another use for Talos was with an anti-radiation homing head, allowing them to destroy radar sites in North Vietnam. But their hulls and steam plant were ageing fast and in August 1976 the

Columbus was struck off the effective list and her two sisters have now gone the same way.

By 1968 the original conversions were considered unsuitable for defending the Fleet against air attack because of the obsolescence of the BW-1 Terrier missile systems. Paradoxically, they proved extremely useful off Vietnam because they had retained their forward triple 8-inch guns. Both they and unconverted heavy cruisers served on the 'gun-line' in Vietnam, pounding enemy positions far more effectively than ground attack aircraft. The virtue of naval bombardment has always been that it can be sustained for as long as ammunition lasts, and its methodical and repetitive nature has a worse effect on enemy morale than occasional air strikes, however devastating.

The advantage of converting cruisers was exactly the same as it had always been; they had useful endurance and their size meant that they could carry a worthwhile number of missiles. Once the US Navy had shown the way others followed suit. The Royal Netherlands Navy rebuilt the *De Zeven Provincien* on similar lines, with a twin Terrier launcher and fire control in place of the after turret, while the Italians did much the same for the old light cruiser *Giuseppe Garibaldi*.

All these conversions of World War II cruisers suffered from the inherent problems of pressing new wine into old bottles, but

Left: The nuclear-powered cruiser *Virginia* looks under-armed but because of her elaborate fire-control systems is a very powerful warship indeed.
Top right: The old French cruiser *Jeanne d'Arc* and behind the more modern *La Resolue*, seen in 1964.
Right: The carrier *Nimitz* and the cruisers *California* and *South Carolina* seen at Norfolk Navy Yard.
Below: The profile of the French *Suffren* is dominated by her radar systems.

Above: The Soviet *Sverdlov* Class cruiser *Aleksendr Suvorov* seen during a Soviet exercise in the Philippine Sea area.
Left: The *Kresta II* Class cruiser *Marshal Voroshilov* photographed in 1979.
Below: The Soviet *Kirov* nuclear-powered, guided-missile cruiser on her trials in 1980. This large and powerful ship has weapons systems suited to a range of air defense, surface and antisubmarine missions.

they wrung a few more years service out of ships which might otherwise have gone to the scrapyard, and showed that the cruiser could adapt to modern warfare. In the 1950s it had been fashionable to predict that the cruiser would soon follow the battleship into obsolescence. Nobody made such a suggestion after seeing the exceptional performance of the missile cruisers in the Vietnam War.

Although most navies gave up the idea of big gun-armed cruisers after World War II there was one exception. The Soviet Union had been expanding its navy before the German invasion in June 1941 and although much of the new construction had been destroyed either by enemy action or by the Russians to keep it out of German hands, a number of hulls survived in 1945.

Joseph Stalin's naval Commander in Chief, Admiral Kuznetsov was given funds to complete five of the *Chapaev* Class. These were improved editions of the prewar *Kirov* Class, and like them had been designed with Italian technical assistance. While work was being restarted on the *Chapaev* Class a new class of slightly improved and enlarged ships was laid down. This was the handsome *Sverdlov* Class, also mounting four triple 150mm (5.9-inch). The *Sverdlov* made a big impression in the West and speculation was rife about her capabilities, but her essentially old-fashioned features were overlooked. Looked at today, her optical range-finding equipment and low-angle main armament stamp her as a prewar design. It is doubtful if she would have made much of an impression against Western navies, but in the 1950s it was fashionable to talk luridly of the 'Sverdlov cruiser-threat.'

In all 20 *Sverdlov* keels were laid but after the death of Stalin a mood of reaction set in. Kruschev admitted as much when he told the West that he was scrapping all his cruisers and recommended them to do the same. As with other Soviet pronouncements this was not quite what happened, and only six incomplete hulls were scrapped. Unlike other navies' cruisers those surviving were not reconstructed, although three were given experimental guided-missile installations aft.

In 1957 an entirely new type of ship was laid down, the *raketny kreiser* or 'rocket cruiser.' Known to the West under the code-name *Kynda* but actually called the *Grozny* Class, four were built between 1957–65. It is possible that as many as 12 were planned, but with eight very large missile tubes on deck, reloads in the superstructure, a surface-to-air missile launcher and

massive radars it is almost certain that severe stability problems were encountered, so the program stopped at four ships. To Western observers the massive surface-to-surface missile, code-named SS-N-3 or *Shaddock*, with its range of 170 miles gave the Soviet Navy a big advantage. Immediately they were seen to be successors to the *Sverdlov*, roaming the oceans and hunting down American aircraft carriers.

A closer look at the *Kynda* raises some doubts about the role assumed for them by most Western commentators. For one thing the 170-mile range for the SS-N-3 missiles could only be achieved if the missile received mid-course guidance, and as the *Kynda* design does not include a helicopter it must be assumed that she was intended for waters dominated by Soviet air power – not the world's oceans. This limitation is confirmed by the lack of a high-performance search radar, and the much-praised doubling up of fire-control radars, two sets were fitted, now seems to be a reflection of their lack of reliability, not a doubling of efficiency. Another interesting point is that although they were built for the Northern Fleet they were subsequently modified to reduce topweight and sent to the less demanding Pacific and Black Sea areas.

During the 1950s and 1960s there was a tacit assumption that the day of the cruiser was over. To many observers the only justification for all the cruiser conversions was their capacity to take the bulky first generation surface-to-air missiles such as Terrier and Talos.

All this changed in 1957 when the United States Navy laid the keel of a 14,000-ton nuclear-powered cruiser (CLGN-160, later redesignated CGN-160 and finally CG-9) to be called *Long Beach*. Not only was she the first cruiser built since 1945 but was also the world's first nuclear-powered surface warship and the first to be armed with nothing but guided missiles. The planned displacement was to have been 7800 tons but this rose to 11,000 tons after a second Terrier missile system was added to the design. A subsequent decision to add the long-range Talos aft (both Terrier systems were forward) pushed standard displacement up to 14,200 tons.

Having reactors to provide steam meant that uptakes and funnels were dispensed with, and for the first time designers could lay out the superstructure to suit themselves. The result was a big square block of bridgework with unique 'billboard' radar arrays on the outer faces, free from corrosive funnel gases and sited for maximum efficiency. Although the speed of 30 knots was modest it was constantly available and so the *Long Beach* was an ideal carrier escort. In fact after she was completed in 1961 she operated with the nuclear-powered attack carrier *Enterprise* and it was soon realized that conventionally-powered escorts were simply not suited to the task as they used so much fuel in the high-speed steaming required to keep up with the *Enterprise*.

The C1W reactors in *Long Beach* were similar to the A2W type in the *Enterprise*. Work had also started on a prototype reactor small enough to be installed in a 'destroyer-sized' ship. In 1959 the keel of the first nuclear-powered DLG or frigate was laid. The *Bainbridge* (DLGN-25) displaced 7600 tons and differed from

the *Long Beach* principally in having her two Terrier missile systems at either end of the ship, but no Talos. She also had rotating radar scanners on tall lattice masts instead of the 'billboards.'

The commissioning of the *Bainbridge* in 1962 gave the US Navy the world's first nuclear task force with the *Enterprise* and *Long Beach*, and there was talk of an all-nuclear navy. However, the cost was staggering, $332.85 million for the *Long Beach* and $163.2 million for the *Bainbridge*. Fiscal Year 1958 therefore included money for three 'fossil-fuelled' frigates, and six more were authorized the following year.

There was a return to nuclear power in 1962 when DLGN-35 was authorized, later to commission in 1967 as the *Truxtun*. She was in effect a nuclear edition of the *Belknap* Class, but with the 5-inch gun forward and the Terrier missiles aft. All 20 frigates in commission were reclassified as cruisers on 30 June 1975, a change which was confusing at the time, but entirely logical because of their role as fast carrier escorts.

The Soviet Navy, having pioneered the surface-strike cruiser in the *Kynda* Class, decided to rectify their more obvious faults in the next class. Work apparently started in 1964, code-named *Kresta* by NATO. When she first appeared in 1970 the *Vize-Admiral Drozd* looked quite different from her predecessors, with a massive central mack and tall radar tower. Instead of the fore-and-aft quadruple missile tubes the *Kresta* carried two pairs, one on either side of the bridge. Current Western thinking is that no reloads for the SS-N-3 *Shaddock* missiles are carried, although there might well be space for four reloads in the forward deckhouse. Two important deficiencies in the *Kynda* design were rectified; a helicopter hangar is provided right aft and the big air-warning radar is sited on the mack. The *Hormone-B* helicopter carries a radar and could provide mid-course guidance for the *Shaddock*.

The appearance of a modified version of the *Kresta* in 1970 complicated assessment of this Soviet design. The *Kronstadt* was code-named *Kresta II*. The main external difference from the four *Kresta I* was the redesign of the pyramidal tower amidships

Above: Stern view of HMS *Bristol* showing her Sea Dart missile system and Type 909 radar.
Left: The Soviet 'antisubmarine cruiser' *Kiev* in 1976.
Below left: HMS *Tiger* in 1977 with hangar and flight deck aft.
Below: The Italian helicopter cruiser *Vittorio Veneto*.

Above: Old gun-armed cruisers were used to provide shore bombardments during the Vietnam War. This is the *Canberra.*

to carry a new 3-D radar antenna and the replacement of the horizontal missile tubes by missile launchers in quadruple boxes angled up at 20 degrees. For some years this was reputed to be a new surface-to-surface missile, code-named SS-N-10. However it is now believed to be the SS-N-14, an antisubmarine missile with a range of up to 30 miles. This helps to explain the Soviet designation for the *Kresta II, Bolshoi Protivo Lodochny Korabl* or large antisubmarine ship, but it casts doubt over the ship's ability to defend herself or pose a threat to Western surface ships.

The *Kresta II* is clearly more successful than the *Kresta I* for 10 ships have been completed since 1970. They have been superseded by the similar but larger (8200 tons) *Kara* type. The armament of the *Kresta II* has been repeated in roughly the same layout but instead of the rather ugly mack there is a big square funnel. Although some Western authorities credit the *Kara* type with massive power and speed these are probably grossly overestimated; on roughly the same dimensions as an American nuclear cruiser capable of 30 knots she is claimed to have double the power and 34 knots.

In mid-1967 the Russians produced their first helicopter carrier, the 14,500-ton *Moskva.* She and her sister *Leningrad* are officially described as *Protivo Lodochny Kreiser* or antisubmarine cruisers. In general layout they resemble the French *Jeanne d'Arc* in having a center-line superstructure and conventional guided-missile cruiser bow, but a flight deck aft as if two different ships have been joined together. Unlike the British *Invincible* Class they are obviously not intended to operate anything but helicopters. Clearly the Soviet Navy was providing itself with a more effective antisubmarine arm by taking more ASW helicopters to sea.

Of even more significance was the next class of 'antisubmarine cruisers,' the *Kiev* Class. When she appeared late in 1976 she threw Western observers into a fever of speculation for she was clearly intended to operate fixed-wing aircraft. The presence of a flight of Yak-36 *Forger* VTOL aircraft on her flight deck immediately sparked fears that the Soviet Navy was intending to take on the US Navy on the high seas and by developing a much greater offensive capacity.

On closer examination the *Kiev* proves to be as much of a hybrid as the *Moskva,* with a heavy battery of eight SS-N-12 surface-to-surface missiles, a surface-to-air missile launcher and a twin 76mm gun mounting on the forecastle. The Yak-36 also has severe limitations as a shipboard strike aircraft in that it cannot make a short take-off, only vertical. This means that it must have much lower endurance than the Harriers used by the US Marines or the Royal Navy. In many minor respects the flying arrangements take second place to the 'cruiser' characteristics, particularly in the shapes of the forecastle and superstructure and the sheer weight of armament. The second ship of the class, the *Minsk,* does not display any major changes, so it seems likely that the Soviet designation is an accurate reflection of their hybrid nature as cruiser/carriers.

Far from being tempted to follow the Soviet line the US Navy remains convinced that the functions of aircraft carriers and their cruiser escorts are best kept apart. As long as nuclear carriers continue to be built there is a need for nuclear-powered cruisers to keep pace with them and protect them, conversely using the carrier's aircraft as part of their own defenses. This concept was amply proved in the late 1960s, when the carrier *Enterprise* and the *Long Beach, Bainbridge* and *Truxtun* operated together in the Vietnam War. The authorization of a second nuclear carrier, the *Nimitz* (CVN.68) in 1967 was therefore accompanied by approval for a nuclear cruiser, followed a year later by funds for a second ship.

The USS *California* (CGN.36) and *South Carolina* (CGN.37) are two of the most powerful warships in the world, and as the epitome of modern design deserve a closer look. At first glance they seem devoid of armament, with only two single-arm launchers for the Standard SM-1 missile and two lightweight 5-inch gun mountings. However, their fighting power cannot be gauged by counting gun barrels and launchers. The sensors, the surveillance and tracker radars and the massive bow-sonar, combined with a comprehensive computer suite to process their data, enable the weapons to be used far more effectively than ever before. For example the SPG-60 radar can acquire air targets at a range of 75 miles and track them automatically. It provides a fifth channel to back up the four SPG-51D missile-control trackers, and its computer can handle up to 120 different targets automatically. Thus, although only five missile targets can be engaged *simultaneously,* the computer allows rapid shifts from track to track and selection of the most urgent targets. When the more advanced SM-2 missile is available the system will become even more potent, because the missile's guidance system only requires assistance in the initial and terminal phases of its flight.

Two more nuclear carriers, the *Dwight D Eisenhower* and *Carl Vinson,* followed the *Nimitz.* To provide them with escorts four more nuclear cruisers have been built, the *Virginia* Class. They are basically similar to the *California* Class, but with many minor improvements such as a helicopter hangar and an improved missile launcher capable of launching both Standard surface-to-air and Asroc antisubmarine missiles.

The next step forward was a major improvement in weaponry based on a new fleet defense system called Aegis. The heart of Aegis is a new fixed-array radar which sends out pencil-like beams; as soon as one picks up a target several nearby beams are directed to it as well. This enables the Aegis SPY-1 radar to start a smooth tracking of the target within one second, when a conventional radar would still be completing its first rotation. With four SPY-1 radars an Aegis system provides complete coverage which the SPG-62 trackers and the SM-2 missiles can exploit to the full.

In 1968–69, when development of Aegis was well advanced, the US Navy started to plan for a fleet of 30 nuclear Aegis ships. These were to have included destroyers with only one missile launcher and cruisers with two launchers, but of these only the four *Virginia* Class were authorized between 1971 and 1975. Delays in the Aegis program then resulted in the *Virginias* getting a conventional outfit of radars and missiles.

Above: Talos on the cruiser *Chicago* in 1967 off Vietnam. Two views of the Talos surface-to-air missile system.
Below: A missile is fired during maneuvers.

From 1975–77 Congress debated building a 17,000-ton 'Strike Cruiser', or CSGN. She was to be nuclear-powered and armed with Aegis, surface-to-air missiles and Tomahawk surface-to-surface cruise missiles, but the cost was a staggering $1500 million. Despite the vociferous claims of the nuclear lobby led by Admiral Rickover, in May 1977 the Senate Armed Services Committee gave its final verdict that the ship was too costly and over-designed for its role as a carrier escort.

The alternative was to resurrect the Aegis-armed destroyer, based on the hull of the *Spruance* Class destroyers. On a displacement of 9000 tons these destroyers are seaworthy enough to carry out a cruiser's duties, and late in 1979 the *DDG-47* Class became the *Ticonderoga* Class (CG-47). However this did not stop the authorization of four Aegis-equipped Modified *Virginia* Class in place of the eight strike cruisers requested in 1976. To help make up the numbers of Aegis systems Congress also urged that the existing *Virginia* Class should be refitted with the system as soon as possible.

As always the Soviet Union came up with a bigger and more impressive answer. In 1978 it was revealed that the Zhdanov yard in Leningrad was building a powerful 22,000-ton 'battle-cruiser' to be called *Kirov*. She is nuclear-powered and armed with air-defense and long-range surface missiles, and is presumably intended to screen the big aircraft carrier reported under construction in the Black Sea. Also building are three 12,000-ton cruisers, an expansion of the *Kara* design reputed to be called the *Sovietski Soyuz* Class. And so the cruiser-story comes full circle, with a new generation of super-cruisers about to dominate the oceans. This development, coupled with growing doubts about the cost and validity of the big strike carrier, may yet give the cruiser the prestige of being the most powerful warship type ever built.

Below: The US light cruiser *Trenton* in dry dock in the 1920s.

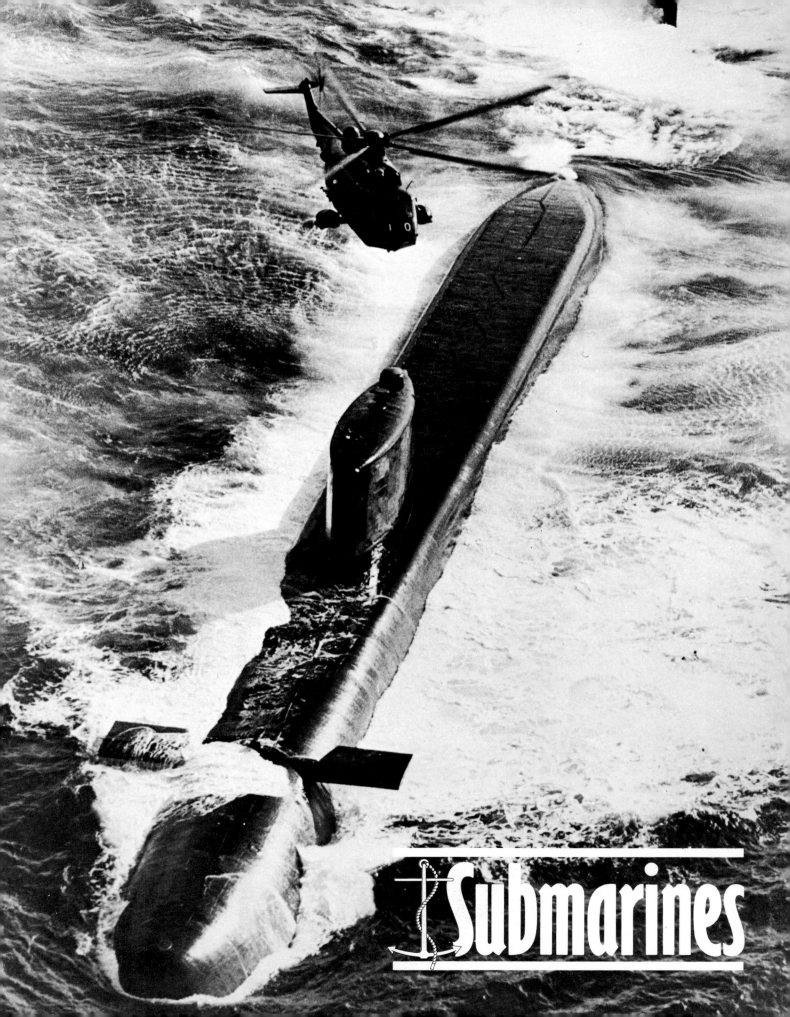

Submarines

Submarines

Previous page: A British Polaris submarine sets out on patrol from a Scottish base.
Page 201: A Sea King helicopter hovers over a British nuclear submarine.

THE FIRST U-BOATS

For centuries designers dreamed of submarines but the first practical design did not appear until 1578 when an Englishman, William Bourne described a submersible boat. He mastered a concept which eluded many later submarine designers by providing a simple mechanical means of varying the boat's total weight. He also solved the lack of fresh air by providing a hollow mast, but there is no record in his description of any form of propulsion, nor of any purpose, peaceful or otherwise, for his boat. The Dutch physician, van Drebbel, went a step further, and in 1624 built two submersibles propelled by oars. The purpose of submarines up to the middle of the eighteenth century was largely restricted to salvage or construction work on the sea bed, in other words an extension of the diving bell's capability.

An American, Robert Fulton, took the submarine a step further with his *Nautilus* in 1799 but despite convincing demonstrations neither the French or the British wanted anything to do with him. With nothing but hand-propulsion available and only the crudest of close-range weapons it was still nothing more than a toy.

In 1850 a Bavarian artillery sergeant called Wilhelm Bauer produced a submarine called the *Brandtaucher* or 'Fire Diver.' The first voyage in December 1850 was successful but little more than a month later the *Brandtaucher* was lost in Kiel harbor. Bauer was not discouraged by this setback, however, and produced a number of other designs for underwater craft. In 1855 he was allowed to build an improved 52 feet submarine called the *Seeteufel* or 'Sea Devil' for the Imperial Russian Navy.

The 'Davids,' built during the American Civil War by the Confederate States to break the Federal blockade, marked the next step forward. The original 'David' was hardly a submarine rather a submersible torpedo boat but she was driven by a steam engine. The 'Davids' did score some successes but their cost was exorbitant; two warships sunk and a third damaged for the loss of two submersibles (which had each sunk once before during training, with the loss of their entire crews).

In 1878 a Liverpool clergyman, the Reverend George Garrett, built a small egg-shaped boat and a year later started a second boat, christened the *Resurgam*. It was 40 feet long and used steam on the surface. Before submerging a full head of steam was raised to provide latent heat in special storage tanks. The Swedish arms manufacturer Thorsten Nordenfelt put up fresh capital to allow the building of a new boat at Stockholm to a design by Garrett. This boat was sold to Greece in 1883 and Turkey ordered two more in 1886 but they were not a success. They were, however, the first to use the Whitehead automobile torpedo. For the first time a submarine could attack a target from a safe distance.

The submarine still needed a workable means of underwater propulsion. The answer lay in the electric motor but early electricity generators were too heavy. The accumulator battery was also very heavy, but it did offer a way around the problem. A young Spanish naval officer designed a boat in 1886, powered by two 30hp electric motors using current stored in accumulators. The French soon grasped the implications and started work on designs of their own. In April 1887 the first submarine, the *Gymnote* or 'Eel,' was laid down. Her armament was a single 14-inch torpedo tube in the bow, and her electric batteries drove her at a theoretical maximum speed of 6½ knots. However the *Gymnote* relied totally on her accumulator batteries and these had to be recharged by a generator ashore or in another ship.

The next submarine ordered, the *Gustav Zédé*, was much larger. Although she gave a lot of trouble she provided invaluable experience, and convinced the French that the submarine was worth developing. In February 1896 the Minister of Marine proposed an open competition to produce designs for a 200-ton submarine with a range of 100 miles on the surface, and no

Below: The CSS *C L Hunley*, a hand-cranked submersible, sank the Federal sloop *Housatonic* during the American Civil War.

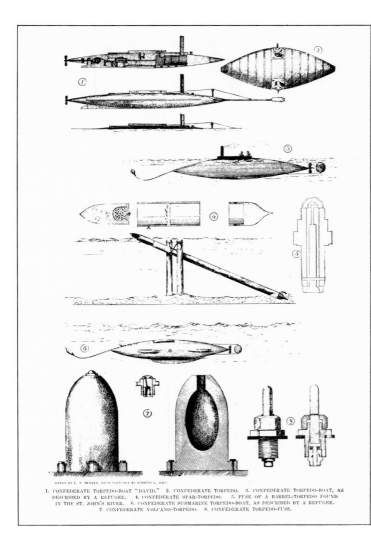

1. CONFEDERATE TORPEDO-BOAT "DAVID." 2. CONFEDERATE TORPEDO. 3. CONFEDERATE TORPEDO-BOAT, AS DESCRIBED BY A REFUGEE. 4. CONFEDERATE SPAR-TORPEDO. 5. FUSE OF A BARREL-TORPEDO FOUND IN THE ST. JOHN'S RIVER. 6. CONFEDERATE SUBMARINE TORPEDO-BOAT, AS DESCRIBED BY A REFUGEE. 7. CONFEDERATE VOLCANO-TORPEDO. 8. CONFEDERATE TORPEDO-FUSE.

Above: A modern model of Bushnell's *Turtle* incorporates the results of the latest historical research.
Left: Confederate 'torpedoes' and torpedo boats included not only submersibles but mines as well
Below: The French *Amphitrite* (1906) served for twenty years.

Top: The Italian FIAT firm built the 'F' Class to the designs of General Laurent.
Above: The *Naiade* of 1901 was too small to be effective and was out of service by 1914.
Below: French submarines like the *Clorinde* (1907) were noted for their low silhouette.

fewer than 29 designs were submitted from all over the world. The winner was a Frenchman, Maxime Laubeuf, whose remarkable boat, the *Narval* had two propulsion systems, a 220hp steam engine for surface running and an 80hp electric motor for running underwater. But most important of all, the steam engine could also run a dynamo to recharge the batteries, and so the effective range of the *Narval* was much greater than the all-electric boats.

Despite the importance of Laubeuf his fame has been eclipsed by that of John P Holland, who had been designing submarines since 1875. In 1893 he entered a United States' Navy competition to choose a submarine design. Only two other inventors submitted designs, Lake and Baker. The Baker boat quickly dropped out of the competition and as Simon Lake did not complete his prototype promptly the Ordnance Bureau awarded the contract to Holland. The boat, called the *Plunger*, was launched in 1897 after a number of changes and delays. So many changes were made against the designer's wishes that he withdrew from the contract and ordered his Holland Boat Company to build a second submarine at his own expense. His faith was justified by the total failure of the *Plunger* to pass her trials; the boat was never accepted by the Navy and the contract was cancelled. The trials of the *Holland*, by comparison, were a great success, and the US Navy bought her in 1900. By a year later a further seven of similar type were building and the British had taken out a license to build five for the Royal Navy.

The *Holland* design differed from the French *Narval* in several ways. She also had a dual propulsion system, but used a 45hp gasoline engine for surface running, giving more power for less weight as well as more reliable starting and stopping. This produced two advantages, the boat could be smaller and it could dive faster than the French boat.

The Germans, of all the major naval powers, were the last to show an interest, for Admiral Tirpitz saw submarines as a threat to his plans for a big battle-fleet. However the firm of Krupps built a small submarine for Russia in 1902–03, and were then asked by the Russians to tender for three more boats. These were known as the *Karp* class, and a fourth unit, almost identical, became the German *U.1* in 1906. She had a Körting kerosene engine, which was better than the gasoline engine of the Hollands. It had one severe drawback, however. It gave off dense clouds of smoke which gave away the submarine's position, and only when the Diesel engine was perfected was surface propulsion satisfactory.

By 1904, therefore, the broad outlines of the modern submarine were settled. The three big advances, the electric accumulator battery, the diesel engine and the self-propelled tor-

Above: The German 'UB' Class of small U-Boats proved to be useful in the North Sea. *UB.4* is pictured at Zeebrugge, an important German submarine base in World War I.

pedo were to be steadily improved as the years went by, but no other fundamental change was necessary for another 50 years. The submarines of 1904 were essentially the types that would revolutionize naval warfare in 1914, yet ten years earlier only two workable submarines existed. It had been a remarkably short period of gestation.

Although much lip-service had been paid to the effect of submarines on naval warfare the world's navies in 1914 had little idea of how to use them. All the belligerents and the neutrals regarded themselves as bound by the provisions of International Law and the Hague Convention of 1899 concerning the conduct of war at sea. It was assumed that a sub-

marine, like any other warship, was not permitted to fire on an unarmed merchant ship not acting in a hostile manner. The submarine would have to stop the merchant ship and examine her papers to ascertain that she was in fact trading on behalf of the enemy. If the papers indicated that she was carrying contraband the ship would have a prize crew put aboard to sail her to a port of examination. The submarine could, of course, sink the ship and forego the prize money, and if the weather was too

rough for taking to the boats the crew were to be taken aboard the submarine as prisoners.

The Prize Regulations, as they were called, favored the British and the French with their large merchant fleets, but they took little account of the peculiar nature of the submarine. To stop and search a merchant ship the submarine had to come to the surface, thereby forfeiting her principal advantage. Her tiny crew was too small to allow a prize crew to be spared and there was no room aboard for prisoners.

A submarine which endeavored to keep to these rules would either expose herself to counter-attacks from enemy warships or would be able to sink no more than one or two ships on each cruise. In spite of these drawbacks, however, some thought had been given to using submarines against commerce, and on 20 October 1914 *U.17* made history by capturing the small steamer *Glitra* off Norway.

Most naval officers still regarded the enemy's warships as the true target for the submarine, and the first successes bore out this belief. As soon as war broke out both the British and Germans sent out submarines to observe and report on warship movements. The British set up a patrol line in the Heligoland Bight, and acting on reports from these submarines planned a successful raid on the German light forces late in August 1914. Similarly the Germans sent their U-Boats out on an offensive patrol as far north as the Orkneys, to find out what the British were doing.

Both sides were disappointed. The British found that their torpedoes were running under their targets because the warhead was heavier than the pre-war practice head, while the Germans found that extended cruising put an unexpected strain on machinery. The limited field of vision through a periscope

made target identification much harder than anyone had imagined in peacetime, and there were many wrong guesses. The early successes against warships were as much the result of the victim's carelessness as the skill of submariners.

On 22 September a single U-Boat, *U.9*, sank three armored cruisers, the *Aboukir*, *Cressy* and *Hogue*. These three old ships, with little protection against modern torpedoes and carrying large crews of reservists, were known to be vulnerable and the order cancelling their patrols was already drafted. The senior officer of the squadron assumed that the first ship had been mined, and so Kapitänleutnant Otto Weddigen was given time to reload his torpedo tubes and work *U.9* into an ideal attacking position between the two remaining cruisers, with both forward and after tubes bearing. Weddigen's reputation as the first U-Boat 'ace' was confirmed when three weeks later he torpedoed another old cruiser, the *Hawke* off Aberdeen. Yet here again, the British cruiser was lying stopped in the open sea to transfer mail, and there were other examples of ships piping 'Hands to Bathe' or steaming slowly in waters known to be patrolled by U-Boats.

The Royal Navy had moved its main fleet base from the southern dockyards to a new base at Rosyth before the war, but on the outbreak of war the Grand Fleet moved to Scapa Flow, a large natural anchorage in the Orkneys. The news of the U-Boats' foray to the Orkneys was followed by a submarine scare in the Flow itself, and although no U-Boat got into Scapa Flow throughout the war the fear was enough to paralyze the Grand Fleet. Until Scapa Flow could be defended with nets, blockships, guns and searchlights it was necessary to send the whole fleet away to the west coast of Scotland. This was the first major strategic victory scored by submarines, for they had forced an entire fleet away from its chosen area of operations, and had the Germans been in a position to take advantage of it they might have caught the Royal Navy badly off balance. As things turned out there were not enough U-Boats and those that

Below: *E.6* was one of the famous 'E' Class, which formed the backbone of the Royal Navy's submarine force in World War I.

existed were not yet reliable enough to be risked far from their bases, while the High Seas Fleet did little to take advantage of the British withdrawal. The chance passed, and once the Grand Fleet returned to the Orkneys it refastened its grip on the German Fleet; its base remained inviolate right to the end.

When war broke out the German Navy had 29 U-Boats (U-Boat = *Unterseeboot*) in service. The original boat, *U.1* had been developed into the *U.27* Class, of which *U.30* was still to complete, but a further 20 boats were on order. This modest program reflects the German High Command's obsession with the surface fleet, and for a long time the admirals continued to think that the main role of their U-Boats was to wage a war of attrition against British warships, either by direct attack or by using the surface fleet to draw the British fleet into a 'submarine trap.'

The German Navy's submarines proved to be well-designed and the current class was put into quantity production. A new small or coastal type, the 'UB' Class was also started to make use of available Körting kerosene engines, and the first mine-layers or 'UC' Class were also ordered. In the summer of 1915 the British were mystified by reports of damage to merchant ships, but in July 1915 a steamer reported that she had collided with a submerged object, and when divers went down they found that the newly completed *UC.2* had blown herself up with her own mines.

The sinking of the *Glitra* by *U.17* encouraged the German naval staff in the growing belief that submarines could and should be used against British shipping. The ruthlessness with which Great Britain enforced the blockade also weakened any scruples entertained about violation of international law. For example the British even declared foodstuffs to be contraband, claiming that the German government had commandeered all food supplies. Allied propaganda made good use of any mistakes made by the U-Boats; for example the sinking of the SS *Amiral Ganteaume* by *U.24* off Cap Gris Nez in October 1914 was de-

Above: Early U-Boats are moored at Hamburg, including (from left) *U.22, U.20, U.19* and *U.21.*

nounced as an atrocity because she was carrying Belgian refugees, but knowing how little the U-Boat's commander could have seen through his periscope it is more likely that he mistook her for a French troopship. The time for a torpedo shot was often limited to a few seconds, during which the submarine CO was supposed to count numbers of people on board, boats, guns and even where they were positioned; guns mounted forward were classed as offensive armament whereas guns mounted aft were defensive.

Even without any flouting of the Germans' self-imposed

Below: The German U-Boat *U.35* sinks the British merchantman SS *Parkgate* by gunfire.

restrictions, the losses were heavy, 32,000 tons of British and 15,900 tons of French and neutral shipping sunk in January 1915 alone. By March the total had risen to 80,700 tons for that month, and two months later to 185,000 tons. Neutral opinion was outraged, and the United States was particularly angry, because the needs of the British and French war economies had opened new markets to all countries exporting war material of any kind. There was a residue of anti-British feeling in the United States, and the blockade did prevent some American exporters from sending goods to Germany, but the vast increase in British and French demands more than replaced the lost German markets. In addition there was a sentimental attachment between France and the USA which went back to the days of Marquis de Lafayette, Admiral de Grasse and the War of Independence. American public opinion was violently inflamed against Germany by stories of the rape of Belgium, and the deaths of American citizens in torpedoed ships did nothing to help.

On 4 February 1915, Germany announced that a War Zone existed around the British Isles, in which British and French ships would be sunk without warning. The declaration added that it would not always be possible to avoid attacks on neutral shipping; in other words the U-Boats could now sink merchantmen 'at sight' unless they saw a neutral flag. If the neutral countries could have been persuaded to forbid their ships to trade with the Allies the German gamble might have paid off, but the British blockade meant that a refusal to trade with the Allies would mean virtual bankruptcy for most shipping companies as there was not enough trade with other countries to keep everyone in business.

A great help to the U-Boat offensive was the German Army's conquest of bases on the Belgian coast. After the initial German land advance was held at the Battle of the Marne the front stabilized with its flank resting on the Flanders coast at Nieuport. The German Navy set up a completely new naval base at Ostend, with light forces based there and at Zeebrugge. U-Boats were based at the inland port of Bruges and reached the open sea by canals to Zeebrugge and Ostend. These Flanders bases reduced the distance and increased the time the U-Boats could spend on patrol in the Western Approaches and the Bristol and St George's Channels, their best hunting-grounds. British minefields and net-barriers in the Dover Straits were not effective as the U-Boats soon learned to make the passage on the surface at night, when the chances of being spotted were slim. To encourage the British in their belief that the Dover Straits were blocked U-Boats from German ports making the 'north-about' passage around the Orkneys were even ordered to show themselves occasionally to the patrols. Part of the problem was the lack of an efficient British mine, as later experience was to

Above: The end of the road: *UC.91* and a sister boat are tied up alongside one of the giant U-Cruisers after being surrendered in 1918. Below: A German submarine takes the lifeboat of a sunk enemy steamer in tow, April 1917.

show that minefields were an important weapon against submarines. Above all there was no adequate way of sinking a submarine even if she gave away her presence, the principal tactic for a surface ship being to ram or try to hit the U-Boat with gunfire. Both these methods pre-supposed that the submarine was either submerging or running at periscope depth; once a submarine dived deeper she was not only immune but undetectable.

The Allies' answer to the U-Boat offensive of 1915 was to increase the number of patrols by impressing all manner of ships into service. The battle fleet was screened by destroyers, whose speed and maneuverability gave them some chance of racing to the spot where a submarine had dived. They could then ram or try to hit the conning tower with a lucky shot from their guns. After the initial losses no major warships moved anywhere without her destroyer escorts, and as a result no battleship of the Grand Fleet was torpedoed by a U-Boat at sea throughout the war, but there were not enough destroyers to spare for

Above left: A wartime scene shows UB III U-Boats tied up alongside a temder.
Left: Two U-Boats keep a mid-ocean rendezvous.

Above: *U.35* loads torpedoes before leaving for a wartime cruise in April 1917.
Above right: A U-Boat runs on the surface.

escorting merchant ships. The Auxiliary Patrol was formed out of the large number of steam yachts, trawlers and drifters available, and after being armed with guns they were sent off to hunt for submarines. But the Atlantic and the North Sea are large areas, and no matter how many patrols were maintained there was always space in which submarines could hide. The huge volume of shipping in and out of British ports meant that the U-Boats merely had to wait for their victims to come to them – if a patrol vessel appeared the submarine could submerge and wait until it was safe to come up again and begin the process of destruction again.

Nothing more clearly illustrates how easy it was than the tragedy of the *Lusitania*. Most British transatlantic liners had been taken over by the Royal Navy in August 1914 for conversion to armed merchant cruisers or troopships, but the *Lusitania* was kept in commercial service between Liverpool and New York.

Much has been made of the fact that the *Lusitania* was carrying explosives, according to her manifest 5500 cases of small-arms ammunition and fuse nose-caps, totalling 37 tons. It has

even been claimed that she was armed, despite the absence of any evidence. The *Lusitania*'s small cargo (as a passenger liner she had in any case very little cargo-capacity, despite her size) comprised the most inert form of munitions in existence, and short of the ship catching fire there was little likelihood of it exploding.

When in due course on 7 May 1915 the *Lusitania* was torpedoed by *U.20* off Southern Ireland both sides for their own reasons tried to claim that the sinking had been planned. To the British it was all part of a plot to sink innocent ships, while the Germans claimed that as they knew of the *Lusitania*'s cargo their submarine was quite entitled to sink her. What both sides chose to ignore was that Kapitänleutnant Schwieger's own report showed that *U.20* had stumbled on the liner by chance.

The U-Boat had patrolled unsuccessfully in the Irish Sea for some days, and Schwieger had moved southwards to find more targets. He had been ordered to look out for troopships arriving from Canada and so headed for the Old Head of Kinsale, a popular landfall for transatlantic shipping. Schwieger was not disappointed, and soon saw smoke on the horizon. He was puzzled by the target's four funnels belching smoke, and assumed that he had stumbled on a submarine's worst enemy, a whole flotilla of destroyers. But then the 'flotilla' altered course, and to his joy Schwieger saw the massive bulk and four funnels of a

215

Above left: A blazing schooner sinks after being hit by gunfire from a U-Boat in mid-Atlantic.
Above: The 'commercial' U-Boat *Deutschland*.

large ship in the graticules of his periscope. On the assumption that most large liners were serving either as armed merchant cruisers or troopships, and as she carried no Red Cross markings to indicate a hospital ship he ordered one torpedo to be fired. The report made no mention of seeing guns, and as we have already mentioned, a submariner could see so little through a periscope that he would not have been looking for them, but it did mention a second explosion. This has been claimed to be the cargo of munitions 'tearing the heart out' of the ship, but any ordnance expert can testify to the fact that a quantity of rifle bullets and nose-caps some distance away from an explosion are unlikely to cause a further detonation. Schwieger himself attributed the second bang to boilers, coal or munitions, without further comment. If he was correct in thinking that his torpedo hit level with the funnels the more plausible explanation is that seawater rushing into the boiler-rooms caused an implosion of the boilers. A big liner of that vintage, with her numerous boiler-rooms, was doomed once flooding started on a large scale and the *Lusitania* went down rapidly with heavy loss of life. *U.20* slipped away unseen.

Below: The *R.2* was a British forerunner of the fast submarines of the post-1945 era. These streamlined craft exceeded 14 knots underwater as early as 1918.

Among the many dead were 159 American citizens, and the US government reaction was stronger than it had been previously. A note from Washington to Berlin demanded that U-Boats should refrain from torpedoing passenger ships. The Germans did not handle the diplomatic crisis tactfully, and maintained that they had warned passengers of the dangers, thereby giving further credence to the 'conspiracy' theory. The British, who had believed that the Germans would never dare to sink the *Lusitania*, were not averse to making capital out of the incident. Carefully skating round the point about the cargo (the contents of the manifest were published after the First World War), they connived at the idea of a planned sinking, although if anyone thought about the security implications, they would have realised that German agents would have had to be in command of the ship herself to achieve such a perfect interception.

The outcry forced the German government to slow down its onslaught on shipping, but in 1916 losses climbed steadily once more, until the monthly total reached over half a million tons. The Allies responded with 'Q-Ships,' decoy vessels fitted with concealed guns. The Q-Ship loitered in a likely area with the intention of luring an U-Boat to the surface for an easy sinking with her deck gun. If all went well a 'panic party' abandoned ship, leaving gun-crews aboard who would open fire as soon as the U-Boat came within range. Although a few spectacular suc-

cesses were scored the Q-Ship idea was greatly over-rated, and tied up skilled seamen who were needed elsewhere, without sinking enough submarines to justify itself. A variation on the decoy theme was to use trawlers and submarines together to stop U-Boats from shelling the fishing fleet. Among the trawler fleet would be one trawler towing, instead of a trawl, a small submarine. The submarine was in touch with the trawler by means of a telephone link, and could cast off the towing wire. The idea actually worked twice, although each time technical snags nearly ruined everything, and the submarines each sank a U-Boat.

The Allies also armed merchant ships to enable them to fight off U-Boats. In practice the provision of a small gun on the poop of a tramp steamer did little but boost the crew's morale. However bad the shooting from a submarine's deck-gun the shooting from the average steamer was probably much worse.

The arming of merchant ships inevitably led the Germans into upgunning their submarines. The 'cruiser-submarine' with her medium-caliber guns had a tremendous moral effect, and in Britain there was even talk of having to arm merchantmen with 6-inch or 7.5-inch guns. What the advocates of big submarine guns ignored was that against the thin plating of a merchant ship a 4-inch shell is as good as a 6-inch, bearing in mind that a submarine had such poor fire-control that she would have to approach relatively close to allow her gun-crew to achieve hits.

The theory of the cruiser-submarine was that she could drive off small warships by out-ranging their guns, but in practice no submarine was likely to win such a contest. One hit or near miss from a shell could damage the submarine sufficiently to prevent her from diving, whereas the submarine's shooting would have to be exceptionally good to cripple even a small warship.

The first German cruiser-submarines were actually converted from a series of big mercantile submarines, built in 1915–16 to run cargoes through the blockade. Their purpose was two-fold: to bring in special materials needed for the armaments industry and to prove to neutral opinion that Germany was not being strangled by the blockade. Unlike other submarines the cargo-carrying submarines were named, and the first, *Deutschland*, left Kiel in June 1916 carrying a small cargo of mail, chemical dyes and precious stones for Baltimore. She presented a tricky legal problem for the US Customs authorities but as she was clearly not armed she was entitled to be treated as a commercial vessel. The effect on the Americans was tremendous; crowds flocked to see the submarine after her arrival on 9 July, and again when she sailed for Bremen three weeks later, loaded with copper, nickel, silver and zinc. Although the size of her cargo would never have made her a commercial proposition the *Deutschland*'s propaganda value to Germany was enormous, but an attempt to repeat the performance backfired.

A second cargo-submarine, the *Bremen*, set out, bound for Newport, Rhode Island. She was accompanied by *U.53* under Kapitänleutnant Hans Rose, who had orders to 'blow a path' for the *Bremen* through any British warships which tried to bar her passage. Unfortunately British mines were more effective in doing the job and the *Bremen* disappeared without trace somewhere off the Orkneys, with the result that *U.53* arrived at Newport on 7th October by herself. The US Navy suddenly found itself with a belligerent nation's submarine lying off one of its naval bases, a situation for which the rule book did not cater. While the Navy frantically badgered the State Department and everyone else for instructions, Hans Rose finished

Far left: Crewmen of a U-Boat are wrapped up to keep out the cold and the damp.
Left: U-Boats pictured at their base at Bruges. Many German submarines were based at captured Belgian ports.
Right: A U-Boat crew strikes down a torpedo.
Below: *U.8* sinks after being damaged by a British destroyer in March 1915.

the amusing chat that he had been having with the naval officers at Newport and left as quietly as he had arrived. But what followed undid any goodwill that *U.53*'s visit might have engendered, for the U-Boat started to sink shipping within sight of Nantucket lightship. Rose was convinced that his mysterious visit had left the US Navy and Government with a deep impression of how powerful Germany's submarines were; before he had left Germany he had been told by Commodore Hermann Bauer (the chief of the U-Boat Arm) that bold action would silence the anti-German party in America and would result in the restrictions on the U-Boats being lifted. The reasoning behind this forecast is hard to follow, and the Germans evidently understood very little of American attitudes. In fact the Americans became even more worried about German intentions, while the US Navy started to take the submarine threat seriously indeed. Germany's leaders, furthermore, did not feel that the time was right to launch a second unrestricted U-Boat campaign, and so the second attempt to break the British blockade was also a failure. The *Deutschland* was converted to a military submarine with two torpedo tubes and four guns. Six more were ordered in February 1917, and the class were numbered *U151–157*, the *Deutschland* becoming *U.155*.

Not until February 1917 was permission given for unrestricted U-Boat warfare. It was a gamble, for the High Command knew that it was only a matter of time before the Americans came into

the war to rescue the French and British. If they could force the British to sue for peace the attitude of the Americans was irrelevant. With German submarines in command of the North Atlantic the Americans could not intervene in Europe, and Germany would then be free to deal with France at her leisure. It was an appealing proposition and one that the Navy favored. The High Seas Fleet knew that after the Battle of the Skagerrak (Jutland) in May 1916 that it could never win, and that it had been extremely lucky to escape destruction. Thereafter its best officers, petty officers and seamen were drafted to U-Boats and torpedo-boats in increasing numbers. The U-Boats ordered since 1914 were also coming into service, and the daily average of boats at sea was rising steadily from no more than 10 in mid-1915 to 30 by the end of 1916. In mid-1917 the figure would exceed 40 U-Boats, with more to come, and the Germans knew that the time had come to act.

The first results justified all the claims made by the U-Boat Arm. Within weeks the shipping losses rocketed to nearly 800,000 tons (April 1917). The British countermeasures proved quite inadequate, and no matter how many warships, auxiliary patrol vessels and Q-Ships were deployed, one ship in every four that entered the War Zone was certain to be sunk. When the United States entered the war in the same month, Admiral Sims of the US Navy went to London to confer with Sir John Jellicoe, the First Sea Lord, and was appalled to hear that the naval war was being lost, and that food stocks in the British Isles would only last six weeks. Every weapon that could be used against the submarine had been tried, and the Admiralty no longer knew which way to turn.

Yet the oldest weapon of all had not been tried, the sailing of merchant shipping in groups under the protection of warships. Convoy had been in use from the fourteenth century until the end of the Napoleonic Wars but somehow the impact of more recent technology had blinded naval officers to the simple fact that an attack on merchant shipping was easiest to defend against if the merchant ships were concentrated in groups. It seems an obvious statement to make, but the sea is a big area, and individual merchantmen could never conceivably be allocated their own escort. Convoy was the only way in which a limited number of warships could hope to protect the Allies' vast merchant fleet.

The argument over convoy took time to resolve. The British Prime Minister was in favor after hearing the views of the Cabinet Secretary, Maurice Hankey, and naval officers in the Trade Division. The Admiralty Board fought hard against it, however, and it was only French insistence in February 1917 that resulted in coal ships sailing from England to France being convoyed. During the April crisis the French colliers were suffering a loss rate of 0.19 percent as against 25 percent elsewhere. Reluctantly the Admiralty allowed the first ocean convoy to sail at the end of April, and much to their surprise a miracle occurred: within a month the loss rate fell from 25 percent to 0.24 percent. By November 84,000 ships had been convoyed, of which only 257 were sunk.

For the U-Boats' convoy meant the end of easy pickings, for they could no longer lie in wait for whatever ship might come along. When smoke was seen on the horizon it heralded the arrival of 10 to 20 merchantmen surrounded by destroyers, sloops and patrol vessels, and often accompanied by an airship. All the U-Boat commanders' reports bear out the fact that the seas suddenly emptied, and an important side-effect was that U-Boats could no longer rely on the gun as a cheap and quick means of sinking ships. Now it was numbers of torpedoes carried which determined the endurance of a U-Boat, and this alone helped to reduce the tonnage sunk.

The British and their Allies took the offensive against the

Above: U-Boats accounted for the majority of their victims with gunfire in World War I.
Above right: A UB I boat cruises on the surface, showing how small these 'tin torpedoes' were.
Below: British Auxiliary Patrol trawlers stand by a torpedoed merchantman in 1918.

U-Boats in 1917, using a new type of horned mine modelled on the high lethal German 'egg' mine with its electro-chemical Herz horn. Using information gained from cryptanalysis, destroyer-minelayers and submarines laid mines in the exit-routes from Heligoland and Flanders. As soon as a new route was selected for the U-Boats the minelayers would promptly mine it, and in this way the minelaying UC-Boats operating out of

Flanders were finally neutralized. In 1918 an even more sinister weapon was introduced, the first magnetic mine.

The U-Boats kept up the pressure until the end, but the combination of convoy and other measures prevented them from ever getting back to the position that they had enjoyed in April 1917. When the Armistice was signed in November 1918 one of its most important clauses related to the U-Boats, all of which had to be surrendered in Allied ports. The German Navy had built some 360 submarines during the war, and a further 400 had either been cancelled or lay incomplete in the shipyards. The U-Boat Arm sank over 11 million tons of shipping and damaged a further 7½ million tons, but to achieve this 178 U-Boats were lost, and 5364 officers and men, nearly 40 percent of personnel.

FORCING THE DARDANELLES

After the first timid beginning the submarine war in the Mediterranean took a new turn with the Anglo-French attack on the Dardanelles. The Allies could not get surface warships through the Straits, and so looked to their submarines to achieve something, while the Germans felt that they ought to make some effort to help their new Turkish allies.

The only submarines available were three old British 'B' Class boats and the French *Brumaire* and *Circé*, which had all been sent to the Dardanelles at the end of 1914 to help maintain the blockade of the Dardanelles. On 1 December *B.11* left on a perilous journey up the Straits to see if a submarine could breast the 4–5 knot current and dive through the five rows of mines known to exist at Chanak (Cannakale). She had an exciting passage through the Narrows but she was rewarded by finding the old armored cruiser *Messudieh* lying at anchor, apparently safe from attack. A single 18-inch torpedo was enough to sink the target, hardly an outstanding victory but one to offset the recent successes of the U-Boats in the North Sea.

As a direct result of *B.11*'s exploit the British and French sent more modern submarines to the Dardanelles and their arrival coincided with the Allied landings. The Anglo-French offensive was not going well and any interference with the Turks' supply-routes through the Sea of Marmora would benefit the hard pressed troops at Gallipoli. But forcing the Dardanelles was still very dangerous, even for a modern submarine.

The *E.15* tried it and ran aground, followed by the French *Saphir*; the Australian *AE.2* got through on 26 April only to be sunk, but her sister *E.14* followed her a day later. The French *Joule* was mined on 1 May, making the loss rate four submarines for every one that arrived in the sea of Marmora. But when the news got through that *E.14* had sunk three ships the Allies redoubled their efforts, and soon another six British submarines and the French *Turquoise* reached the Sea of Marmora.

The German *U.21* under Kapitänleutnant Hersing had also made a safe passage of the Dardanelles from Cattaro. Six of the small UB-Boats and four UC-Boats were sent to the Adriatic by rail to be reassembled at Cattaro, and three of the UB-Boats were sent to the Dardanelles to join Hersing at Constantinople. Two arrived safely but it was *U.21* which scored the first success. On 25 May Hersing spotted the old battleship *Triumph* firing at Turkish positions near Gaba Tepe. He had to wait two hours for a favorable shot, but when it came a single torpedo sent the *Triumph* down. Two days later he came upon another old battleship, HMS *Majestic* off Cape Helles, at anchor. She was surrounded by colliers and patrol vessels, but the man who had waited two hours to get the *Triumph* was not easily put off, and eventually a gap opened. Again a single torpedo sufficed to send the *Majestic* over on her beam ends. The obsolescence of the ships was immaterial; they had been sunk in full view of the troops fighting ashore and Hersing's feat was therefore all the more

Above: A view of the interior of the German submarine *Deutschland* showing the control room.
Below: *U.35*, the command of the 'ace' Arnauld de la Perière, about to submerge.

dramatic. The bombarding ships had to be withdrawn to Mudros, and at a crucial moment the presence of *U.21* put fresh heart into the Turkish troops.

Italy joined the war on the side of the Allies on 24 May 1915. Her large surface fleet offered the Austrian and German U-Boats tempting targets, but as she had only declared war on Austria the German submariners at Cattaro were in a difficult situation. The solution was a simple one; the German boats pretended to be Austrian until such time as Italy chose to include Germany among her enemies. *UB.15* and *UB.1* were among the boats reassembled at Cattaro, and they were nominally commissioned as *X* and *XI*, (in October 1915 the Austro-Hungarian Navy adopted the U-prefix with Arabic numerals). Among their successes in the Adriatic were the sinkings of the Italian submarines *Medusa* and *Nereide* and the armored cruisers *Amalfi* and *Giuseppe Garibaldi*.

The five small U-Boats sent to Turkey had been formed into a half-flotilla under Otto Hersing as senior officer. Her pursued a vigorous policy in the Black Sea and in the Sea of Marmora but had too few boats to deal with the Russian Fleet as well as the Allied submarines in the Sea of Marmora. The British submarines' campaign against the Turks is a classic of economy of effort, for a handful of submarines was able to dominate both land and sea communications for eight months. It was discovered that trains could be bombarded with deck-guns, and so British submarines followed the German trend towards heavier

guns. The campaign only ended in January 1916 when the Allies evacuated the Gallipoli Peninsula, but in that time submarines had virtually stopped all seaborne communication between Istanbul and the Gallipoli Peninsula.

The Mediterranean remained a good hunting ground for U-Boats right to the end. Some of their most notable successes were scored there, including the torpedoing of the battleships HMS *Cornwallis* and the French *Danton*. The introduction of convoy in 1917 brought the losses under control just as rapidly as it did in the Atlantic.

If British submarine operations in the North Sea were humdrum the same could not be said about the Baltic, where they equalled their achievements in the Sea of Marmora. The situation was similar to that in the Dardanelles: Russia was under pressure from the German Navy as well as on land, and any diversionary effort by the Royal Navy would reduce some of the strain. In October 1914, therefore, two 'E' Class submarines left their East Coast base bound for the Baltic via the Kattegat. Their port of destination was Libau (now Liepaja) but when the two boats arrived they found a scene of utter confusion. The Russians were blowing up ammunition and port installations before evacuating Libau in the face of the advancing German armies. The submarines were given a new base at Lapvik in the Gulf of Finland, and here they were able to repair the minor damage and wear and tear before getting down to business.

The Western Baltic was virtually a German lake, and it was used for training by the High Seas Fleet. The first boat, *E.1* had already fired at the cruiser *Viktoria Luise* but missed; *E.9* was more successful when she sank the destroyer *S.120* off Kiel. However, German warships were not the prime targets for the

Below: The Italian steamer SS *Stromboli* sinking in the Mediterranean in a picture taken from the attacking submarine.

Above: The salvaged hull of *UC.5* seen in dry dock at Harwich, showing her mine chutes.

two submarines, but rather the merchant ships carrying iron ore from Sweden. The Germans were soon convinced that a whole flotilla of boats was operating, and even convinced themselves that a mysterious depot ship was operating in the Western Baltic. In August 1915 the first reinforcements arrived at Lapvik. In addition four of the old 'C' Class were sent as deck cargo to Arkhangelsk, and then by canal barge and rail all the way down to Lapvik where they were reassembled.

By October 1915 the nine British submarines were ready to resume the offensive, and with the help of Russian submarines they inflicted heavy losses. But after the Menshevik or 'February' Revolution in March 1917 the efficiency of the base-support at Lapvik declined steadily. When the Bolsheviks signed the Treaty of Brest-Litovsk they agreed to surrender the British submarines to the Germans, but this the British would not allow at any price. On 8 April 1918 one of the few Russian ships which was still 'friendly' forced a passage to allow the submarines to reach open sea. By this time the seven survivors were based at Helsingfors (now Helsinki) and once they reached deep water scuttling charges were detonated.

By the end of the First World War the submarine had undergone much the same sort of transformation as the aircraft. From being a rather quaint instrument of limited potential it blossomed into a most advanced and complex weapon. Its special requirements acted as a spur to industry to improve every item of its equipment, the diesel engine, the periscope and the torpedo to name only three. Its unexpected flexibility as a weapon changed the nature of sea warfare completely. The British admirals at the Battle of Jutland could not maneuver freely through fear of being torpedoed by submarines. Their depredations among the world's merchant fleets in 1915–17 nearly bankrupted the British Empire, and certainly hastened its decline, but it had other side-effects. One of their saddest achievements was the virtual extinction of the sailing ship, many of which had been trading profitably in 1914. The blockade of Germany and the U-Boat campaign between them inflicted near-starvation and malnutrition on poor people in both Britain and Germany, and even neutral Europe suffered from the widespread food shortage. Even today the ruthlessness of U-Boat warfare raises a shudder, but in fairness we must admire the courage of the men who took their small submarines to sea in all weathers. Submarine warfare was and will always be a mixture of bravery and utter ruthlessness.

WOLFPACKS UNLEASHED

When World War II began on the morning of 3 September 1939 both British and German submarines were already at their war stations. The Royal Navy had eight boats based at Dundee, six at Blyth, and a further 16 on training duties, in addition to a pair of old boats being brought forward from reserve, five in the Mediterranean and 15 in the Far East. The Germans had sent 21 U-Boats to sea with the pocket battleships *Deutschland* and *Graf Spee* a month earlier. Their boats were based on Kiel (25 boats divided between four flotillas), 17 boats in two flotillas at Wilhelmshaven and 12 boats for training at Neustadt. The French Navy's Division des Sous-Marins (DSM) had also alerted its flotillas; apart from submarines abroad there were 28 boats based on Toulon, 17 at Bizerta and 12 at Casablanca.

Both sides were wary, and the Germans in particular had strict orders not to deviate from the Prize Regulations. It may seem mildly quixotic of Hitler to insist on the observance of such rules after violating almost every other rule of international law but he was well aware of how important it was to give American opinion no opportunity to turn against Germany. The results were ludicrous, all the more so because the chief beneficiaries of this policy, the British, did not even expect it to be followed. British Merchant Navy captains had been instructed to the effect that a 'sink at sight' policy would be followed immediately, and were told to ignore the Prize Regulations. Yet most U-Boat captains made an effort to carry out their orders. When Kapitänleutnant Lemp, in *U.30* identified the liner *Athenia* wrongly as a troopship he reported his mistake to Admiral Dönitz, who promptly threatened him with a court martial. Unfortunately the Propaganda Ministry then took a hand, accusing the Royal Navy and Winston Churchill of sabotaging the *Athenia* to discredit Germany and to support this story the U-Boat's logbook and other material evidence was suppressed. Some commanders, like Herbert Schultze in *U.48* went so far as to send messages 'in clear' to the British to give them positions of lifeboats.

Even when the U-Boats were restrained in their attacks on Allied shipping they sank 114 ships totalling 421,156 tons between 3 September and 31 December 1939. The Prize Regulations were held not to apply in the North Sea from the end of September, and on 2 October U-Boats were given permission to attack any ship sailing without lights off either the British or French coasts. On 4 October the exemption from the Prize Regulations was extended to longitude 15 degrees West and two weeks later U-Boats were given permission to attack all ships identified as hostile. The last prohibition, forbidding attacks on liners was removed on 17 November and unrestricted submarine warfare was back.

The most spectacular U-Boat successes were, however, against warships in these first weeks of the war. On 12 Septem-

Above: The Type VIIB *U.101* comes alongside a tender.
Left: A heavily retouched view of the secret *K.21*, which claimed to have torpedoed the *Tirpitz*.
Far left: *U.557* with an interned Dutch liner.
Below: The British *Syrtis* off Liverpool, 1943.

ber *U.29* sank the aircraft carrier HMS *Courageous* which was ironically on antisubmarine patrol in the Western Approaches. A large, fast warship is not an easy target for any submarine, and Kapitänleutnant Schuhart had to wait for nearly two hours before the carrier turned into wind to allow her aircraft to land. Had the *Courageous* not detached two of her four destroyers to help a sinking merchant ship *U.29* might still have been frustrated in her attack, but Schuhart was too skilled a submariner

to let the chance slip, and at 1950 three torpedoes tore into the ship and sent her down with the loss of more than 500 men. Two days later the new carrier *Ark Royal* had a lucky escape west of the Hebrides, when she was missed by torpedoes which passed astern. This time the destroyers detected *U.39* on Asdic and sank her with depth charges, but it was clear to the Admiralty that big fleet carriers could not be hazarded on such dangerous work, and they were withdrawn.

Exactly one month later Günther Prien in *U.47* achieved one of the most outstanding submarine exploits of all time. Knowing from aerial reconnaissance that the winter gales had opened gaps in the blockships which had been sunk in one of the eastern entrances to Scapa Flow, the U-Boat Command gave permission for an attempt to penetrate the defences. Prien was undertaking a mission fraught with danger but his courage was rewarded when he found himself in the Flow. The main anchorage was empty because most of the Home Fleet was no longer there, but to the North Prien found the old battleship *Royal Oak*. He fired a bow salvo of three torpedoes, and was mortified to hear only a small explosion, so slight that people aboard the battleship thought it was either a collision or an internal explosion. Prien turned to fire his stern tube at the battleship but missed, and was forced to reload his forward tubes. This time all three torpedoes ran true and exploded underneath the *Royal Oak*'s hull, and 13 minutes later the 25-year old veteran of the Battle of

Left: British 'T' Class boats in the Gareloch.
Right: *U.561* passes through a lock gate in the Kiel Canal heading for the North Sea.
Below right: *U.558* lies in dry dock under camouflage netting.
Below: Günther Prien aboard *U.47*.

Jutland rolled over suddenly and sank, taking 833 officers and men with her.

However elderly and out-of-date the *Royal Oak* might be, her loss was a blow to the Royal Navy's prestige and a reminder that the Home Fleet's main base was not properly protected. The Home Fleet was forced to move to Loch Ewe on the west coast of Scotland, in precisely the same manner as the Grand Fleet had been dispersed in 1914. Once again a single submarine had brought about a major shift of surface fleets and affected seriously the conduct of operations at sea. At a crucial moment the Home Fleet had to move away from its theater of operations and so leave the vital exit route to the Atlantic unguarded. But the German Navy was in no better a position to exploit its victory than it had been 25 years before, and the chance was lost again.

The Admiralty suffered no doubts about convoy such as they had in 1917, and drew up elaborate plans for the immediate convoying of merchant ships. All that was lacking was sufficient escorts, and to economize on warships for this purpose 'close'

Left: *U.557*'s 10.5cm gun undergoes maintenance.
Right: HM Submarine *Shark* surrendered to German trawlers in the Kattegat in 1940.
Below: The *Shcha* Class of boat was one of the more successful Soviet designs.
Bottom: The famous Free French submarine *Rubis*, 1946.

escort was not provided for convoys further west than 15 degrees. In coastal waters constant aircraft patrols were effective in keeping the U-Boats under control, and when the new coastal escorts or Flower Class corvettes began to come into service in the spring of 1940 they proved very effective. To avoid this concentration of counter-measures the U-Boats moved further west, and as a result the convoy escort limit had to be moved out to 17 degrees West in July, and again to 19 degrees West from October 1940. Similarly on the other side of the Atlantic the Canadians had to extend their convoy limit from 56 degrees to 53½ degrees West, but in between was the 'Black-Gap' in which merchant ships had neither air nor surface escorts. However, the U-Boats were still far from winning an outright victory because of their own shortage of numbers; many had to be retained for training, others were refitting between patrols, and sinkings by British antisubmarine forces were keeping abreast of new construction.

The respite gave the hard-pressed British and French navies time to develop their convoy organisation and to complete and convert more escort vessels. In addition deep minefields were laid in the English Channel to block it to U-Boats and so force them to use precious fuel and time on the northern passage to the Western Approaches. In the previous war the Dover Barrage had taken four years to perfect, but this time it worked completely; only one U-Boat got through and three others were mined in the first month.

British submarines were active in the North Sea, but the absence of major targets meant that they could do little more than watch or try to attack the occasional U-Boat on passage. The principal bases for these operations were Blyth and Dundee on the East coast of Scotland, but in October 1939 the Admiralty decided to concentrate the submarines temporarily at Rosyth until they could be better defended against air attack. They were reinforced by two Polish boats, the *Wilk* and *Orzel* which had escaped from the Baltic after the defeat of Poland. Another

base was established at Harwich, using the new 3rd Flotilla, created from boats withdrawn from the Mediterranean.

The British flotillas got their chance for action with the opening of the Norwegian Campaign in April 1940. The British Government was anxious about the extent to which German ships were taking iron ore from Norwegian ports. Although the traffic itself was perfectly legal the German ore-ships were able to take full advantage of Norway's military weakness by infringing her neutrality in a number of minor ways. The British finally reached a decision to lay a 'declared' minefield (that is one whose area and extent were notified to all neutrals)

Above: Ratings stow torpedoes in the forward torpedo room of a British submarine.
Below: A 'T' Class submarine enters harbor.

Above left: A censored view of HMS *Sturgeon* arriving home in 1940 after sinking a German transport.
Above: A Soviet sailor works on a torpedo.

as a retaliation for German breaches of Norwegian neutrality. This move coincided with Hitler's decision to occupy Norway to forestall the British invasion that he felt was inevitable. The result was that British and German naval forces encountered one another in a state of mutual ignorance and surprise.

The first intimation of what was afoot came when the Polish submarine *Orzel* sank a German transport off Christansand at noon on 8 April. Yet, although soldiers picked up by Norwegian craft admitted that they were on their way to occupy Bergen, and in spite of this news reaching the Admiralty that evening, nothing was done to alert the other submarines in position. Even when the submarines were given the vital information they were hamstrung by the same Prize Regulations as had hampered the U-Boats earlier. Even to the British Cabinet such hair-splitting was finally unacceptable; Allied submarines were given permission to sink transports on 9 April, and two days after that they were freed to attack any ship sighted up to ten miles from the Norwegian coast.

The results were spectacular and in less than a month 18 transports, tankers and other mercantile vessels were sunk, as well as the cruiser *Karlsruhe*, the gunnery training ship *Brummer* and a U-Boat. In addition submarine-laid mines accounted for another 13 ships, and the 'pocket battleship' *Lutzow* was badly damaged by HMS *Spearfish*. The losses were not unduly heavy, considering that nearly 100,000 tons of scarce German shipping had been sunk; 3 boats were sunk and one lost in a collision.

By comparison the U-Boats did not do well. The magnetic pistols for their torpedoes were adversely affected by an unforeseen change in the Earth's magnetism in the high latitudes off Norway, and so U-Boat commanders were robbed of a number of targets. Most of the U-Boats had been withdrawn from the Atlantic for the campaign, and so the resulting lull took the pressure off the Royal Navy at a crucial time, with nothing to compensate for it elsewhere.

While the Germans were consolidating their gains in Norway their main armies were preparing to invade France and the Low Countries. As soon as news of the German invasion of Belgium was heard on 10 May the bulk of the Allied submarine force was withdrawn from Norway, leaving only the British *Severn* and *Clyde*, the Polish *Orzel* and the French *Rubis* to harrass the Germans. All other submarines were redeployed to prevent German surface forces from making any incursion into the southern North Sea in support of their land forces.

The fall of first Holland and then France meant that Dutch and French submarines fled to British ports. Strenuous efforts were made to get submarines out of Brest and Cherbourg, and in some cases submarines completing refits or even still under construction were towed away. In all the giant *Surcouf* and six smaller submarines reached England.

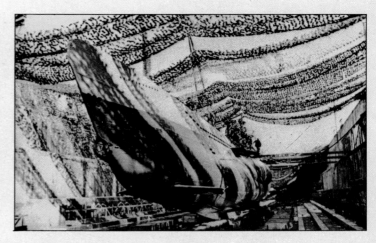

Above: *U.558* lies camouflaged in dock to avoid the incessant Allied air raids.
Right: The Soviet *D.2* at Polyarnoe, near Murmansk.

But under the armistice conditions agreed by Marshal Pétain, French naval officers were ordered to take their ships back to France, where they would be kept out of German hands. Not unnaturally the British, knowing just how valuable the French Navy would be to make good the deficiencies of the *Kriegsmarine*, doubted that the French would be allowed to keep their end of the bargain. After Dunkirk the British Government knew that it was fighting for survival, nothing less, and feeling that it dared not gamble once again on a written agreement, took over all French warships lying in British ports.

Within hours of the fall of France Admiral Dönitz and his staff were ready with plans to exploit the situation. Road transport was commandeered to move heavy equipment such as air compressors and torpedoes from Germany down to the French Atlantic coast. From Lorient, Bordeaux, Brest, St Nazaire, La Rochelle and La Pallice, U-Boats could now reach

Left: Ratings man the Finch gun aboard a British 'S' Class boat.
Below: The 'T' Class submarines had two 21 inch torpedo tubes beneath the conning tower, but these were later resited.

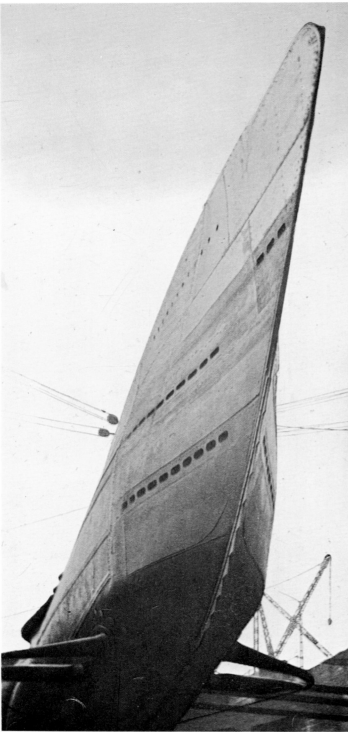

Left: A U-Boat in dry dock displays the knife-edged lines of its hull.
Below: An ensign flutters above a surfaced U-Boat.
Bottom: A U-Boat's hull is examined for damage.
Far right: A U-Boat's lookouts scan the horizon as the boat runs on the surface.
Below far right: U-Boat crew members parade for inspection.

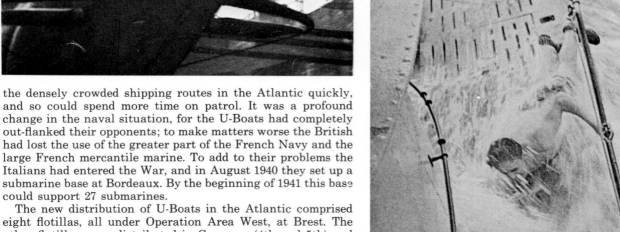

the densely crowded shipping routes in the Atlantic quickly, and so could spend more time on patrol. It was a profound change in the naval situation, for the U-Boats had completely out-flanked their opponents; to make matters worse the British had lost the use of the greater part of the French Navy and the large French mercantile marine. To add to their problems the Italians had entered the War, and in August 1940 they set up a submarine base at Bordeaux. By the beginning of 1941 this base could support 27 submarines.

The new distribution of U-Boats in the Atlantic comprised eight flotillas, all under Operation Area West, at Brest. The other flotillas were distributed in Germany (4th and 5th) and Norway (11th and 13th).

Had the Italian submarines been better suited to Atlantic conditions their reinforcement of the U-Boats might have been decisive, but they achieved comparatively little. Operating mainly off the Azores, they sank about 1,000,000 tons of shipping between January 1941 and September 1943. This was an average of approximately 31,000 tons sunk by each of the 32 boats involved; by comparison the 14 Type IXB U-Boats which operated in roughly the same area sank 40 percent more. But the U-Boats also suffered from problems. The Type VII U-Boat was found to be on the small side for operating so far out into the Atlantic, and special 'milch-cow' U-tankers were designed, which could transfer diesel fuel and spare torpedoes to other U-Boats at sea. Only ten of these underwater supply vessels were completed in 1941–42, and as all were made the object of special attention by Allied antisubmarine forces they were all early losses. The big Type IX boats had more endurance, but their bulk and slow diving made them particularly vulnerable in the Western Approaches. They were mostly employed away from the main convoy routes, where the escorts were less active and many of their victims were unescorted. Largely because of this the IXB Class accounted for approximately 10 percent of the entire mercantile tonnage sunk by U-Boats.

Between June and November 1940 British and neutral shipping losses from U-Boats rose to 1,600,000 tons. This was the heyday of a new generation of 'ace' U-Boat commanders, men like Otto Kretschmer and Günther Prien, who sank more than 200,000 tons apiece. Kretschmer in *U.99* was the leading exponent of a brilliant new tactic, the night attack on the surface. Taking advantage of her low silhouette and relatively high speed on her diesel motors, a U-Boat could actually penetrate the columns of a convoy of merchant ships undetected, from which position her CO could fire his torpedoes with impunity. The escort commanders were usually on the flanks of the convoy, and unless an exceptionally alert lookout, watching in the least likely quarter, happened to spot the trimmed down conning tower, the chances of detection were slim. Radar put an end to this practice, but in 1940 no convoy escort had a radar set, and the only answer was to provide artificial illuminating rockets known as Snowflakes, which could act like starshell and turn night into day.

Even the efforts of the 'aces' were not enough for Admiral Dönitz. Realizing that there would never be time to train a new generation of commanders of the quality of Kretschmer, Schepke and the others, he developed a concept which had been suggested over twenty years earlier by Commodore Bauer. This was the mass-attack or 'wolf-pack' idea (German *Rudeltaktik*), in which a force of 20 or more U-Boats could swamp a convoy's defences. Briefly the sequence of a wolf-pack attack would be as follows:

1. A pack of U-Boats is disposed in a wide curve across the probable route of a convoy.
2. Any U-Boat sighting the convoy signals its course, speed and composition, as well as its own position to U-Boat HQ.
3. The U-Boat then shadows the convoy without attacking, and merely reports any change in course and speed.
4. U-Boat HQ orders all other U-Boats in the pack to make contact with U-Boat No. 1.
5. When all U-Boats have made contact with the shadower a coordinated attack is made on the convoy after dark.
6. At daybreak the pack breaks off the attack leaving one shadower to maintain contact, while the others recharge batteries and load fresh torpedoes.
7. At nightfall the pack renews its attack.

The wolf-pack system had the advantage that it made the best use of the newly trained and relatively inexperienced U-Boat captains and crews, and inevitably it wrought havoc among the poorly escorted convoys of 1940. The new methods were introduced gradually between October 1940 and March 1941, but by then the British had in any case scored such success against the aces that it became obvious to Dönitz that pack-tactics were the only effective method left.

In March 1941 the escorts got Prien in *U.47*, and then Schepke in *U.100* and Kretschmer in *U.99*, all sunk while attacking convoys. It was a heavy blow to the U-Boat Arm, for these three men alone had sunk 111 ships totalling over half a million tons. They had fallen victim to the new weapons and techniques of convoy escort, for the British had introduced surface search radar, radio direction-finding and a series of new weapons and tactics. There were two great weaknesses in the wolf-pack system: all depended on the shadower and on communications between U-Boat HQ and the pack, and if any means could be discovered of hindering either of these the defenders could hold their own.

The simplest means of dealing with shadowers was to maintain an aircraft patrol astern of the convoy, so that the shadowing U-Boat was forced to dive, and could therefore no longer keep up. The most urgent need, therefore, was to provide air cover for convoys all the way across the Atlantic, but until the end of 1941 there were neither the aircraft nor the aircraft carriers to spare for this. In mid-1941 the Admiralty began to convert an experimental escort carrier, a small merchant ship with an extemporized wooden flight deck, but she was not ready until the end of the year. In 1917–18 Allied cryptographers had eavesdropped on the large volume of radio traffic between the U-Boats and their bases, but in 1940–41 German codes and cyphers were secure against this. However, the source could be located by a sufficiently sensitive high-frequency receiver. Unknown to the Germans, the British were successful in producing a set small enough to be fitted in a small warship; using it, an escort could pinpoint the position of a U-Boat to within a quarter of a mile, and so escorts could drive off shadowers or even sink them.

When a corvette went to sea in May 1941 with the first Type 271 surface warning radar set she was able to detect a conning tower at night at $2\frac{1}{2}$ miles. This was the countermeasure which enabled escorts to deal with night attacks at last, and it was put into quantity production immediately. In May 1941 a British boarding party captured code-books and an Enigma cypher machine intact from *U.110* before she sank, probably the greatest intelligence 'pinch' of the War. Hitherto the German B-Dienst or cryptographic service had enjoyed considerable success in locating convoys, but as soon as the secrets of the *U.110* haul were unravelled the advantage passed to the other side.

In 1941 a number of new antisubmarine weapons were introduced. At last an efficient aerial depth-charge was available, and ships were given extra-heavy depth-charges designed to sink faster. The standard Asdic set could not hold a submarine in its beam directly underneath, and so contact was lost in the final moments of an attack. To remedy this the Hedgehog ahead-throwing weapon was devised to hurl 24 small bombs in a pattern forward, while the escort still held the U-Boat in contact. Despite all these countermeasures 1941 saw the loss of more than 2,000,000 tons of shipping, 432 ships in all. The British, even allowing for the neutral nations' shipping which was available, could not stand losses of this order. The German attack on Russia in mid-1941 did little to ease the situation because the Russians were in no position to offer any naval assistance or draw off any substantial number of U-Boats. All now depended on the Americans, who alone could provide the shipping to offset the huge losses inflicted by the U-Boats.

The attitude of the United States had been pro-Allied right from the start of the War, but of course as a neutral she could not lend direct support to any belligerent. However, President Franklin Roosevelt was resolved to offer 'all aid short of war,' and had already lent the British 50 old destroyers for escort purposes in return for base-rights in British colonial possessions. The later Lend-Lease Act of March 1941 was a fiction to allow war material to be made available 'on loan' to Britain but however it might enrage Hitler, his orders to Admiral Dönitz were to avoid provoking the Americans into a declaration of war. In September 1941 the US President went a step further and ordered the US Navy to escort American merchant ships bound for the British Isles to a Mid-Ocean Meeting Point, (MOMP) and warships were given orders to attack any submarines which appeared to be attacking American ships. As the meeting point was near Iceland, where British escort vessels were based, it was not long before incidents occurred between U-Boats and American ships.

On 4 September the old destroyer USS *Greer* picked up a submarine contact on her Sonar (the USN equivalent of Asdic), and following standard orders tracked and shadowed it without making an attack. But the *Greer* was broadcasting in clear and soon a British shore-based aircraft arrived and dropped depth-charges. Under the impression that the *Greer* had attacked him, the CO of *U.652* lost his patience, ignored his orders and fired a torpedo at the destroyer. Although it missed the *Greer*, she went to action stations and counterattacked, but without success. The next incident was on 10 October, when a U-Boat torpedoed the US destroyer *Kearny*, whose silhouette was very similar to the British escort destroyers operating in the area. The *Kearny* did not sink but the attack whipped up anti-German feeling to a new pitch. Worse was to follow, for on 31 October the old destroyer *Reuben James* was sunk, but still the United States was so reluctant to get involved in World War II that President

Top: Lookouts on *U.86*'s conning tower.
Above: The French boat *Circé*.
Above right: The view from a U-Boat's 21cm gun platform.
Below: *U.27* was photographed from *U.26* during a prewar training cruise.

Roosevelt could do nothing but express his indignation. For his part Hitler was adamant in his decision to avoid hostilities with America, and refused to lift the restrictions on the U-Boats. The undeclared war continued without further major incidents until the Japanese attack on Pearl Harbor on 7 December. Two days later Hitler removed all restrictions on attacks against American shipping, and two days after that declared war on the United States. The Battle of the Atlantic was about to enter an even fiercer stage.

MEDITERRANEAN LIFELINES

The Italian Navy had built a large force of submarines before the outbreak of war, and the Italian High Command or *Supermarina* had high hopes of denying the British the use of their main base, Malta. With some 90 submarines at their disposal and being very close to Malta, they should have been a decisive factor in the naval war but in fact it was the British submarines which took this honor from them.

When Italy declared war on France and Great Britain in June 1940, the British were in the process of reforming their submarine flotillas after withdrawing all but two submarines for training. With boats transferred from China it was possible to base six at Alexandria and six at Malta, but none could be spared for Gibraltar. The boats sent were too large for the Mediterranean and before the end of the first two weeks of operations the *Grampus*, the *Odin* and *Orpheus* were lost. Visibility in Mediterranean waters is so good that an aircraft can spot a submarine 50 feet down in calm weather, and the fact that the three submarines had recently come from China could have meant that their COs had not yet learned how to cope with these difficult conditions. Another factor may have been the tendency for the British 'O' Class boats to disclose their positions by fuel leaks from their saddle tanks outside the pressure hull.

The Italian lines of communication in the Mediterranean were vulnerable to submarine attack, and the dangers had to be taken into account if the British were to offset their numerical inferiority in surface ships. The targets were mainly the shipping carrying men and supplies to the North African colonies, but it was not until February 1941 that British submarines were allowed to attack all shipping at sight. In spite of this handicap and poor aerial reconnaissance the British submarine flotillas sank a number of transports and warships, for the loss of one French and nine British boats. During the same period Italian submarines achieved very few successes, and sank no warships at all. The reasons for this failure were partly the transfer of most of the top Italian submarines to France and partly the design of the boats themselves, which were also too large and clumsy for Mediterranean operations.

In many ways the campaign resembled the 1915 campaign in the Sea of Marmora, with the gun being used as much as the torpedo. Submarines were used to land raiding parties and to bombard shore targets such as trains. In the early part of 1941 British land forces were doing well against the Italians in North Africa, and the depredations of the Malta submarines added to the problems of the *Regia Navale* in escorting supply-convoys. But when the *Luftwaffe* came to the rescue of the Italians they were able to make life much harder for British submarines. Aircraft minelaying caused losses, and heavy air attacks on Malta made it almost untenable as a base. Losses were heavy, but the Axis armies were seriously hampered by the attacks on their supply-lines. Between January and May 1941 the Germans and Italians lost 100,000 tons of shipping to submarines alone, nearly a third of their total losses to surface and air attack, mines and other causes. Between June and September they lost another 150,000 tons, but the total fell to half that figure between October and December reflecting the reversal of British fortunes in the Mediterranean. The Italian merchant fleet was reduced by 30 percent in a year, a rate of decline which would eventually

prove disastrous for the Axis position in the Mediterranean.

Until the autumn of 1941 there were no U-Boats in the Mediterranean as Admiral Dönitz refused to allow any of his precious boats to be withdrawn from the Battle of the Atlantic. He rightly felt that the war would be won or lost in the Atlantic, and maintained that the Italians should have been capable of looking after the Mediterranean by themselves. But the successes of the British Mediterranean Fleet and the ceaseless harrying of convoys by the Malta submarines threatened to bring about the collapse of the Italians, and so Hitler over-ruled Dönitz. During September six U-Boats left the Biscay ports, and another four passed successfully through the Straits of Gibraltar in October. Dönitz was resigned to losing them permanently, for the eastward current and thermal layers in the Straits which made it relatively easy for a submarine to get into the Mediterranean made it correspondingly hazardous to get out again.

All the U-Boats were eventually hunted down, as Dönitz had foreseen, but they gave a good account of themselves. On 13 November *U.81* sank the famous *Ark Royal* near Gibraltar and so robbed the Gibraltar forces of their only carrier. On 25 November the battleship *Barham* was torpedoed by *U.331*, and blew up with the loss of 862 officers and men. As Admiral Cunningham ruefully commented, the British antisubmarine forces had become a little rusty as a result of only having to deal with Italian submarines, and the U-Boat managed to get right through the Battle Fleet's destroyer-screen without being detected.

British submarines suffered heavily in the summer of 1942, for they were operating in areas almost entirely dominated by hostile air power. Many were sunk and others were damaged in harbor. Malta's situation became so precarious that the submarines had to supply the garrison with such diverse stores as high octane gasoline, kerosene, machine-gun ammunition and glycol coolant for Spitfires. The use of submarines for this vital purpose had started in May 1941, and in some cases conversion involved the removal of one battery to provide more space. It was the big minelayers like the *Rorqual* which carried cargo most easily on their capacious mine-decks, but the *Clyde* carried 1200 tons on one trip. All in all some 65,000 tons of supplies were landed by submarines before the crisis was over. Even so the submarines were forced to lie on the bottom of the harbor during daylight, and could only surface at night. Every submarine engaged on supply-runs was a submarine not available for attacking Italian and German supply ships; it is quite clear from German records that submarines accounted for over half the tonnage of shipping sunk in the first half of 1942, and that those losses rose after Malta was relieved by the big Pedestal convoy action in August and after the Battle of El Alamein brought the coast of North Africa under Allied control once more.

Above: The *Sturgeon* returns to Dundee, September 1940.
Right: *U.505* is preserved at Chicago, Illinois.
Below right: *U.995* is today preserved at Laboe, outside Kiel in West Germany. This view shows the boat's forward torpedo room.
Bottom: The control room of the preserved *U.995*.
Below: The Italian wartime submarine *Marcello* is pictured in harbor.

THE BLACK GAP

Hitler's declaration of war on the United States in December 1941 came as no surprise to the U-Boat High Command for Admiral Dönitz and his staff felt that it was inevitable. Plans were ready for Operation Drumroll or *Paukenschlag*, and by 25 December six U-Boats were on their way across the Atlantic to attack American shipping.

The US Navy had been in close touch with the Royal Navy, and all reports on antisubmarine tactics and equipment were available. Yet the fierceness of *Paukenschlag* took the USN completely by surprise and an amazing lack of preparedness led to the loss of 500 ships in the first six months. U-Boat commanders had referred to the period June–December 1940 as the 'happy time,' and now they rejoiced at the return of the happy time as they slaughtered ships sailing independently. Destroyers steamed in every direction on 'offensive' patrols, so regularly that they could be timed by the U-Boats, ships broadcast their positions in clear and shore lights gave the U-Boats easy navigational bearings. The US Navy had been suspicious of the efficacy of convoy, despite its deep involvement in the defeat of the U-Boat offensive in 1917–18, and some senior officers felt that the task of escorting a convoy plodding along at 10 knots was too humdrum. It might be right for the stolid British and Canadian character but it did not suit the more dashing American temperament, or so it was claimed. Attractive though this line of reasoning might be it was totally wrong. Nor was it unique to the Americans; it had been used frequently between 1915 and 1917 by the British to prove that convoy was too defensive a measure for a navy inbred with the Nelson spirit. More important, developments in Sonar had not kept pace with

the British Asdic, and considerable leeway had to be made up quickly by the US Navy. Although the need for special escort vessels had been foreseen, financial limitations had prevented the Navy from placing any orders, but fortunately the British had already placed an order for destroyer-escorts (DEs) under Lend-Lease. The programme was immediately expanded from 50 to 250 DEs, and it was possible for the Royal Navy to transfer 25 corvettes as a temporary measure. The British had also designed a new escort vessel specially for the North Atlantic, the 'River' Class High Endurance Escort (later called the frigate), and an American copy was put into production. All these measures took time, and all the while the U-Boats were adding to their scores.

During 1942 the monthly average shipping loss was 650,000 tons, and in that year the U-Boats sank 6 million tons. By December Admiral Dönitz had 212 U-Boats operational, and the war was entering a critical phase. In simple strategic terms the U-Boats could cut the United States off from Great Britain and the Mediterranean, and so make it impossible for her to bring her vast resources to bear anywhere in the European Theater. If this had happened, and Dönitz estimated that a monthly average loss of 800,000 tons of shipping would do it, not even the wealth and industrial might of America would have been any use to her. She might have been able to deal with Japan in the Pacific, but her entire Eastern Seaboard would have been vulnerable to seaborne attack. Thus the Battle of the Atlantic came to mean much more than the survival of Great Britain; it was the decisive theater of the western half of World War II, and the victor would win the war.

There were several factors balancing the enormous losses of shipping. By mid-1942 the American shipyards were able to provide the first purpose-built escort carriers, and in the fall

Below: A Type VIIC U-Boat lashed by depth-charges and cannon fire sinks by the stern.

the first Very Long Range Liberator antisubmarine patrol aircraft came into service, and these measures did much to close the Black Gap by providing continuous air cover to convoys. British shipyards were also beginning to turn out larger numbers of escort vessels, and it was possible to form the first Support Groups in September of that year. These were groups of well-trained escorts, usually destroyers and frigates or sloops, which operated independently of the convoys to break up concentrations of U-Boats and to harry them on passages to their patrol areas. If they sound suspiciously like the old discredited concept of offensive patrolling this is erroneous, for the support group supplemented the convoy system and was intended to reinforce any convoy that was hard-pressed, as well as hunting further afield. One of the drawbacks of convoying was that an escort which had detected a submarine was often forced to break off the attack prematurely in order to catch up with her convoy. The support group was free to spend hours or even days if needed on a lengthy hunt to destruction.

The climax of the Battle of the Atlantic might have come in the fall of 1942, for all the tactics and weaponry on both sides had been perfected, but political decisions at a high level resulted in the escort carriers and support groups being withdrawn to cover the Allied invasion of North Africa, Operation Torch. The U-Boats were not slow to take advantage of this weakening of the Allied effort in the Atlantic but the effect was delayed by the winter weather, which hampered the U-Boats as much as it did the escorts. Furthermore in the first two months of 1943 the Germans encountered difficulty in locating convoys, due to the Admiralty's success in rerouting convoys to avoid wolf-packs whose position was known.

The first big battle was in March, when two groups of U-Boats tried unsuccessfully to trap convoy SC-121. In a battle lasting five days 13 ships were sunk, despite the fact that the convoy slipped through the patrol line. Later that month, after the German B-Dienst cracked the current convoy cypher, Admiral Dönitz concentrated 40 U-Boats against the slow convoy SC-122

Above: A U-Boat puts to sea, getting the 'send off' which Admiral Dönitz knew was essential for morale.
Below: Two U-Boats are moored in their bomb-proof 'pen' at St Nazaire.
Bottom: The successful *U.48* takes on a torpedo.

Above: The conning tower and periscope details of *U.776* photographed in the London Docks after World War II.

Right: A German photograph of a U-Boat running on the surface.
Far right: U-Boats pictured under construction during World War II.

(52 ships) and the fast HX-229 (25 ships). Both convoys were heading eastward, and on 16 March they were about 120 miles apart. HX-229 was the first to be attacked, and in a space of eight hours 12 ships were torpedoed, *U-338* managing to sink four ships with only five torpedoes. In a desperate attempt to fight off the ceaseless attacks the escorts ordered the two convoys to combine, but even so 140,000 tons of shipping was sunk, and only one U-Boat was sunk by the escorts. A similar attempt was made against the next Halifax convoy, HX-230, but the weather was so bad that it lost only one straggler, while an American escort carrier helped SC-123 to pass through a gap in the U-Boats' patrol line by using her high-frequency direction-finding gear to locate the U-Boat which was transmitting the sighting reports.

The support groups which had been withdrawn for Operation Torch were now being thrown back into the Battle of the Atlantic. By the end of March there were five support groups and three escort carriers in the Western Approaches. They were just in time, for Admiral Dönitz had almost achieved his great dream of shattering the convoy system. After the disastrous battle around HX-229 and SC-122 the Admiralty nearly abandoned the convoy organisation, for it seemed that the U-Boats had found the answer. Half a million tons of shipping was sunk in the first 20 days of March, far more than the Allied shipyards could make good if losses had continued at that level. Just as the U-Boats sensed that victory was within their grasp it eluded them, and they were overtaken by a stunning defeat.

The reasons behind this dramatic reversal were complex. In an attempt to cope with the growing weight of air attack the U-Boat Command had introduced a radar search-receiver, the Metox, which could detect some radar pulses and so warn a U-Boat before the aircraft came into range. So much confidence was placed in the Metox that some U-Boats were even fitted as 'flak-traps' with a heavy antiaircraft armament. Although the ruse was successful against the first unwary Sunderlands and Liberators which came in too close it was not long before aircraft took to circling just outside gun range, while calling up the nearest support group. If the U-Boat tried to break off the action by diving the aircraft immediately switched to the attack.

In March a U-Boat reported that she had been attacked at night by a Wellington bomber, and that the Metox receiver had not recorded any radar emissions. It was this action which prompted the order to stay on the surface and fight it out with enemy aircraft, but a month later came a whole series of night attacks which were undetected by the Metox. In response to urgent requests the scientists replied that there was no possibility of an Allied breakthrough in radar. A chance remark by

a British navigator to the effect that the Metox receiver produced a signal which could be traced by Allied aircraft was sufficient to throw everybody off the scent. Convinced that the Metox was giving away the positions of the U-Boats, the Germans ordered all sets to be removed, whereas this offensive piece of equipment was simply incapable of detecting short waveband (10-cm) radar pulses.

A similar error had been made in 1942, when U-Boat captains had first reported that they were being attacked as soon as they started to transmit their sighting reports. Then they had been disbelieved because the scientists did not think that a high-frequency direction-finding set could be installed in a ship. But this time the lack of liaison between the *Kriegsmarine* and its scientists proved fatal, and U-Boat losses rose alarmingly.

Shipping Losses and U-Boat Sinkings July 1942–June 1943

Month	*No. of Ships*	*Tonnage*	*U-Boats Sunk*
1942			
July	96	476,000	11
August	108	544,000	10
September	98	485,400	11
October	94	619,000	16
November	119	729,100	13
December	60	330,800	5
1943			
January	37	203,100	6
February	63	359,300	19
March	108	627,300	15
April	56	327,900	16
May	50	264,800	41
June	20	95,700	17

Defeat was conceded when the U-Boats were ordered to withdraw for 'regrouping'. There was no disguising the fact that the U-Boat Arm had been shattered by the pounding it had received, and it was necessary to restore morale with new weapons and tactics before committing the U-Boats again. There was also the problem of U-Boat construction to consider, and Hitler and Admiral Dönitz met in a series of conferences to

Right: A floating dock at Kiel holds the hulls of three scuttled Type XXIII coastal U-Boats, after the German surrender.
Below: *U.249* was the first of the U-Boats to surrender to the British on 9 May 1945.

DIE
WEHRMACHT
HERAUSGEGEBEN VOM OBERKOMMANDO DER WEHRMACHT

Die Schläge der deutschen U-Bootwaffe hat jetzt auch die nordamerikanische Schiffahrt zu spüren bekommen

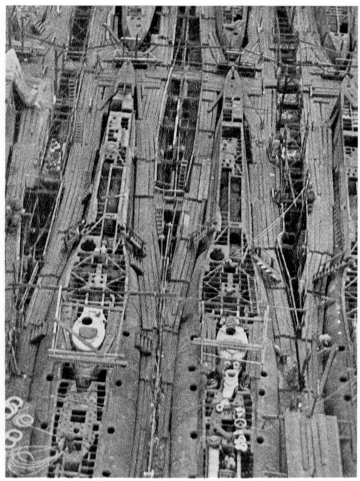

decide on naval policy. In April 1943 it was established that by the second half of the year production of Type VII boats would be increased to 27 per month, and that this rate could be maintained even if the more complex VIIC$_{42}$ design was built. By 1945 it was hoped to increase production to 30 boats per month, but Dönitz reminded the Führer that the program was using 4500 tons of steel per month for the hulls, and a further 1500 tons for torpedo-bodies.

In June the vexed problem of manpower was discussed, and Dönitz pointed out that even if 40 U-Boats could be delivered each month this would merely exacerbate the shortage of personnel. The current allocation was 102,984 men, whereas the requirements would be for 437,822 men, a shortfall of nearly 335,000. If 634 U-Boats were to be manned 62,000 men would be needed for their crews alone. The Admiral pointed out that since April 1942 the *Wehrmacht* had received the major share of manpower, leaving the *Kriegsmarine* short of 200,000 men. The officer-candidates who had entered the navy in the fall of 1939 were now being given commands, and it would be necessary to transfer officers from the other two services. If the personnel were not found the U-Boat Arm could function but at the cost of manning none of the new surface craft such as motor torpedo boats completed after January 1944.

In July 1943 Dönitz made the first mention to Hitler of a startling new project, the so-called electro-submarine. Known as the Type XXI, it was a fully streamlined boat with a novel 'figure 8' hull and enlarged battery-capacity to give it a much higher underwater speed. Another important feature of the design was the provision of automatic torpedo-reloading gear, which enabled a Type XXI boat to fire torpedoes rapidly at a series of targets, unlike the older boats which had to retire to reload, with each torpedo taking half-an-hour to load. This feature alone made the new submarine a lethal weapon against convoys, and Hitler demanded that the *Konstruktionsamt* should try to improve on the November 1944 delivery date for the first. Albert Speer was told to authorize three-shift working in the shipyards in order to get production up to 20 per month, and it was hoped that these new U-Boats would eventually win back the initiative from the Allies.

Another advanced design was in hand, the Walter turbine design known as the Type XVII. The Walter turbine burned enriched hydrogen peroxide and oil fuel with a catalyst to release sufficient oxygen, thus providing a 'closed cycle' to dispense with the need for outside oxygen. This provided a very high underwater speed, 20 knots or more, because of the great heat produced during the decomposition of the hydrogen peroxide. The fuel was known as *T-Stoff* (abbreviation for *Trieb-Stoff*), Ingolin or Aurol, and proved both difficult and expensive to manufacture. An experimental boat, *V-80*, ran trials in 1940, and *U.791* (ex-*V.300*) was the first U-Boat to be fitted with a Walter turbine for trials in 1942. The first production model was the Type XVIIB coastal boat displacing 312 tons, which needed 55 tons of Aurol to reach 21½ knots for 150 miles.

The Walter turbine boats must, however, be judged an aberration, despite their advanced technology. The German Navy was already badly behind in its submarine building-programs, despite all the efforts made in the shipyards, and the Walter boats rank with some of Hitler's tank projects as pipe-dreams which frittered away resources and delayed production of more useful equipment. There is no doubt that 50 Type XXI U-Boats in mid-1944 would have done more to redeem the situation than 200 Walter boats in 1945. To compound the error the shipyards were allowed to continue the construction of the now-obsolescent Type VIIC, and 'diluted' or mixed skilled and semi-skilled labor was used to build the highly complex Type XXI boats. Heavy Allied bombing on shipyards also held up

Left: The incomplete hulls of Type XXI U-Boats lie amid the devastated shipyards of Hamburg after the city's surrender in May 1945.

production, and as a result only four Type XXI boats had been completed when Germany surrendered in May 1945. The first, *U.2511*, did not finish her training and shakedown until the week before the surrender. A simplified version with a single hull, known as the Type XXIII was also built, and the small numbers of boats completed proved quite successful in British coastal waters but so few were available that they could not affect the outcome of the war.

The only other countermeasures that could be initiated in 1943 were the provision of new weapons and tactics. New acoustic torpedoes were introduced to allow U-Boats to attack escorts, but technical problems made them less dangerous than first thought.

In the search for an answer to the danger from aircraft someone remembered the Dutch *schnorkel* device which had been installed in submarines which had been captured in 1940. The device was by no means perfect, and had to be modified by the Germans because the air induction pipe and the exhaust 10 feet below the surface created a clearly visible wake. This problem was successfully tackled, and the *schnorkel* device was soon made a standard fitting for U-Boats.

The *schnorkel* achieved its aim, but it made life extremely uncomfortable for U-Boat crews. In rough weather the valve shut constantly, and each time the diesels sucked in enough air

Right: The schnorchel head of *U.516*, a Type IXC.
Below: Two Type XXIII boats, *U.2336* and a sister, lying at Lisahally, Northern Ireland, in 1946.

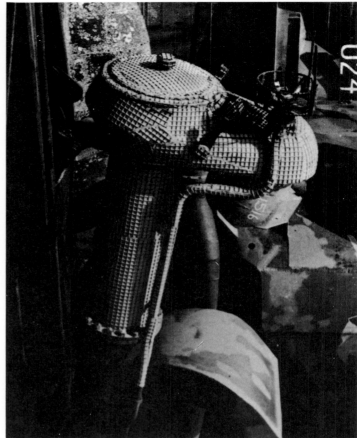

Above right: A blazing merchantman settling by the stern is viewed from the attacking U-Boat.
Above, far right and right: Following a mid-ocean rendezvous between two U-Boats, a life raft ferries mail to one of the boats.

to create a partial vacuum which made ears and eyes pop. It also had the effect of making the U-Boats 'keep their heads down' for longer periods, so that although they became harder to sink, in turn they sank fewer ships. But the U-Boats never gave up, and they remained dangerous right to the end. More than 32,000 officers and men out of a total of 39,000 died on active service. The balance sheet was a grim one:

U-Boats built:	1162
U-Boats sunk:	784
Allied Warships sunk:	175*
Merchantmen sunk:	2828*
Merchantmen sunk:	14,687,231* tons

*These figures include sinkings by Italian and Japanese submarines, but they form only a small part of the total.

No figures exist for the total number of merchant seamen lost, because the Allies' merchant fleets included vessels from so many neutral nations, but some idea of the scale of losses can be gauged from the fact that the British Merchant Navy alone lost 30,248 men in action.

On 7 May 1945 Admiral Dönitz, now the Führer as well as Commander in Chief of the German Navy, transmitted orders to all U-Boats to cease hostilities. For the second time in 30 years the U-Boats had failed in their bid to defeat the world's navies and were destined to finish their careers in enemy ports. Some refused to accept the surrender orders and scuttled themselves, while *U.977* went to South America to be interned rather than surrender, but the majority surfaced, hoisted the black distinguishing flag agreed with the Allies, and handed themselves over to the nearest warship to be escorted to port.

THE WAR AGAINST JAPAN

When the Japanese attacked the US Pacific Fleet at Pearl Harbor without warning on the morning of 7 December 1941, it was envisioned that submarines would play their part in supporting the aircraft carrier strike. The Submarine Force was to move to the vicinity of Hawaii in order to provide reconnaissance for the Carrier Striking Force and to attack any US warships which presented themselves. One unit was detailed to launch midget submarines against Pearl Harbor itself, but as we shall see the attack was unsuccessful and all were sunk.

At the outbreak of war the Japanese submarine fleet numbered about 75 operational units. A large construction program was in hand, with 18 boats to be ready by the end of 1942 and a further 11 to be ready by the end of 1943. What was lacking was any real grasp of the importance of standardizing and streamlining production, such as the German, British and American Navies had already achieved in their submarine programs. The Japanese High Command seemed to be unduly obsessed with the potential of their big boats, but whatever designs were chosen the shipyards were not able to build fast enough. The *RO.35* Class was intended to be a standard medium design, and the first was laid down in October 1941 and completed in March 1943, but 8 out of the 18 ordered were not completed until 1944. A large number of additional boats authorized in 1941 were cancelled in 1943, never having been laid down. By comparison a typical American *Gato* Class boat, the *Barb* was laid down in June 1941 and completed a year later, and the British were taking 18 months to complete a 'T' boat.

The American Navy had gone to the opposite extreme. Having developed their fleet submarines through a series of logical improvements to the 'T' and 'G' Classes of 1940–41, they were content to put the 'G' Class into quantity production as the *Gato* Class. Then when war-experience dictated improvements the new *Balao* Class and their successors the *Tench* Class were kept as similar as possible. Although only four builders undertook the construction of the *Gatos* they proved well able to meet the challenge. Two other yards had to take some of the burden

when orders were placed for a total of 366 *Balao* and *Tench* Classes but this does nothing to diminish the remarkable American achievement of 228 submarines completed in four and one-half years.

Unlike the Japanese the Americans had no chance to use their submarines in conjunction with the battle fleet. After Pearl Harbor there was no American battle fleet in the Pacific, and the submarines were the only units which could fight back. For a while the attack was blunted because of a high incidence of failures affecting the Mark 14 torpedo. In some cases the

gyroscopes failed, and in others the warhead pistol failed to function, and until these problems were identified and cured the submarine offensive was only partially effective. But once an improved torpedo was available American submarines began to make enormous inroads into Japanese shipping.

Although American submarines did not hesitate to attack warships they were given instructions to concentrate on mercantile shipping, particularly oil tankers. The Japanese had carved a seaborne empire for themselves, and their large merchant fleet was needed to supply the garrisons in all the outlying islands. Furthermore, Japan imported 20 percent of its food, 24 percent of its coal, 88 percent of its iron ore and 90 percent of its oil. The Japanese Navy had not foreseen that this fragile structure could be so vulnerable to a concerted submarine attack, and had failed to devote any resources to antisubmarine warfare. As a result US submarines were not subjected to the full weight of countermeasures that were the lot of a U-Boat in the Atlantic or a British submarine in the Mediterranean. At the end of the war the Americans were amazed to learn that the Japanese claimed to have sunk 486 submarines. The actual losses were 37 sunk by enemy action and 23 through miscellaneous causes such as grounding.

In 1943 American submarines first used wolf-pack tactics against Japanese shipping. Because of the lack of convoying and the poor antisubmarine measures used by Japanese escorts there was no need for the large packs used by the Germans in the Atlantic, and the Americans found that groups of three were suitable. Under such titles as 'Ben's Busters,' 'Donk's Devils,' 'Ed's Eradicators' and 'Laughlin's Loopers' the packs ranged far and wide across the Pacific in search of targets. Their names

Right: The launch of a new submarine for the US Navy. US shipyards built over 200 boats in 1942–45.
Below: The *Sea Devil* (SS.400) rescues aircrew from a rubber dinghy in the Pacific.
Bottom: The USS *Cavalla*, a *Gato* Class fleet submarine runs on the surface.

derived from the aces who led them, and several boats like *Barb*, *Rasher*, *Silversides* and *Tang* sank over 90,000 tons of shipping. The highest scoring US submarine was USS *Tang* (SS.306), with 100,231 tons, and by 1945 the Japanese had lost over 4,000,000 tons of shipping.

American submarines were able to attack on the surface at night, just as the U-Boats had in 1940, but unlike the British escorts the Japanese did not get radar sets until very late. Using their own radar the US submarines could choose their position for attacking, and dodged the escorts with ease. Some daring commanders were expert in the 'down-the-throat' shot, which involved firing a full salvo of six torpedoes at an attacking escort at close range.

As the Japanese came to rely more and more on small junks and coasters for shipping cargoes the big American boats found themselves short of targets. But by early 1944 the British and Dutch had established three flotillas in the Far East. Although smaller and shorter on range, the British and Dutch boats proved capable of operating within the 10-fathom line. Their most notable successes were the sinking of the cruisers *Kuma* and *Ashigara*, but they also achieved the destruction of a large number of minor vessels.

The American submarines, in addition to their onslaught on merchant shipping, performed a vital role in reporting enemy fleet movements. Time and again fleet commanders received vital intelligence from submarines, and it was these patrolling submarines which scored some of the greatest successes of the Pacific War. In 1944, just on the eve of the Battle of Leyte Gulf the *Darter* and *Drum* ambushed a Japanese heavy cruiser squadron, sinking the *Atago* and *Maya* and damaging the *Takao*. In June 1944 the *Albacore* torpedoed the new carrier *Taiho* during the Battle of the Philippine Sea, causing severe damage which led to her loss, and five months later the incomplete *Shinano*, a 62,000-ton converted battleship, was torpedoed by the *Archerfish* in Japanese home waters.

The Japanese submarine force, from which so much had been expected, had little to show by comparison. By concentrating on attacking well-defended formations of warships they exposed themselves to the efficient antisubmarine tactics of the Americans, while their neglect of mercantile targets reduced the burden of escort. American antisubmarine measures were very much better than the Japanese, as demonstrated when a newly commissioned destroyer escort, the USS *England* sank six submarines in 12 days in 1944. On 19 May the *England* sank *1.16*, 140 miles northeast of Choiseul Island in the Solomons, and acting on the likelihood that the submarine was one unit in a patrol line she moved west. On 22 May she made another sonar contact 250 miles north of Kavieng in New Ireland, which turned out to be *RO.106*. A day later she sank *RO.104* in the same area, followed by *RO.116* the day after that, 25 miles south. At about midnight on May 26, north of Manus Island she caught *RO.108*, but for her last kill she moved back to the scene of her earlier successes, and sank *RO.105*, 200 miles north of Kavieng.

Against this, credit must be given for some outstanding Japanese successes, particularly the sinking of the damaged carrier *Yorktown* by *I.168* during the Battle of Midway and *I.19*'s destruction of the carrier *Wasp* south of the Solomons in 1942. The battleship *North Carolina* was damaged by a hit from *I.26* and one of the greatest successes came right at the end of the war, when on 30 July 1945, the heavy cruiser USS *Indianapolis* was sunk by *I.58*. The Americans had become so used to

Top: The USS *Ray* (SS.271) under refit at Mare Island, with alterations ringed in white.
Above right: Submarines built at Manitowoc, Wisconsin, were launched sideways into the narrow river.
Above: The *Argonaut* (SS.475) in April 1945.
Below: The famous USS *Barb* (SS.220) leaves Mare Island, California, on her last war patrol, July 1945.

enjoying immunity from submarine attack that they had allowed this valuable warship to travel without escort between Guam and Leyte, and even failed to notice that she was missing for three days.

As things got worse for the Japanese they turned to desperate measures. Submarines were sacrificed in useless attacks on invasion fleets or used to run supplies of goods and ammunition to garrisons of small islands. Although this misuse of submarines was justified in the case of Malta in 1941–42 the Japanese had so many garrisons that they were forced to use more and more of their submarines for this subsidiary purpose. A special supply-submarine was developed the *I.361* Class, which could

steam 15,000 miles on the surface and carry 82 tons of cargo. Nor did the dispersion of resources end there; the army started to build its own submarines for supplying its garrisons. By 1945 most of the fleet submarines were converted either to supply craft or transports for *Kaiten* midgets.

When World War II ended in August 1945 it also brought to a close the most successful submarine campaign in history. Only 231 Japanese merchant ships survived out of a prewar total of 2337 ships listed in *Lloyd's Register*. In all 190 submarines were completed for the Japanese Navy by August 1945, but only 55 were surrendered, a loss rate of more than 70 percent. It was a heavy price to pay for so little.

THE MIDGETS

The Italian Navy was the first in the field with midget submarines in 1912, with two 18-feet boats designed for the defense of Venice. During World War I the Italians built a further 12 midgets for harbor defense, but nothing further was heard of midgets until the mid-1930s, when the Japanese started work on two at Kure Dockyard. The result was the Series A, numbered *Ha.3* to *Ha.44*, 78-feet, battery-driven craft armed with two 18-inch torpedoes. They were designed to be carried by seaplane tenders and fleet submarines, and were intended for the penetration of enemy harbors. Their first operation was a disaster, an attack on Pearl Harbor intended to coincide with the main air strike. No midget got into the harbor and four were sunk. An attempt to attack Sydney Harbor, Australia, in May 1942 was also unsuccessful, although a torpedo intended for the US cruiser *Chicago* did sink a ferryboat. An attack 24 hours earlier on Diego Suarez in Madagascar had greater success; two midgets from the submarines *I.16* and *I.20* hit the British battleship *Ramillies* and a tanker.

More midgets were built, but mainly for local defense, in which role they achieved little. In 1944 the growing realization that the Empire of the Rising Sun was coming ever closer to defeat led to the construction of a new series, the Type D or *Koryu*. A total of 540 were planned but by August 1945 only 115 had been finished. As a counterpart to the *Kamikaze* tactics of the Air Force the Imperial Navy produced the *Kaiten* series, basically the body of a Type 93 24-inch torpedo adapted for one-man control. The prototype could travel 26,000 yards at 30 knots, or as much as 85,000 yards at 12 knots, and had a massive 1½ ton warhead. Later models used a hydrogen peroxide motor in place of the gasoline and oxygen motor, giving a maximum speed of 40 knots, but the shortage of engines meant that many *Kaitens* ended up as fuel tanks. The *Kairyu* midgets were more like the original Type A and carried torpedoes slung underneath the hull. Over 200 were built at Yokosuka Dockyard but like the other types, they did little to stave off defeat.

The Italians also revived the midget submarine just before World War II, and even entertained an ambitious project to ship one on board a submarine to attack the US east coast harbors. But their most noteworthy achievement was the *Maiale* or 'pig,' a small midget submarine which had two saddle-positions for its crew. Although known as a 'human torpedo' (*Siluro a Lenta Corsa* = Slow-running Torpedo) the 'pig' bore no resemblance to the Japanese *Kaiten*; it merely looked like a torpedo, and the 'warhead' had to be detached by the operators and clamped to an enemy ship's hull. In December 1941 three 'pigs' from the submarine *Scire* succeeded in penetrating Alexandria Harbor, and disabled the British battleships *Queen Elizabeth* and *Valiant*. In fact the battleships were sunk, and the Italian Navy had eliminated the entire British battle fleet in the Mediterranean, but because they were resting upright on the bottom of the harbor Italian Naval Intelligence erroneously assumed that they had only suffered minor damage, and so a great victory was therefore thrown away. The other success scored by Italian 'pigs' was against shipping in Gibraltar. In an elaborate undercover operation the Italian crews operated from the tanker *Olterra* in neutral Algeciras harbor. Two freighters were sunk and one damaged by this attack in early August 1943.

Ironically the skill of the Italians was put to best use against their own ships. After Italy negotiated an armistice with the Allies in September 1943 several Italian warships fell into German hands, and Italian crews were used to sink the cruisers *Gorizia* and *Bolzano* at La Spezia in June 1944.

The British had shown no interest in midget submarines until the Alexandria attack in 1941, which led to a series of special underwater assault craft. Two were ideas which had already been put forward, a one-man midget, and a four-man midget, the third was a straight copy of the Italian pig, code-named the Chariot. The one-man midget was known as the Welman Craft, and was designed to attach its 560 pound charge to the target by magnetic clamps. The Chariot was transported in a cylinder welded to the casing of a submarine, as in the Italian submarines.

The large midgets were known as X-Craft, and they differed from all other navies' midgets in not using torpedoes. Instead they were fitted with two 2-ton side charges which were faired into the saddle tanks. Once under the targets the X-Craft could release the charges internally and merely drop them on the floor of the harbor; with charges of such a weight there was no need for them to be exploded in contact with the hull to inflict serious damage. A slightly enlarged version known as the XE-Series

Above right: This *Seehund* midget submarine is preserved at Washington Navy Yard.
Right: Two surrendered *Seehunden* on road trailers enabling them to be rapidly deployed.
Far right: A section of a Type XXVIIB *Seehund* midget submarine.
Below: This Japanese Kaiten midget is preserved at Washington Navy Yard.

was built later for Pacific operations, with air-conditioning to improve habitability.

Chariots were used in October 1942 in a daring attempt to cripple the German battleship *Tirpitz*, which was hiding in a fjord north of Trondheim. A Norwegian trawler managed to tow two Chariots past the German outposts, but a sudden squall made them unmanageable, and they had to be abandoned. In September 1943 six X-Craft were sent to attack the *Tirpitz* and the *Scharnhorst* in Kaafjord. One, *X-8* had to be scuttled on the way to Norway and *X-9* dived and was never seen again, but *X-5*, *X-6*, *X-7* and *X-10* left their towing submarines to begin the 50-mile voyage through minefields and nets. Unfortunately *X-10* had to abandon the attack when she was only six miles from the battleship's anchorage, leaving three to make the final attack. *X-5* came to grief about a mile from the *Tirpitz* but *X-6* and *X-7* laid their charges underneath her giant hull before being scuttled by their crews; both were damaged and had no chance of escaping back down the fjord. When the charges went off they inflicted heavy damage on the *Tirpitz*, and although she was patched up she never put to sea as a battleworthy unit again.

In November four Welman craft attacked shipping in Bergen without success. These little midgets were unreliable, and never achieved any results; like the Chariots their operators suffered from the extremely cold temperatures experienced in northern waters, whereas the X-Craft, although uncomfortable, afforded reasonable protection to their crews. In April 1944 the submarine *Sceptre* towed *X-24* to Bergen, where the midget attacked a floating dock and a transport. The transport was sunk and so *Sceptre* and *X-24* returned for a second time in September; this time the floating dock did not escape.

Chariots were successfully employed in the Mediterranean. In January 1943 five penetrated Palermo harbor in Sicily, sinking the liner *Viminale* and the incomplete light cruiser *Ulpio Traiano* at their moorings. Only prompt action by their crews in removing limpet mines saved the destroyer *Grecale*, the torpedo boat *Ciclone* and the submarine *Gemma* from damage. In the Far East the *Trenchant*'s Chariots sank a transport at Phuket, in Thailand, and *XE-1* and *XE-3* attacked the heavy cruiser *Takao* in Singapore in July 1945.

Olterra in neutral Algeciras harbor.

K-Craft (*Kleine Kampfmittel* = Small Assault Units) as a countermeasure against invasion but they never played a decisive role. There were several types. The *Neger* was a one-man torpedo with a torpedo slung underneath, which ran awash with the operator in an open cockpit. About 200 were built, and later models had a perspex dome over the cockpit. The *Marder* was similar but could run submerged. *Negers* claimed two patrol vessels off Anzio and a destroyer off Normandy, while *Marders* sank the Polish cruiser *Dragon*, four landing craft and four minesweepers off the Normandy beaches. About 300 *Biber* one-man midgets were built, 29 feet craft armed with two under-slung torpedoes. They could be carried on deck by U-Boats and are credited with sinking 95,000 tons of shipping in the Scheldt estuary between December 1944 and April 1945.

The most successful German midgets were the Type XXVIIB *Seehund* type, which were developed from the XXVIIA or *Hecht* type. They were 39 feet craft propelled by a single-shaft diesel-electric plant, and when extra fuel tanks were fitted had an operational radius of 500 miles at 7 knots.

A swivelling rudder made them extremely maneuverable, and it was found that depth-charge attacks tended to throw them violently aside without sinking them – an experience which must have been extremely unpleasant nonetheless for the two-man crew. *Seehunds* sank the French destroyer *La Combattante* and a British LST in the Thames Estuary in February 1945. Nearly 300 were completed and several served in the Soviet and French navies after World War II.

Left: The nuclear submarine HMS *Repulse* has a Deep Submergence Rescue Vehicle (DSRV) perched on the after casing.

Above: A British XE-Craft is pictured running in Sydney Harbor in 1945.
Right: A Japanese Type A midget lies stranded on a Pacific island beach, 1943–44.
Bottom: The depot ship *Titania* with the X-Craft carrying submarine *L.23* lying alongside.

THE NUCLEAR AGE

As soon as German resistance ceased in May 1945 teams of American, British and Soviet submarine experts converged on German dockyards and shipyards. They had only one aim, to locate and recover as much information as they could on the new Walter boats. The British and Americans each raised a sunken Type XVIIB boat, and the Soviets certainly recovered at least one.

Everybody knew how far the Germans had progressed with their revolutionary designs, and it was solely a question of who got there first. In the end the British and Americans got the lion's share as they occupied the principal yards and harbors well to the west of the advancing Soviet armies. A share of the British tonnage was, however, later handed over to the Soviets in 1946.

It was the Walter hydrogen peroxide engine which interested everybody, despite the problems associated with it. Both the British and Americans succeeded in making their captured boats work, and the British even built two improved versions subsequently, but the Russians are believed to have abandoned their efforts after a lengthy period of trials. Looking back now it can be seen as a waste of time and money for the unstable nature of the fuel combined with its bulk made the submarine the dangerous and short-legged weapon that it had been before the introduction of diesel engines. Nevertheless it was the only means at the time of producing the high speed needed to counter the ascendancy of antisubmarine tactics.

The basis of the Walter system was the chemical hydrogen peroxide, a relatively unstable compound which breaks down easily into water and oxygen, the breakdown being accompanied by the generation of considerable heat. In normal industrial use a 35 percent solution could be produced, but any greater concentration needs stabilizers which form protective layers around any contaminating particles such as dust or rust. High Test Peroxide (HTP) was the name given to the very high concentrations of hydrogen peroxide needed by the Walter turbine. The fuel was a colorless liquid considerably more viscous than water, and liable to explode if its temperature rose above 200° Fahrenheit. To make matters worse a fire could not be put out by smothering it with foam or even sand, as the oxygen generated in the reaction was sufficient to maintain combustion, and the only way to deal with it was to dilute the HTP with water and so stabilize it.

Despite all the problems the British pressed on with their two HTP-fuelled boats, the *Explorer* and *Excalibur*, built in 1952–58, but they spent their time as 27-knot underwater targets, acting as stopgaps until the first British nuclear submarine could give antisubmarine forces similar target-speeds.

The influence of the Type XXI design was ultimately far more important than that of the Walter boats. The Type XXI characteristics were incorporated in new construction as fast as possible. The Soviets designed their *Whiskey* Class and its later variant the *Zulu* type to incorporate virtually every feature. Other navies, notably the Americans, adapted the design as far as possible to fit in with their own ideas. In 1946 the US Navy began its 'Guppy' program, named from the acronym for Greater Underwater Propulsive Power; as an alternative to building

Below: A Soviet 'Foxtrot' Class diesel-electric powered submarine edges through the Arctic pack-ice in 1973.

Above: 'Whiskey' on the rocks: this Soviet submarine grounded off Karlskrona, Sweden, in December 1981.
Right: A Soviet 'Charlie' Class nuclear cruise missile submarine in the South China Sea, 1974.

large numbers of new submarines nearly 50 of the 200 wartime submarines of the *Gato*, *Balao* and *Tench* Classes were rebuilt to incorporate Type XXI characteristics.

The basic approach in the 'Guppy' program was to streamline the hull and increase the underwater power. They lost their conning towers and instead were given a streamlined 'sail' which enclosed the periscopes and a schnorkel mast. The characteristic buoyant bow was replaced by a round bow and

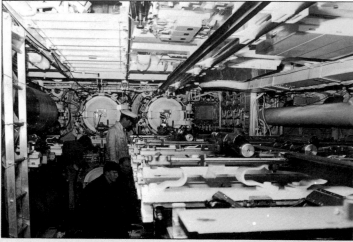

every conceivable piece of equipment likely to cause resistance was either removed or made retractable, down to deck-cleats. Internally it was much harder to find space for a bigger battery as the wartime fleet submarines were by no means spacious.

The success of the prototypes led to a further 22 *Balao* Class boats being converted. There was even a 'Pearl Harbor Guppy' a simple conversion undertaken at the Pacific Fleet base which involved removal of deck guns and platforms and crude streamlining of the periscopes.

The 'Guppy' configuration became standard for submarines throughout the world. The British converted their 'T' and 'A' Class boats similarly, and even when navies could not afford the expense of a full conversion the deck gun was sacrificed and the conning tower became a slender fin. The schnorkel or 'snort' (its British name) also became a standard fitting but with many improvements over the original German version.

Nothing had come of a German project late in the Second World War for U-Boats to tow submersible rafts across the Atlantic to act as launching pads for V-2 rockets, but the US Navy pushed ahead with the idea of firing guided missiles from submarines. In 1947 a submarine fired the first surface-to-surface cruise missile, the Loon. This small missile, an improved version of the German V-1 'doodlebug,' could be carried in a watertight 10 feet by 30 feet canister on deck, much like the old aircraft hangars of the 1920s, and then launched from a collapsible ramp by a rocket booster; it was assembled on deck and then 'flown' by radio signals, either from its parent submarine or another boat to its target. Although a crude weapon in that it could be jammed or even shot down by existing antiaircraft defences, the submarine-launched Loon and the later Regulus I and II were the forerunners of the most lethal submarine weapon of all, the underwater-launched ballistic missile.

Apart from experimental conversions of older *Gato* Class boats to such exotic uses as cargo carriers, underwater oilers and amphibious transports the other major effort the US Navy was making was the most revolutionary idea of all, the use of nuclear propulsion. Work on a reactor capable of harnessing the immense power of nuclear fission at a controllable rate had started in January 1948. Development of the associated tech-

Top: 'Foxtrot' submarines number some 60 boats and they are seen world-wide.
Above: The torpedo compartment of a modern British nuclear submarine, showing the reloading gear.

Above: The hull of the first Trident missile submarine, the USS *Ohio*, dwarfs even a 4000 ton *Los Angeles* SSN.
Below: A Soviet 'Foxtrot' is shadowed by an American destroyer in the Mediterranean.

Left: The British nuclear submarine HMS *Dreadnought* approaches the derelict chemical carrier *Essberger Chemist* preparing to torpedo her, June 1967.

and the *Nautilus* (SSN.571) was launched by Mrs Eisenhower on 21 January 1954 at Groton, and only eight months after that she was commissioned. She was an immediate success, and in her first year steamed over 62,000 miles. Apart from the streamlining of her hull she was very conventional in her design, with two shafts driven by steam turbines using superheated steam provided by a single nuclear reactor. An electric motor and batteries were provided for emergencies; by a strange quirk of history steam propulsion had finally justified itself in submarines.

From the moment at 1100 hours on 17 January 1955 when she slipped her moorings and signalled to the Submarine Force Commander 'Underway on nuclear power' the *Nautilus* began to set records and to break many long-standing ones. On her shakedown cruise she made the longest submerged cruise at the highest speed, 1381 miles to Puerto Rico at an average speed of 16 knots. By 27 November the same year she had logged 25,000 miles, and Rickover, now a Rear-Admiral, could claim that 'The *Nautilus* is not merely an improved submarine, she is the most potent and deadly submarine afloat. She is, in fact, a new weapon. Her impact on naval tactics and strategy may well approach that of the airplane.' And yet, technically, she was no more than an enlargement of the previous *Tang* Class, with six 21-inch bow torpedo tubes and a big BQS-4 passive sonar in the bow. But the figures speak for themselves: in April 1957 when the uranium core of the reactor was replaced she had logged 62,562 miles, while the second core lasted another 91,234 miles.

Of all the exploits of the *Nautilus* none caught the world's imagination like her voyage to the North Pole. On 23 July 1958 she left Pearl Harbor, passed through the Aleutians and the Bering Sea and surfaced only when she reached the shallow Chukchi Sea. She submerged when she spotted deep water alongside the pack ice and headed north along the 12,000 feet deep Barrow Sea Valley. Two days later Commander Anderson told his crew that *Nautilus* had reached 90 degrees North, the exact site of the North Pole, but that there could be no flags or landing parties for the submarine was underneath a 35 feet thick roof of ice. Film of the adventure gave an impression of a translucent cloud of fantastic shapes, dimly lit by the 24-hour sunlight above. Only on 5 August, two days after reaching the Pole, could Anderson announce to the world 'Nautilus Ninety North'. She had been submerged under the polar ice for 96 hours and had travelled 1830 miles.

It had been a risky business, and had only succeeded after five attempts between August 1957 and June 1958. There was the obvious risk of collision by surfacing underneath the ice pack but much more serious was the risk of colliding with unknown hazards in the deep Arctic channels. These were totally uncharted waters and the *Nautilus* was travelling virtually blind, with no navigational aids beyond echo-sounders and a TV camera to allow the captain to look up at the ice. If she had been badly holed by a pinnacle of rock or had damaged her propellers far under the icecap there was no other submarine in the world capable of reaching her, and her crew would have shared the fate of a previous generation of polar explorers.

More experimental nuclear submarines followed, to evaluate different types of reactor. A fifth, the giant 5450-ton *Triton* (SSN.586), broke all previous records by having two reactors; in 1960 she made an incredible underwater voyage around the world lasting 84 days. She submerged off Long Island on 16 February and proceeded to the St Peter and Paul Rocks in mid-Atlantic where the circumnavigation began on 24 February.

nology was in the hands of a group of scientists and engineers at the Naval Reactors Branch of the Atomic Energy Commission, led by Captain Hyman G Rickover of the US Navy. The penalty for failure would be immense for not only was a large amount of money involved but also the prestige of the United States, but Rickover and his team never showed the slightest hesitation.

On 12 December 1951, when the Navy Department was satisfied that the time had come to order the hull it announced that the name chosen would be *Nautilus*. This commemorated not only two previous US submarines but also the mythical boat of Captain Nemo in *Twenty Thousand Leagues Under the Sea*. Her keel was laid on 14 June 1952 by President Truman at what had now become the Electric Boat Division of General Dynamics, the birthplace of the Hollands. Work progressed rapidly

Left: The new nuclear attack submarine *Jacksonville* (SSN.699) lies alongside the Trident missile submarine USS *Ohio* at the Electric Boat yard, Groton, Connecticut.

The circumnavigation was completed on 25 April and she surfaced on 10 May.

Despite such feats the early nuclear submarines did not have the most efficient hull-forms for underwater speed, largely because they were derived from existing ideas on streamlining. At about the same time as the final designs for the *Nautilus* were being prepared work started on a small submarine designed to test new hydrodynamic principles. She was the *Albacore*, and when she appeared at the end of 1953 her appearance caused a great deal of surprise. She had a whale-backed hull with no deck-casing, and even the streamlined 'sail' had given way to a much thinner dorsal fin. Her two propellers were contra-rotating on a single shaft, and she bore a noticeable resemblance to the original British 'R' Class of 1918, with a hull made up of tapering circular sections, much like a small airship or 'blimp.' In fact many of the ideas tested by the *Albacore* derived from earlier aerodynamic research on dirigible shapes. Since refined into the standard 'tear-drop' form, the new hull-form provides significantly higher speed and maneuverability from the extra power now available.

The Soviet Navy had been very impressed by the massive U-Boat campaign in the Atlantic and spent the years after World War II in building up a large fleet to replace the one which had performed so dismally in the war. The lessons of the German Type XXI and Type XVII boats were absorbed, but the HTP experiments were discontinued after some years of abortive investigations. Like the Americans the Soviets grasped the

Right: The Polaris boat *Van Steuben* (SSBN.632) returns to Charleston Navy Yard, South Carolina, at the end of an extended deployment in 1965.
Below: The 1000-ton Swedish submarine *Näcken* is small enough to be lowered into the water by crane.

The 'tear-drop' hull design became standard, but another problem had to be overcome, that of noise. The first nuclear boats like the *Nautilus* were very noisy, partly because of the turbulence caused by the inevitable holes in the casing and the design of propellers. Propellers 'sing' from the effects of cavitation, and today a computer can scan the recorded 'signatures' of all types of ship to give a quick identification of ship-type and the speed at which it is travelling. Russian submarines have the reputation of being very noisy, the old *Whiskey* type being compared to an express train passing in the distance. Sound travels far underwater, and the *Nautilus*, for example, could be heard ten miles away when using pumps to cool her reactor. Great emphasis is now placed on propeller-design to eliminate cavitation, but the need to let water into ballast tanks means that a submarine must have a number of holes in its outer hull.

However impressive the tally of nuclear submarine building by the two Super-Powers it would be wrong to assume that there is no future for the conventional submersible. Not only are the 'nukes' expensive to build, they also make demands on skilled manpower which all navies are finding hard to meet. The inevitable bulk of the reactor and the steam machinery needed for high speed makes the nuclear submarine very big, yet there are areas like the Baltic, the North Sea and Mediterranean and Black Sea where a 3000-ton submarine is at a severe disadvantage on account of her draught and size. The Russians are rumored to be considering a new conventional class for defense and the smaller navies still rely on them to defend their coasts.

It is hardly surprising that the nation which has made the most original contribution to conventional submarine design is Germany. Although the Federal German Navy was not permitted to build submarines when it was first formed as part of NATO in 1954 this restriction was soon waived to permit 350-ton boats. The Federal German Navy had no need to repeat the effort of the 1920s to conceal its researches, for NATO gave its blessing to a rapid re-forming of a U-Boat Command. Two Type XXIII U-Boats which had been scuttled in the Western Baltic were raised in 1956, and as the *Hai* (Shark) and *Hecht* (Pike) they were recommissioned in 1957 for training. At the same time a Type XXI boat, the former *U.2540* was raised and put back into service as a non-operational trials vessel under the distinguished name *Wilhelm Bauer*.

Above: The British nuclear hunter-killer HMS *Churchill*.
Far left: The SSBN HMS *Repulse* enters Portsmouth.
Left: A circular hull-member for the first Trident SSBN is lowered into place at Groton, Connecticut.
Right: The ultimate sanction, an A.3 Polaris missile.

potential of nuclear power, and in 1958 they completed the first of the *November* Class, 3500-tonners. The *Victor* Class which appeared in 1967–68 were much quieter than the *Novembers* and are believed to be capable of 30 knots underwater.

The only other countries to embark on the construction of nuclear submarines were Great Britain, France and possibly the People's Republic of China. The British and French both have surface fleets of considerable size, and wished to develop the nuclear submarine not only as a defense against Soviet nuclear submarines but also to give their antisubmarine forces proper experience. It is becoming more and more obvious that the hunter-killer submarine is not only the best craft to catch another submarine but also the ideal Sonar platform. During operations in the Arctic in World War II, Allied escorts noticed that U-Boats were often able to hide under 'thermal layers' formed by layers of water of differing temperatures. When water changes temperature it changes density, and this can deflect sonar pulses. Surface ships have to be equipped with variable-depth sonar to avoid this effect, whereas a submarine simply changes depth. She is also relatively unaffected by rough weather as there is virtually no wave effect below periscope depth.

A Soviet sailor conducts maintenance work on a submarine torpedo late in World War II.

AIRCRAFT CARRIERS

AIRCRAFT CARRIERS

Previous page: The USS *Kitty Hawk*. Among the aircraft on deck are
McDonnell Douglas Phantoms and Grumman Hawkeyes.
Page 265: The *Kitty Hawk* refuels the destroyers *McKean* and *Harry E.
Hubbard* in an exercise in 1962.
Below: A Grumman Hellcat comes in to land on an American carrier in
the Pacific late in World War II.

270

WINGS FOR THE FLEET

The aircraft carrier is an anomaly, the most vulnerable of warships and also the most powerful. As late as 1940 she was regarded by many naval men as ancillary to the battleship, yet only five years later she outclassed the battleship in importance. Thirty years after that, the carrier's own future is under discussion, and many feel that she is a doomed dinosaur.

Even during World War II the latest carriers cost as much to build and needed more men to man them than a battleship. Today the cost of the *Carl Vinson*, *Eisenhower* and *Nimitz* averages out at about 2 billion dollars each and they need over 6000 men apiece.

The aircraft carrier is a hybrid creation which enables Man to conquer both sea and air simultaneously. The sea forms two-thirds of the Earth's surface and when Man learned to control the use of that sea, great power passed into the hands of those who achieved control. The conquest of the air also promised power to anyone who could exert the most influence, but the sea proved to be intractable, for its distances were too much for the first aircraft. There were other problems too, and even today's long-range aircraft find peculiar problems when operating at any distance from land. The air may be indivisible, but the oceans have proved baffling to many land-based air forces, and will continue to do so.

The first aircraft carriers did not take long to appear and their

potential was realized very quickly. Even in the late Nineteenth Century some balloonists talked of using captive balloons from ships. From the moment that the Wright brothers made their first flight, therefore, the question of how to use powered aircraft from ships was bound to be pursued. When Clement Ader published his *L'Aviation Militaire* in 1909, he talked of the indispensable need for a ship to operate aircraft.

The naval requirement for aircraft stemmed from one basic requirement which had been valid since Nelson's day: reconnaissance. There is a practical limit to visibility with the naked eye and even a lookout at the tallest masthead, using the most powerful binoculars or telescope, could not see more than 40 miles in perfect conditions. To provide the vital information

Below: The first shipboard landing was carried out by Eugene Ely, flying a Curtiss pusher biplane, on a platform built over the stern of the cruiser USS *Pennsylvania* on 18 January 1911.

Above: Ely prepares to take off from the *Pennsylvania* after his hazardous landing.

about enemy movements 'scouting' cruisers had to be stationed in patrol lines, near enough to remain in visual contact with one another to be able to pass signals. The invention of radio had helped to reduce the dependence on visual signalling, but there was still the problem that an individual ship could not hope to find anything outside her limit of visibility.

In 1910 the US Navy gave permission to fly an aircraft from a warship and in November that year work started on the new light cruiser *Birmingham* to install a platform over her bows.

Below: Ely's biplane leaves the *Pennsylvania*'s improvized flight deck on 18 January 1911.

Early on 14 November 1910 a Curtiss pusher biplane piloted by Eugene B Ely was hoisted aboard the USS *Birmingham*, ready to roll down the 83-foot long wooden platform built over her forecastle. The *Birmingham* duly steamed out of Hampton Roads into Chesapeake Bay and in the middle of the afternoon the weather cleared enough to allow the trial to begin. As the cruiser ploughed steadily on at 10 knots Ely raced his engine and started to roll down the ramp. Despite some damage to the propeller the aircraft began to climb clear of the ship and vanished into the drizzle. The world's first flight from a ship was a success.

The effect on the Navy was instantaneous. Ideas flooded in for launching platforms on the gun-turrets of battleships, and other novel concepts, but the main result was that in December the US Navy's first pupil pilot, Lieutenant Theodore G Ellyson was chosen to be trained by Glenn Curtiss.

The next step was for Ely to land on the big cruiser *Pennsylvania*. This was a much harder operation, and the risks were considerable. A platform nearly 120 feet long was erected over the cruiser's stern, sloping from the mainmast back aft. Ely was to touch down on this deck while the ship was under way, allowing the speed of the wind over the deck to give him better control. His plane had no brakes but a crude 'arresting' gear of 22 wires weighted with sandbags was provided.

On 18 January 1911 the weather in San Francisco Bay was poor and as the *Pennsylvania*'s captain also felt that his ship had too little room to maneuver, the ship remained at anchor with the wind behind her. This was the worst possible combination for any pilot but Ely flew out to the ship, making a low approach to her stern. He pulled the plane up just short of the platform and then cut the engine; his momentum and the tail wind took him right over the first 11 cross wires before the hooks on his under-carriage engaged, bringing him to a stop in 30 feet.

Eugene Ely's feat marked the first quickening of naval aviation, but the high hopes were premature. For one thing Ely was a well-trained exhibition pilot, a 'stuntman' who was pre-

pared to gamble his life in a highly dangerous landing. It would be a long time before the US Navy would have sufficient pilots and aircraft to be sure of repeating his performance every time. For another the aircraft itself was still at a crude stage of development, with no means of communicating with the ground or of conveying anything more lethal than a hand grenade. This helps to explain why the next step was away from landplanes capable of landing on decks, towards development of the seaplane, also called the floatplane or hydroaeroplane. This was either a specially designed aircraft with floats or a landplane fitted with airbags around its wheels to permit it to float on water. Having been launched from a ramp as before, the floatplane would land on the water close to its parent ship and then be hoisted back on board by crane. This was done in February 1911 and a month later Congress voted 25,000 dollars for the Navy to allow aviation experiments to continue. A series of giant strides had been taken inside a year. Photographs had been taken from aircraft, they could stay aloft for several hours and it had been proved that floatplanes could be recovered in a moderately calm sea.

By April 1914, when the United States became embroiled in yet another dispute with Mexico, the US Navy had 12 hydroaeroplanes, and six of them were sent to Vera Cruz to provide reconnaissance. They were carried on board the battleship *Mississippi*, and they provided valuable scouting for the landing parties.

Meanwhile the Royal Navy was also becoming enthusiastic about naval aviation. Captain Reginald Bacon, one of the Navy's most talented technical officers, had been sent to Reims in 1908 to report on an international aviation exhibition and the following year he was appointed to a Government advisory committee. In 1909 the building of a rigid airship for the Navy was authorized, and another gifted technician, Captain Murray Sueter, was appointed Inspecting Captain of Airships.

The reason for the British bias towards airships at this stage is not hard to deduce. Across the North Sea was Britain's arch-rival, Germany, building a fleet of dreadnoughts clearly intended to match the Royal Navy's in size, and Germany was the world's leading builder of airships. It seemed a logical aim to keep abreast of Count Zeppelin's developments, although as we shall see later, the answer to the airship lay elsewhere.

Permission was given shortly afterwards for five officers to train as pilots, and the first British waterborne takeoff was made by Commander Oliver Schwann on 18 November 1911, although he crashed while trying to land on water. It was left to Arthur Longmore to achieve success two weeks later in a Short S.27. Lt Charles Samson was keen to emulate Eugene Ely and flew off the forecastle of the battleship HMS *Africa* on 10 January 1912; he then repeated the feat at a naval review at Weymouth the following May, from the battleships *Hibernia* and *London*.

May 1912 was a turning point in British naval aviation. In that month the influential Committee of Imperial Defence called for the establishment of an aviation service. The service was to be called the Royal Flying Corps, but there were two separate army and naval wings, but within two years the naval wing was renamed the Royal Naval Air Service.

At the end of that year the Admiralty took a further step by ordering the old light cruiser *Hermes* to be converted as a 'parent ship' for naval aircraft. This involved fitting her with platforms forward and aft for launching and stowing. The brash young First Lord of the Admiralty, Winston Churchill, showed particular interest in naval aviation, and even intervened to ban the clumsy term hydroaeroplanes; he much preferred the simpler 'seaplanes' and the name has stuck.

The *Hermes* took part in the Annual Maneuvers in 1913. So successful was the old cruiser that plans were approved to buy a mercantile hull on the stocks and convert her to a proper seaplane carrier capable of accommodating ten seaplanes.

Below: Lt C R Samson RN flew this Short S.27 floatplane from HMS *Africa* on 10 January 1912.

When war broke out in 1914 the British Government immediately ordered the dispatch of nearly all the Army's aircraft to France, soon to be followed by a squadron of RNAS seaplanes under Samson. The new carrier *Ark Royal* was not yet ready, but to get seaplanes to sea the Admiralty requisitioned three cross-Channel steamers for conversion. They were fast, which met the principal requirement, and with the promenade and boat decks cleared there was room for a large canvas hangar and cranes to handle four seaplanes. In response to a request from the Grand Fleet a larger and faster ship was also bought, the old record-breaking Cunard liner *Campania*.

It was not long before Winston Churchill prodded the Admiralty into planning a bombing raid on the Zeppelin sheds in Cologne and Dusseldorf. The raid, on 8 October 1914, destroyed not only a shed but the Zeppelin inside, for the loss of one aircraft. Flushed by this success the Royal Navy decided on something much more ambitious, an attack across the North Sea on the German base at Cuxhaven. This meant using the three new carriers *Empress*, *Engadine* and *Riviera*, each with three seaplanes embarked, and a large screening force of light cruisers, destroyers and submarines.

Four seaplanes reached Cuxhaven safely, but found low cloud obscuring the Zeppelin sheds. The crews of three seaplanes were rescued by a submarine and the fourth was interned in Holland. The failure of the Cuxhaven raid did not discredit the concept of seaplane carriers, however, and the Admiralty pressed ahead with the conversion of more ships.

Naval aviation by November 1918 had reached a crossroads. Many ideas had been tested and others were ready to be tried, but the pace of development was to be checked sharply. While the War lasted no expense was spared in testing new concepts, but in peacetime not only would the civilian authorities be unwilling to sanction expenditure on untried-ideas but in addition there would be fierce opposition from traditionalists in the services. There would also be a vociferous new lobby for land-based air power, seeing naval aviation as a rival to its claims for money.

Below: At the end of World War I HMS *Furious* had a flying-off deck forward and a landing-on deck aft, but the latter proved to be unusable.
Right: A Fairey floatplane mounted on HMS *Slinger*'s experimental catapult.
Below right: A Sopwith 1½ Strutter takes off from HMS *Australia*'s turret platform.

TRIUMPH AT TARANTO

The British held a commanding lead in naval aviation at the end of the war in 1918 but they had already made a disastrous decision. Following two damaging daylight raids on London in 1917 the Cabinet had panicked, and had decided to unify both air forces. A new Air Ministry was formed in November 1917, followed by the formation of the Royal Air Force on 1 April 1918, the world's first independent air service.

The Admiralty realized the dangers of losing control over naval aviation, and in 1924 the Fleet Air Arm was reestablished within the RAF as a branch in its own right. Senior RAF officers particularly Trenchard became increasingly concerned to safeguard the independence of the Royal Air Force, and in their zeal they fastened on the role of strategic bombing as the main or even the only role. The debate on air power became more and more unreal, with parrot-cries of 'the bomber will always get through' – from which followed the logical conclusion, that there was no point in building fighter aircraft! At every turn the politicians and press were bombarded with claims that every ship would be blown out of the water by high-level precision bombing.

The US Navy also had its fair share of problems. After the Armistice the Army aviator Brigadier-General William Mitchell started to agitate for an independent air force along the lines of the Royal Air Force. The first practical bombing tests were carried out by the US Navy in November 1920, when the old pre-dreadnought battleship *Indiana* was subjected to a series of tests. She was first loaded with aircraft bombs placed in vital positions on board, and then attacked with dummy bombs. Billy Mitchell had been invited to watch the tests, and he was delighted to see that the old battleship sank, but what he would not admit was that the on-board detonations had sunk the ship, because the air-dropped bombs had been dummies. What was equally relevant was that the *Indiana* was a small and obsolete warship, never intended to withstand aerial bombardment.

Mitchell continued to agitate publicly for a separate air department, and the US Navy Department was put under strong pressure from Press and Congress to give the aviators a chance to prove their point. The Navy agreed to stage a series of tests.

On 21 June 1921 the first test began, with three Navy flying

boats attacking a U-Boat. Next it was the turn of the old battleship *Iowa*, a contemporary of the *Indiana*; she was attacked by Navy aircraft with dummy bombs. The destroyer *G.102* and the light cruiser *Frankfurt* were both sunk by heavy bombing.

The three ships sunk so far had either been very old or small, but the final test was to be against a modern battleship, the 22,800-ton dreadnought *Ostfriesland*. On 20 July Navy and Marine Corps aircraft dropped 34 light bombs on the *Ostfriesland* of which six hit. An inspection should have followed, but without warning six Army bombers arrived on the scene and dropped a number of 600lb bombs, of which only two hit. This time the inspection was carried out properly and the ship was found to have no appreciable damage between decks. Next day eight Army bombers each dropped two 1000lb bombs and scored six hits, but

the inspecting team reported that the ship was still seaworthy.

The Army bombers returned in the afternoon, this time armed with 2000lb bombs, the biggest in the world. One bomb bounced off, two missed and the fourth hit. Even so the *Ostfriesland* took the rest of the day to sink, with no fire-parties or damage-control parties to control the flooding. Nor had the ship put up any sort of resistance, even by maneuvering to avoid the bombs, for she was an inert hulk. But these points did not matter, for as Mitchell

Above: After World War I HMS *Furious* was reconstructed as a flush-decked carrier. She remained in service until 1945.
Below: The sinking of the former German battleship *Ostfriesland* by US Navy and Army aircraft in 1921 was a powerful propaganda victory for the advocates of air power.

278

boasted, he had sunk a battleship by air attack, and had 'proved the ability of aircraft to destroy ships of all classes on the surface of the water.'

Mitchell had done a great deal of good, and in the long run assured the future of the carrier, but he had also done a great deal of harm. He focused attention, not only in the United States but elsewhere, on high-level precision bombing at the expense of torpedo attack. All the experience of World War II and since has shown that no major warship of any navy has been sunk by high-level free-fall bombs while under way. In World War II the RAF's faith in high-level bombing proved totally misplaced, as did that of the Italian *Regia Aeronautica*. Only those air forces which showed an interest in dive-bombing and torpedo-dropping achieved any significant results.

In 1922 the Washington Naval Disarmament Treaty reduced the number of battleships building in Japan and the US. The result was that the United States and Great Britain agreed to retain 15 capital ships each, Japan accepted a limit of nine and France and Italy accepted a total of five ships each. Largely as a sop to their wounded pride the navies concerned were allocated tonnage totals for aircraft carriers, 135,000 tons to the US and Great Britain, 81,000 tons to Japan and 60,000 tons to France and Italy. This was specifically to permit the British, Americans and Japanese to convert cancelled hulls to avoid unemployment in their shipyards, but it provided the excuse to build carriers at a time when funds would have been extremely hard to find.

The fine print of the Washington Naval Disarmament Treaty also provided the first formal definition of an aircraft carrier; a warship with a standard displacement in excess of 10,000 tons but not more than 27,000 tons, designed for the specific and exclusive purpose of carrying, launching and landing aircraft, with guns no bigger than eight-inch caliber. As a special exception the Japanese and Americans were each permitted to convert two carriers of 33,000 tons to make use of existing hulls. These were the rules which were to govern carrier design for nearly two decades, and only Pearl Harbor would sweep them aside.

Right: A formation of Blackburn Baffin torpedo-bombers fly over HMS *Furious* in the mid-1930s.
Below and below right: The bombing trials carried out against the *Ostfriesland* were in many ways unrepresentative of operational conditions.

When the British ultimatum to Nazi Germany expired on 3 September 1939 the strategic situation remained very much what it had been at the beginning of the previous conflict. The Home Fleet was based in the Orkneys at the same base in Scapa Flow, guarding against a German attempt to break out into the Atlantic, while defense of the Mediterranean was largely left to the French Navy. The main difference was the existence of air power, and there were many who looked to German and Italian shore-based aircraft and submarines to wipe out the traditional British advantage of a superior fleet.

First events seemed to bear this out. On 14 September the new carrier *Ark Royal* was operating west of the Hebrides when her lookouts spotted the tracks of torpedoes passing astern. Her destroyers counter-attacked and sank *U.39* but the carrier had been lucky to escape. Three days later the *Courageous* paid the penalty when *U.29* scored three torpedo hits and sent her to the bottom. The remaining carriers were immediately withdrawn, for big fleet carriers were not suited to such work.

The German invasion of Norway in April 1940 provided the aircrews of the Home Fleet carriers with invaluable experience. The first into battle was the *Furious*, which had landed her aircraft for intensive training. Pausing only to embark two Swordfish torpedo-bomber squadrons, she sailed from the Clyde on 9 April, two days after the invasion, and two days later her aircraft made their first air strike, an unsuccessful attack on a destroyer.

Although the *Ark Royal* and *Glorious* arrived to relieve the strain on the *Furious*, there was little they could do to reverse the trend of events ashore. The collapse of the Norwegian Campaign was inevitable, for already the Battle of France had been lost. On 7 June the *Glorious* was ordered to recover the surviving RAF Gladiators and Hurricanes from Bardufoss. Despite the fact that none of the pilots had ever landed on a carrier, all landed safely. But next day the unlucky *Glorious* was intercepted by the battle-cruisers *Scharnhorst* and *Gneisenau* west of Narvik. With her deck still crowded with the Gladiators and Hurricanes there was no time to fly off a strike of Swordfish before 28-cm shells started to fall on the flight deck from a range of about 28,000 yards. By about 1720 hours the carrier was burning, and twenty minutes later she rolled over and sank.

The *Ark Royal* emerged from the Norway debâcle with a considerable reputation for efficiency. She had already become well-known to the public, both in England and Germany, as the German propaganda broadcasts plaintively repeated the question, 'Where is the *Ark Royal*?' As early as October 1939 a Luftwaffe pilot had been awarded the Iron Cross for sinking her, and the question became a British catch-phrase.

The inherent flexibility of the carrier was amply demonstrated when Swordfish from *Ark Royal* attacked targets in Sardinia and her Skuas shot down shadowers. This provocation was not enough to stir the Italian Fleet to defend what Mussolini had claimed as *Mare Nostrum*.

Life was, however, becoming uncomfortable for the Italians with a hostile aircraft carrier in the Mediterranean. The *Eagle* had been refitted at Singapore and was sent to join Admiral Cunningham's Mediterranean Fleet at Alexandria. On 9 July 1940 the Mediterranean Fleet encountered the Italian Fleet in the Battle of Calabria, during which the hard-worked aircrews of the *Eagle* had to shadow the enemy, spot for the battleships, defend their own ships against high-level bombing and try to mount strikes against the Italian ships. Not surprisingly, they failed to slow down the Italians, who were lucky to escape with minor damage, but the determination shown by the *Eagle*'s pilots convinced Cunningham that he could take the offensive with a modern carrier.

Cunningham's request was granted and on 30 August the brand-new armored carrier *Illustrious* and a powerful escort left Gibraltar. Her air group was small, only 15 fighters and 18 bomber aircraft, but she had one of the first air-warning radars, and this gave her a big advantage in fleet defense as she could detect and track hostile aircraft and give her aircraft time to gain altitude.

With *Illustrious* under his command Cunningham could now take the offensive, and the *Eagle* and *Illustrious* rampaged

Top right: The British aircraft carrier *Illustrious*.
Above right: A Sea Hurricane fighter is lifted by elevator to HMS *Argus*' flight deck.
Above left: A Blackburn Skua dive bomber moments before touchdown.
Below: An Albacore leaves the flight deck of HMS *Victorious*.

282

through the central Mediterranean, bombing airfields, hitting shipping between Italy and North Africa and mining harbors. But these were only pinpricks, and Cunningham and his staff were eager to implement a plan formulated at the end of the previous war, a torpedo strike against a fleet in harbor. The plan was to attack the main fleet base at Taranto on Trafalgar Day, 21 October. But a fire broke out in *Illustrious'* hangar while her air group had been flown ashore for maintenance, and then *Eagle*'s fuel-supply started to give trouble, a legacy of previous damage from near-misses. The damage to *Illustrious* was not serious, and so it was decided to transfer Swordfish and crews from *Eagle* to strengthen her air group for the attack. *Illustrious* finally mustered a total of 21 Swordfish, 14 Fulmars and four Sea Gladiators for the attack, now scheduled for the night of 11/12 November.

The Swordfish took off for the attack on Taranto in two waves an hour apart. The coordination of the attack was good, with flares dropped to illuminate the anchorage and dive-bombing of subsidiary targets to create a diversion. Two 18-inch torpedoes ripped into the new battleship *Littorio* and a third hit the *Conte di Cavour*. An hour later the second wave of eight aircraft arrived, and they hit the *Littorio* a third time and damaged another battleship, the *Duilio*. The subsidiary attacks were also successful as oil storage tanks were set alight and the seaplane base was wrecked.

The powerful *Littorio* was out of action for more than six months, the *Duilio* would not be fit for action inside eight months, and the *Conte di Cavour* proved to be beyond repair, all for a total of 11 torpedoes and the loss of two Swordfish. But the biggest blow was to Italian morale, for half their fleet was out of action. The surviving heavy units were withdrawn to more northerly bases, and were ever afterwards handled with great caution.

The pressure from the Mediterranean Fleet and Force H on the Italians was now so severe that the Germans were forced to lend

Below: HMS *Ark Royal*, which was launched in 1937, was the Royal Navy's most modern carrier at the outbreak of World War II. She is pictured with a formation of Fairey Swordfish.

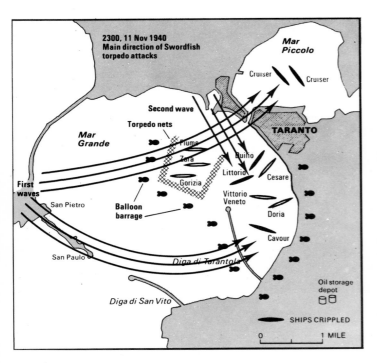

Above: A map of the FAA's attack on Taranto.

a hand. *Fliegerkorps X*, a special force of Ju 87 Stuka dive-bombers trained to attack shipping, was moved to Sicily in January 1941 with the specific task of sinking the *Illustrious*. What followed was an outstanding example of a coordinated attack catching the defense off balance. When the carrier was sighted about 55 miles west of Malta a pair of Italian torpedo-bombers made a feint attack to draw off the air patrol of four Fulmars. The British fighters took the bait and pursued the Italians for 20 miles, but another attack was developing, in the opposite direction and at a height of 12,000 feet. Although another four Fulmars were 'scrambled' they had no hope of intercepting this new force, *Stukageschwader 1* and *Stuka-geschwader 2*.

Illustrious paid dearly for her over-confidence. Within ten minutes six bombs of various sizes hit her. Three hits forward did relatively little damage, but two of the three bombs aft nearly sank her, hitting the after lift and starting serious fires in the hangar. With her steering gear crippled the carrier was a sitting duck for further air attacks, but her armored deck had limited the extent of the damage, and when the steering was repaired she was able to shape a course for Malta. The fires continued to burn and the engine rooms were filled with smoke and fumes, but she worked up to 18 knots and even managed to avoid most of the subsequent dive-bombing attacks. With a fierce AA barrage from two battleships providing some protection, the battered *Illustrious* finally crawled into Malta late that night. The fires were not extinguished for another five hours, but she had survived the worst punishment, and was ready for the voyage to Alexandria by 23 January. From there it was a relatively quiet trip to Norfolk, Virginia, by way of the Suez Canal for massive repairs.

The Mediterranean Fleet was now without an armored carrier but the second of the *Illustrious* class, HMS *Formidable* had just completed her work-up. On 10 March she passed through the Suez Canal and joined the Fleet. The effect was immediate: on 28 March Cunningham was at sea with his fleet, hunting for the Italians. In the afternoon came the exhilirating news that one of the *Formidable*'s torpedo-bombers had scored a hit on the battleship *Vittorio Veneto*, and that her speed had dropped to eight knots.

Cunningham pushed his ships forward at maximum speed in the hope of catching the crippled battleship. What nobody knew was that although the *Vittorio Veneto* had managed to effect

some repairs and had increased speed to 19 knots, an Albacore had managed to torpedo the heavy cruiser *Pola* at dusk. Thanks to the efficient air patrol of the carrier's Fulmars, the Italian Admiral Iachino had no idea of the whereabouts of the British main fleet and he felt safe in ordering the *Pola*'s sisters, the *Fiume* and *Zara* to turn back with an escort of two destroyers to try and help her. The result was the Battle of Cape Matapan, in which the three hapless Italian cruisers were surprised by Cunningham's three battleships and destroyed. But the credit was entirely due to the *Formidable*, whose air-crews had accomplished all that was asked of them; they had found and immobilized the main enemy units, they had defended their own fleet and had denied intelligence to the enemy.

This was the zenith of British carrier operations, for events were in train which would all but sweep them from the Mediterranean. The *Formidable* was badly damaged during the battle for Crete, this time by Stukas from North African airfields. Her damage was less extensive than *Illustrious*', but she too had to go to the United States for repairs. Thereafter shortage of spares and unsuitable aircraft meant that *Eagle* and *Ark Royal* made considerably less impact on operations than they could have.

Events had taken an even more serious turn in the North Atlantic. On 22 May news was received that the new battleship *Bismarck* had sailed from Bergen, bound for the shipping routes of the North Atlantic. Immediately the newly-commissioned carrier *Victorious*, was told to prepare a torpedo strike using nine Swordfish and six Fulmars.

On 24 May it was learned that the *Bismarck* had sunk the battlecruiser *Hood* and had shaken off the battleship *Prince of Wales*. It was imperative that some effort be made to slow her down and at about midnight nine Swordfish from *Victorious* attacked. By outstanding luck they had managed to score a single hit amidships, but what demanded even more skill and a large measure of luck was to find the carrier again and land safely. Yet it was all in vain, for the 18-inch torpedo could do no more than inflict superficial damage on a battleship's main belt and the *Bismarck* was only shaken by the blast.

There was one more trump to play, the *Ark Royal* which was steaming north at full speed. As soon as the position was reported by a Catalina flying boat on the morning of 26 May she was ready to fly off a strike of Swordfish. Unfortunately the first strike of 15 Swordfish mistook the cruiser HMS *Sheffield* for the *Bismarck* in thick visibility, and attacked her with torpedoes. The weather was so bad during the attack that the torpedoes

plunged, detonating their sensitive magnetic fuses. Eleven torpedoes were fired at the *Sheffield* and although the cruiser was somewhat affronted at having to dodge 'friendly' torpedoes she was able to signal to the *Ark Royal* that several of them dropped had detonated prematurely, and to signal sardonically to the Swordfish, 'Thanks for the kippers.' It was then an easy matter to rearm the Swordfish for a second strike, using a contact setting for the torpedoes.

This time the Swordfish made no mistake, and they picked up the target on their own radar, attacking individually. Despite fire from a flak-battery of 68 guns ranging from 105mm down to 20mm the biplanes lumbered on, seeming to fly almost into the *Bismarck*'s superstructure in some cases, to make sure of dropping their torpedoes at the right point. Miraculously they escaped the hail of tracers and shell-fragments and dropped 13 torpedoes. One hit the main belt, as before, and did little damage, but the second hit right aft and wrecked the rudders. This single hit made the German ship impossible to steer, and sealed her fate. Next morning the final gun-duel began between the *Bismarck* and the two battleships of the Home Fleet which finished her off.

The *Ark Royal* returned to the Mediterranean, where she fought in the repeated attempts to get aircraft and supplies into Malta. Her luck finally ran out on 13 November 1941; she was less than 50 miles from Gibraltar when *U.81* slipped through the screen and hit her on the starboard side with a single torpedo. She started to list, but there was every reason to hope that she could be towed to safety, but the pumps failed to keep pace with the flooding, and next day it became clear that she was going to go down. Finally she gave up the struggle after staying afloat for 14 hours, less than 30 miles from Gibraltar.

Above left: The British escort carrier HMS *Campania* served with Arctic convoys from mid-1944. An Albacore is shown aboard HMS *Victorious*, with Fulmar fighters parked behind.
Left: A Swordfish from HMS *Indomitable* drops a sleeve gunnery target onto the deck of the parent carrier during exercises in June 1942.
Below: A formation of Seafires over *Indomitable*. This naval version of the Spitfire was not a very successful fighter.

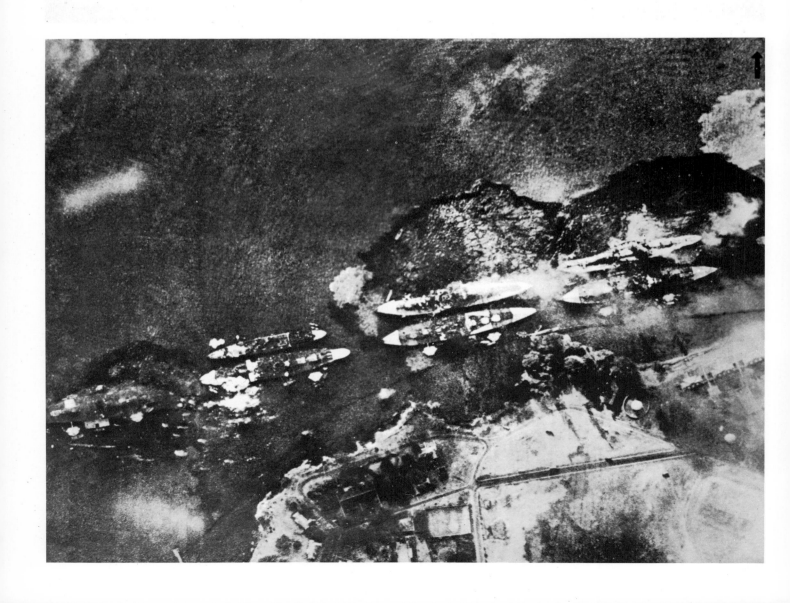

THE CARRIER COMES OF AGE

The lesson of Taranto had been studied with great interest by the Japanese. It put the finishing touches to their plans for dealing with the American Pacific Fleet, which had been a long time maturing.

The arguments for a surprise attack on the American Fleet were strong ones. There was the disparity in numbers; major reductions in American strength were needed to put the two surface fleets on an equal footing. The clinching argument was the need to keep the war short, to prevent America from mobilizing her industrial might.

As everyone knows the attack on Pearl Harbor was a devastating success. Taken completely by surprise, the US battleships were rapidly put out of action. The *Arizona* blew up, the *Oklahoma* capsized, the *California* and *West Virginia* sank in shallow water, and the *Nevada*, *Maryland*, *Tennessee* and *Pennsylvania* were all more or less seriously damaged. A second strike destroyed numerous aircraft on the ground and caused many casualties; a third strike might have inflicted further damage on the ships but the cautious carrier admiral would not allow it.

However disastrous Pearl Harbor was a milestone in the history of American carrier-warfare. Without a battle-fleet there was no longer any possibility of 'battleship tactics' taking precedence over pure 'carrier tactics', for there was no other way of taking the offensive against the Japanese. Henceforward the Americans would have to base everything on the carrier task force rather than the battle-line, an idea that had been tried out but had never been official doctrine.

However all this was hidden at the time and for nearly six months after Pearl Harbor it seemed as if the Japanese were unstoppable. The next target was the Philippines, for which the *Ryujo* and four seaplane carriers were allocated. No carriers

were provided for the fleet covering the invasion of Malaya, for the slender British naval forces had no carrier with them. The capital ships *Prince of Wales* and *Repulse* were sunk with relative ease by shorebased torpedo-bombers as they had not even a vestige of shore-based air support.

As soon as the fast carriers got back into action they struck at the East Indies. On 20 January they struck at Rabaul in New Britain from their new base at Truk in the Carolines. Despite heroic efforts by the Australian defenders, which caused Nagumo to order a second strike, Rabaul was invaded three days later. The *Hiryu*, *Soryu* and *Zuiho* covered the invasion of Ambon, while *Ryujo*'s aircraft attacked a force of American, Australian, British and Dutch cruisers off Sumatra. On 15 February the fast Carrier Division 1 struck at Australia itself, with an attack by 188 aircraft on Darwin and Broome on the North coast.

The only Allied carrier in striking distance of Java, the veteran USS *Langley*, was transporting aircraft. She was caught by the land-based bombers on 26 February and was sunk *en route* to Tjilatjap with crated fighters on board. From 1 to 3 March the Japanese carrier aircraft roamed at will, sinking warships and merchant ships trying to escape to Australia. Three destroyers, less than 100 naval aircraft and a number of transports and naval auxiliaries was a small price to pay for the oil, rubber and mineral wealth of the Philippines, Malaya and the East Indies.

On 26 March Nagumo's carriers went on the rampage again. This time it was the turn of the British in the Indian Ocean as the *Akagi*, *Hiryu*, *Soryu*, *Shokaku* and *Zuikaku* struck at the Royal Navy's main base at Trincomalee and Colombo. There was on paper a balanced Eastern Fleet to defend India and Ceylon, three carriers and five battleships under Vice-Admiral Sir James Somerville. Two of the carriers were modern but the *Hermes* carried only a dozen Swordfish. The *Formidable* had 16 modern fighters, while the *Indomitable* had 21, scarcely enough to defend against the Japanese, let alone escort an attack. Nor were the battleships any sort of match for the Japanese surface fleet.

Above left: Japan's superb Zero carrier fighter.
Left: Battleship Row under dive bomber attack.
Below: The battleship *Nevada* ablaze.

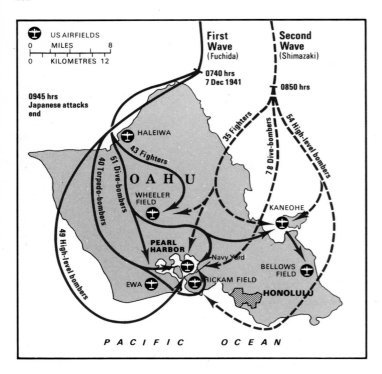

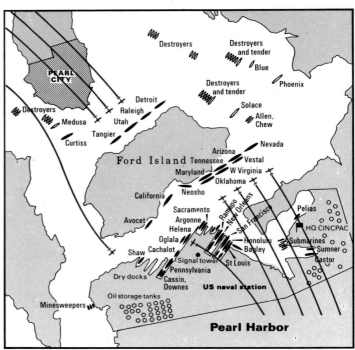

Above: A map of the Japanese attacks on Oahu.
Above right: A map of the Pearl Harbor base.
Below: Vice-Admiral Chuichi Nagumo commanded the carrier force which attacked Pearl Harbor.

Somerville intended to stay out of reach by day and only to close with the Japanese by night, using the advantage of radar. He also had the advantage of having a new base in the Maldive Islands, nearly 500 miles west-south-west of Colombo, whose existence remained secret.

Unfortunately the plan went wrong. When Nagumo's carriers failed to show up at the estimated time on 2 April Somerville interpreted it (somewhat optimistically) as evidence that Nagumo had withdrawn in the face of his concentration. He therefore sent his Fast Division, the two armored carriers and the battleship *Warspite*, to refuel at Addu Atoll in the Maldive Islands, leaving the *Hermes* and two destroyers in the vicinity of Trincomalee. He was thus caught on the wrong foot when the Japanese arrived over Colombo on 5 April. Damage to the port was relatively light, but the heavy cruisers *Cornwall* and *Dorsetshire*, hurrying south to Addu, were sunk by dive-bombers from *Akagi, Hiryu* and *Soryu*.

The Eastern Fleet was caught out of position again three days later. While it was refuelling Nagumo's carrier-aircraft struck at Trincomalee, on the other side of Ceylon. As at Colombo, there had been sufficient warning from reconnaissance aircraft to disperse shipping and so comparatively light damage was done to the base. But a second wave of aircraft was held back when a floatplane from the battleship *Haruna* sighted HMS *Hermes* and a number of ships, only 65 miles from Trincomalee. Within two hours 85 dive-bombers sank the *Hermes*, a fleet oiler and two escorting warships.

In the Central Pacific, American attempts to regain the initiative were getting underway. The *Yorktown* was sent through the Panama Canal early in January 1942 and rendezvoused with the *Enterprise* to accompany a convoy of troopships to Samoa. This brought the total of United States carriers to four, but on 11 January the *Saratoga* was damaged by a torpedo from a Japanese submarine southwest of Oahu, and had to be sent back to the United States for repairs. She was, however, quickly replaced by the *Hornet* and so the planned raid against airfields in the Gilbert and Marshall Islands was not held up.

The carriers were now grouped in three task forces: TF 8, built around *Enterprise* under Admiral Halsey, TF 11 under Rear-Admiral Brown in the *Lexington* and TF 17 under Rear-Admiral Fletcher in the *Yorktown*. TF 8 and TF 17 were to effect the strike while TF 11 was to cover them from a position east of Wake Island. The first strike was by TF 8 against Kwajalein Atoll in the Marshalls group and inflicted slight damage on shipping in return for light losses from defending Zeroes. The strike by TF 17 on the Gilberts accomplished even less and lost seven aircraft. The raid was later described as an extremely expensive form of pilot training and it showed up several weaknesses in the US Navy's carrier tactics. The worst was the lack of IFF (Identification Friend or Foe) in the F4F Wildcat (the same aircraft known to the British as the Martlet), which prevented the Flight Direction Officers from distinguishing even the strike aircraft from the patrol aircraft and 'friendlies' from 'hostiles' on their radars. Another was the lack of good long-range radios, which meant that two-way radio contact could not be guaranteed outside a range of 30 miles.

The new carrier *Hornet* was earmarked for an unusual task, flying Army bombers to drop bombs on Tokyo as a reprisal for Pearl Harbor. When Admiral King's Air Operations Staff discovered that a B-25 Mitchell two-engined bomber could just manage a carrier takeoff approval was given for the raid. As it was impossible to land again, it was hoped that America's ally China would provide a landing strip for the bombers at the end of their mission.

The Chief of the Army Air Force, General 'Hap' Arnold was enthusiastic about the plan and selected Lieutenant Colonel James Doolittle to lead the raid. After a hectic period of preparation the *Hornet* left San Francisco on 2 April 1942 with 16 B-25s lashed to her flight deck. There was no way of concealing them and it was put about that the carrier was employed on a ferrying mission. She carried most of her normal air group stowed in the hangar, but would have had difficulty in defending herself as most of the aircraft had to be dismantled to leave room for the Army Air Corps maintenance teams. The *Hornet* would have her sister *Enterprise* as an escort for the most dangerous part of the mission, and the two carriers made their rendezvous north of Hawaii 11 days later, forming Task Force 16 under Halsey's command.

On 18 April the B-25s were spotted ready for takeoff, leaving only 467 feet of flight deck for takeoff. A 40-knot gale was blowing, making the Hornet pitch violently, but at 0820 hours Jimmy Doolittle opened the throttles and, keeping his wheels within the 'tramlines' painted on the deck to guide the Army pilots, took off safely. The rest of the B-25s lumbered off at four-minute intervals and, as soon as they were seen to be safely in formation and shaping course for Japan, Task Force 16 withdrew at high speed.

The Japanese were aware of the impending raid, partly from analysis of American radio traffic and partly from a signal flashed by a small patrol vessel before she was sunk by TF 16's escorts. But the use of B-25s was unsuspected and, basing their estimates on the range of single-engined aircraft, the Japanese defenses expected the raiders a day later. They arrived on a spring afternoon and 15 of the bombers dropped their bombs on their chosen targets. A stunned defence failed to intercept them and they headed for mainland China. Four B-25s crash-landed near Chungking and the crew of one was interned by the Russians after landing near Vladivostok, but only three of the original 80 aircrew were killed.

The military results of the Doolittle Raid were negligible, but it provided a tremendous boost to morale after the unbroken run of defeats. President Roosevelt, when asked where the raid had started from, referred to James Hilton's novel and claimed that the B-25s had flown from a secret base called Shangri-La. To commemorate the exploit one of the new *Essex* Class carriers was renamed *Shangri-La*.

The next encounter, the Battle of the Coral Sea, came about because Admiral Yamamoto's cherished decisive battle had not yet come about. His strategy had worked well so far. The US Pacific Fleet had been destroyed and a chain of island bases had been established to protect the new conquests. But still the American carriers eluded him, as the Doolittle raid on Tokyo showed only too clearly. It was recognized by the Army that Australia was an important base for any counter-offensive aimed at their own base at Rabaul. Yamamoto did not believe

that the Southwestern Pacific would provide the decisive battle (his staff was planning for that in a strike against Midway), but he acquiesced in the Army's plans. It all looked so easy to him after the staggering series of victories and the Japanese were becoming drunk with success.

The operation included an amphibious invasion of Port Moresby and the capture of Tulagi in the Solomons. The Carrier Strike Force, under Rear-Admiral Takagi, comprising the *Shokaku* and *Zuikaku* left Truk on 1 May and by the afternoon of 5 May it was in a position to attack any American strike against the Port Moresby invasion. Its opposition was Task Force 17 with *Lexington* under Rear-Admiral Fitch and *Yorktown* under Rear-Admiral Fletcher. The Americans had a slight edge, with the same number of fighters as the Japanese, fewer torpedo bombers but more dive-bombers. They also had radar, and *Yorktown* had just received the first IFF equipment for some of her fighters, but above all they had the benefit of superior intelligence about the Japanese dispositions. Not only had the Americans broken the code, so that Admiral Nimitz and his staff knew exactly what the Japanese objectives would be, but there was a constant flow of reports from the Australian 'coast-watchers', who reported sightings of Japanese forces.

First blood went to the Americans, when the invasion transports in Tulagi harbor were sighted. On the morning of 4 May the *Yorktown*'s aircraft swept over Tulagi sinking four ships and damaging three more. On 6 May an Army bomber sighted the small carrier *Shoho*, which was refuelling at Bougainville while acting in support of the invasion forces. Before noon the next day the *Yorktown* and *Lexington* air groups had sunk her with bombs and torpedoes. It was realized too late that this could not be the Strike Force and that the attack had revealed the presence of Task Force 17, but this could not be helped.

Admiral Takagi, meanwhile was operating well to the north of TF 17, but equally unaware of its position. Early on the morning of 7 May he received a sighting report of a carrier and a cruiser and ordered an all-out strike from the *Shokaku* and *Zuikaku*. The

Below: The British carrier *Hermes* was sunk by Japanese dive-bombers off Ceylon on 5 April 1942.

290

Above: The B-25 Mitchell bombers which carried out Doolittle's Tokyo Raid on 18 April 1942 are parked on the flight deck of USS *Hornet*.
Above left: B-25s positioned for take off.
Left: A B-25 climbs away from *Hornet*'s flight deck en route for Tokyo.

targets turned out to be the oiler *Neosho* and her escorting destroyer, USS *Sims*, and they put up such a defense that 51 aircraft took two-and-a-half hours to sink them. Five precious hours were lost in this uncharacteristically inept affair and Takagi lost his chance to locate and engage TF 17, which was at that moment in the process of preparing to sink the *Shoho*. In a belated attempt to save the day, the Japanese launched another strike at the *Yorktown*, but an error in calculating the target's position led the strike astray. On their way back they were hammered by the *Yorktown*'s Combat Air Patrol (CAP), which shot down nine aircraft for the loss of two of their own. The survivors then lost their way and four even tried to land on *Yorktown* in error, until the carriers opened fire. The Japanese had wasted 17 percent of their strength on the first day of battle, all for an oiler and a destroyer, and still the American carriers had not been located.

The Japanese carriers turned northwards, while the *Yorktown* turned southeast to clear a patch of bad weather which was hindering flying, but during the night the Japanese reversed their course so as to be able to engage shortly after dawn. They kept in touch with the *Yorktown*'s movements and were able to launch a dawn search in the right sector next morning at 0600 hours, with a strike to follow as soon as the target was located.

Rear-Admiral Fletcher had no such confidence, for he had no idea where Takagi's carriers were. He handed over tactical command to Rear-Admiral Fitch in the *Lexington*, who ordered a big search to be flown off at 0625 hours. At about 0800 hours a Japanese plane radioed a sighting report which was intercepted by the Americans and passed to Fitch, but almost immediately this disquieting news was followed by a report that the Japanese carriers had been found. A combined strike of 84 aircraft was put up by the *Lexington* and *Saratoga*, but 30 minutes earlier the Japanese had launched their own strike of 69 aircraft. The world's first carrier-versus-carrier battle had started.

The two American carriers' strikes were about 20 minutes apart and so *Yorktown*'s CVG-5 struck first, nine torpedo-bombers and 24 dive-bombers. The torpedo strike was a failure, but two bombs hit *Shokaku*, one forward which started an avgas (aviation fuel) fire, and one aft which wrecked the engine repair workshop. *Lexington*'s group made a navigation error and so failed to find the target; after nearly an hour's search only four dive-bombers and 11 torpedo-bombers had sufficient fuel left for an attack when they sighted the smoke from the burning *Shokaku*. Only one bomb hit, on the starboard side of the bridge, which caused little damage and five aircraft were shot down by the Japanese.

The Japanese attack began at 1118 hours, 51 bombers and 18 fighters operating as a single unit. The raid was detected at nearly 70 miles' range on *Lexington*'s radar, but a series of errors put the eight Wildcats of the CAP at 10,000 feet, between the dive-bombers at 18,000 feet and the Zeroes and torpedo-bombers at 6000 feet. To make matters worse they were not stationed at a reasonable distance from the carrier, so that only three fighters made contact before the attack developed. There were also 12 Dauntless dive-bombers stationed at 2000 feet three miles outside the screen to try to break up the torpedo-bombers' attacks. Unfortunately the Japanese torpedo-bombers were flying much higher than anticipated, and they simply flew over the Dauntlesses to take up their dropping height inside the carriers' destroyer screen.

The *Yorktown* was lucky not to be hit by a torpedo, and her maneuverability helped here, but a 250kg bomb hit inboard of the island and penetrated three decks before bursting. The longer and less maneuverable *Lexington* was attacked by six torpedo bombers, three converging on each bow, and had little chance to dodge them. She was hit once on the port side forward and a second time amidships, and subsequently by two hits from 60kg bombs, which caused only slight damage.

The *Lexington* appeared to be holding up well despite her torpedo hits. Three fires were burning, but these were being dealt with by fire-parties, but the real damage had been done to her avgas system by the colossal 'whip' of the hull under the blast. About an hour after the attack a spark set off a big explosion, followed by several minor explosions and a further fire. At 1445 hours a second big explosion shook the ship and 30 minutes later

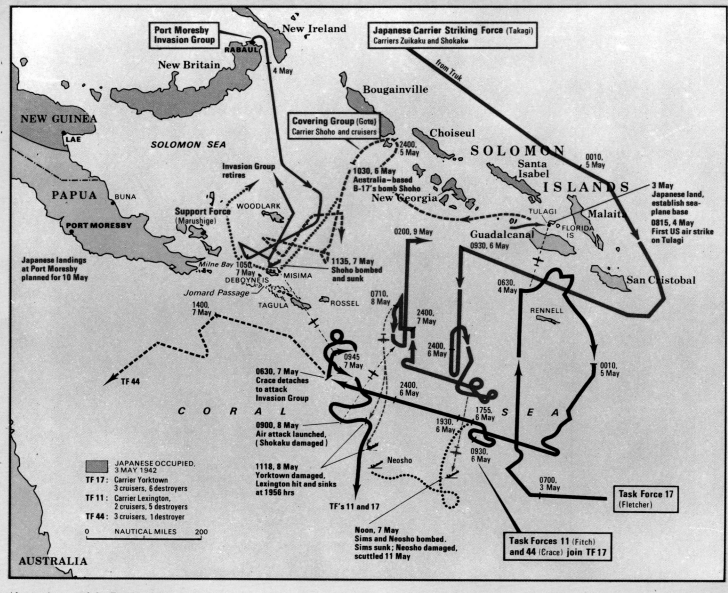

Port Moresby Invasion Group

RABAUL

4 May

New Ireland

New Britain

Japanese Carrier Striking Force (Takagi)
Carriers Zuikaku and Shokaku

from Truk

NEW GUINEA

LAE

SOLOMON SEA

Bougainville

Covering Group (Goto)
Carrier Shoho and cruisers

2400, 5 May

Choiseul

SOLOMON

Santa Isabel

0010, 5 May

ISLANDS

3 May
Japanese land,
establish sea-
plane base

1030, 6 May
Australia–based
B-17's bomb Shoho

New Georgia

Invasion Group retires

PAPUA

BUNA

WOODLARK

Support Force
(Marushige)

Milne Bay 1050,
7 May
DEBOYNE IS

1135, 7 May
Shoho bombed
and sunk

0200, 9 May

TULAGI

FLORIDA IS

Malaita

Guadalcanal

0930, 6 May

0630, 4 May

0815, 4 May
First US air strike
on Tulagi

San Cristobal

Japanese landings
at Port Moresby
planned for 10 May

PORT MORESBY

MISIMA

Jomard Passage

TAGULA

ROSSEL

0710, 8 May

RENNELL

0010, 5 May

1400, 7 May

TF 44

0945
7 May

0630, 7 May
Crace detaches
to attack
Invasion Group

2400, 7 May

2400, 6 May

2400, 6 May

1755, 6 May

SEA

CORAL

0900, 8 May
Air attack launched,
(Shokaku damaged)

1118, 8 May
Yorktown damaged,
Lexington hit and sinks
at 1956 hrs

1930, 6 May

0930, 6 May

0700, 3 May

Neosho

TF's 11 and 17

JAPANESE OCCUPIED,
3 MAY 1942

TF 17: Carrier Yorktown
3 cruisers, 6 destroyers

TF 11: Carrier Lexington,
2 cruisers, 5 destroyers

TF 44: 3 cruisers, 1 destroyer

0 NAUTICAL MILES 200

AUSTRALIA

Noon, 7 May
Sims and Neosho bombed.
Sims sunk ; Neosho damaged,
scuttled 11 May

Task Force 17
(Fletcher)

Task Forces 11 (Fitch)
and 44 (Crace) **join TF 17**

Above: A map of the Battle of the Coral Sea.

she suspended flying operations. After 1700 hours she was abandoned and three hours later a destroyer scuttled her with torpedoes.

The *Yorktown* had been luckier. Her fires were soon brought under control and at no time was her operational efficiency seriously impaired. But the elated Japanese pilots had seen her burning furiously and reported that both she and the *Lexington* had been sunk. The *Shokaku*, badly damaged by fire, was unable to recover her aircraft, but she limped back to Japan with so much water on board that she nearly capsized in a gale. Her sister *Zuikaku* also needed attention for minor defects and so the two best Japanese carriers were out of action for some time.

The Americans had won an important strategic victory on the first day of the battle, but suffered a tactical defeat on the second. They had stopped the invasion of Port Moresby, but had lost a big fleet carrier in exchange for a small carrier. The Japanese had performed better because of their experience, but they had been reckless with their aircraft and their superb aircrews, and at a crucial stage Admiral Yamamoto was robbed of his two best carriers. The Coral Sea marks the high-water mark of Japanese naval aviation, the last in that chain of success which had started just five months before at Pearl Harbor.

Above right and below: USS *Lexington* sustained damage from torpedo- and dive-bomber attack at the Coral Sea and she was abandoned when the fires aboard became uncontrollable.

DECISION AT MIDWAY

The Coral Sea operation had been in Japanese eyes little more than a side-show. Although the Army still wanted to capture Port Moresby as a prelude to the invasion of Northern Australia, Admiral Yamamoto and the Navy saw their prime task as the annihilation of the American carriers.

The small island of Midway was the key to Yamamoto's plans. Its name indicated its position, almost exactly in the center of the Pacific. By itself it was of little importance, but the little atoll was an important advanced post for the Americans from which reconnaissance aircraft could watch the Central Pacific. In Japanese hands it would drive a wedge into the American defensive triangle which had its base on the west coast and its apex at Pearl Harbor, and Yamamoto knew that the Pacific Fleet must come out to defend it. Fighting at such a distance from Japan would pose problems, but the Combined Fleet staff knew that the chance of luring the American carriers into a trap was well worth the risk. The Doolittle Raid added weight to the argument for although the American carriers had achieved very little so far it was clear that nothing but mischief would follow if they were not sunk.

The plan was complex but sound. Four fast carriers would provide air strikes on Midway, with a powerful surface force backing it up. To make doubly sure the Aleutian Islands 1500 miles to the north were to be attacked and two islands occupied to provide bases for aerial reconnaissance in case the Americans should try to attack the Kurile Islands, to the north of Japan. This force would have two light carriers and a covering force comprising three battleships and a light carrier would be in position 500 miles southwest of the Aleutians and 1150 miles northwest of the Midway carrier force. This covering force also had the task of watching for any American force trying to

outflank either the Aleutian or the Midway striking forces. The plan called for a rapid occupation of Midway to allow bases for reconnaissance aircraft to be set up and so two seaplane carriers were allocated to the surface forces covering the assault. It was expected that the Americans would take a day to react to the first attacks, leaving two days clear for occupation and preparation for the decisive battle.

There were however two major snags to the plan. The first was that it all hinged on surprise and the second was that the Japanese had poor intelligence on the number and whereabouts of the US Navy's carriers. The naval code had been broken some months before and so Admiral Nimitz knew that a major operation was planned for the Central Pacific. Possession of this code

Right: The USS *Yorktown*, accompanied by a fleet oiler, steams toward Midway.
Below: Repair parties and firefighters work on the crippled *Yorktown* during the Battle of Midway.

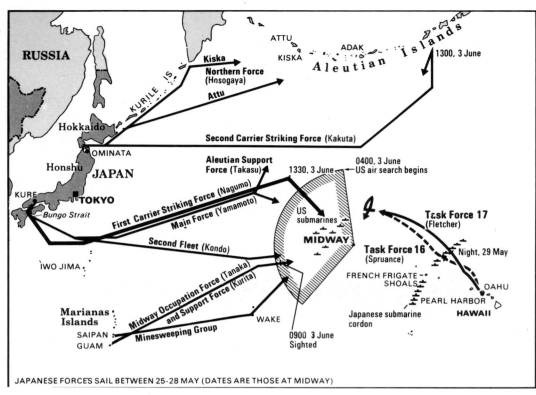

RUSSIA

ATTU
ADAK
KISKA
Kiska
Northern Force
(Hosogaya)
1300, 3 June
Aleutian Islands

KURILE IS.

Attu

Hokkaido

Second Carrier Striking Force (Kakuta)

OMINATA

Honshu   JAPAN

Aleutian Support
Force (Takasu)

1330, 3 June
0400, 3 June
US air search begins

TOKYO

KURE
Bungo Strait

First Carrier Striking Force (Nagumo)

Main Force (Yamamoto)

US
submarines

MIDWAY

Task Force 17
(Fletcher)

Second Fleet (Kondo)

Task Force 16
(Spruance)

Night, 29 May

IWO JIMA

FRENCH FRIGATE
SHOALS

Marianas
Islands

Midway Occupation Force (Tanaka)
and Support Force (Kurita)

WAKE

Japanese submarine
cordon

PEARL HARBOR

OAHU

HAWAII

SAIPAN
GUAM

Minesweeping Group

0900 3 June
Sighted

JAPANESE FORCES SAIL BETWEEN 25-28 MAY (DATES ARE THOSE AT MIDWAY)

also helped the Americans to foil a plan to fly a large seaplane over Pearl Harbor to check on ship movements in and out. As a result the Japanese had no news from that source and, to make matters worse, the patrol line of 13 submarines was positioned between Pearl Harbor and Midway after TF 16 and TF 17 had passed on their way to Midway. This was the last chance that the Japanese had of finding out the strength of the Americans and they remained convinced that only two carriers were operational in the Pacific.

The most important piece of information which eluded the Japanese was the fact that the *Yorktown* was not only afloat but in fighting trim. She had arrived at Pearl Harbor on 27 May bearing the scars of her bomb-damage in the Coral Sea battle and it was estimated that it would take three months to repair her. With the knowledge that the Japanese were heading for Midway, Nimitz ordered the Navy Yard to make every effort and the *Yorktown* sailed three days later, after 1400 men had worked on her round the clock. She was not 100 percent repaired but was battleworthy.

The Americans had been forced to make changes in their command. Rear-Admiral Fletcher continued to fly his flag in the *Yorktown* as commander of TF 17, but Halsey had fallen ill and the command of TF 16 passed to Rear-Admiral Spruance. Although not an aviator Spruance had commanded the screen

under Halsey and backed up by Halsey's highly competent air staff he was to prove an able task force commander.

The Japanese could muster the *Akagi*, *Kaga*, *Hiryu* and *Soryu* for the Carrier Strike Force. The small carrier *Hosho* was to sail with the main body of the fleet, the *Ryujo* and a new light carrier the *Junyo* were with the Aleutian invasion force and the light carrier *Zuiho* was to accompany the Support Force. The Aleutian diversion robbed the Midway force of the *Ryujo*'s air group (37 aircraft) and the 77 aircraft carried by the *Junyo* and *Zuiho*.

The early warning of the attack enabled TF 16 and TF 17 to be in position covering Midway, 400 miles to the northeast, and also enabled Admiral Nimitz to ignore the diversionary attack on the Aleutians. On 3 June a Catalina sighted the invasion force under Admiral Kondo about 800 miles west of Midway and that afternoon a series of air attacks started from the aircraft based on Midway, most of them ineffectual. By nightfall the two opposing carrier forces were closing on Midway, neither aware of the other's whereabouts, and by dawn on 4 June they were only 248 miles apart, the Americans to the east of the Japanese. The only difference was that the Americans knew they were looking for carriers; the Japanese were not even certain that any American carriers could be in the vicinity. Admiral Nagumo launched 108 aircraft for the first softening up of Midway's defences, but he cautiously held back *Kaga*'s air group in case any American ships were sighted. Fletcher took much the same precaution by launching only ten Dauntlesses from the *Yorktown* to search to the north, just to make sure that the Japanese task force had not turned his flank.

At 0602 hours Admiral Fletcher learned from a Catalina that the Japanese carriers had been sighted 207 miles northeast of

Far left: A map of the Battle of Midway.
Left: Frank Fletcher (seen here as a Vice-Admiral later in the war) commanded Task Force 17 at the Coral Sea and Midway.
Below: Douglas TBD Devastator torpedo-bombers suffered appallingly heavy losses at Midway.

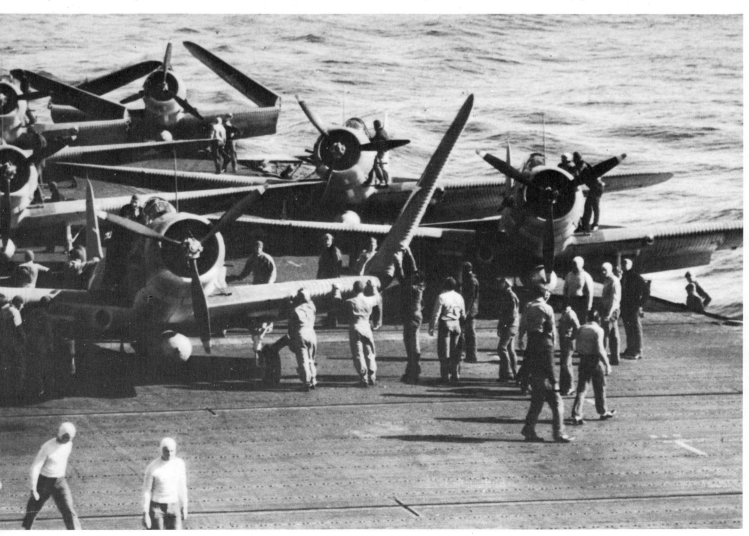

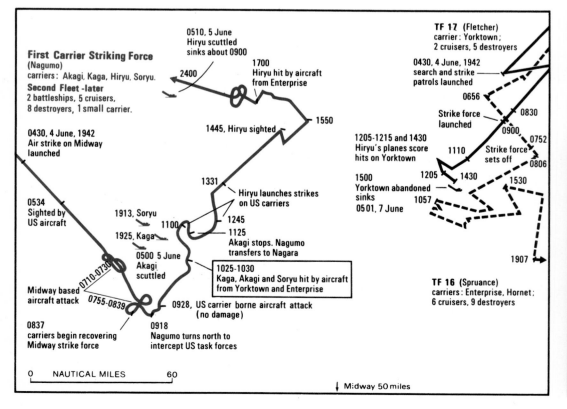

First Carrier Striking Force
(Nagumo)
carriers: Akagi, Kaga, Hiryu, Soryu.
Second Fleet -later
2 battleships, 5 cruisers,
8 destroyers, 1 small carrier.

0430, 4 June, 1942
Air strike on Midway
launched

0534
Sighted by
US aircraft

Midway based
aircraft attack

0837
carriers begin recovering
Midway strike force

0918
Nagumo turns north to
intercept US task forces

0710-0730

0755-0839

1913, Soryu

1925, Kaga

0500 5 June
Akagi
scuttled

0928, US carrier borne aircraft attack
(no damage)

1100
1245
1125

0510, 5 June
Hiryu scuttled
sinks about 0900

2400

1700
Hiryu hit by aircraft
from Enterprise

1550

1445, Hiryu sighted

1331

Hiryu launches strikes
on US carriers

Akagi stops. Nagumo
transfers to Nagara

1025-1030
Kaga, Akagi and Soryu hit by aircraft
from Yorktown and Enterprise

TF 17 (Fletcher)
carrier: Yorktown;
2 cruisers, 5 destroyers

0430, 4 June, 1942
search and strike
patrols launched

0656
0830
0900
0752
0806

Strike force
launched

Strike force
sets off

1110
1205
1430

1205-1215 and 1430
Hiryu's planes score
hits on Yorktown

1500
Yorktown abandoned
sinks
0501, 7 June

1057
1530
1907

TF 16 (Spruance)
carriers: Enterprise, Hornet;
6 cruisers, 9 destroyers

0 NAUTICAL MILES 60

↓ Midway 50 miles

Midway and five minutes later he ordered Spruance to launch a strike from *Enterprise* and *Hornet*. He himself would launch *Yorktown*'s aircraft as soon as the Dauntlesses had been recovered and refuelled. Spruance's Chief of Staff decided not to fly a reconnaissance mission to confirm the Catalina's sighting, but to attack straight away to catch the Japanese carriers in the middle of recovering and refuelling the Midway strike. It was a rash move, for as we know, Nagumo had kept back over 90 aircraft, but as yet he had no idea that the two carriers were so close.

Although the American attacks were made piecemeal their frequency and tenacity kept up the pressure on Nagumo. At 0707 hours four bombers and six torpedo-bombers attacked *Akagi* and *Hiryu*, but the Japanese CAP mauled them severely and seven aircraft were lost without scoring a hit. Nagumo now reached the conclusion that Midway's defences had not been silenced sufficiently and ordered a follow-up attack using the aircraft held back for strikes against ships. This meant striking down the B5Ns to the hangars for removal of the torpedoes and rearming with bombs. Then at 0728 hours, just 14 minutes after the order had been given, came a report from a floatplane to say that TF 16 had been sighted. The report was vague and did not mention the carriers or the fact that they were flying off aircraft. Nagumo hesitated, asked the floatplane to amplify its report and then suspended the bombing-up of the remaining B5Ns.

Meanwhile the attacks from Midway started again. The first was at 0755 hours on the *Hiryu* and *Soryu*, the second came at 0810 hours and the third at 0830 hours. They achieved nothing, but the third attack coincided with the return of the first Midway strike aircraft and this delayed the recovery of the aircraft to such an extent that ditchings and crashes of damaged aircraft pushed the total losses up to 36 aircraft, or 33 percent of the strike. The final aircraft was not safely back on board until 0917 hours. The delay was fatal, for at 0820 hours Nagumo had

Left: SBD Dauntless dive-bombers played a major part in the victories at Coral Sea and Midway.
Below left: The carrier air strikes at Midway.
Right: *Yorktown*'s funnel and tripod mast were damaged by the second Japanese bomb to hit her.
Below: A new *Yorktown* joined the fleet in 1943.

received his first intimation that the mystery task force sighted at 0728 hours might include a carrier.

Nagumo had been outmaneuvered and knew it, but he finished the recovery of his aircraft and resolutely turned his carriers 90 degrees north to get in position for a strike against TF 16. Even the arrival of the first wave of attackers at 0925 hours had little effect on these preparations for as before they were unco-ordinated. The first wave of 15 Devastators from *Hornet* was shot down by the CAP and flak, then *Enterprise*'s strike went in with 14 Devastators, scored no hits and lost 10 aircraft. Finally *Yorktown*'s 13 Devastators attacked and were beaten off with the loss of 10 more. Of the other aircraft in the strike, 35 dive-bombers and 10 escorting fighters failed to find the Japanese ships. All the fighters had to ditch when they ran out of fuel and only 11 bombers reached Midway. Another 59 Dauntlesses had over-flown the estimated position and had turned back towards *Enterprise* when they sighted a lone Japanese destroyer heading back to the carriers. The Air Group Commander correctly interpreted her movements and sighted the carriers at about 1005 hours. They were in a diamond formation, with *Hiryu* leading.

The 12 aircraft began a diving attack on *Kaga*, while the remaining aircraft went for the flagship *Akagi*. The third squadron attacked *Soryu* four minutes later.

The concentrated attack was a brilliant success. The *Akagi* was hit twice, once by a 1000-pounder which hit the edge of the center lift and burst in the hangar and by a 500-pounder which burst on the after end of the flight deck and set fire to parked aircraft. The *Kaga* was hit by four 1000-pounders of which three penetrated the hangar. The *Soryu* took three 1000-pounders in a line down the center of the flight deck and two penetrated the hangar. All the dive-bombers survived the attack, although 18 of the aircraft from the *Enterprise* were either shot down on the way home or had to ditch because they could not find their ship.

Of the three stricken carriers the *Kaga* was the worst hit, with the forward part of the ship set on fire. The third bomb hit just in front of the island and killed nearly everyone on the bridge, including the captain. The flight officer, the only surviving officer on the bridge, took over command and tried to fight the fires, but nothing could make any impression on them. The ship was abandoned about three hours after the attack. The *Soryu* was set on fire from end to end, and shortly after 1040 hours lost rudder control. Her captain gave the order to abandon ship at 1045 hours, but the blazing hulk continued to drift for another eight hours before sinking with the loss of about 700 of her crew. The *Akagi* was racked by fire and explosions, but stood up better to the damage. Her captain took energetic measures to fight the fires and gained time for Admiral Nagumo to shift his flag to a light cruiser. At 1130 hours all survivors except the damage-control parties were evacuated, but even they abandoned ship at 1915 hours.

Despite the disabling of three of his carriers, Nagumo still had a trump card in the undamaged *Hiryu*. She was ordered to launch an immediate counter-strike, with the certain knowledge that the Americans had used all but 17 of their strike aircraft and that the 60 Devastators and Dauntlesses which had just departed would need at least four hours to refuel and rearm for a second strike. *Hiryu* had her problems as well, for she had lost 10 out of the 27 bombers sent to Midway, and the survivors needed repairs and servicing before they could take off. Thus she could not launch a coordinated bomb- and torpedo-attack.

The *Yorktown* was the only American carrier with search aircraft left and so she launched ten Dauntlesses at 1130 hours before recovering her strike aircraft. Half an hour later her radar detected the *Hiryu*'s strike and her defending Wildcats were vectored out to intercept at 15 to 20 miles. Aboard the carrier last-minute precautions were taken; refuelling was stopped and the avgas supply system was flooded with carbon dioxide gas to damp down the deadly vapor.

A lethal dogfight developed over the *Yorktown*, with many of the attackers jettisoning their bombs, but eight of the D3A 'Vals' did not, and broke out of the dogfight to streak in through the screen. Six were shot down but three bombs hit the carrier. One burst on the flight deck and set aircraft ablaze; the second burst in the funnel and blew out the fires in five out of the six boilers, while the third penetrated three decks before bursting. An avgas fire was started, but fortunately the magazines were promptly flooded, the cofferdams surrounding the fuel tanks were flooded with carbon dioxide gas, and the fire did not spread. But the ship had lost nearly all power and by 1220 hours was stopped.

Admiral Spruance detached two cruisers and two destroyers from TF 16 to provide extra AA cover for the crippled carrier and by 1320 hours she had three boilers working and could make 20 knots. The fire was still burning but was under control. She had flown her CAP to the other carriers, but was now able to resume the fuelling and arming of her remaining strike aircraft. About an hour later one of the screening cruisers reported that she had detected *Hiryu*'s second strike, the ten B5N torpedo-bombers and six escorting Zeroes. They were heading for the *Yorktown* rather

Left: The carrier *Hiryu* maneuvers to avoid the bombs of B.17s flying from Midway Island.
Right: *Hiryu* ablaze after attack by Dauntless dive-bombers. She sank the following day.
Below: USS *Wasp* was lost off Guadalcanal.

Above and right: USS *Hornet* was crippled by air attack during the Battle of Santa Cruz in October 1942. She was abandoned by her crew and finished off by Japanese destroyers.

than the two undamaged American carriers, and so once again fuelling was stopped and the fuel system was flooded with carbon dioxide, but there was time to fly off eight fighters.

This time the CAP was not so successful in breaking up the attack, and only two 'Kates' were shot down before they reached an attacking position. The CAP then chased the 'Kates' through their own AA barrage and stopped them from dropping more than four torpedoes, but two of these struck the *Yorktown* on the port side. Only five 'Kates' returned to *Hiryu* to report that they had sunk the carrier. The Japanese, well aware of what had happened to their own carriers that morning, could not believe that the carrier they had seen burning at noon could have been operational so soon, and so they jumped to the conclusion that they had just inflicted torpedo hits on a second carrier. As we know, they credited the Americans with having only two carriers fit for sea and so they were now certain that they had wiped out both of them. By a coincidence the three carriers of TF 16 and TF 17 were sisters and virtually identical in appearance.

The *Yorktown* was battered but still afloat. Once again power was lost and the ship lay dead in the water. She had already diverted her Dauntlesses to the *Enterprise*, and the fight continued to check the flooding. By 1500 hours she was listing 26 degrees to port and the order was given to abandon ship.

While the attack on *Yorktown* was developing one of the ten Dauntlesses which she had launched earlier reported the position of the *Hiryu* and so TF 16 prepared a forlorn hope strike with all its remaining aircraft. These were pitifully few, 4 Devastators and 24 Dauntlesses from *Enterprise* and 22 Dauntlesses from *Hornet*, with 50 fighters. *Enterprise* started to launch her strike, 24 Dauntlesses, at about 1530 hours, followed 30 minutes later by 16 Dauntlesses from *Hornet*. The Wildcats were all held back for the CAP, and none could be spared to escort the strike.

The *Hiryu* was preparing for a third strike against the *Yorktown* at 1630 hours, but it had been postponed until 1800 hours to give time for the exhausted crew to have an evening meal. That meal was never finished, for without warning 13 dive-bombers attacked

out of the sun, while others attacked her escorts. The first three bombs missed but then four hit, two forward of the island and two amidships. Once again there was a searing explosion of fire in the hangar, and the warheads and bombs stored in readiness for the next strike began to explode. Despite this damage the *Hiryu* continued to steam at 28 knots. Nothing could stop the flames for the bomb blast had destroyed the fire-fighting equipment and the fires gradually spread through the ship. She burned through the night, and the order to abandon ship was not given until 0230 hours the next morning. Despite a torpedo from an escorting destroyer to scuttle her she was still afloat next morning, but sank at about 0900 hours.

To Admiral Yamamoto on board his flagship, the giant battleship *Yamato,* the situation was surprisingly still hopeful, although he was stunned by the loss of the four magnificent carriers. He ordered the Second Mobile Force in the Aleutians and Admiral Kondo's Second Fleet to meet the Main Body northwest of Midway. This would give him in little over 24 hours a concentration of force, with the light carriers and the *Hosho;* even after the sinking of *Hiryu* the Japanese had as many aircraft left as the Americans. But the Japanese had no experience of being on the losing side and Yamamoto's estimate of the time needed to concentrate such a large force was too low; only Admiral Kondo's two battleships joined Nagumo by the morning of 5 June, and even the Commander-in-Chief himself was still out of touch. In any case Spruance had very prudently withdrawn his two carriers to the east at dusk, so there were no carriers to be sunk by the Japanese, although their reconnaissance aircraft had swung from one extreme to the other and were now reporting four carriers present.

Early on the morning of 5 June Yamamoto conceded defeat by ordering the withdrawal of the invasion forces, although the covering forces to the north were told to devote their attention to the assault on the Aleutians. As soon as the withdrawal was noticed the American carriers gave chase, but inaccurate reporting resulted in the air searches missing opportunities to inflict further damage. It was a disappointment to Spruance and Fletcher but they had just won the most important single victory of the war in the Pacific and had more than enough laurels.

The implications of the Battle of Midway were far-reaching. Although the war had not been lost the Japanese had been given a severe shock. It is said that Imperial headquarters was sunk in black despair for several weeks, fearing an immediate American attack on Japan itself. The loss of the carriers was bad enough, but at least 260 aircraft had been lost, and 45 percent of the air-

crews. These losses could have been replaced but now a fatal rift between the Army and the Navy opened up. Even when the full losses became known the Army continued to plan for further expansion as if Midway had not happened. The Navy was now forced to overextend its resources at just the moment when it should have been resting and rebuilding its strength. For the Americans it was an obvious strategic victory and, although the loss of the *Lexington* in the Coral Sea and the *Yorktown* at Midway were hard blows, the first of the new *Essex* Class was not far from completion. The worst of Admiral Yamamoto's fears had come to pass: the big battle had been fought without accomplishing the destruction of the main American fleet and now it was to be a war of industrial production, which in the long run the Japanese must lose.

There were in fact to be only two more genuine carrier-to-carrier battles, the Eastern Solomons on 24 August and Santa Cruz on 26 October 1942. These were brought about because of the Japanese Army's insistence on occupying the Solomons. That precipitated the ferocious struggle for Guadalcanal and the two battles were part of the struggle for domination of the area. In the first engagement the *Ryujo* was sunk and the *Enterprise* was damaged, and as at Midway the Americans won a strategic victory by preventing an invasion. Then on 31 August the *Saratoga* was damaged by a torpedo from submarine and had to return to the United States for repairs. On 15 September the *Wasp* was also torpedoed, but this time the 'whip' of the hull ruptured avgas lines and fire mains and the carrier was gutted by fire. Within 30 minutes she was abandoned and sinking, leaving the *Hornet* the only carrier in the front line for a while. Fortunately the *Enterprise* returned to active duty only two days before the Battle of Santa Cruz, for the two carriers were faced by Nagumo's Striking Force, comprising the *Shokaku, Zuikaku, Zuiho* and *Junyo.* Their last success was to be the sinking of the *Hornet,* in a classic attack by dive-bombers and torpedo-bombers. Although she stood up nearly as well as her sister *Yorktown* to the widespread damage she eventually had to be scuttled to avoid capture. The *coup de grâce* was administered by Japanese destroyers.

Santa Cruz was a technical victory for the Japanese, for on paper they had only suffered damage to the *Zuiho* and *Shokaku.* But they had lost over 100 aircraft and most of their crews, thanks to prodigal use of them over Guadalcanal. When the Guadalcanal campaign finally petered out at the beginning of February 1943 it was clear that a turning point had been reached. Although the US Navy had lost two carriers, eight cruisers and 14 destroyers, the Japanese Naval Air Force had lost a thousand front-line aircraft and with them most of the crews. In the long run these losses were to outweigh even the staggering losses on land. What makes them even more significant is the fact the Japanese Navy was pursuing no important strategic aim but merely supporting the Army.

Above left and below: USS *Wasp* was torpedoed by a Japanese submarine off Guadalcanal on 15 September 1942 and was abandoned. The *Wasp* had previously served in the Mediterranean.
Left: A bomb hit *Enterprise* abaft the island and blew two SBDs off the flight deck during the Battle of Santa Cruz.

THE FAST CARRIERS

The intervention of hurriedly converted mercantile escort carriers in the Battle of the Atlantic in March to May 1943 had been decisive and by the summer of that year the declining U-Boat threat allowed the British to switch more of their naval air strength to the offensive.

As early as 1941 German communications in Northern Norway had been a priority target, in order to take the strain off the convoys which carried vital war material to Russia. In March 1942 the *Victorious* and her Albacores had a rare chance to attack the battleship *Tirpitz* at sea but failed to hit her. Despite the small scale of the attack the *Tirpitz* had a close shave and even if the Royal Navy was disappointed by the result the *Kriegsmarine* was highly impressed. On Hitler's orders the *Tirpitz* was told not to remain at sea if a carrier was known to be at sea.

In 1943 the *Furious* was the backbone of the Home Fleet's carrier force, for the *Victorious* was sent to the Pacific at the end of 1942 to make up numbers after the loss of the *Hornet* and *Wasp* and the disabling of the *Enterprise*. The other big carriers were usually in the Mediterranean, apart from the *Indomitable*, which after July was under repair. Only three offensive operations could be undertaken in 1943, and the USS *Ranger* took part in the third, the only American carrier strike in Northern European waters. Her air group attacked German shipping at Bodo on 4 October 1943 and her Dauntlesses and Avengers sank or damaged 10 ships for the loss of five aircraft.

On 3 April 1944 the Home Fleet mounted Operation Tungsten, using the *Furious* and *Victorious* and the escort carriers *Emperor*, *Searcher*, *Pursuer* and *Fencer* to strike at the *Tirpitz* in Kaafjord. Careful planning and rehearsal enabled the Barracuda dive-bombers to take the Germans completely by surprise. The *Tirpitz*

Above: The ungainly Fairey Barracuda was designed to operate both as a torpedo- and dive-bomber.
Above right: The US Navy's SBD Dauntless dive-bomber served throughout World War II.
Below: The veteran *Saratoga* was retired in 1945.

Above: Grumman F4F Wildcats test-fire their guns during preparations for the Torch landings.
Right: Flying operations from USS *Monterey* (CVL.26) are viewed from her open compass platform.

was hit by 14 bombs and suffered over 400 casualties and only two Barracudas and a Hellcat were shot down. The Hellcats and Wildcats had supported the strike by strafing the target and suppressing the enemy flak, while fighter cover was given by Corsairs. Had the Fleet Air Arm had something bigger than the 500-pound bomb the *Tirpitz* might have been sunk but the RAF still insisted that there was no need for anything heavier.

In July and August the Home Fleet carriers struck again, but on both occasions the *Tirpitz* was surrounded by smokescreens in time to foil the attack. The main problem in all these attacks was the shelter provided by the steep side of the fjord; the aircraft had a severely limited sector in which to make their bombing run, while the extensive nets prevented a torpedo-attack.

Other operations were mounted in Norwegian coastal waters to interrupt the coastal shipping, and 100,000 tons of shipping was sunk by the fleet carriers alone. Right up to the end of hostilities in Europe in May 1945 there were of course convoys to and from Murmansk and escort carriers sailed regularly with the convoys from February 1944. Their operations also helped to whittle away German resources, and several U-Boats were sunk in the Arctic.

In the Pacific the time for defensive fighting was over too, and by the end of 1943 it was possible to form a Fast Carrier Force, Task Force 50. With its six fleet carriers, five CVLs and 700 aircraft, screened by six battleships and six cruisers it was the most powerful fleet in the world. It was divided into four Task Groups, TGs 50.1, 50.2, 50.3 and 50.4.

The Carrier Interceptor Group (TG 50.1) had as its first task in November 1943 to hit islands in the Marshalls group to prevent them from reinforcing Tarawa and Makin. The Northern Carrier Group supported the Makin landings while the Southern Carrier Group attacked Rabaul and Tarawa in turn. The Relief Carrier Group was charged with supporting the landings in the Solomons and then made a very successful strike on Rabaul which inflicted severe damage.

On 6 January 1944 TF 50 was renumbered TF 58 and put under the command of Rear Admiral Marc A Mitscher, one of the US Navy's most skilled aviators. The new carriers were coming forward in such numbers that it was now possible to provide six fleet carriers and six light fleet carriers.

The new Fast Carrier Force destroyed all the aircraft defending the Marshalls in a strike against Kwajalein at the end of January, so that not a single ship was hit by air attack during the landings on Kwajalein and Namur. Then it was the turn of Eniwetok and on 17–18 February the first attack was made on Japan's 'Gibraltar of the Pacific', the fortress of Truk in the Carolines. Truk had been the base of the Combined Fleet for nearly two years and it was hoped that an attack on such an important target might even force the Japanese fleet to try a surface action.

In fact the attack turned out to be a sort of Pearl Harbor in reverse. Despite alerts and even a radar warning very few aircraft took off in time to cope with the raiders, and nearly 200,000 tons of shipping was sunk or damaged. A fierce air battle developed but the Japanese lost over 50 aircraft and a further 100 or more destroyed or damaged on the ground; the losses were four Hellcats and nine Avengers. Truk was no longer usable as a base and the news was received in Tokyo with consternation for it meant that the whole defensive perimeter was in ruins. The only consolation was that a strike by six 'Kates' on the night of 17 February broke through the screen and put a torpedo into the stern of the *Intrepid*. But the *Essex* class were tough ships and, although her rudder was jammed, the *Intrepid* was able to return to Majuro Lagoon at 20 knots.

With the arrival of the British carrier *Illustrious* in Ceylon it was possible to stir up more trouble for the Japanese. Task Force 70 was formed with the *Saratoga* and *Illustrious*, to operate in the East Indies against Japanese oil and rubber supplies. Under the command of Admiral Sir James Somerville the new Eastern Fleet celebrated by a devastating raid on the oil refinery at Sabang in Sumatra on 19 April 1944.

Operations showed up weaknesses in the British carrier organization. For one thing the air group was small and for another the strike aircraft, the Fairey Barracuda had poor performance. Nor was the vital importance of a brisk turn-around of aircraft in the hangar and on the flight deck appreciated at first by the British, who had to learn the advanced techniques from the battle-hardened *Saratoga*. Eventually the Barracudas were exchanged for TBF Avenger torpedo-bombers, and with these the *Illustrious* and *Sara* were able to launch a second successful strike in May. This time the target was a refinery outside Surabaya on the island of Java and only one plane was lost. The results were not as impressive as those achieved by the Fast Carrier Force in the southwest Pacific but they compounded the problems of the Japanese High Command and distracted attention from the drive against the Marianas in the Central Pacific.

It has already been said that there were only five great carrier-versus-carrier battles, and the greatest of these was the Battle of the Philippine Sea. But it was not the close-run affair that Coral Sea, Midway, the Eastern Solomons or Santa Cruz had been. The American carriers were more numerous and their aircraft and pilots much better than they had been two years before, whereas the Japanese had squandered their magnificent force of pilots with no heed for the real danger that was developing.

Once again the Japanese tried to bring on a decisive battle in the vicinity of the western Caroline Islands. The trigger was the American landing on Saipan on 15 June, for this island was the key to the new 'inner ring' of defensive islands which had to be held to keep Japan out of range of long-range bombers. It was hoped to make up for the shortage of naval aircraft by bringing the Americans to battle west of Saipan within range of land-based aircraft, flying from Guam, Yap and Rota.

A big reorganization had taken place at the beginning of March, with the Combined Fleet replaced by something similar

Below: Fire parties deal with a blaze among F4F Wildcats. This was a particular hazard on crowded flight deck parks and hangar decks. Stringent precautions were always necessary.

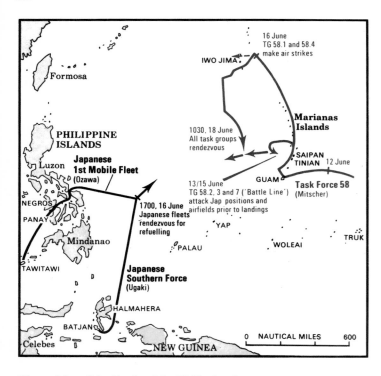

Above: Map of the Battle of the Philippine Sea.

the *Chitose* was hit by two 'dud' torpedoes. The threat was so great that the First Mobile Fleet was forbidden to put to sea for maneuvers and as there was no airfield at Tawitawi the unfortunate aircrews could not improve their proficiency.

The land-based air support for Ozawa was to be provided by Vice-Admiral Kakuji Kakuta, commanding the Base Air Force in the Marianas. Because Japanese carrier aircraft were designed without the 'luxuries' of armor protection for the pilot and self-sealing fuel tanks, they could outrange American aircraft by as much as 210 miles and so Ozawa knew that he could stay out of range and still launch a strike of his own as soon as the attacks from the Marianas had whittled down the enemy's numbers. In fact Ozawa intended to fly his carrier aircraft on to Guam to be refuelled and rearmed and to make a second strike on Task Force 58 on the way back. He was also banking on the easterly tradewinds, which would allow him to launch and recover planes while steaming towards the enemy, whereas the American carriers would have to turn into wind every time they operated their aircraft, particularly when recovering them. The plan also provided much better reconnaissance than at Midway, for Ozawa was determined to avoid the mistake of not locating all hostile carriers.

Task Force 58 formed part of the 5th Fleet under Admiral Spruance, whose proverbial caution had not only provided the victory at Midway but had certainly avoided a defeat. Spruance correctly saw his main duty as the protection of the Saipan invasion force and he disposed his four Task Groups to block any attack by Ozawa, with special precautions to prevent the Japanese from slipping past to the north or south. An innovation was to pull the battleships out of the task group and put them into a Battle Line under Admiral Lee. The Japanese aircraft would first have to face a 'picket line' of heavy AA fire before going on to tackle each Task Group, its CAP and individual AA defences.

The First Mobile Force left Tawitawi on 14 June and was

to the American task forces. The First Mobile Fleet was put under the command of Vice-Admiral Ozawa, with three carrier divisions.

The carriers were sent to Singapore for a short refit and were then moved to their forward base at Tawitawi, in the Sulu Archipelago in the northeast of Borneo. Here they were supposed to exercise their inexperienced aircrews, but this proved virtually impossible. Enemy submarines were very active, and on 22 May

Below right: The badly damaged USS *Franklin*.

Right: The Curtiss SB2C Helldiver was an unpopular aircraft with its crews.
Below and bottom: Maps illustrating the fighting on 19–20 June 1944 during the Battle of the Philippine Sea. This engagement was known to US naval airmen as The Great Marianas Turkey Shoot.

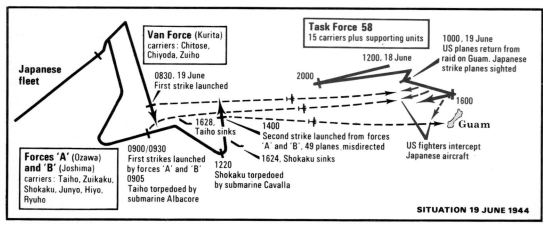

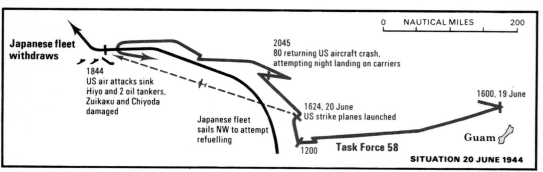

Above: USAAF Republic Thunderbolt fighters are ferried to Saipan aboard a carrier.
Above right: Fire parties struggle to isolate a blaze among parked Grumman TBF Avengers (left).
Right: The Grumman Hellcat began to replace the Wildcat aboard US carrie4s in 1943.

spotted by two American submarines next day, which alerted the 5th Fleet. Land-based reconnaissance planes had made contact with TF 58 as early as 11 June and to forestall the inevitable attacks a massive sweep of 208 carrier fighters was made over the Japanese airfields, the first of a series of devastating raids. The staging posts of Iwo Jima and Chichi Jima were put out of action as were Guam and Rota, by nearly continuous fighter attacks. The luckless Ozawa would face the fast carriers with their strength virtually unimpaired, but to complicate his problems Kakuta for some unfathomable reason refused to tell him the bad news. From his base on Tinian, Kakuta continued to tell Ozawa that his aircraft had inflicted heavy losses in aircraft and ships, when in fact every attack had been beaten off with heavy loss. He continued to attempt the hopeless task of covering all the other bases against diversionary raids, despite the fact that everything depended on the 'stocking' of Guam with 500 aircraft. Despite the fact that he had only managed to get 50 aircraft to Guam by the night of 18–19 June he reported to Ozawa that the island was secure and well-supplied with aircraft.

Unaware that he was facing a completely unharmed adversary Ozawa took up his battle formation early on the morning of 18 June, with his Van Force under Vice-Admiral Kurita and the light carriers *Chiyoda*, *Zuiho* and *Chitose* in line abreast, 100 miles ahead. His Main Body, with the *Shokaku*, *Taiho* and *Zuikaku* in one group and the *Hiyo*, *Junyo* and *Ryuho* in a second group, brought up the rear.

The first strike was launched at about 0900 hours the next day and was detected on radar by the Battle Line about an hour after that. It was a disastrous failure, for the curtain of flak and the superior tactics and training of the American fighter pilots smashed the attack decisively. Out of the 69 aircraft which took off only 37 survived. A second strike was launched by the main body just after, with 110 aircraft, but it too was torn to ribbons by the massed gunfire of the Battle Line. Only 31 aircraft survived,

and all they had to show was a near miss on the *Wasp*.

Ten minutes after the departure of the second strike a major disaster befell the Japanese when the submarine *Albacore* slipped through the destroyer-screen and hit the flagship *Taiho* with a torpedo. The explosion jammed the forward aircraft lift and ruptured fuel lines and this allowed the deadly vapor to fill the hangar. She did not catch fire however and for over six hours it looked as if the damage-control parties would be able to save the ship. The captain turned his ship into wind and maintained 26 knots and to help clear the hangar of the avgas fumes ordered all hatches to be opened. This permitted the avgas vapour to spread even further, and at 1530 hours it is believed that a starter-button on an electric pump provided the fatal spark for an enormous explosion. It is assumed that the avgas explosion set off a chain reaction, for the *Taiho* literally erupted in flame. She burned so fiercely that no other ships could approach her, and when she sank at 1728 hours only 500 out of a crew of 2150 men could be rescued.

Another submarine the *Cavalla* hit the new flagship *Shokaku* with four torpedoes at 1222 hours. She was engulfed in flames and finally blew up and sank at 1510 hours. Ozawa had already shifted his flag twice and finally moved to the *Zuikaku*. He was still determined to force a battle with the Americans and as he did not know of the failure of the land-based attacks he felt that his 102 remaining aircraft could tip the balance. From Kakuta's reports he believed that several American carriers had been sunk and that a reasonable number of his aircraft had reached

Guam. None of it was true, particularly not the massive strike that Kakuta led him to believe was about to be made against TF 58.

The two fleets drew apart for a while and although Spruance's carriers had a speed advantage he did not sight Ozawa until the following afternoon. The news was intercepted by the Japanese and immediately Ozawa stopped his refuelling, increased speed and prepared a strike. The sighting had been made at 1540 hours, which put Spruance in a quandary. If he launched a strike at this hour of the day and at a distance of more than 300 miles the aircraft would have to land in the dark and some might run out of fuel. However the chance to inflict a really crippling blow on the Japanese was not to be missed and at 1620 hours he ordered an all-out strike with 85 fighters, 77 dive bombers and 54 torpedo-bombers. Only 16 minutes later the entire strike was airborne.

It has already been said that flight deck procedure and turn-around time was the key to carrier operations and it is significant that the Japanese had got only 80 aircraft airborne by 1840 hours, when the first of TF 58's massive strike arrived. The *Hiyo* sank after hits from two torpedoes, while the *Junyo*, *Zuikaku* and *Chiyoda* were badly damaged. As for the aircraft and air-crew losses, the exultant American pilots dubbed the battle 'The Great Marianas Turkey Shoot.' The final total came to some 400 carrier aircraft, 100 land aircraft and a number of float-planes, as well as the large majority of their pilots. It was effectively the end of the Japanese Naval Air Force.

It almost dealt a crippling blow to the Americans as well. The carrier aircraft were at the limit of their endurance and it was a case of finding the shortest route back. In ones, twos and threes they made their way, as the light faded. Admiral Mitscher ordered the carriers to close the gap as best they could and the pilots throttled back to conserve fuel, but it was 2230 hours before the first aircraft were within range of the carriers' homing beacons. In the darkness it was impossible to make out more than each carrier's wake, and with aircraft flying around in confusion it was only a matter of time before some collided. Others ran out of fuel and as their engines died had to go down into the sea.

To an ex-pilot the scene was agonising, and eventually Mitscher quietly gave the order, 'Turn on the lights.' To illuminate the flight decks and mastheads was to run the risk of being torpedoed or even to be attacked by Japanese aircraft and it had never been done since the war began, but Mitscher knew that the pilots could not land without illumination. Soon the whole of TF 58 was a blaze of lights, with glow-lighting on the edges of each flight deck, masthead lights and recognition lights to identify the individual carrier. Some ships even fired starshell, while the flagship of each task group burned a searchlight straight up into the sky as a beacon. Many aircraft crashed on landing and there was little attempt to find the right carrier as there was so little time. In all 100 of the 216 aircraft sent off that day were lost, but fortunately the loss of pilots was much lower as many managed to ditch near ships or were picked up by flying boats and surface ships. Some measure of the carnage is that only 20 of the aircraft lost were shot down in combat with the Japanese.

The Battle of the Philippine Sea was the last and greatest of the carrier battles and it wiped out the Japanese air groups. But Spruance had his critics, who felt that he should have sunk more of Ozawa's fleet and the aftermath of the battle was an unedifying scramble by other commanders to indict him for his alleged timidity. It must be remembered that Spruance did not know exactly what Ozawa's dispositions were at the closing stages and there was still a chance that a detached force of Japanese ships might break through to attack the Saipan invasion forces. Another fact that is ignored is the exhaustion of the air crews, who had flown to the limit of their endurance, in every sense of the word. The critics also forget what happened four months later at Leyte, when aggressive tactics by Halsey led to a mad chase after a decoy force of light carriers. This opened the way to an attack by Japanese surface forces against the invasion transports and only a desperate stand by the destroyers and escort carriers saved the day.

Leyte was hardly a carrier battle, but the stand of the 'jeep carriers' off Samar on 25 October 1944 showed how much punishment these little ships could take. Their air groups were armed for softening up beach obstacles and strong-points, not battleships and heavy cruisers, but still the pilots made dummy runs at the Japanese ships. The CVE *Gambier Bay* was sunk by numerous hits from shells and her sister *Kalinin Bay* was badly damaged. Eventually Admiral Kurita called off his attack just as he seemed certain to break through.

A more sinister manifestation of Japanese power declared itself at Samar, when the first *kamikazes* or suicide aircraft attacked the CVEs. The *Santee* was jumped by a Zero which dived straight onto her flight deck and blew a huge hole. Seconds

Right: *Zuiho* under attack on 25 October 1944.
Below: Escorts attempt to screen the 'jeep carriers' during the Battle of Samar.

later another Zero broke into a suicide dive over the *Suwannee*, and a third made for the *Petrof Bay*. Both of these attacks missed, but later the *Suwannee* was hit by a Zero which plunged into her and killed 71 men and injured 82. Further attacks followed, but the only fatality was the CVE *St Lô*, which blew up and sank after a Zero had set off her ammunition and avgas.

In March 1945 TF 58 struck the first blow against the Japanese home islands since the Doolittle Raid three years before. While 55 miles off the coast of Kyushu the *Franklin* was hit by two bombs dropped by a low level bomber, both of which detonated in the hangar and set fire to the fully fuelled and armed aircraft. A minute later the first of a series of explosions rocked the ship and these continued for five hours. But she did not sink and the fight to get her home began. The carrier was unable to steam, but next day she was able to make two knots and this allowed the cruiser *Pittsburgh* to get her in tow. Fires broke out intermittently but two days later she was able to work up to 22 knots and she crept back to Ulithi for more permanent repairs. The casualties were on a horrific scale, 832 dead and 270 wounded and the *Franklin* proved so badly crippled that she was never put back into service.

The landings on Okinawa in April 1945 provoked a great onslaught from the *kamikazes* and as at Leyte they made the carriers their prime target. The *Enterprise*, *Intrepid*, *Bataan* and *Bunker Hill* were all hit, the last-named suffering a terrible ordeal. Like the *Franklin* she was never repaired, but the fast carriers were not sunk and the invasion was not delayed.

Into this witches' cauldron came the newly formed British Pacific Fleet. Although small in numbers its four armored carriers *Illustrious*, *Indefatigable*, *Indomitable* and *Victorious* were formed into Task Force 57 and given the task of forming a buffer to stop the Japanese forces in the Ryukyus from attacking the Okinawa invasion. The *kamikazes* attacked them as avidly as they had the American carriers and in turn the *Indefatigable* and *Illustrious* were hit. But the armored flight decks stood up to the impact and the two carriers were back in action almost immediately. On 4 May the *Formidable* was hit by a Zero and although the flight deck was holed and 11 aircraft were destroyed she was back in action less than 30 minutes later. Two days later she was hit again and lost seven aircraft, but the fire was out within a few minutes.

All arms played their part in defeating the Japanese but there can be no doubt that the fast carriers decided the outcome. Without their support the 'island-hopping' strategy could never have been developed and only when the Marianas had been captured could B-29s begin to bomb Japanese cities. What was even more important was that the carriers had stopped the Japanese at Midway, an essential prelude to the drive across the Pacific. One could go further and say that had the atom bomb not been dropped on Hiroshima and Nagasaki the fast carrier task forces acting in support not only of round-the-clock aerial bombing but also of aerial and submarine minelaying could have brought Japan to surrender within three months.

Left: The flight deck crew manhandle an F6F. The Hellcat was a robust and maneuverable fighter.
Below left: US Navy ordnancemen load a torpedo onto a Grumman Avenger.
Below: From their quadruple 40mm Bofors mounting, a guncrew watches an F6F Hellcat make its approach.

THE NUCLEAR AGE

The title of capital ship definitely passed from the battleship to the aircraft carrier after VJ-Day. The massed AA batteries of the battleships had been useful to protect the fast carriers, but their 16in guns were far outclassed by the torpedoes and bombs of carrier aircraft. There was no doubt about which would go first and a few months after the end of hostilities the first battleships went into reserve or in the case of the oldest, straight to the scrapyard.

There was serious doubt however about the future of the carrier. The dropping of the atom bomb had led to a renewed frenzy of speculation and claims that 'The Bomb' had made all ships obsolete at a stroke. The old *Saratoga* and the damaged CVL *Independence* were among the target-ships at Bikini in 1946 and although the *Sara* sank several hours after the second test many valuable lessons were learned.

Scrappings of the old carriers and sale of many of the CVEs whittled the US Navy's carrier strength down considerably, but this left the mighty *Midway* class and the whole *Essex* class, apart from the incomplete *Oriskany*. This unit was suspended to allow a study to be made of improvements and she would not complete until 1950. By the end of 1947, there were 20 carriers active in the Fleet, 11 attack carriers, two CVLs and seven CVEs.

The only other navy with a flourishing naval air arm was the British, but the end of hostilities had seen the cancellation of many ships. All the older carriers were scrapped, as well as the damaged *Formidable*, leaving three *Illustrious* class and two *Implacable* Class as the front-line strength.

The French still had the old *Béarn*, which was in service as an aircraft transport, and a CVE on loan from the British. To give the *Aéronavale* a chance to re-establish itself, the British trans-

ferred the new light carrier *Colossus* in 1946 and she became the *Arromanches*. The Netherlands Navy was given her sister HMS *Venerable*, under the new name *Karel Doorman*. Another of the class, HMS *Warrior* was lent to the Canadians to enable them to build on the expertise they had acquired by manning two CVEs in the Battle of the Atlantic. The fourth country to acquire one of these ubiquitous small carriers was Australia, which renamed the *Terrible* HMAS *Sydney* in 1948, followed later by HMAS *Melbourne* (ex-*Majestic*). The Canadians later took the *Magnificent* in place of the *Warrior* and then the *Bonaventure* (ex-*Powerful*).

The big question immediately after the war was how to operate jet aircraft from carriers, for many experts considered them too fast and dangerous for the job. Three Ryan FR-1 Fireballs were operated from the USS *Ranger* in 1945 and from the CVE *Wake Island* to test the feasibility and as the landings were made with partial assistance from the piston engine they do not count as true jet landings. This honour goes to a British Vampire fighter, which landed on board HMS *Ocean* on 3 December 1945. Just over seven months later the first jet took off from the *Franklin D Roosevelt*.

As early as 1945 there had been discussion of the possibility of arming carrier-borne aircraft with nuclear weapons. The idea might have remained on the drawing board but for a coincidence. The 'Fat Man' bomb dropped on Nagasaki weighed about 10,000lb, which happened to be the payload specified for a new carrier-borne bomber. This would ultimately be the AJ Savage, a twin piston-engined bomber delivered in 1949. As an interim nuclear bomber the P2V-2 Neptune (later a highly successful

Above: F-4 Phantoms aboard the USS *Coral Sea*.
Below: USS *America* (CVA.66) pictured during her 1965 shakedown cruise.

maritime patrol and anti-submarine aircraft) was pressed into service and it first flew from the *Coral Sea* on 27 April 1948.

Even the *Midways* were a tight squeeze for such aircraft; it was said during one of the first Neptune landings that if anything went wrong the US Navy would have a flush-decked carrier whether it liked it or not! This was a reference to the Congressional approval in 1948 of a new 60,000-ton carrier to be called the *United States*. She would be the largest warship ever built, 1090ft long and 130ft wide at the waterline and driven by steam turbines at 33 knots. To facilitate flying there would be no island, merely Japanese-style funnels projecting to port and starboard and, as in the old *Hosho* and *Argus*, the navigating bridge would be hoisted up hydraulically when needed. There would be no centerline lifts, but four deck-edge lifts to leave space for four catapults.

The keel was laid at Newport News on 18 April 1949, ten days after the purchase of 39 giant six-engined B-36 bombers was announced. The Air Force was well aware that the purchase price of 234 million dollars would be challenged by Congress and compared unfavorably with the estimated cost for CV.58 of only 189 million dollars. It was war to the knife and the Air Force went so far as to claim that the Navy was lying in quoting the price, for it 'knew' that the real cost would be close to 500 million dollars.

The US Navy was premature in demanding that scarce resources should be diverted when the feasibility of carrier-based nuclear bombing had only just been demonstrated. The argument had to be centered on strategic bombing because military planners were convinced that the next war would be decided by bombing alone. It had not yet become a four-minute affair of ICBMs, but 'conventional' forces like armies and navies were seen as having no future against nuclear attack.

The verdict of history must be that in principle the Air Force was right, for it could deliver more nuclear weapons at less cost. The Navy was right to insist on a new carrier but wrong to pin its arguments on strategic bombing, for the carrier's most deadly power lies in her ability to destroy an enemy's control of the sea.

Fortunately the Navy's obsession with nuclear strike did not preclude modernization of existing carriers. Half of the *Essex* Class were earmarked for modernisation to allow them to operate jet aircraft, with a stronger flight deck, larger catapults, more powerful lifts, more fuel stowage and better radars.

The prototype, the USS *Oriskany* commissioned in September 1950, after two years of work, just in time for the Korean War. The 'conventional' conflict that the pundits had said could never happen again had arrived and the only way of dealing with it was to mobilize Western seapower, to offset the enormous local preponderance of North Korean ground troops. Not only the carriers were needed but even the battleships played their part in bringing seapower to bear on the land war. Korea is moun-

tainous, making it difficult to establish airfields quickly and so carrier aircraft were able to give much-needed support.

The United States carriers were backed up by four British light fleet carriers and the Australian *Sydney* operating at various times. In November 1950 a US Navy F9F from the *Philippine Sea* shot down the carriers' first MiG-15 while one of the HMS *Ocean* Sea Furies shot down one in 1952. At the end of April 1951 Skyraiders from the *Princeton* torpedoed the Hwachon reservoir dam. Air Force B-29s had failed to hit the dam with guided bombs, but the eight Skyraiders scored six hits with torpedoes set for a surface run. The older *Essex* class on occasion even took a hand in shore bombardment with their 5in guns.

The Korean War had a salutary effect on airy talk about the

Above: USS *Point Cruz* (CVE.119) operated as an ASW ship in the 1950s, with HO4S helicopters.

321

end of conventional forces. The Cold War which followed had to be fought with a mixture of nuclear threat accompanied by conventional capability and for this the carrier proved ideal. As a result ten more *Essex* class were commissioned by 1953.

Meanwhile the British had been quietly pursuing a number of interesting developments, all aimed at improving the ability of carriers to handle jet aircraft. The first of these was a flexible rubber deck installed on HMS *Warrior* in 1948. The idea was to dispense with the weight of the undercarriage in the aircraft and the weight of arrester gear in the carrier, but first trials were carried out using a Vampire fighter with its wheels retracted. It died simply because it would have meant a reduction of flexibility; naval aircraft would only be able to land on land bases equipped with flexible runways and thus the fundamental advantage of being able to move aircraft from a land air base out to a carrier and back would be lost.

The next suggestion was for an angled deck. The biggest risk in deck landings was still overshooting after missing an arrester wire. Even if the aircraft did not crash into the deck park at the forward end of the flight deck, it was unlikely to survive hitting the crash-barrier without serious damage. To avoid this it was proposed to skew the flight deck at 10 degrees to the centerline, so that if an aircraft should overshoot the pilot could merely open his throttle and go round for another attempt.

The light fleet carrier *Triumph* carried out a series of trials in February 1952. When similar trials were held on board the USS *Midway* and proved equally successful the USS *Antietam* was taken in hand in September 1952. When she reappeared she had her flight deck extended out to the deck-edge lift, allowing an 8 degree angled deck with the arrester wires aligned on the new axis.

The next improvement was to the catapult, for the catapults used by both the British and the Americans were no longer adequate to launch the latest aircraft. The Royal Navy produced a design for a catapult using a piston driven by steam from the ship's boilers, with the aircraft attached to a connection between the pistons by means of a 'bridle' which dropped clear after take-off. The reserve of power is more than enough to cope with any foreseeable aircraft and for the first time since World War I it became possible to launch aircraft even while the carrier was at anchor. In a series of joint Anglo-American trials 140 launches were made and the first US carrier fitted was the *Hancock*, in 1954.

A third invention came forward at this time, a mirror device which gave the pilot precise information about his attitude and height above the flight deck. By eliminating the 'batsman' and reducing pilot-error the mirror landing device cut the percentage of human error significantly. The basic idea is simple; lights are focused into a mirror to produce a pattern which can only be seen in line if the pilot is coming in at the right height and with

his wings level. Some years ago the US Navy admitted that the two inventions, angled decks and landing sights, had saved an enormous sum of money by halving the previous ratio of aircraft damaged or lost in deck-crashes.

By the 1950s the West had retreated from its stance on nuclear weapons as the only guarantee of world peace. The explosion of the USSR's own nuclear device showed that some degree of parity had to be accepted and with that admission came the realization that 'conventional' forces still had a role to play. In the United States the decision against the big carrier had been reversed during the later stages of the Korean War, when in July 1952 the keels were laid of the first two of a class of 60,000-ton carriers: *Forrestal* (CVA.59) and *Saratoga* (CVA.60). From

Above: The modernized USS *Hancock* (CV.19).
Below: The ASW carrier *Tarawa* (CVS.40) sails off the coast of Cuba in July 1957.

Far left: Although automatic approach aids have replaced the batsman's signals, an LSO still monitors all carrier landings.
Left: The British V/STOL carrier *Invincible* under construction in 1978.
Below: The nuclear-powered USS *Nimitz* (CVN.68) embarks an air wing of some 90 aircraft.

that year the designation CVA was adopted for Attack Carrier and this classification was extended to all the modernized *Essex* class as well as the *Midway* class.

The *Forrestal* class represented a quantum leap in carrier technique and it owed much to the earlier studies for the *United States*. The centerline lift disappeared entirely and was replaced by four deck-edge lifts, one to port and three to starboard. Three features were reminiscent of British carriers: the closed hangar, the defensive guns sited in groups at the corners of the flight deck and the hurricane bow.

The number of CVAs was fixed at 15 in commission and it was hoped to build a dozen *Forrestals* to replace the *Essex* class eventually. This figure was maintained faithfully, although the cycle of refits and movements on and off station sometimes reduced it to 14 or up to 16 carriers. Two CVAs were kept with the 6th Fleet in the Mediterranean and three with the 7th Fleet in the Western Pacific, but to enable them to be relieved every six months another two carriers had to be maintained, either coming forward after refit or in dock. To keep up the tempo a third *Forrestal*, the *Ranger*, was laid down in 1954 and the *Independence* a year later. They were followed by the new improved class, the *Kitty Hawk* and *Constellation* laid down in 1956–57. Two more were ordered in 1961 and 1964 to this design, the *America* and *John F Kennedy* bringing the total up to eight.

The next step was a logical improvement, the provision of nuclear propulsion. Apart from the obvious advantage of virtually unlimited endurance nuclear power had specific advantages for carriers. First, it provided unlimited steam for the catapults, whereas a steam-powered carrier has to maintain a full head of steam while flying is in progress. Second, the elimination of funnel gases making landing easier, for a steamdriven carrier has considerable turbulence at the after end of the flight deck in most conditions, when the hot smoke drifts back. Third, the island can be redesigned for maximum convenience to personnel and flying requirements and radar arrays can be placed where they work best, with no fear of corrosion from funnel-smoke.

The new ship was ordered in Fiscal Year 1958 and was given the honored name *Enterprise*. The keel was laid in February 1958 and she was launched in September 1960. When she commissioned at the end of 1961 she was the largest warship ever built, displacing 85,350 tons at full load, 1123 feet long and 252 feet wide across the flight deck. With her air group embarked the complement rose to 4600 officers and enlisted men, and eight nuclear reactors allowed her to make over 30 knots continuously. Her configuration followed the lines of the *Forrestal* and *Kitty Hawk* classes, the most obvious difference being the compact, square island; this had specially designed 'planar array' radars with fixed flat aerials on each face of the bridge, and a round 'turban' top carrying fixed aerials. The combination of a circular array and the four planar arrays gave a 360 degree coverage, but without the maintenance problems associated with rotating antennae.

The 'Big E' had one big drawback. Her cost was a staggering 451,000,000 dollars, more than twice the cost of the first *Forrestals*, and although she required less frequent docking she needed more men with more specialized training to run her. The shock was so great that Congress would not vote funds for another carrier in Fiscal Years 1959 or 1960. For the second time the wisdom of building big carriers was questioned, but this time it was the Treasury rather than the Air Force leading the opposition. The Navy was divided on the issue; many senior officers wanted an all-nuclear navy but others argued that if nuclear propulsion was going to cost over 100,000,000 dollars extra then it was better to have conventional or 'fossil-fuelled' carriers rather than none at all.

The problem with running a nuclear carrier is that only nuclear-powered escorts are really suitable to operate with her. Her ability to move at high speed for long periods rapidly outstrips the endurance of an oil-fired DDG or DLG and having to wait while her escorts refuel from an oiler means a greater risk of attack from submarines or surface-to-surface missiles. At least an oil-fired carrier can refuel her escorts while under way, but a nuclear carrier does not carry suitable fuel. The cost of nuclear power is all but prohibitive and to date there are no signs of it becoming cheap enough to make any significant difference to the argument. The only point in its favor (as far as cost is concerned) is the longer time between machinery overhauls. Whereas steam boilers need cleaning and eventual retubing, the *Enterprise* ran for three years and logged 207,000 miles before her reactors had to be 'refuelled' with new enriched uranium cores. In 1965–69 she logged 300,000 miles on these new cores and the cores installed in 1969–71 are expected to last for 10 to 13 years.

Congress compromised on the issue of carriers by authorizing a further two *Kitty Hawk* class in FY 1961 and 1963, the *America* and *John F Kennedy*, after a bitter wrangle. Then the nuclear lobby succeeded in getting five nuclear-powered carriers authorized in Fiscal Years 1967, 1970, 1974 and 1980–81, the *Nimitz*, *Dwight D Eisenhower*, *Carl Vinson* and *CV.71–72*. But time was running out, with inflation pushing up costs every year and labour shortages in the shipyards extending the building times. The *Nimitz* and *Eisenhower* took seven years to build (three years more than *Enterprise*) and cost an average of about 2,000,000,000 dollars each.

A number of navies turned to helicopter carriers. The French built an interesting hybrid cruiser-carrier, the *Jeanne d'Arc*, with a conventional bow and centerline superstructure forward and a flight deck aft, while the Spanish acquired the old CVL *Cabot* and renamed her *Dédalo* after a ship which had carried autogiros in the 1920s. The British ran their carrier *Hermes* as a fixed-wing carrier for several years, but then converted her to ASW, and the small carriers in the Australian, Argentine and Brazilian navies replaced strike aircraft either partially or totally with Tracker ASW aircraft and ASW helicopters.

The British were working on a revolutionary new aircraft, a Vertical/Short Take Off and Landing (V/STOL) machine called first the P.1127, later the Kestrel and ultimately the Harrier. This unique fixed-wing aircraft has four swivelling exhaust ducts which can be rotated downwards for a vertical takeoff and landing, in much the same manner as a helicopter, but once aloft it becomes a conventional turbojet strike aircraft. The prototype flew in 1960 and only three years later a series of trials was conducted aboard HMS *Ark Royal*. Since then the Harrier has landed and taken off from a bewildering variety of ships, from helicopter platforms on the sterns of small ships

Below: Task Group Alpha was formed around the unmodernized *Essex* Class carrier *Valley Forge* to evaluate antisubmarine warfare tactics.

and the wooden flight deck of the Spanish *Dédalo*, to the flight deck of the Italian helicopter-carrying cruiser *Vittorio Veneto* to show its versatility.

The problem with V/STOL is that at this early stage of its development the aircraft are limited in performance by the weight devoted to the V/STOL capability and the heavy consumption of fuel. In other words, there are jobs which only a big fixed-wing aircraft can do, such as high-speed interception. The Harrier is the pioneer of a new generation of V/STOL aircraft but for the moment it is the only one available and its limitations have to be accepted.

The Royal Navy pressed on with its plan to build an anti-submarine helicopter carrier to provide some sort of screen for its ships. Officially the idea of a big carrier was dead and the Sea Harrier was only a design on a drawing board, but the people responsible for drafting the new design courageously decided to make sure that the new ship would be capable of operating the Sea Harrier when and if it was approved.

The ever-expanding Soviet Navy finally decided to provide itself with a naval air arm, having previously relied on land-based aircraft. In 1968–69 two helicopter carriers were commissioned, the *Leningrad* and *Moskva*, and in 1971 the keel of a much more ambitious ship was laid. She emerged in 1976 as the cruiser-carrier *Kiev*, a 40,000-ton ship with a surface-missile armament forward and a nearly full-length angled flight deck. The arrival of the *Kiev* on the scene in 1976 threw Western naval observers into paroxysms of excitement, for on her flight deck were four Yak-36 Forger V/STOL strike aircraft. Suddenly the Soviet Union seemed to be getting into the carrier game after conspicuously ignoring it for over 50 years.

After a more careful appraisal the hybrid nature of the *Kiev* is more apparent. For one thing the flight of Forgers appears to have been embarked for evaluation rather than as part of an operational unit. For another they fit so tightly into the after lift that the design of future V/STOL aircraft for the *Kiev* Class will be badly restricted. The second ship, *Minsk* has appeared, and the third ship, *Komsomolets* appears to be still under construction. There is now evidence that the Soviet Navy is planning a big carrier on American lines. It is strange irony that one of the continuing arguments against carriers for the US Navy used to be that 'the Russians don't have them, so why should we?'

Above: A Vought A-7 Corsair II is launched from USS *Ranger*'s waist catapult during operations off Vietnam in January 1968.
Below: The crowded hangar deck of USS *Enterprise* (CVAN.65) illustrates some of the problems of aircraft maintenance aboard a carrier.

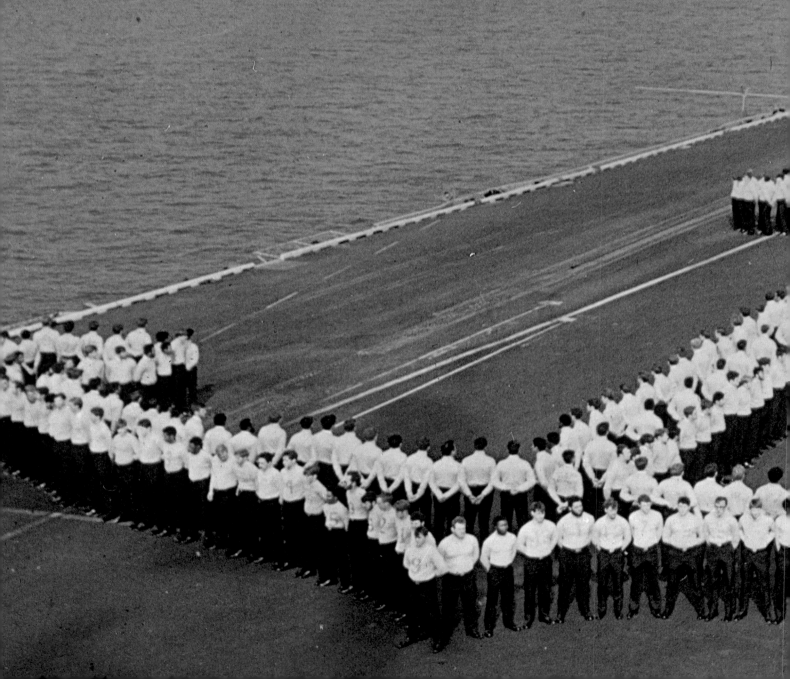

Far left: Seamen work aboard USS *Lexington* (CVA.16).
Left: An AV-8A Harrier of the US Marine Corps carries out trials aboard the amphibious transport dock USS *Coronado* (LPD.11).
Right: France maintains two attack carriers, the *Foch* and *Clemenceau*.
Below: Men of the *Coral Sea* form an anchor to commemorate her fourth Golden Anchor award for retaining personnel.

Below: The veteran carrier *Coral Sea* (CVA.43) in San Francisco naval shipyard in 1962.

STRIKE CRAFT

STRIKE CRAFT

Previous page: One of the many patrol boats that played a vital role in the island battles of the Pacific War.
Page 329: Soviet Osa missile boats in line ahead.
Below: Two Royal Navy MGBs in the English Channel during World War II.

THE GIANT KILLERS

Just over a century ago the safe and secure world of the big warship, the battleship and the cruiser, was threatened by the small torpedo boat. Today navies feel equally threatened by small missile boats and the wheel has turned full circle.

To understand how it all started we must go back to 1864, when a British engineer, Robert Whitehead, working for an Austrian engineering company was approached by an elderly retired Army officer, Captain Giovanni Luppis. It appeared that he had an invention for attacking ships, a small 'mobile spar torpedo' or explosive charge which could be steered by two wires. The spar torpedo, a weapon which had been proven in the recent American Civil War, was a canister of guncotton mounted on a pole over the bows of a small steam launch. The spar torpedo had sunk two ironclads and damaged a third during the Civil War, but it had one great drawback: its success virtually guaranteed the destruction of the attacker.

Clearly the invention of Captain Luppis promised an improvement over the spar torpedo and Whitehead was sufficiently impressed to make a model, but he subsequently decided that it would not work. However his fertile brain came up with a much better idea, an 'automobile torpedo' which could detonate below a ship's water-line. By 1866 the prototype was ready, a cylindrical vessel driven by a compressed air engine for 300 yards at 6½

knots. Little else is known about the weapon as Whitehead had cannily kept all the details to himself, confiding only in his 12-year old son and an elderly workman.

Two years later Whitehead produced two new models, with improved depth-keeping, capable of running at about seven knots for 700 yards. The Austro-Hungarian Navy showed a lot of interest but had no money to spare, but when British officers saw the trials at Fiume in 1869 they recommended that Whitehead be invited to England to demonstrate his torpedo to the Admiralty. Following exhaustive trials a year later the Royal Navy bought the rights to manufacture the 'Whitehead torpedo,' followed by a series of torpedo boats.

The lead was given by the British boatbuilder John Thornycroft, who adapted the design of his fast steam launches to the new weapon. In 1877 his Chiswick boatyard delivered HMS *Lightning*, the first seagoing boat to be armed with the Whitehead torpedo, but she was closely followed by the French

The steam yacht *Turbinia* was a floating test bed for the Parsons steam turbine. Her success showed the way towards higher speeds for all ships towards the end of the 19th century.

Above: Captain Luigi Rizzo was responsible for one of the major strike craft successes of World War II when *MAS.15* torpedoed and sank the Austro-Hungarian battleship *Szent Istvan* in June 1918.
Below: An Italian MAS-boat of the series MAS.204-217 running trials in 1918. They could be easily converted to MGB's by the addition of a 57mm gun as shown here.

Torpilleur No. 1. By the early 1880s all the leading navies had invested in large numbers of torpedo boats, some of them little more than wooden launches for harbor defense, but others were capable of making long voyages. The French in particular put their faith in the torpedo boat as a weapon to offset the vast superiority of the Royal Navy, deploying large numbers around the Channel ports. It was widely believed that these torpedo boats would be able to force their way into harbors and sink even the most powerful battleships with impunity and many influential commentators prophesied the end of the big ship.

There were however drawbacks to the torpedo boat which prevented it from achieving such success. The light reciprocating steam engines were liable to break down frequently, while their thin steel hulls proved very fragile. To achieve the high speed necessary to overhaul big ships the engines were running at maximum revolutions and the hulls had to be kept narrow, while the silhouette was kept low to avoid being seen at night, all requirements which aggravated their inherent faults.

Although the torpedo boat was by and large a failure, there was no doubt about the ability of the torpedo to sink a ship if it hit, and so torpedo-carrying warships continued to be built. For a while the trend was towards bigger ships, resulting in the torpedo boat destroyer, but as soon as the lightweight internal combustion engine was available thoughts turned once again to producing small torpedo-craft. In 1904 the first 'motor' torpedo boat appeared, a private design built by Comte Recepe; it had a 14-inch torpedo-tube built into the bow. Two years later the Italian FIAT company went one better with a multi-purpose motor boat, armed with a 47mm gun, two machine guns and two 14-inch torpedo-tubes. Her twin 80hp gasoline engines drove her at 16 knots and after successful trials the Italian Navy bought her.

The British firm of Thornycrofts, having pioneered the steam torpedo boat, was naturally interested in finding a successor. The *Dragonfly* could make 18 knots on her single 120hp engine and launched a single 14-inch torpedo sideways, using a folding discharge-chute. The US Navy looked at ways of equipping battleships with steam torpedo boats, but when the craft turned out to be too heavy for the battleships' boat-cranes the motor torpedo boat was seen as the only alternative. The engineer A T Chester produced a novel design in which the torpedo was dropped through a hatch in the keel, but in spite of this the idea

of motor torpedo boats was not pursued. The problem was that the internal combustion engine was not yet sufficiently developed to permit big, reliable units, and so size had to be kept down. This in turn suggested that the true role of small torpedo craft would be to be transported aboard larger warships. This resulted in a number of unsatisfactory compromises between power and size, a problem exacerbated by the fact that the torpedo was a very heavy weapon.

In peacetime no navy can afford the large sums needed to invest in unproven craft such as motor torpedo boats and so none of these experiments bore fruit. But there was another force capable of pushing the design of hulls and engines forward. Since the 1890s the sport of motor boat racing had gained ground. Like powerboat racing today, it was a rich man's sport offering more excitement than traditional yachting. As early as 1900 a gasoline-engined boat won the International Motor Boat Show race in Paris and three years later Lord Harmsworth established the British International Trophy for motor boat racing.

The influence of competition showed in a steady improvement in hull forms, resulting in higher and higher speeds. The first stepped planing hull, the French *Rapiere III*, was built in 1908 and two years later the English *Miranda IV* from Thornycrofts reached the remarkable speed of 35 knots. The German Lürssen yard, on the other hand, developed round-bilge hulls and their boat won the two top championships in 1911.

The years before World War I saw the paradox of the disappearance of the traditional torpedo boat but the failure of the motor torpedo boat to take its place. And yet, as we have seen, giant strides had been taken in the design of fast hulls, and these developments were all to have their effect much sooner than anyone expected.

Shortly before entering World War I the Italian Navy sounded out various firms to obtain designs for motor torpedo boats and prudently enquired about American gasoline engines. By March 1915 it was possible to place an order with the Societá Veneziana Automobili Navali (SVAN) for two 15-meter boats driven by gasoline engines on two shafts, capable of 30 knots and armed with two 18-inch torpedoes. They were christened Motorbarca Armata SVAN o Silurante (SVAN torpedo-armed motor boats) and numbered *MAS.1* and *MAS.2*. On trials they were not an outstanding success, largely because extra weight added

during construction had slowed them down and because the method of launching the torpedoes over the stern was clumsy. However this did not stop the Italian Navy from forming a national volunteer corps, the Corpe Nazionale Voluntari Metonauti (CNVM), although *MAS.1* and *MAS.2* were rearmed with guns in November 1915 and were demoted to submarine chasers.

Before the two prototypes were complete the Navy ordered 20 more boats, *MAS.3* to *MAS.22*, from SVAN. Once again speed proved disappointing, for additional weight brought the maximum smooth-water speed down to as little as 21 knots. But this did not deter the Navy from pushing ahead with plans to use them offensively in the Adriatic. *MAS.5* and *MAS.7* were fitted with 14-inch torpedoes and dropping gear, much like the old torpedo boats and on the night of 6/7 September 1916 attacked Austrian shipping lying off Durazzo (Dubrovnik). The attack was a success and the two MAS-boats escaped after sinking the small steamer *Lokrum*. The enemy had been taken completely by surprise despite the noise made by the gasoline engines.

The solution to the noise problem was to provide electric motors for the approach and *MAS.20* and *MAS.21* were modified in September 1916. On the night of 1/2 November *MAS.20* and two larger warships approached the boom at Pola (Pula) and the tiny craft managed to get across the nets without being sighted. Unfortunately the battleship she was trying to attack had already left the anchorage and after a search lasting two hours all she could find was the old harbor defence ship *Mars*. It was clearly not her lucky night for both torpedoes were caught in anti-torpedo nets, but *MAS.20* still managed to get back safely through the gap in the boom.

The first major success was scored by *MAS.9* and *MAS.13* on 9/10 December, when Captain Luigi Rizzo took them into the roadstead off Trieste to attack the battleships *Wien* and *Budapest*. These two old ships had been a thorn in the side of the Italians because of their persistent bombardments of shore positions and this was not the first attempt to sink them. This time all went well and both MAS-boats got within 200 meters without being detected, after cutting through three 2½-inch hawsers with hydraulic shears. Both *MAS.9*'s torpedoes hit the *Wien* amidships and the old battleship rolled over and sank a few minutes later. The other boat's torpedoes missed the target, but

once again both assailants were able to creep away unseen in the confusion.

All the time the MAS operators were perfecting their tactics. Groups of two or three boats were towed by larger torpedo boats and destroyers to the area of operations, thus saving fuel and providing some protection *en route*. The destroyers could also provide covering fire if the defense tried to put off their retreat. Smoke floats were introduced to make it harder for the defenders to fire at the MAS-boats during the withdrawal. The biggest nuisance was aircraft, particularly the big Austro-Hungarian seaplanes, and on one occasion one of them succeeded in recapturing a motor boat from *MAS.19* off Trieste.

Once convinced of the value of MAS-boats, the Italians threw themselves energetically into the task of building hundreds. Other firms joined SVAN in the hunt for higher speed and heavier armament. Orlando of Liverno produced the first design for an interchangeable motor torpedo boat/gunboat, *MAS.91* in January 1917; she was armed with two 18-inch torpedoes or a 47mm quick-firing gun, but most important, speed was increased to 27 knots. The American Elco type was also imported and by 1918 the Baglietto-built *MAS.397* boat had exceeded 28 knots. When the Armistice was signed in November 1918 over 400 boats were in service or under construction.

Undoubtedly the finest hour of the MAS-boats was the sinking

Below: The Baglietto-built 'D' Type MAS-boats 397-400 were capable of 28 knots, a speed which rose to 33 knots when armament was reduced.

of the dreadnought battleship *Szent Istvan*, an event known the world over because it was the earliest motion picture sequence of a big ship sinking. On 10 June 1918, as the Austro-Hungarian Navy's battleships were steaming off Premuda Island they were attacked by *MAS.15* and *MAS.21* under the command of Luigi Rizzo. The first salvo fired at the *Tegetthoff* missed but *MAS.15* hit the next astern, the *Szent Istvan*, twice. As the flooding spread unchecked the 22,000-ton ship slowly listed to starboard. Her consorts tried to take her in tow and strenuous efforts were made to save her, but after two-and-a-half hours she gave up the struggle and capsized, hundreds of sailors scrambling over the giant keel. It was a convincing demonstration of the power of the motor torpedo boat and to make the victory even more complete the escorting destroyers had not been able to score a hit on the escaping MAS-boats, let alone catch them.

The Italians hoped to develop MAS tactics even further and four months later planned a large-scale raid on Pola. The old battleship *Re Umberto* was to push a large raft equipped with net-cutters and paravanes through the nets and minefields and then as many as 40 MAS-boats would sweep into the inner harbor. Nothing came of this audacious plan as the Austro-Hungarian Empire was now visibly on the point of collapse, but there could be no doubt in the minds of Italian naval planners about the need to continue with development of bigger and better craft.

The Austrians, with neither the resources to develop motor torpedo boats nor the opportunity to use them, were nonetheless aware of their potential and produced a revolutionary craft.

This was the Müller-Thomamühl air-cushion hydroplane, built in 1915 to the design of a young naval officer. Although she carried two 18-inch torpedoes and achieved 32 knots in the same sea-states as the early MAS-boats, the high command decided that she was no use for naval operations. It was a curious decision for the MAS had already shown their potential and only a few months later another inventor, Szombathy, was ordered to develop another design for a hydroplane torpedo boat. It was completed only two months before the Armistice and had no chance to prove itself before the Dual Monarchy crumbled.

The British, having found their surface warships restricted in their freedom of movement by the threat of U-Boats and minefields, turned to other ways of taking the offensive against the German High Seas Fleet. At about the same time as the Italians were looking into the matter, proposals were put forward by young officers at Harwich for carrying small motor torpedo boats in the davits of light cruisers. It was intended that these boats should be dropped outside the Heligoland Bight and then attack at high speed across the minefields. A speed of 30 knots was regarded as the minimum.

The technical problems were considerable. For one thing, the only light power unit capable of developing the power needed was an aero engine, which would need modification before it could be used in a boat. For another, the hull would have to be strong enough to be hoisted up in a cruiser's davits and yet not exceed the 4¼ tons that they could lift. The Royal Navy also stipulated an armament of one 18-inch torpedo, the smallest which could inflict serious damage on a battleship.

Naturally the Admiralty turned to the firms which had been building fast racing craft before the war and it is hardly surprising that John I Thornycroft's proposals won approval. Using the *Miranda IV* as a model, Thornycroft proposed a 'stepped' hull which would plane easily at high speed, reducing drag and damping down the bow wave. After experiments with other means of launching, it was finally decided to launch the torpedo stern-first from a trough in the after part of the boat. At top speed the torpedo would sink underneath before starting up and reaching its correct depth, by which time the boat would have turned away. There was some risk that the torpedo might be damaged by enemy fire or that the torpedo might overrun the boat, but these were regarded as minor objections.

The craft which resulted was called the 40 foot Coastal Motor Boat or CMB, a designation intended to hide its true purpose. The hull was built of American elm, even the frames, and the prototype *CMB.1* made 33½ knots on trials. The engine was adapted from an aero unit and to save weight reversing gear was omitted. The trials were a great success and a dozen more boats were ordered immediately.

Although experiments were carried out with CMBs hoisted aboard light cruisers this was quickly abandoned and the first operational units were sent to Dunkirk. In any case, the constant demand for better speed, armament and seakeeping was pushing up weight all the time and before long the weight-limit was dropped. In 1917 a much larger 55-foot CMB was built, capable of launching two torpedoes and planing at 40 knots and this was put into quantity production. An even larger 70-footer was under construction at the end of the war, capable of minelaying.

There were plenty of targets for CMBs in the English Channel and off the Flanders coast. In April 1917 four attacked German torpedo boats off Ostend, sinking *G.88*; a second torpedo boat might have been sunk as well, but the torpedo was a 'dud.' On 23 April 1918 a large force of CMBs joined in the attempt to block Zeebrugge and Ostend. Their task was to add to the diversionary effect by laying smokescreens, firing torpedoes at enemy 'targets of opportunity' and even firing mortars at shore positions. In the confusion they were able to do little more than harass the defenders but they escaped without loss.

An unusual engagement took place off the River Ems in August 1918, when a force of six CMBs was attacked by eight German seaplanes. The CMBs fought back, using their machine-guns and trying to throw off the seaplanes' aim by tight turns at high speed, but although they shot down two of their attackers all were badly damaged. Time was to show that aircraft were the deadliest enemy of small craft.

The British attempt to oppose the Russian Revolution in 1919–20 took the Royal Navy into the restricted waters of the Baltic, an ideal operating area for CMBs, and they were also used at Archangel and on the Caspian Sea. They even proved useful as river gunboats, stripped of torpedoes and fitted with bullet-proof plating around the wheelhouse and extra machine-guns. The biggest operation was however a daring raid on the Soviet ships in Kronstadt, the heavily defended base outside Leningrad. The idea was generated after a single CMB under Lieutenant Agar had sunk the light cruiser *Oleg* and as a result seven more were sent out to the Gulf of Finland.

On the night of 17/18 August 1919 the seven CMBs entered the North Channel off Kronstadt, timing their arrival to coincide with a bombing raid on the base. Their targets were the battleships *Andrei Pervozvanni* and *Petropavlosk*, the light cruisers and a submarine depot ship, the *Pamyat Azova*, and any other targets which would immobilize the Baltic Fleet. Although greatly reduced in effectiveness since the Revolution two years earlier, the Russian ships were still a danger to the British light forces operating in the Baltic and Admiral Cowan hoped to neutralise them.

The CMBs approached the harbour in line ahead, engines throttled back to cut down both noise and the bow-wave. Two of the forts opened fire but failed to hit the CMBs as they crept by. The seven boats split into three groups, *Nos. 79, 31* and *88*

leading the main attack, *Nos. 86, 72* and *62* following, and *No. 24* attacking the guardship, the destroyer *Gavriil*. Lieutenant Bremner in *CMB.79* led the attack, heading straight for the *Pamyat Azova*, while Lieutenant Dobson in *CMB.31* attacked the *Petropavlovsk*. Both lots of torpedoes hit their mark; the depot ship listed rapidly to starboard and sank, while the battleship was severely damaged. The CMBs were so close that the officers on the bridge of *CMB.88* were stained yellow by the picric acid in their torpedo's warhead when it hit the other battleship, the *Andrei Pervozvanni*.

So far the attack had been a success, although Lieutenant Dayrell-Reed of *CMB.88* had been shot through the head. But *CMB.24*'s torpedo had passed underneath the *Gavriil* and the destroyer retaliated by blowing her small opponent in half with gunfire. Then *CMB.62* collided with *CMB.79*; the former was entering the harbour and the latter was leaving it. Such was the presence of mind of both COs that Lieutenant Brade kept *CMB.62* at full speed, so that the two boats remained locked together long enough for Bremner in *CMB.79* to fire a demolition charge before jumping clear. *CMB.62* had drawn clear, but she failed to hit the *Gavriil* with her torpedo and was in turn sunk by the destroyer's guns. *CMB.86*'s engines broke down before she entered the harbor and *CMB.72*'s torpedo-firing gear was put out of action by a shell splinter. Unable to fire the torpedo, Lieutenant Bedley broke off his attack but succeeded in towing *CMB.86* to safety.

Despite the loss of two CMBs the attack was a success, for the three ships were out of action – only the dreadnought *Petropavlovsk* was repaired, and the Baltic Fleet was effectively reduced to a handful of destroyers and submarines. Six British officers and nine ratings had been killed, while another three officers and six ratings were taken prisoner.

The German Navy made surprisingly little effort to develop an equivalent to the CMB and the first LM-boats were not ordered until the beginning of 1917. The principal problem was the lack of suitable engines, as the Zeppelin engines used proved less than satisfactory. Another development was the FL-boat, known to the British as a DCB or 'Distance Controlled Boat,' a wire-guided pilotless boat with a large explosive charge in the bows. These were guided from shore, using information provided from an overhead aircraft, to attack the British monitors operating off the Belgian coast. One of these 43-foot craft, *FL.8* was destroyed while attacking the monitor *M.23* in September 1917, but a month later *FL.12* hit HMS *Erebus* full amidships. The big monitor stood up surprisingly well to the 1500lb charge of TNT, but she and all other monitors were later fitted with guard-rails to prevent the DCBs from riding up on top of their 'bulges.' Subsequent attacks by DCBs were not successful, but they showed technical ingenuity a good 20 years ahead of their time.

It might be expected that all the major navies would immediately start building large numbers of motor torpedo boats. They had after all just demonstrated that they were a deadly and cost-effective means of waging war, needing only further refinement of engines and hulls to exploit their capabilities. Instead the opposite happened and few navies showed any interest in them. The British allowed their CMBs to be disposed of, the Americans made no attempt to create even the nucleus of a force, and it was left to the Italians to continue experiments. The reasons for this were mainly financial, but the main cause was their very simplicity and cheapness; it was felt that a force of motor torpedo boats could be recreated in a short space of time, just as the British and Italians had in 1915–16.

Time was to show how wrong this was. It takes time to perfect the right sort of engines and, like weapons and tactics, they must be developed at sea rather than on the drawing board. It is significant that the German Navy which paid the most attention to engine-development, entered World War II with the most

Above left: Luigi Rizzo's *MAS.15* being hauled out of the water at Ancona after she had torpedoed the battleship *Szent Istvan*.
Below: By the 1930s the specialist Italian shipyards were producing the '500' series MAS boats which could reach 47–50 knots.

successful designs of all. Similarly the Italians produced a most successful petrol engine and showed the way to more advanced hull-forms. The real problem for the major navies was that the money and manpower available during times of financial retrenchment did not stretch to cover what were seen as 'luxuries.' Small strike craft may be cheap to build, but they require large investments in research and development and large numbers of skilled manpower to operate.

The German Navy on the other hand was hamstrung by the Treaty of Versailles and looked on the motor torpedo boat as a means of making up for the weakness of the Fleet. At first in secret and later more openly, designs were tested to establish a good hull-form and by 1928 it was clear that Lürssen's designs were the basis for development, being both robust and seaworthy. It was also necessary to find a good engine and so development contracts were given to the leading firms, MAN and Daimler-Benz, to produce a reliable high-speed diesel. Once this was achieved the new *Schnellboot* could truly be regarded as the first satisfactory small fast torpedo boat. Although not as fast as the planing craft still favoured in other countries, she had more endurance and could face the rough weather encountered in the Baltic and the North Sea.

The Royal Navy gave no such lead to British industry, but this did not stop the British Power Boat Company and Vosper from building their own craft. Finally in 1936 the first MTBs or Motor Torpedo Boats were ordered, marking the rebirth of Coastal Forces. But the Admiralty had left it too late and the lack of a suitable British engine meant that Isotta-Fraschini petrol engines had to be imported from Italy. Although powerful aero-engines were available, there was no equivalent of the German Daimler-Benz V-20 diesel.

The French had virtually ignored the motor torpedo boat in 1914–18 and had done little beyond building a handful of prototypes, known as VTAs and VTBs (*Vedette Torpille* Type A and Type B), to distinguish small boats from large. More of the larger VTB type were ordered from 1930 onwards, but like the British, designers were hampered by the lack of suitable engines. There was however considerable cooperation with British firms and performance was steadily improved.

As the victims of the 1919 Kronstadt attack, the Russians were very impressed by the potential of the motor torpedo boat. Using the wreck of a CMB from Kronstadt and another captured in the Caspian, the distinguished aircraft designer Andrei Tupolev was able to produce an effective design known as the G5. They were years ahead of their time in having Duralumin hulls for lightness, but this caused severe corrosion.

The US Navy tried to make up for its neglect by launching a public competition in 1937, calling upon designers and builders to submit designs for small craft, including wood- or metal-hulled 60 to 70-feet torpedo boats. The winning designs, a 60-footer by Hewey and Nevins Inc and a 70-footer from Sparkman & Stevens, were immediately ordered, six hulls with various engines. To compare performance two official Bureau of Ships designs were also ordered and the British Power Boat 70-footer which had been bought by the Electric Boat Company (Elco) was also purchased. In spite of political pressure to support US industry the Navy went ahead with an order for 23 of the British design from Elco. Although originally referred to as Motor Torpedo Boats, these craft were given a designation which would become famous: Patrol Torpedo Boats, or PT-Boats.

It is surprising to find that the Japanese, who took such a pride in building powerful and unorthodox warships, should have shown little interest in developing MTBs. Perhaps in their case the strategic emphasis on a major fleet battle blinded them to the potential of strike craft. Maybe they felt, like the Americans, that the vast distances of the Pacific were not suited to small craft, but whatever the reason very little was done. Only in 1939 did the Imperial Navy order an experimental MAS-type from Italy and the six MTBs developed from this design did not enter service until after Pearl Harbor.

Significantly the smaller navies favored the MTB, usually because their geography lent itself to ambush tactics and because big warships were a drain on their slender resources. Much the same reasoning led small navies to acquire steam torpedo boats 50 years earlier; countries like Sweden and Yugoslavia can hide light craft behind the screen of islands along their coasts and indulge in hit-and-run tactics.

The real problem which lay ahead was not one of material, but one of tactics. The truth was that every navy which possessed motor torpedo boats had ideas about their worth, by no means all of them valid. In the words of a senior British officer, 'Very few people knew much about coastal forces and very few had any idea of what they were going to do.' A handful of dedicated specialists thought that they would be able to do almost anything, but the majority looked on them as nothing more than toys. But on one issue almost all were united, to build a lot of MTBs would cost too much money and as a result all too few had been ordered.

Above: Hundreds of sailors abandon ship as one of the *Szent Istvan*'s sisters stands by to rescue survivors.
Below: The dramatic moment as the 20,000-ton *Szent Istvan* rolls over after being torpedoed by *MAS.15*.

E-BOAT ALLEY

The German Navy's *Schnellboote* soon found employment in the North Sea and the English Channel. Until the fall of France in June 1940 there were French coastal convoys and of course the British moved much of their heavy cargo such as coal by means of coasters. To the British the German motor torpedo boats were known as E-Boats and the East Coast convoy route was known as 'E-Boat Alley.' Any night that was calm and moonless was likely to bring an attack from these sleek, menacing craft and if the lookouts and gunners were not alert the attackers would get away undamaged.

In one of these confused encounters *S.31* torpedoed the British destroyer *Kelly*, captained by Lord Louis Mountbatten. The Allied evacuation from Dunkirk should have given the S-Boats their greatest opportunity, but surprisingly they only hit the French destroyers *Jaguar*, *Cyclone* and *Sirocco* and the British destroyer *Wakeful*, sinking three out of the four. The collapse of France brought the S-Boats closer to the English coast and before long the casualty lists began to grow. Nor were the attackers limited to using their torpedoes, for the S-Boat was ideal for clandestine minelaying, with eight magnetic or acoustic mines stowed on the after deck.

As more S-Boats became available the weight of attacks was stepped up. As an example of what could be done, on the night of 25/26 July 1940 six S-Boats attacked a Channel convoy in conjunction with aircraft. After the convoy and its escort had been badly shot up, the S-Boats left their base at Boulogne and sank three ships, in addition to seven already sunk by the bombers. The destruction of this convoy forced the Admiralty to suspend the Channel convoys for a while, proof of how dangerous the S-Boats could be when used correctly.

The Admiralty for its part reacted as promptly as it could by expanding Coastal Forces as soon as possible. The first MTB base on the East Coast opened in January 1940 and by the time that Coastal Forces were officially established as a separate command in November that year three more had been set up. After June 1940 the supply of Isotta-Fraschini engines dried up, but it proved possible to obtain supercharged Hall-Scott engines from the USA and so the building programme was not delayed. An innovation was the Motor Gun Boat, a similar hull to the MTB but heavily armed with guns to provide a greater volume of fire for the defense of convoys.

When the flotillas were up to strength it was at last possible to take the offensive and on 8 September 1940 two MTBs scored the first British success, an ammunition ship sunk and a cargo ship damaged, off Ostend. But until mid-1941 the bigger and better-armed S-Boats generally had the better of such exchanges. Nor

Above: *PT.212* entering a dry dock on the north coast of Sardinia in May 1944.
Below: PT Boats were active during the D-Day landings in Normandy. Here *PT.509* stands by the sinking minesweeper USS *Tide* off Omaha Beach.

Above: *MTB.538*, a convertible prototype built by Vosper. Here she is armed as an MTB with four 18-inch torpedo tubes and twin power-operated 20mm gun.

could the British MTBs and MGBs achieve the sort of spectacular sinkings notched up by their German counterparts, for there was a much smaller volume of coastwise shipping in Europe.

All the while tactics were being learned. Apart from a handful of prewar specialists the majority of S-Boat and Coastal Forces personnel were wartime volunteers new to the job. The prewar image of dashing in at high speed, firing torpedoes at a line of dreadnoughts and getting away scot-free was largely to blame for the amateurish way in which many attacks were made. The first lesson was that torpedoes had to be fired at relatively slow speed, or else they dived straight to the bottom. Next, torpedoes had to be fired at fairly close range; if fired at a mile or more the torpedo would probably miss or its wake would be spotted by the enemy. But the worst problem was noise, for if the approach was made at high speed enemy lookouts were bound to spot the MTB before she was within range. The S-Boat was better in this respect for the Daimler-Benz diesel discharged its exhaust underwater and for British MTBs the solution was to creep in on a quiet auxiliary engine. The main virtue of high speed was to enable the attackers to break away rapidly after the engagement, rather than in attack. Another tactic developed was to lie

Below: *MTB.48* was built by J Samuel White in 1940. Her three Sterling gasoline engines gave her a speed of 39 knots.
Below right: *S.128* was one of the wartime German 'E Boats.' They differed from the earlier *Schnellboote* in having an enclosed forecastle.

in wait ahead of a convoy, with engines shut down, while MGBs were often used to engage the convoy's defenders, allowing the MTBs to approach from a different quarter undetected.

Whatever tactics were used these encounters were brief, hair-raising and frequently bloody. An attack called for split-second judgement and iron nerve and once battle began it was an affair of multicolored tracers flying in all directions, punctuated by explosions. The petrol-engined boats were liable to catch fire and blow up from a single tracer bullet and this respect the diesel-driven S-boat had another advantage. Many new weapons were developed specifically to deal with S-Boats, notably the 'Headache' gear for monitoring radio messages and rapid-firing guns for destroyers. Royal Navy destroyers in 'E-Boat Alley' were given a light 'bowchaser' gun right up on the forecastle and later a twin 57mm mounting was developed.

What is remarkable is that even as late as June 1941 there were only four flotillas of S-Boats operating in the North Sea, some 25 boats. Yet during the first six months of that year they were able to sink 16 merchant ships totalling 28,000 tons. There were so few S-Boats that when Hitler decided to invade Russia three out of the four flotillas had to be withdrawn to support German operations in the Baltic.

The pattern of operations was repeated, starting with an audacious mine-laying operation in the eastern Baltic on the night that Operation 'Barbarossa' was launched. For a while the S-Boats had things their own way, but poor cooperation with the Luftwaffe robbed them of greater successes. Finally after only two months the Kriegsmarine decided, probably rightly, that other areas were more important to the German war-effort; two flotillas returned to the North Sea while one went to the Black Sea and the other to the Mediterranean. Surprisingly the

Above *S.18* was one of the last of the German prototypes for war production. She was followed by the S.38 type.

Baltic operations had shown up several weaknesses in the design of S-Boats, particularly minor technical faults which tended to put the whole boat out of action. One of the flotillas, for example, had no more than five or six operational boats out of a total strength of ten.

A new flotilla was formed to serve in the Arctic from October 1941, with a view to hindering any British attempt to send supplies to north Russia and to attack Soviet shipping off Murmansk. The operation was plagued by bad luck, one of the S-Boats running aground and two more colliding with one another. With only two craft operational little could be achieved, and reinforcements did not arrive until the following summer. Even that did not improve matters and apart from a series of mine-laying trips to the Kola Inlet the flotilla was inactive. Their

problem was the long Arctic summer twilight, which robbed them of the ability to operate under cover of darkness for most of the summer. Nor did the end of summer allieviate matters as the onset of autumn was certain to produce weather too bad for extended operations. Finally the flotilla was disbanded in July 1942, having been wasted in a basically hostile environment.

The growing number of S-Boats coming forward from the shipyards enabled more effort to be put into the North Sea and Channel areas in the early months of 1942. But the British were getting the measure of S-Boat countermeasures, and they too had plenty of reinforcements. The basic Vosper 70-footer was

Below left: *MTB.238*, a Vosper 72½-footer, was armed with two 21-inch torpedoes, a 20mm gun and twin .5-inch machine guns.
Below: *MGB.510* was an experimental type armed with a 6-pdr (57mm) gun, two twin machine guns and two 18-inch torpedo tubes.

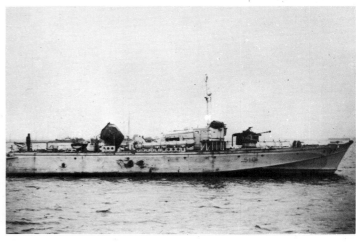

Above: One of the original Vosper 70-footers, *MTB.34*, returning home after an active night in the Channel.
Above right: The British Power Boat-built MGBs 107-176 were reclassified as MTBs and renumbered in 1943. *MTB.449* however has still to receive her two 18-inch torpedo tubes.

enlarged and fitted with new weapons and some of the US Navy's Elco type PT-Boats were made available under Lend-Lease. Radar was now available, not only to the aircraft of Coastal Command but to Coastal Forces, and this enabled more interceptions to be made. The result was a series of fierce actions fought to establish mastery.

Two actions demonstrate the nature of this struggle. The first was fought in July 1942, when seven S-Boats set out from Cherbourg to attack shipping passing through Lyme Bay. Early on the morning of 8 July the flotilla found its quarry, a long line of merchantmen escorted by armed trawlers, and the S-Boats immediately fanned out into an attacking formation. On silenced diesels, four approached to within 500 yards before their main engines burst into life with a shattering roar. The four S-Boats leapt forward like greyhounds loosed from the leash and eight torpedoes sped away towards the enemy. In the confusion it was impossible to tell which boat hit which ship, but the defending fire was wild and as the attackers turned away to reload their torpedo-tubes the remaining three roared into a second attack. The result of this catastrophic action was

six ships sunk, four cargo ships, a tanker and one of the escorting trawlers.

In contrast Coastal Forces had warning of a sortie by R-Boats (the German equivalent of MGBs) from Calais on the night of 16 August. Two MGBs were already at sea and they were joined by three more from Dover; both groups were ordered to join forces in mid-Channel and attack the German force, now known to include at least 20 R-Boats. When they came upon a group of six R-Boats the British force opened fire first at a range of less than 100 yards, damaging them severely. *MGB.330*, with nearly all guns out of action, rammed an R-Boat deliberately and sank her. The other four MGBs continued firing at the enemy, hitting several and setting them on fire. From German survivors it was later learned that the MGBs had sunk two R-Boats outright and damaged another so severely that it had to be abandoned. In addition two more were badly damaged and the action marked a clear victory for the British.

On the opposite side of the Channel the German convoys were having considerable success in running the gauntlet until early in 1942. The 'Channel Dash' by the battlecruisers *Scharnhorst*

Above: *MTB.376* leaves war-damaged Grand Harbour, Malta.
Above right: *MTB.476*, an ex-MGB, is armed with a 6-pdr gun and two 18-inch torpedo tubes.
Below: *MTB.80*, a Vosper 72½-footer at speed, showing the hardchine hull lifting clear of the water.

and *Gneisenau* in February 1942 is well known, but what is often forgotten is the part played by MTBs and S-Boats. The battlecruisers' screen included a strong force of S-Boats and R-Boats, which succeeded in beating off an attack by five MTBs from Dover, one of the last chances the British had of stopping the operation. In March the disguised raider *Michel* succeeded in brushing aside massed attacks by destroyers, MTBs and MGBs, when she made her way from Kiel to Brittany. Yet when the *Stier* made the same run in May her escorting torpedo boats were both sunk.

The British were able to form new flotillas with the large number of craft now available. A novel addition to their strength was a force of Steam Gunboats, virtually small destroyers capable of reinforcing the MTBs and MGBs. Initially known by SGB-numbers, they were given the names *Grey Goose*, *Grey Owl*, *Grey Shark* etc, under which they achieved considerable renown. The SGB Flotilla was taken over by Lt-Cdr Peter Scott, who brought a new dash and vigor in the handling of coastal forces. Another addition to the strength was a new type of long-hulled craft, the Fairmile 'D.' Here at last was a craft with sea-worthiness to match the S-Boat, although the petrol engine was still a weak point. These 'Dog-boats' were capable of functioning as MGBs or MTBs, according to the needs of the moment, a major advance in operational flexibility and of course their larger hulls permitted a heavier scale of armament than the short-hulled boats.

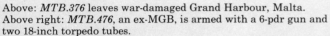

Far left: The Fairmile 'B' Type Motor Launches (MLs) performed a useful support task. Over 500 were built.
Center left: *MTB.422* passes wrecked shipping in Livorno. She was one of five American 'Higgins' Type PT.Boats made over to the Royal Navy under Lend-Lease.
Near left: A Vosper 73-footer, *MTB.381*. This flush-decked design carried an armament of four 18-inch torpedo tubes, a 20mm gun and six machine guns.

Another factor contributing to Coastal Forces' growing dominance over the S-Boats was air power. As the Allied air forces gained mastery in the air over the Channel, it became more and more hazardous for German light craft. The equipment and tactics which had already begun to end the freedom of the U-Boats to recharge their batteries on the surface at night could equally be used against craft moving under cover of darkness. Radar was now available in sufficient quantity to allow both Coastal Forces and RAF Coastal Command to be properly equipped with the latest surface search radars.

There was a final ingredient: better training. When Commander Peter Dickens took command of the 21st MTB Flotilla he realised that part of the problem for Coastal Forces was a lack of coherent tactical thought. He pioneered the concept of the unhurried approach, like a hunter stalking his quarry, and began to analyse results in a way which had not been done before. An example of his tactical innovation was the procedure to be followed if a force of MTBs or MGBs was sighted; one craft would start firing and maneuvering at high speed, drawing enemy fire and allowing the others to approach quietly from a different direction. If the remainder was sighted the decoy then slowed down in turn and started to make a silent attack.

The combination of Dickens' torpedo tactics and MGB tactics developed by the other great Coastal Forces leader, Robert Hichens, proved the key. When they finally worked together as respective Senior Officers of the MTB and MGB flotillas at Felixstowe, tactics could be worked out jointly and although Hichens was subsequently killed the procedures which he had refined with Dickens became standard for Coastal Forces.

As Coastal Forces grew in strength and confidence their area of operations was extended. During the winter of 1942 a force of Norwegian-manned MTBs began to raid shipping in Norwegian waters and landed Commandos. These operations were carried out with the new 'Dog-boats,' which also began to operate off the coast of Holland with considerable success.

In contrast the S-Boats' position deteriorated throughout 1943. Although the German Navy had been keen to develop S-Boats as a means of attacking British shipping in 1940, it had not occurred to the Naval Command that its own coastwise shipping would ultimately come under attack. The disruption of the iron ore imports through Rotterdam forced the Germans to send much of the traffic through Emden in river-barges, imposing a severe strain on an already overloaded canal-system. Both Spain and Sweden were becoming reluctant to charter merchant ships for the iron ore trade with Germany and this forced the Third Reich to use its own scarce mercantile tonnage.

It would be wrong however to talk of the S-Boats having been defeated. In the autumn of 1943 they switched to new tactics, using the maximum number of boats for one large sortie, rather than attacking in small numbers over a wide area. At the end of September three flotillas attacked a convoy off Harwich and a month later no fewer than 28 S-Boats launched a massed attack from Ijmuiden against a convoy off Cromer. It was later estimated that the battle which ensued broke down into 16 separate actions, as the S-Boats vainly tried to penetrate the convoy's defenses. When dawn came the British had lost an escorting trawler and the Germans had lost two S-Boats but the convoy was unharmed.

Left: *MTB.447* and her sisters had three Packard gasoline engines developing 4050hp, producing a smooth water speed of 39 knots.

352

Above: One of the early Vosper 70-footers *MTB.23* firing her torpedoes
at speed. Wartime experience however showed that torpedoes must be
launched at low speed to prevent them diving too deep.
Below: *MTB.297* returning to port at full speed after she and *MTB.228*
had torpedoed the old cruiser *Niobe* (formerly *Dalmacija*) in the
Adriatic in December 1943.

Another innovation was to adopt direct attacks. Instead of relying on silence the S-Boats now took to attacking at high speed, hoping to out-distance the escorting destroyers. It could also be unwise to pursue a fleeing S-Boat too far, for they had a trick of luring a pursuer almost to the Dutch coast and then turning on him.

During the build-up before the Normandy invasion in June 1944 emphasis switched back to the English Channel. For the first time a force of American PT-Boats was used in Northern European waters, but they were intended primarily for 'cloak and dagger' operations rather than attacks on German shipping. However for D-Day itself three PT-Boat squadrons were employed to guard the flanks of the beachhead. With their Allied counterparts they joined in a series of fierce night actions, preventing the S-Boats from harassing the huge invasion armada lying off the beaches.

When one remembers that there were literally thousands of targets available, the S-Boats' efforts were a dismal failure. During the first week of the invasion they sank only a dozen or so ships and lost three of their own. Air strikes took out four more and then on the night of 14 June a massive bombing raid on Le Havre sank 11 and damaged three, a blow from which the Channel flotillas never recovered.

Right to the end the S-Boats remained dangerous. As late as March 1945 they were able to sink two merchant ships in the Scheldt estuary, while the mines that they laid sank 11 more. Not until Germany itself was crumbling did the S-Boats give up the struggle. At the surrender only 15 boats were still operational – as against over 300 craft in Coastal Forces.

Above left: A Fairmile 'B' Type, *ML.145* carried a variety of weapons and also laid mines.
Left: *MGB.673*, a Fairmile 'D' Type, bristles with guns. These 115-footers were capable of 31 knots.

BATTLE FOR THE MED

In the autumn of 1941 the German Navy, faced with the need to prop up its Italian ally, decided to move an S-Boat flotilla to the Mediterranean. As activity in the Baltic was virtually at an end the 3rd Flotilla was earmarked for the Mediterranean, while the 1st Flotilla was to be sent to the Black Sea to keep up pressure on the Soviet Union.

The journey of the 3rd Flotilla was a minor epic, involving ten S-Boats and all their spares and support equipment moving all the way from the North Sea to the Mediterranean without going through the Straits of Gibraltar. From Rotterdam the flotilla went up the Rhine to Strasbourg, where they transferred to the Rhine-Rhône Canal. Passing through 167 locks and the famous Burgundian Gate, they then traversed the River Doubs and the Saône, finally joining the Rhône at Lyons. Even a S-Boat was a tight fit in the locks on the Rhine-Rhône Canal and it was necessary to use the slightly smaller type, with 16-cylinder engines, to get through the locks.

Security was strictly maintained throughout the operation. The 20mm gun was removed, the torpedo-tubes were covered over with sheet metal and a dummy funnel was built on deck. The wheelhouse had to be cut off to pass underneath the low bridges, and was carried on deck. The Reich Service flag was worn instead of the naval ensign and the crews wore civilian clothes, as the cover-story was that a force of air-sea rescue launches was in transit.

The Flotilla moved in two divisions; the first was operational at Augusta in Sicily by December 1941, while the rest joined them a month later. From Sicily they could harass Malta, laying mines and picking off unwary small craft. In May 1942 they moved to Derna in North Africa, a forward base for attacking the big 'Vigorous' convoy to Malta. During the evening of 14 June they sank the destroyer HMS *Hasty* and damaged the cruiser *Newcastle*. They were also able to interdict the evacuation from Tobruk, sinking a minesweeper and several small vessels and even capturing a tank landing craft.

In theory the Italian MAS-boats should have been able to make a considerable nuisance of themselves, even without German reinforcements, for there were some 60 boats operational. But the Type 500 boats were not sufficiently robust and even their weapons were unsatisfactory. Nevertheless they achieved successes, notably the sinking of the cruiser HMS *Manchester* in August 1941 and the submarine *Turbulent* in March 1943. In the Red Sea *MAS.213* hit and damaged the anti-aircraft cruiser HMS *Capetown* in April 1941.

Above: *MAS.534* and her sister *MAS.533* in December 1941. The former was later sunk by German air attack in the Adriatic.
Below: Two Italian Series 500 MAS-boats at high speed. In spite of their outstanding performance, the MAS failed to achieve many significant results during World War II.

In spite of their weaknesses the Italian Navy deployed its MTBs wherever the Axis needed reinforcement, even as far afield as Lake Ladoga, outside Leningrad. In January 1942 the Naval Command answered a German request for help by sending MTBs, midget submarines and explosive motor boats to the Black Sea. This called for as much ingenuity as the S-Boats' trip from Germany; they were taken by large road-transporters from Venice to Vienna and from there towed to Galatz. They then made their own way down the Danube, reaching the sea at Constanza before crossing the Black Sea to Yalta in the Crimea. The 19th MAS Flottiglia became operational in May 1942, and three months later scored a major success by blowing the bows off the cruiser *Molotov*.

What could have been the proudest chapter in the story of the MAS turned out to be a disaster. On 26 July 1941 a coordinated attack was planned on Malta, using MAS, midget submarines and aircraft. The plan was audacious, typical of the daredevil temperament which had led the Italians to develop the MAS way back in 1915. The frigate *Diana* led a force consisting of *MAS.451* and *MAS. 452*, each carrying a *Maiale* or 'pig' human torpedo, and eight explosive motor boats. The latter were known as *Barchini Esplosivi*, but had a camouflage designation, *Motoscafi da Turismo Modificati* (modified tourist motorboats or MTM). They were piloted within range of the target and the operator locked the controls before making his escape, or so the rule book said. The British defenders were alerted by their surface radar, so that the coastal artillery was ready for the attack. In spite of that Major Tesei, leading the assault, was able to destroy the boom and it looked as if the attack would succeed. But the attackers did not allow for the detonation blowing up the St Elmo lifting bridge on the breakwater; the wreckage collapsed and stopped the remaining *Barchini* from getting into Grand Harbour. Early next morning the two MAS were caught by RAF fighter-bombers and destroyed, a devastating end to what could have been a shattering blow to the British.

The S-Boats which went to the Black Sea went from Kiel to Hamburg, and then up the Elbe to Dresden. From there they were taken by road-transporters along the autobahn as far as Ingolstadt, where they were once more put afloat on the Danube. For the journey they were stripped to the bare hull and even the engines had to be removed to reduce weight, but even with a delay caused by ice in the Danube the first four boats of the 1st Flotilla were operational in May 1942. They were just in time for the siege of Sevastopol, during which they were able to inflict several casualties.

The work done by the comparatively small number of S-Boats was tremendous, especially as they were heavily outnumbered by Soviet forces. Whereas the Soviet heavy units were handled cautiously, they used light forces aggressively, particularly in support of commando-type operations behind enemy lines. The Russians fought desperately to save the great naval base and fortress of Sevastopol and thereafter there was heavy fighting in the Straits of Kerch and the Sea of Azov. When the German Army broke through to Novorossiisk in September 1942, the Black Sea Fleet's light forces had to help transport men and supplies from Poti to Tuapse in a frantic effort to stem the advance. Losses were heavy, particularly in action with German and Italian light forces.

An outstanding action was the seizure on 10 September 1943 of Novorossiisk by Russian MTBs (known as TKA or *Torpedny Kater*). Three groups of TKA, 26 in all, based on Gelendik were given the task of entering the harbor and capturing a bridgehead for the landing of three army brigades. The Russians later admitted that the operation had been successful but costly, with the loss of five gunboats, eight motor launches and two minesweepers.

The pattern of operations in the English Channel was repeated

Left: Italian MTS boats at sea. These two-man craft carried a short 17.7 inch torpedo in the stem and could travel for a distance of about 120 miles.

as the Soviet air force gradually won air superiority and the navy's MTBs and gunboats were able to defeat their Axis opponents. However Soviet operations were normally characterized by a lack of imagination and there are many examples of the High Command's failure to exploit the potential of their light strike craft. For example, nothing was done to interrupt the German evacuation of Odessa and Nikolaiev, nor was the evacuation of the Crimea an excuse for unleashing the light forces. Instead the emphasis was put on supporting the army, an important role but only one of the functions for which MTBs and MGBs were suited.

In the Mediterranean Axis light forces reached their peak in August 1942 and thereafter their fortunes declined dramatically. The British victory at El Alamein, followed by the 'Torch' landings in Algeria and Morocco, soon led to the destruction of the S-Boats' bases in North Africa. Then came the Allied landings in Sicily, which forced the S-Boats to move from Taranto to Viareggio. Although they succeeded in sinking an American destroyer, the USS *Rowan*, off Salerno, it is interesting to read in German records that the S-Boat flotillas felt that they had been abandoned by the Naval Command. Even so, their discipline and dedication made them formidable opponents. Even when forced to evacuate Taranto in September 1943 one of them laid mines as she left and one of these sank the British minelayer HMS *Abdiel* next day, with heavy loss of life.

Two S-Boats left for the Adriatic and there they managed to wage what amounted to a private war. On 11 September 1943 they sank the Italian gun boat *Aurora* off Ancona and on the same afternoon they captured a troop transport and torpedoed the destroyer *Quintino Sella* south of Venice. By now almost out of fuel, they then persuaded the garrison of Venice to surrender to them, having convinced the Italian defenders that they were supported by dive-bombers and tanks.

In October 1943 two flotillas (11 S-Boats) moved into the Adriatic, having travelled through northern Italy via the River Po. There were rich pickings in the form of numerous small craft running arms and supplies to the Yugoslav partisans and many of them were sunk. Gradually however the process of attrition wore them down to eight boats and when hostilities ended in May 1945 only five were left at Pola. It had been a hard-fought battle.

The British had been able to reinforce the Mediterranean flotillas in the spring and summer of 1943, particularly with the new Fairmile 'D' type. They had been able to make the journey by sea, having been modified to carry extra fuel in deck-tanks. They were joined by American PT-Boats as well, but they suffered from the dearth of targets. This is reflected in the extraordinary variety of subsidiary duties performed by light craft in 1943–44. Only when action flared up in the Adriatic and Aegean did they begin to justify their existence.

An unusual feature of the small-ship combat during this period was the use by both sides of converted landing craft as inshore gunboats. The Germans used F-lighters and the British used their Landing Craft, Gun (LCG) to provide heavy firepower in support of inshore operations. The F-lighter was a particularly doughty opponent when upgunned and armored and its light automatic 37mm and 20mm guns were usually supplemented by 88mm flak guns which could smash a PT-Boat or MTB into matchwood. The American PT-Boats were particularly valuable in these operations because of their superior surface-search radar. They normally provided reconnaissance and targeting information for MTBs and MGBs.

One of the most successful operations was a patrol by three PT-Boats in June 1944, patrolling out of the base at Bastia in Corsica. Between La Spezia and Genoa they picked up what appeared to be two escorts and tracked them for half an hour, running on silenced engines. The three PT-Boats then each fired two torpedoes and turned away, still creeping on silenced engines. Suddenly the leading target blew up, the second started firing wildly and then the radar-screens went blank. Postwar research showed that the six torpedoes had accounted for the small destroyers *TA.26* and *TA.30*, both ex-Italian Navy ships operating under German control. The action encapsulated all the lessons and improvements of wartime experience and lived up to the ideal attack as envisaged by people like Peter Dickens, not only to attack undetected but to leave the scene still undetected.

Below: *MS.15* and other Series I *motosiluranti* were copied from German designs.
Right: *MAS.539* being winched out of the water. The small size of these craft allowed maintenance to be carried out on shore.

PT-BOATS IN THE PACIFIC

Contrary to expectations the new PT-Boats of the US Navy were not hurled into the Pacific War. For a start, events had moved so fast after Pearl Harbor that there hardly was time to get forces moved into the Central Pacific. Another factor was the immense distances covered by the carrier task groups; the big battles of Coral Sea and Midway had been fought well away from land and the rival ships had not even seen one another. Only when the time came to make an amphibious landing would there be any chance to attack Japanese warships on anything like equal terms.

That chance came at last in August 1942 when the far-reaching decision was made to invade the Solomon Islands. The landing planned for Guadalcanal was certain to stir up a hornet's nest and in that sort of close-range fighting the PT-Boat was likely to prove vital. The only PT-Boats in the Pacific were Squadron 2's 14 boats at Panama and these were divided into two squadrons and shipped out to Noumea in New Caledonia as deck-cargo aboard cargo ships.

Left: A PT-Boat escorts landing barges at Nassau Bay, New Guinea, July 1943.
Below: PT-Boats take evasive action under a Japanese air attack during the Leyte Gulf landings, October 1944.

Inevitably the initial attempts to set up a forward base were chaotic. There was great difficulty in getting the 50-ton hulls off the cargo ships for there was no crane available for three weeks. Once afloat the boats had to move with their tender, the converted yacht *Jamestown*, to Tulagi. Their new operational base was only 35 miles across the water from Guadalcanal, where the US Marines were locked in a bloody struggle to stop the vital airstrip from falling into Japanese hands. Night after night Japanese warships came down the 'Slot' from Rabaul to bring in reinforcements of men and ammunition and to bombard the American positions. With their superior training in night-fighting the Japanese had already inflicted severe casualties and it was now absolutely vital that the PT-Boats try to redress the balance.

The crews worked hard to set up their new operating base on 12 and 13 October and the four boats, *PT.38, PT.46, PT.48* and *PT.60*, were ready when at 0200 hours the following morning the alarm sounded. A force of Japanese warships had come down the 'Slot' and were busily bombarding the Marines' position. Intelligence was as poor as the tactical appreciation of what PT-Boats could do – at first, when it was thought that only three destroyers were coming, the PT-Boats' commander thought that they were not sufficiently worthy opponents!

Above: *PT.1* shipped as deck cargo on the seaplane tender USS *Pocomoke.*

Such illusions were shattered as soon as the PT-Boats cleared Tulagi harbor on that moonless night. Apart from the distant flash of gunfire nothing could be seen in the inky blackness and nobody realised that the four boats in line ahead had already passed through a picket line of eight Japanese destroyers. The squadron became separated, with *PT.60* well ahead of *PT.46* and *PT.48*, and *PT.38* several miles away to the east. *PT.60* fired two torpedoes at what she identified as a cruiser and then turned and ran for home, oblivious of the fact that she was running into the destroyers. Two of them gave chase, but were unable to hit the small target and, although she was subsequently damaged on a reef while waiting for a patrolling destroyer to move away, she escaped without further damage.

PT.46 and *PT.48* had a much more frightening time, being illuminated by searchlights and bracketed by heavy shells, but miraculously both escaped. They had however found no targets because, as the reports put it, by the time a Japanese destroyer was sighted the PT-Boat was too close to fire a torpedo. Being so far away, *PT.38* avoided the fire which had been directed at her squadron-mates, but when she tried to fire her torpedoes only one of the four got into the water. Two stuck in the tubes and one damaged its fins by striking the deck as it shot out (the humid air in the Solomons had affected the powder-charge), but the fourth ran straight and apparently exploded. So confused was the whole series of actions that the US Navy was convinced that *PT.60* and *PT.38* had each sunk a cruiser, but postwar research is quite clear that no Japanese warships were hit that night. The problem was one that affected all actions involving small strike craft – from a small bridge only a few feet above the waterline very little can be seen and often torpedoes exploding on hitting the seabed or the seashore were mistaken for hits.

Until the PT-Boats could be fitted with radar they could do very little except harass the Japanese, who proved much more proficient at the deadly game of night-fighting. Even allowing that they caused confusion merely by appearing on the scene, contemporary accounts show that an equal amount of confusion was created among the PT-Boats. In fact, far from being a menace to the bigger warship, PT-Boats proved frighteningly vulnerable to destroyers. In the best-known of such incidents a destroyer cut *PT.109* in half and very nearly put paid to the career of Lieutenant John F Kennedy.

The main target of the PT-Boats' attentions was the famous 'Tokyo Express,' a nightly supply-run from Rabaul to Guadalcanal. It was led by a man widely reckoned to be the finest Japanese commander of World War II, Rear-Admiral Raizo Tanaka. His light cruisers, destroyers and fast transports made their runs as regularly as any express train. For the Japanese it was the only hope of preventing the Americans from gaining a vital foothold in the Solomons and equally for the Americans, 'derailing the Tokyo Express' was given top priority.

For the PT-Boat crews the strain became almost unbearable. Not only were they continually frustrated in their attempts to surprise the Japanese, but also the enervating climate of the Solomons was beginning to wear them down. To be out three nights in four was not uncommon and it was normal for the officers and men to catch a few hours sleep and then to work all day on the engines for the following night. Mechanical faults were inevitable, given the strain the boats were under and it was not unusual for five out of the eight boats at Tulagi to be incapable of going to sea. By December 1942 the efficiency of the squadron was seriously affected by the strain. Most personnel had succumbed to a combination of malaria, dengue and dysentery and were way below the tough mental and physical standard required for operating light strike craft, yet these 'zombies' still managed to show what they could do.

On the night of 9 December *PT.59* and *PT.44* were sent to investigate an intelligence report that a Japanese submarine would be landing men on a clandestine mission. As predicted the submarine was there and *PT.59* was the best placed to fire two torpedoes. They ran true and the *I.3* disappeared in a shower of debris. Although the submarine had been a sitting duck it was heartening to the crews back at Tulagi to know that PT-Boats were as deadly as they had been claimed.

Only two nights later they scored another heartening success, when *PT.37*, *PT.40* and *PT.48* set up an ambush for the 'Tokyo Express' off Savo Island. They were lucky that the usual clammy haze of the Solomons had given way to a clear night and so, although they had lost visual contact with one another, the lookouts sighted the Japanese first. They slid out into the channel and took up their firing positions and they fired their spreads of torpedoes almost simultaneously. There was a tremendous explosion and this time there was no false claim for they had torpedoed Tanaka's flagship, the big destroyer *Terutsuki*. The raid was abandoned, for Tanaka had been injured by the blast, and after he had been taken off the *Terutsuki* was left to sink and the 'Tokyo Express' headed back to Rabaul. However the Japanese took their revenge, for two PT-Boats ran into Japanese destroyers shortly afterwards. They had inadvertently allowed themselves to be silhouetted against the burning glow of *Terutsuki* and that was sufficient for the alert Japanese lookouts.

Other actions took place once the 'Tokyo Express' started again, but time was running out for the Japanese. The grim war of attrition was finally wearing them down. On 1/2 February 1943 a last big effort was made by the Japanese, but this time the Express was running empty; the Japanese had decided to pull out from Guadalcanal and a light cruiser and 20 destroyers were coming down the 'Slot.' It was a bad night for the PT-Boats, who failed to hit any of the Japanese ships and suffered in return the loss of three of their number.

In retrospect it can be asked what the PT-Boats had achieved off Guadalcanal. The answer is not much in material terms. However it must be remembered that at a time when US destroyers and cruisers were outclassed and outfought by the Japanese,

Above: A PT-Boat firing her 20mm gun and her .5-inch machine guns at Japanese positions on Biak, New Guinea.
Above right: John F Kennedy and the crew of *PT.109* in 1943.

particularly in view of the overwhelming superiority of the 'Long Lance' torpedo, the PT-Boats were virtually immune to torpedoes; They could also strike back and they posed a threat which the Japanese could never ignore. Without the presence of PT-Boats the Japanese could have had much more freedom of action and that might easily have made the difference between victory and defeat.

At about the time that operations in the Solomons were beginning to go against the Japanese another theater of operations was becoming crucial. The successful outcome of the

Battle of the Coral Sea had frustrated a Japanese drive on Port Moresby, the capital of New Guinea, but the Japanese were still in possession of the northern shore and until they were expelled they remained a threat to Australia.

The battle for possession of New Guinea resolved itself into a struggle to dominate the northern shoreline, for the Japanese had a string of garrisons needing resupply from the sea. Here was an ideal target for PT-Boats and early in 1943 a base was established at Tufi. Their targets were the small barges and lighters used to run in ammunition and food, the best-known being the 46ft Daihatsu type, built originally of steel but later of

Below: Weaponry on the deck of *PT.131* includes short 21-inch torpedoes, rocket launchers and a 20mm Oerlikon gun.

wood. They were armored with bullet-proof steel around the bridge and carried a defensive armament of machine guns. What made them an even tougher nut for PT-Boats to crack was that they drew less than three feet of water and torpedoes would run underneath. Being diesel-powered for the most part, they could absorb much heavier punishment than the PT-Boats and they were to prove doughty opponents.

The first detachment at Tufi numbered only six PT-Boats in January 1943, but eventually the New Guinea PT-Boat Command was expanded to 14 squadrons. They used several bases and were supported by eight mobile tenders. The early 'barge-busting' operations showed just how tough the Daihatsu craft were and there was considerable discussion about the best tactics to deal with them. The initial reaction was to use speed, but eventually stealth was shown to be the right approach, as it had in the Solomons and in the English Channel. In March two PT-boats *PT.114* and *PT.129* tried the new ideas out in a daring attack on Mai-Ami Bay, in Huon Gulf, which was suspected of being a barge-terminal. The two PT-Boats arrived in the area after dark, cut engines and waited to see what would happen. Eventually *PT.129* moved out into the Gulf to see what had happened to the enemy, but *PT.114*'s patience was rewarded when they heard the noise of voices and engines. Although it sounds hard to believe, the incessant tropical rain had blanketed the sound to such an extent that two Japanese barges actually bumped into the PT-Boat without realising what she was.

Being so close the .50 inch machine guns could not depress far enough to hit, but Lieutenant Dean ordered submachine guns to be passed around and with these the men of *PT.114* attacked the barge alongside. As the boat pulled away her guns were able to rake the other barge. At this moment *PT.129* returned at high speed and helped to polish off the remaining four barges.

The next step was to 'acquire' 37mm aircraft cannon and one of these was mounted on the bow to provide more firepower. By July the PT-Boats were moving further up the coast in search of new targets and in that month another unusual action was fought. *PT.142* and *PT.149* found themselves in the middle of a convoy of some 30 barges and were even called up by the Japanese with lamp-signals. Their reply was to open fire and in the murderous exchange which followed six barges were sunk and the PT-Boats sustained hits themselves.

The later boats sent out to New Guinea were armed with the new 40mm Bofors gun, a great improvement over the machine

Above: An aerial view of a PT-Boat at speed. The heavy torpedo tubes have given way to Mark XIII short torpedoes.

Above left: PT-Boats of Squadron 1 pass the carrier USS *Hornet* off Pearl Harbor in April 1942.
Left: *PT.14*, an Elco 70-footer, running trials in 1940. She became the Royal Navy's *MTB.263* in 1941.
Below: The Elco built *PT.105* and two sisters on trial. These 80-footers could make 40 knots in smooth water.

366

Above: PT-Boats of Squadron 13 making their way northwards
through the Inland Passage from Seattle to Alaska in 1943.
Below: An Elco PT Boat fires two of her Mark VIII torpedoes during
exercises off the Newport Torpedo Station.

guns and 20mm cannon previously used. Bofors guns were scrounged wherever they could be found and it was even felt worthwhile to remove two torpedo tubes to permit the extra weight. Another innovation was to move in closer to the shore-line, where interceptions were much easier to achieve. It meant a great increase in the risks from navigational hazards, for the whole area was studded with uncharted rocks and reefs, but the results justified the gamble. Between July and August 1943 the number of barges sunk rose from nine to 45, clear proof that the PT-Boats were getting it right.

It was normally the rule that a PT-Boat could not survive in daylight under air attack, but in December 1943 *PT.190* and *PT.191* showed how an exception proves the rule. Operating off Arawe in New Britain, they were attacked by an estimated 40 aircraft. There was nothing the PT-Boats could do except zigzag violently and hope that their AA fire would put the Japanese pilots off their aim. The impossible happened; four aircraft were shot down and the remaining attacks became more and more ragged. Even so, sheer weight of numbers might have overcome the PT-Boats had not a group of American P-47 Thunderbolts arrived after forty minutes and put the attackers to flight.

It is hard at this distance to remember just how long it took to clear the Japanese out of the Pacific. 'Barge-busting' in New Guinea was not brought to an end until November 1944, when emphasis shifted to the Philippines. The big base at Mios Wendi was closed down and replaced by a new one at Morotai. From here the PT-Boats were to blockade the 40,000-strong garrison on Halmahera, one of the strongpoints 'leapfrogged' by General MacArthur's island-hopping strategy, but still too dangerous to leave unguarded. Nor was Morotai totally secure, for the Japanese defenders had only been pushed to the other end of the island. The base was kept fully engaged to the end of the war, preventing the garrison on Halmahera from reinforcing their comrades on Morotai.

Top: The remains of *PT.323*, almost bisected by a Japanese aircraft off Leyte, December 1944.
Above: *PT.164* minus her bow after an air attack off Rendova in August 1943.

The real business of the PT-Boats however was to support the big amphibious landings in the Philippines. A day after the landings in Leyte Gulf, 45 boats arrived from New Guinea, having travelled 1200 miles with their tenders. As we know a series of misunderstandings and errors in signalling placed the whole invasion force at risk, with a Japanese decoy force successfully luring away the covering aircraft carriers and leaving only six old battleships to stop a task force heading for Surigao Strait. To support Admiral Jesse B Oldendorf there was a slender force of destroyers and 39 PT-Boats, deployed on either side of the strait. Their most important task was to report on numbers and disposition of the Japanese and only then did they have freedom to attack.

The Japanese were alert and their gun crews had little difficulty in beating back the PT-Boats' attacks. Ten were hit, but only one was sunk. PT.137 succeeded in damaging the light cruiser *Abukuma* – with a torpedo which underran its original target! PT.490, PT.491 and PT.493 attacked a destroyer and thought they had scored a hit, but PT.493 was hit twice by heavy shells and had to be run ashore on a coral reef. Further north PT.323 helped to finish off the destroyer *Asagumo*, which was dead in the water, near the burning cruiser *Mogami*.

The PT-Boats had played their part in destroying the Imperial Japanese Navy's last surface fleet, but they still had work to do in the Philippines. The Japanese were always resourceful in supplying their outlying garrisons and from their main base

Above, near right: The crew of *PT.321* haul aboard a waterlogged Japanese survivor in Surigao Strait, October 1944.
Above, far right: *PT.354* mounts a quadruple bazooka armament, a home-grown modification.
Below right: *PT.25*, an Elco 70-footer, is pictured here on her completion.

in Ormoc Bay they were able to feed in small craft carrying supplies and ammunition. Several actions took place between the PT-Boats and the Japanese patrol craft and as late as 12 December a destroyer was sunk. This was the *Uzuki*, torpedoed by *PT.492* and *PT.497* on the west coast of Leyte.

Space does not permit a detailed account of the work done by PT-Boats in the Philippines, but some idea of the scale of operations can be guessed at. By the summer of 1945 the base at Bobon Point, Samar, was operating over 200 PT-Boats and training was starting for the invasion of the Japanese home islands.

It might be thought that the PT-Boat had earned its place in the postwar US Navy, but this was not to be. Out of 212 boats operational in the Philippines in August 1945, no fewer than 118 were immediately surveyed and found to be defective. After being stripped of engines, guns and every useful item of gear they were burned off Samar beach, a sad and undignified end after all they had endured and achieved. Even the boats in the United States were hurriedly disposed of and by 1946 only four new craft were still on the Navy List. Even these were destined to be sold to South Korea in 1952, for the US Navy could see no role for the PT-Boat in warfare dominated by guided missiles and radar. Time was to show how wrong they were.

Below: The sleek lines of *PT.140* are shown to advantage in this photograph taken on a training run off Melville, Rhode Island in November 1943.

THE FAST PATROL BOATS

For many years after World War II the British retained a lead in strike craft, now given the generic title of fast patrol boats or FPBs. The old distinction between MTBs and MGBs had become blurred, with all new craft being designed for interchangeable guns and torpedoes and even so-called torpedo boats carrying a gun-armament far heavier than anything called an MGB in 1941.

The first change was in propulsion. Recognizing that the weak point of their MTBs and MGBs had been the Packard petrol engine, the British decided to exploit their lead in gas turbines and in 1947 a Camper & Nicholson long-hulled FPB, *MGB.2009* went to sea with a Gatric gas turbine. Considering that she was a leap in the dark, when such problems as blade-fatigue and ingestion of salt water were only dimly understood, *MGB.2009* was surprisingly successful. She was purely experimental and did not serve long, but she showed that both noise and vibration could be controlled, despite the enormous increase in power.

Despite this bold step the 'conventional' FPB continued to be built. The British built two large classes, the Packard-engined 'Gay' class and the diesel-engined 'Dark' class. These could be regarded as the last fling of the old short-hulled designs, being only 75ft long – the 'Gay' class were largely wooden whereas the 'Dark' boats were of composite construction, wood planking on aluminum framing. They were like their wartime predecessors noisy and lively, but they carried the exceptionally heavy armament of four 21-inch torpedo-tubes and a twin 20mm gun as torpedo boats or a 4.5-inch gun and a 40mm Bofors as gunboats.

The 4.5-inch gun, otherwise known as the Coastal Forces Mk 1 or the 4.5-inch 8cwt, looked a formidable weapon but it was only a qualified success. In an attempt to follow the successful wartime 6-pounder (57mm) the Admiralty adapted an Army 114mm low-velocity gun which had originally been intended for the demolition of concrete fortifications. On a modified twin Oerlikon power-mounting it encountered a host of teething troubles, but in spite of these it was issued to Coastal Forces postwar. Having very low velocity and a short barrel the gun lacked range and old Coastal Forces hands swore that you could see the shell leave the muzzle and wobble on its way.

The decision to put diesels in the 'Dark' class was based on experience with two ex-*Schnellboote*, *S.208* and *S.212*, which played an unique role in the postwar world. These had been surrendered at the end of the war and were of understandable interest to the British, but once the trials and evaluation were over another use was found for them. The Cold War was as yet an unknown phrase, the Soviet blockade of West Berlin had started and there was no NATO Alliance to defend Western Europe. What was needed was intelligence about the Soviet Navy in the Baltic and so these two S-Boats, minus armament and manned by ex-*Kriegsmarine* personnel, eavesdropped on Russian movements and maneuvers. Nothing could catch them, which was as well, since the German crews would have been executed as spies. No navy recognized them and they could scarcely hope to be granted prisoner-of-war status. The two boats, numbered *MTB.5208* and *MTB.5212*, were for some years fishery protection craft with the British Rhine Army Flotilla.

Below: HMS *Brave Borderer* was one of the last and also one of the most successful British designs. She was armed with four 21-inch torpedoes and two 40mm guns. Her Proteus gas turbines gave her a speed of 50 knots.

Above: The world's first gas turbine powered fast patrol boat was the experimental *MGB.2009*. It was driven by a Gatric turbine.

Performance was all-important and an exciting new British diesel, the Napier Deltic, was tried out in *No. 5212*. This unusual engine, which is still in production for minehunters, took its name from a delta or triangular arrangement of opposed pistons and triple crankshafts. Each Deltic developed 2500 brake horse-power at 2000 rpm and yet with its reverse gear weighed only 10,500lb. Its power-to-weight ratio of 4.2lbs per hp was the best yet achieved in a marine diesel and had the British not invested so much in gas turbines the Deltic would certainly have been

developed for future fast strike craft. However the success of the Gatric in *MGB.2009* coupled with advances in aero-engines pointed inexorably towards the gas turbine.

The next step was to get more gas turbines to sea for evaluation and in 1953 two much larger FPBs were commissioned, the 122-ft long *Bold Pathfinder* and her half-sister *Bold Pioneer*, each driven by a pair of G.2 gas turbines. The opportunity was taken to evaluate hull-forms at the same time. *Bold Pathfinder* trying a round bilge form, while *Bold Pioneer* used the normal hard chine hull-form. With their massive twin funnels set side by side they were impressive craft and were big enough to carry two 4.5-inch guns and a 40mm Bofors or four 21-inch torpedo-tubes and a Bofors gun.

Experience with the Gatric and G.2 showed that the best results would be obtained if a gas turbine was to be specially designed for the marine environment and in 1952 Peter Scott's famous command, HMS *Grey Goose* went into dock for conversion. Her steam turbines were replaced by twin RM-60 turbines

Above: *Bold Pathfinder* was powered by G.2 turbines and could mount two 4.5-inch guns or torpedoes.

developing 50 percent more power than her original steam machinery. In her new incarnation she had twin side by side funnels, as in the 'Bold' boats, but she was no more than a floating test bed and after three or four years of intensive (and highly successful) trials she was scrapped in 1957.

Confidence in gas turbines was gaining rapidly and, once the lessons of the largely experimental 'Bold' class had been absorbed, the Vosper yard at Portchester was given a contract for two composite gas turbines FPBs, known as the 'Brave' class. They were to be driven by three 'marinized' versions of the Bristol Proteus gas turbine. As torpedo boats they carried four 21-inch torpedoes, but instead of the conventional tubes they carried side-launching cradles, an arrangement used in some wartime PT-Boats to reduce weight. The gunboat version was to use the so-called Coastal Forces System Mk 2 or CFS2 gun, a massive 3.3-inch (84mm) gun in a stabilized enclosed shield.

The CFS2 gun system was based on the British Army's Centurion tank gun, the 20-pounder. It used stabilization to compensate for the violent motion and, being designed from the start for the task, had none of the faults of the short 4.5-inch gun. In 1954 one was mounted on a rolling platform at Portland Bill and then it went to sea for trials in the *Bold Pioneer*. It proved popular, giving rise to a new unofficial Coastal Forces motto: 'One Round, One Hit' – a boast that could never have been fulfilled in previous MGBs.

The Proteus was equally successful, proving that the noise of a gas turbine was by no means as severe as its critics had claimed. Its lack of vibration was a marked improvement over the Deltic, which had also been shown to be much noisier. But above all the Proteus offered lightness; with its reversing gearbox fitted, its power-to-weight ratio was still only 1.6lbs per hp. Another clear advantage was its lack of bulk, for the 'Braves' had 25 percent more space available in the engine room than a petrol, or diesel-engined FPB.

The *Brave Borderer* and *Brave Swordsman* attracted a lot of attention, achieving as much as 50 knots in smooth conditions. Denmark ordered six very similar craft in 1962, the *Søløven* class, while the new Federal German Navy ordered a single craft, the *Strahl*. But the hard chine hull proved no better suited to the short, steep seas of the Baltic than it had in the 1930s, when Lürssen had perfected the round-bilge form for the *Schnellboote* and no more were built. What also hamstrung the British

effort to sell their FPB designs was the sudden decision in 1957 to abolish Coastal Forces. It was the old argument: in peacetime fast strike craft are too expensive to maintain as they siphon off funds from more important projects. All the experience and expertise built up since 1939 was thus to be thrown away.

The British decision is even harder to comprehend when it is remembered that other navies showed no such doubt about the efficacy of fast strike craft. Norway, for example, had just placed an order for 12 *Nasty* type, a design which was sufficiently interesting to be evaluated by the US Navy. In Germany the famous Lürssen yard was once again in full production, with the first of 32 *Jaguar* class. Of even more significance was the attention that the Soviet Navy was paying to fast strike craft. Class after class was appearing, *P-4s*, *P-6s*, *P-8s* and *P-10s*, all part of the massive Soviet effort to protect inshore waters. They were fairly small craft, ranging from 82ft to 92ft and armed with two torpedo-tubes. The most successful were the *P-6* type, an estimated 400 of which were built from 1953 to 1960 – a staggering total even by wartime standards.

The first break out of the traditional mould was made by the Royal Swedish Navy. Starting with the 250-ton *Plejad* class in 1950, they enlarged the basic hull to allow a much heavier load of weaponry, associated electronic and a more robust hull. On a hull 157ft long the *Plejad* class (built by Lürssen) mounted six 21-inch torpedo-tubes and two 40mm Bofors guns. In the early 1960s the *Spica* class followed, 141-footers with the same torpedo-armament, but a 57mm Bofors automatic gun in a power-operated enclosed turret and radar-assisted fire control. The *Spicas* and their successors, the very similar *Norrköping* class, displace 200 tons and are driven by three Proteus gas turbines developing over 12,000 horsepower. It is no coincidence that the hull was designed by Lürssen and the seakeeping of the *Spicas* is one of their outstanding features.

The Royal Swedish Navy pioneered the use of very fast (60-knot) wire-guided torpedoes for use against surface targets, at a time when opinion elsewhere was turning against the torpedo. But, whereas the British 21-inch Mk 9 travelled at only 35 knots for 14,000 yards, the Swedish Tp 61, with its hydrogen peroxide fuel, could travel 50 percent further at 60 knots. The guidance-wire pays out very rapidly from a spool in the tail of the torpedo and simultaneously from a spool in the torpedo-tube and the thin wire then floats in the water as it has neutral buoyancy. The advantage of wire-guidance is that the torpedo remains under positive guidance all the way, although in its final run-in it may switch to passive homing on propeller-noise.

The newly formed Federal German Navy had the task of preventing Soviet forces from breaking out of the Baltic and this implied a heavy reliance on strike craft. Following the lead given by the Swedes, in 1970 the Federal German Navy started to equip some of its *Jaguar* class with a new wire-guided anti-ship torpedo known as the *Seeaal* or sea-eel. The ten craft converted were now known as the *Zobel* class and they struck an unusual note in having the two 21-inch torpedo-tubes facing aft. This was to allow the FPB to launch her torpedoes while breaking away and reduced the risks involved in turning under fire.

It was left to the Soviet Union to make the first major break-through. From 1959 reports percolated through to the West of a startling development, a standard P-6 MTB hull armed with two large boxes aft, containing guided missiles. Dubbed 'Komar' by NATO, the new strike craft carried two SS-N-2 'Styx' surface-to-surface missiles and were driven at 40 knots by four-shaft diesel engines. There were many drawbacks to the 'Komar,' however. Because the launch-tubes were open at either end the missiles suffered severely from corrosion and with so much

Above left: The British FBP *Gay Archer,* one of the last gasoline-powered short-hulled boats.
Above: The 'Gay' Class was followed by the 'Dark' Class which were diesel-powered.

armament crammed into an 88ft hull they hardly dared venture outside coastal waters.

The Soviet Navy placed great faith in these missile boats. Many were transferred to 'satellite' navies and both Egypt and the Republic of China built their own versions, but they were only an interim solution until properly designed missile-boats could be built. These started to appear in 1960, the famous 'Osa' class, and scores of them have been built. The 131-ft hull has room for four SS-N-2 'Styx' missiles and, instead of the puny twin 25mm guns of the 'Komar,' the 'Osa' has two twin 30mm automatic mountings. The 'Styx,' although crude by today's standards, was a formidable weapon for its time, a small pilot-

Below: Three British postwar fast patrol boats, *FPB.790* (top), *FPB.5008* and *FPB.5009.*

less aircraft armed with an 800lb warhead. The missile flies under the control of an autopilot, probably with the assistance of commands transmitted from the ship, and has an active-radar homing head or an infrared seeker.

Western navies took little notice of the 'Styx' until 1967. Then on 21 October, during the Six-Day War between the Arab States and Israel, it received its baptism of fire. The Israeli destroyer *Eilat*, an elderly ex-British wartime destroyer, was patrolling off Port Said when she was attacked by two Egyptian 'Komars' lying behind the breakwater. The *Eilat* was a sitting duck, patrolling along a straight line and could offer little more than a token defence from her 40mm guns before being hit amidships by three out of the four 'Styxes' fired. She sank rapidly as flooding spread through an enormous hole amidships and a stunned world realized that the navies of the West had absolutely no defense against such an attack, let alone an equivalent missile.

For a while there was something close to panic in naval circles and the *Eilat* affair was even compared to battles like Lissa or Hampton Roads as a milestone in naval history. In fact the action only resembled Lissa in the sense that it also shed very little light on warfare of the future and created its own mythology. For a start the *Eilat*, in a very exposed position patrolling provocatively off a hostile coast, could have been sunk very easily by other means. For another, the *Eilat*'s fire control and armament were so antiquated that she would have been hard put to defend herself against conventional air attack. Compare what happened six years later, when a force of Israeli FPBs slaughtered a force of 'Osas' during the Yom Kippur War without sustaining more than a small shell-hit during the entire engagement. But the successful use of the 'Styx' in the Indo-Pakistan War of 1971 tended to reinforce the missile's reputation, although the Indian Navy admitted afterwards that they had contented themselves with firing at shipping in harbor rather than fighting an engagement at sea.

Although there were many bitter recriminations about the alleged failure of the West to produce an equivalent to the 'Styx,' the short answer is that the need had not previously been evident. There were, for example, many air defence missiles, but with a large number of aircraft carriers in service in NATO there was no specific requirement for more types of anti-shipping weapons. The French had a project on the drawing-board, later to be known as the Exocet or MM-38 (Mer-Mer 38-km) missile and, as soon as the news of the *Eilat* sinking came through, the manufacturers went ahead with development. In 1970 the first firings at sea were carried out by the small patrol craft *La Combattante* and the trials ship *Ile d'Oléron*. The next step came when the Federal German Navy decided to arm its new Type 148 patrol craft with Exocet MM-38 and the Royal Navy bought it for fitting to frigates. This was the sort of endorsement needed, and by 1977 more than 17 navies had placed orders for over a thousand missiles.

The French were not slow to grasp the opportunity. The Israelis had already approached Lürssenwerft in 1965 for six 45-meter craft armed with 40mm guns, but because the Federal German Government did not wish to anger its Arab customers the order was placed with the French shipyard Constructions Mécaniques de Normandie (CMN) at Cherbourg. These boats were called the *Mivtach* class, but became better-known as the *Saar* class when in 1969 five more of them were impounded in France to conform to a sudden arms embargo. Much to the anger of President de Gaulle all five suddenly escaped from Toulon and reached Haifa in January 1970.

The French now produced their own version of the 45-meter hull, a 47-meter design known for security reasons as the *Combattante II*. Despite this it bore no resemblance to the original laminated wood and fiberglass patrol boat and was virtually identical to the *Saar* class in layout and hull-form. The Federal German Navy wished to buy Exocet for its Type 148 FPBs but France would not permit this purchase unless the *Combattante II* hull was used, with French radar *and* the con-

struction of half the order at Cherbourg, rather than at Lürssen's yard. The German Government, anxious not to disturb the *rapprochement* with France, meekly accepted these rather harsh conditions, and *S.41* to *S.60* were delivered between 1972 and 1974.

The *Combattante II* rapidly carved itself a huge slice of the market, and gave its name to a new generic type. Four were sold to Greece, four to Malaysia, and twelve to Iran. The normal armament is a 76mm OTO-Melara Compact dual-purpose gun forward and two pairs of Exocet launchers angled to port and starboard amidships, but the Iranians chose the American Harpoon missile and the Malaysians favor the Swedish 57mm Bofors gun. The need to accommodate more armament led to the development of the 56-meter *Combattante III* series, usually armed with an additional 76mm gun or a twin 40mm aft and light automatic mountings amidships.

Exocet is fired by one man in the control room. When the FPB enters the battle-zone the magnetron of the homing head is warmed up for about a minute. When the radar detects a target the gyroscope in each missile is run up, requiring another half a minute. Once a target is selected the axial gyroscope must also be aligned and beyond this point the sequence is irreversible. The missile fires itself automatically 2 to 5 seconds after the firing button is pressed, its boost-motor ignites and it accelerates to just below the speed of sound in $2\frac{1}{4}$ seconds. The missile climbs to an average height of 100ft, then pitches over into level flight before descending to its cruising height of 50ft. It is now about $2\frac{1}{2}$ miles away and when it reaches its 'search zone' – a circle from which a target ship travelling at 40 knots could not have escaped during the time of flight – the radar homing head switches itself on. The missile now comes down to a height of

Below: The long-hulled *FPB.5036* armed as a gunboat, with two short 4.5-inch guns and a twin power-operated 20mm.

Above left: *Gay Bombadier* at speed in 1953, armed with two 21-inch torpedoes and a twin 20mm gun.
Above: *Gay Charioteer* alongside the minesweeper HMS *Marvel* in 1956.

less than 25 ft, becoming a 'seaskimmer' until it hits the target or is detonated by a proximity fuze as it flies overhead.

The Israelis, understandably sobered by the loss of the *Eilat*, lost no time in developing their own shipborne missile. Israel Aircraft Industries was given the task of developing a small missile with a range of 12 miles. Known as Gabriel, it was nominally outranged by the Styx, but it apparently has the benefit of superior technology. All twelve *Saars* were refitted to take Gabriel, some with eight launchers and others with five. The next step was to design a bigger boat to take Gabriel, the 58-meter *Reshef* class. Ten of these magnificent craft have been commissioned since 1973, armed with two 76mm Compact guns and five Gabriel launchers. Now they are receiving the Gabriel Mk 2, which has improved guidance and a range of 22 miles, making them even more potent.

It is however the smaller *Saars* which have the distinction of being the only Western FPBs to have fought a missile engagement. Details are very sketchy but it is known that in October 1973, during the Yom Kippur War, a force of *Saars* encountered a large force of Syrian 'Osas' (reputed to be 14 FPBs) off Lattakieh. What is known is that at least six Syrian 'Osas' were sunk without more than a shell-hole in one of the Israeli craft. The

impossible had happened: the 'unbeatable Styx' had been beaten by a missile of half its range.

From various sources it can be deduced that what the Israelis did was to trick the Syrian missile-controllers into firing at long range and too high. This not only caused the 'Styxes' to miss the Israeli boats, but also made them easy to track on radar. The method used was to drop chaff (the metallic strips known in World War II as 'Window') to confuse the tracker head of the missile. Three helicopters flew low over the leading *Saars* and, when the firing of the 'Styxes' was detected, both the helicopters and the FPBs below fired chaff before opening out their respective formations. The missiles were thus seduced into homing onto the biggest radar-image, that created by the floating mass of chaff. The *Saars* were also fitted with the latest jammers and electronic interception and analysis equipment and just how much this helped can only be guessed at. But above all the Israelis had shown that FPBs could hold their own against missile attack and the new weapon had proved itself in battle.

HOVERCRAFT & HYDROFOILS

By the 1960s designers were generally agreed that, however much hull-designs and power units might be improved, there was going to be no significant increase in speeds. If anything, the opposite was true, with a greater emphasis on seakeeping, reliability and robustness, all qualities which are incompatible with ultra-light structures and maximum engine power. Clearly some alternative to the classic 'displacement hull' would have to be developed if the quest for higher speeds was to be pursued.

The answer had already been looked at many years before. In Britain, for example, trials had been carried out on a Canadian design for a ladder hydrofoil as far back as 1921. It was not successful but in 1936 Commander Hampden and the naval shipbuilders J Samuel White produced an 18ft hydrofoil 'runabout.' Although hardly a basis for development, it showed that a hydrofoil, by raising the hull clear of the water, reduced drag to a great extent. The Hampden hydrofoil, on a displacement of 1.34 tons, reached 33 knots, whereas a fast dinghy (1.12 tons) and a fast motor boat (1.78 tons) only reached 24 knots.

The Admiralty was sufficiently impressed by White's proposals for a 67ft hydrofoil MTB to go ahead with an order for *MTB.101* in 1936. She ran her trials in 1940, but the foils and struts produced so much cavitation that she could not get beyond 41.3 knots, no matter how much power was generated. In 1939, the Denny shipyard at Dumbarton put forward a 'semi-hydrofoil' design, using a stepped hull like the old CMBs, but with a single fixed submerged foil at the after end. *MTB.109* was built and on trials in 1944 reached nearly 46 knots. There were however serious practical problems. For one thing it was not possible to fire torpedoes at more than 25 knots and for another, the boat

could not turn safely at high speed. The Admiralty reluctantly decided that these faults prevented *MTB.109* from being accepted and so this interesting craft was broken up.

Although much interest had been generated in German research into military hydrofoils, little was done by the British in the postwar years. They had a new toy to play with, the air-cushion craft or hovercraft, which offered a different solution to the problem of drag by floating the hull on a cushion of air inside a rubber skirt. As soon as the hovercraft demonstrated its unique ability to run ashore over a shelving beach, ideas began to churn forth for strike versions armed with guns and missiles and in 1964 came the first mention of a 'hovership' for the Royal Navy.

Sadly none of these dreams came to anything, for although the hovercraft can do what it claims, it does so at much greater cost than any conventional displacement hull. More important it makes much heavier demands on maintenance, a problem already acute for strike craft. In the early 1970s the Shah of Iran ordered six BH.7 hovercraft, four of which were to be armed with surface-to-surface missiles of an unspecified type. This interesting innovation did not materialize however and nobody else has followed this line of development. Not even the Russians, who made a massive investment in military hovercraft in the 1970s, have tried to use them in the strike role, so for the foreseeable future the strike hovercraft can be discounted. One of their biggest drawbacks is noise, which robs them of any element of surprise.

In contrast the hydrofoil has shown remarkable promise. In the 1950s Russian civilian hydrofoil ferries were developed and they were followed by a large number of 50-ton hydrofoil MTBs.

Below: Although not FPBs as such, the fast target boat *Sabre* and her two sisters were the last British fast strike craft. They had two Proteus gas turbines and were similar to the 'Brave' Class.

Top: The Egyptian missile boat *Khyber* leaves Portsmouth for the long voyage to Alexandria. Six of these 52-meter craft have been built in Britain for the Egyptian Navy since 1977.
Above: The Singaporean Navy's FPB *Sovereignty* is armed with a Bofors 76mm gun forward.

Above left: The new Thai FPB *Witthayarom*, one of three missile boats built in Italy.
Above: Soviet Osa Type missile boats in line ahead, showing the massive SS-N-2 missiles.
Left: The Turkish FPB *Dogan* was built by Lürssen and armed with eight Harpoon missiles.

Known as the *PA-4* class, they had a bow foil to assist in reducing drag at top speed. They were not particularly successful and were replaced by the *P-8* class in the early 1960s. In the mid-1960s the *Pchela* class appeared, roughly the same size but armed with only twin 25mm guns. They were clearly too small for the strike role and most of them were subsequently turned over to the KGB for use in patrolling the rivers and maritime frontiers of the Soviet Union.

In 1973 the first proper strike hydrofoils entered service, the 165-ton *Turya* class. Thirty were built, 123-footers armed with four 21-inch torpedo-tubes, a twin 57mm gun turret aft and a twin 25mm light automatic mounting forward. An unusual feature was a light dipping sonar on the transom stern; as there are no obvious anti-submarine weapons carried this equipment was presumably put in to allow the *Turya* class to cooperate with shore-based helicopters in hunting submarines in coastal waters.

In 1976 a new hydrofoil appeared from the Petrovsky shipyard in Leningrad and it was promptly christened the 'Sarancha' type by NATO. Only one of this class has been sighted, which suggests that she was a test-bed for the new SS-N-9 surface-to-surface missile. Four of those bulky missiles are carried in launching-tubes, two on either side of the bridge, and in addition she is protected against air attack by short-range SA-N-4 missiles and a 30mm 'Gatling' gun. Here was a formidable strike craft, with missiles capable of hitting at a range of 60 miles. The 'Sarancha' was also the first Russian craft with foils forward and aft and her combined gas turbine and diesel propulsion is credited with giving her a top speed of 45 knots.

The next class of hydrofoils, the 129ft *Matka*, started to appear two years later but reverted to the SS-N-2C, an updated variant of the 'Styx' missile. Only two missiles were carried, a reflection of the considerable weight of such weapons, and a 76mm gun forward. The single-foil system of the *Turya* design was retained, suggesting that the design actually predated that of the 'Sarancha.' Western naval opinion sees the ten *Matkas* so far

Above: The Argentinian *Intrepida* is armed with wire-guided torpedoes aft, a 40mm gun amidships and a 76mm gun forward.

completed as replacements for the older 'Osa' boats, which must be approaching the end of their useful lives.

In the last 15 years the People's Republic of China has also built military hydrofoils. The Hutong shipyard at Shanghai turned out the staggering total of 120 *Huchuan* class for the Navy, in addition to another 44 for friendly countries. It has also proved a commercial success, for 16 have been built in Rumania. The 71ft *Huchuan* is armed with twin machine guns and is driven by Russian-designed diesels at a maximum speed of 50 knots and is armed with two 21-inch torpedo-tubes.

The United States took some time to match these impressive achievements by the Communist Bloc. The experimental anti-submarine hydrofoil *High Point* (PCH-1) was completed in 1963 and reached 48 knots on two British Marine Proteus gas turbines. Her antisubmarine qualities were never fully investigated, as she spent most of her time firing Harpoon surface-to-surface missiles and other weapons. In the year that *High Point* came into service, the 328-ton *Plainview* (PCEH-1) was ordered, but she encountered mechanical setbacks and was not commissioned until 1968. She was intended to evaluate the concept of a 'hydrofoil frigate' and carried a variety of weapons during her exhaustive trials.

Both the *Plainview* and the *High Point* were experimental craft and the first intended for operational duties were a pair of prototypes, the Grumman-built *Flagstaff* (PGH-1) and Boeing's *Tucumcari* (PGH-2), which were completed in 1968. Both craft undertook a number of demonstrations around the world, *Tucumcari* going to Europe after a brief trip to Vietnam, while

Flagstaff made such an impression on the Israelis that they ordered the *Flagstaff II* design for their Coastguard.

The *Tucumcari* made an outstanding impression on her European tour and out of this stemmed the 'NATO Patrol Hydrofoil' (PHM) project. This called for 30 advanced naval strike craft to be built jointly by the United States, West Germany and Italy, and it was hoped to use an international weapons-fit. It was an ambitious plan, possibly too ambitious, for in an era of rapid inflation of costs, rising fuel bills and a general

Above: The Saudi Navy's *As Siddiq* en route through the Great Lakes from Sturgeon Bay, Wisconsin.

shortage of defence funds, a missile-armed hydrofoil was felt by many to be an expensive luxury.

In spite of mounting criticism *PHM-1* and *PHM-2* were ordered from Boeing in March 1973, but in August 1975 Congress ordered work on PHM-2 to be suspended. This immediately brought a halt to the NATO PHM programme as well and West Germany abandoned all ideas of building a missile hydrofoil. Italy, on the other hand, felt justified in continuing work to recover the investment already made and a license was taken out to build a slightly enlarged edition of the *Tucumcari* as a prototype for further development. This craft, the *Sparviero*, appeared in 1974 and showed such promise that six more were promptly

Below: Although the US Navy turned its back on FPBs after 1945, the need for inshore craft in Vietnam led to a revival. These 'Nasty' Class boats were bought from Norway.

Above: The Ecuadorean FPB *Quito*, built by Lürssen, is armed with French Exocet missiles.
Right: The Turkish 'Kartal' Class FPBs are armed with Norwegian Penguin missiles aft and two 40mm guns.

ordered. She carries an exceptionally heavy armament for an 80ft craft: two Otomat missiles aft and a 76mm gun forward.

Meanwhile Boeing were permitted to complete *PHM-1*, named *Pegasus*, and she made her first foil-borne trip in February 1975. Since then she has come through every type of trial and test imaginable and has even survived running aground in 1979. She is an impressive craft, 145ft long (with the forward foil retracted) and capable of 48 knots. She is armed with the Italian OTO-Melara 76mm Compact gun and Dutch WM-28 fire-control radar intended for the NATO PHM, and carries eight Harpoon anti-ship missiles aft (only four were mounted during early trials).

The continuing success of the trials with *Pegasus* convinced the doubters and in August 1977 Congress 'unfroze' the funds to complete the PHM program. The change of heart was too late to save *PHM-2*, named *Hercules*; her hull was scrapped and a new one started with the same name and hull-number. The first of the new PHMs to be commissioned is the *Taurus* (PHM-3) and all five are expected to be in service by 1982. Although externally similar to the *Pegasus*, the later PHMs have been completely redesigned internally to take advantage of the lessons learned since 1977.

The results of experience in *Pegasus* make interesting reading. She began her 'shakedown' in April 1977 and two months later she completed her acceptance trials, before commissioning

formally on 9 July. During the next seven months she accumulated nearly 700 hours of running under way, with 262 of those foilborne, a distance of nearly 16,000 miles. This distance compares favorably with US Navy destroyers, which log an average of about 14,000 miles each year. She is fitted with an automatic control system, which provides dynamic control during takeoff, running on the foils and 'landing' or returning to the hullborne state. In addition to stabilizing against the roll, the system controls the height of the hull above the surface of the water and all but eliminates the effect of waves. Foilborne turns are 'banked,' reducing violent motion and further improving the conditions on board. The big submerged foils also act like fixed-fin stabilizers and, if the weather becomes too severe, the commanding officer can always 'land' and turn his vessel back into a conventional 235-ton patrol craft.

As each PHM is completed she is sent to Key West, Florida, where a new PHM Squadron Two was formed in October 1981. There they will be supported by a fleet of mobile logistic support vehicles, allowing them to be independent of major base facilities. It is hoped that they will require no more than a ten-week docking and overhaul every two years, a great improvement over what was previously possible. It is intended to try PHM-RON TWO out in the Caribbean and possibly in the Mediterranean, two operating areas which favor the hit-and-run tactics of a missile-armed PHM. Although there is no reason why the PHMs should not sail across the Atlantic in company, with stops for refuelling in mid-ocean, they are more likely to be towed or carried on board a large merchant ship.

The tactics are still in their infancy, but there are many options open when five or six PHMs are in commission. One way is to use them as part of a larger battle group, with the primary intention of multiplying the number of missile-launching platforms. In this role the PHM's small radar-profile and high speed makes her a difficult target and yet she has the same missile-capability as a much larger ship. The secondary role being looked at is that of controlling 'choke points,' or in other words, ambushing hostile forces trying to push their way through relatively narrow bodies of water such as a strait between two land masses. The PHMs could work with aircraft

Above: The Norwegian FPBs *Glimt* (P.962) and *Gribb* (P.997) tied up alongside.

or by themselves, providing surveillance and a measure of deterrence as well. The high speed of the PHM is particularly valuable when it becomes necessary to investigate suspicious echoes among a large number of friendly ships, as it will enable a large area of water to be patrolled.

While the hydrofoil continues to make such strides it is easy to forget that the conventional displacement-hull FPB is still developing. Modern experience shows that the speed of an FPB has relatively little impact on her efficiency in battle; the difference between 35 and 40 knots will not affect the outcome, especially when speed falls off drastically in rough weather.

What matters is the ability of an FPB to make use of tactical information and to use her weaponry to maximum effect on the basis of that information. This means that precious weight and between-decks space must be given over to equipment for handling communications and target-plotting. Last but not

least, space must be found for generators to power all this equipment. Microminiaturization of electronics has done much to shrink the volume of equipment and there are now 'mini-combat systems' designed specifically for FPBs, capable of presenting the bewildering amount of raw information electronically. Only electronics can provide a speed of response capable of matching a missile travelling at the speed of sound and only electronics can provide a coordinated response to an attack – alerting the commanding officer and at the same time initiating a response, such as the launch of chaff and infra-red decoys, all in one movement.

Another problem is the long range of the latest series of missiles. The Harpoon ranges out to 60km, the MM-40 to 70km, and the Otomat to 150km, and although their manufacturers claim that they can function over the horizon just as efficiently as they do out to horizon-range, there are practical difficulties. At extreme range the target can very easily move out of the 'range gate' after the missile has been launched.

If the missile uses active radar to 'home' onto the target, that radar must be given a wider area to scan in order to pick up the target. If it is a 'fire-and-forget' missile, the triangulation of the relative position of the firing ship and the target becomes even more tricky. At extreme range it is also easier for the target to make use of countermeasures such as chaff and jamming, for the firing ship is too far away to be able to 'see' on radar the correct state of affairs.

The simple solution to these problems is to provide extra data for the missile in flight; the problem is where to get this additional information. The easiest way is to put a radar into a helicopter, which can then relay information back to the FPB,

Left: Soviet 'Stenka' Class boats at sea.
Above right: Captain and lookout on the bridge of a Soviet FPB.
With a vast coastline to protect the Soviet Navy has large numbers of FPBs, hydrofoils and small patrol craft.
Below: Music-loving Soviet sailors on the quarterdeck of a Soviet FPB.
Below right: The first of a new class of 84-foot hydrofoils built for Israel, ready for launching at Lantana, Florida.

The 56-meter Greek FPB *Antiploiarhos Laskos* was built by the French company Constructions Mecaniques de Normandie.

or update the individual missiles in mid-flight. In 1979 Ecuador announced that she would buy the French MM-40 missile for installation in six 660-ton corvettes, and that these would each carry a light helicopter. These *Esmeraldas* class are basically enlarged patrol boats, 204ft long and driven by four-shaft diesels at a top speed of 34 knots. There is no hangar and the helicopter will be lashed down to the small flight deck right aft and this is where the problems begin. Landing a helicopter on a small platform is tricky even in a calm sea, but when the weather is rough the platform is heaving and pitching and the risks multiply. Another problem is that most small helicopters are not suited to the task of operating a sophisticated surveillance radar and passing that information back to a warship or a missile; the power required imposes a considerable load on the generators and every extra pound of gear eats into the helicopter's flying time. Helicopters are notoriously difficult to keep flying – 14 hours of maintenance to one hour of flying time is not uncommon. Their light alloy fuselages are very susceptible to corrosion from salt water and ideally they should be kept under cover for as long as possible.

Whatever the drawbacks of operating helicopters from small craft, the benefits they offer in combat make them indispensable. The new improved version of the Israeli *Saar* class, the 202ft *Alia*, has a hangar amidships, accomodating a Kiowa helicopter. A much larger class of corvettes, 253ft long and displacing 850 tons, will also have a hangar and flight deck, and it has been suggested that their role will be to provide targeting information for the Harpoon missiles which have been retrofitted to the *Reshef* class.

The fast patrol boat, having made its reputation by being small and hard to detect, is now succumbing to that fatal tendency of warships to grow in size. We have seen hulls grow steadily from 220 tons and 147ft in length only ten years ago to nearly 500 tons and over 200ft long today. Such growth is inevitable, for the inherent drawback of the small craft is that its ability to accomodate weapons is much greater than its ability to control them. Modern technology has done a lot to narrow this gap, but at the same time the performance of weapons has been improving steadily and so the gap is virtually impossible to bridge. We can only guess at what the future holds, but many more FPBs of various types will continue to be built, having made themselves a major influence on tactics and strategy.

Sadly there is little permanent record of the thousands of fast strike craft which served in the two world wars. By their very nature they tend to be ephemeral, quickly built and quickly discarded. Wooden hulls tend to rot away the aluminum alloy corrodes very easily and yet there are a surprising number of craft around, for it is at least possible to lift small craft out of the water. One or two wartime MGBs and MTBs have been preserved as war memorials in the Soviet Union, for example, and two CMBs, the 40ft *CMB.4* and the 70ft *CMB.103* survive in Great Britain.

Canada has preserved the experimental hydrofoil *Bras d'Or*, for not for any sentimental reasons. She ran very successful trials in 1969–70 but proved so costly that she was laid up in the dockyard at Halifax, Nova Scotia. There she remains, a forlorn reminder that too giant a stride can be made; it is little use achieving a technical breakthrough which does not make economic sense.

Hundreds of wartime MTBs, MGBs and motor launches survive on both sides of the Atlantic as houseboats. A walk around most backwaters will reveal the unmistakeable lines of a Vosper 70-footer or an Elco PT-Boat. It is a poor tribute to their achievements.

Right: The US Navy's patrol hydrofoil *Pegasus* (PHM.1) at high speed.
Below: The camera's wide angle lens exaggerates the size of the forward foil on the new PHM *Aries*.

Above: A Norwegian 'Storm' Class FPB fires a Penguin missile.
Below: The US Navy's *Pegasus* on trials in Puget Sound in 1977.
Only four Harpoon missiles are on board, the fifth cannister being a
dummy weighted to compensate.

Above: These Norwegian FPBs are armed with small Penguin infrared homing missile.

Below: The 23mm gun and two SS-N-2 Styx launchers on a Soviet *Komar* Class missile patrol boat.

INDEX

Page numbers in italics refer to illustrations.

Acknowledgments

The author would like to thank David Eldred, the designer, R. Watson who compiled the index and Richard Natkiel who prepared the maps. The following agencies supplied the illustrations:
Frank Abelsen: pp 383, 391
Armada Republica Argentina: p 380 (top)
A/S Kingsberg Vapenfabrikk: pp 382-383, 390
Austrian Military Archives: p 343
Author's Collection: pp 63 (bottom), 373 (top left)
John Batchelor Collection: pp 215 (top rt), 221, 226, 241 (top), 253 (top)
Bayer Hauptstaatsarchiv, München: p 219 (top rt)
Bibliothek für Zeitgeschichte, Stuttgart: pp 42-43
Bison Picture Library: pp 35 (lower), 91, 286 (top)
Boeing Marine: pp 388, 389, 390-391
British Official: pp 181, 230, 230-231, 231 (top left), 233 (center), 239 (top), 242 (bottom), 244-245
Charles E. Brown: p 55 (center)
Bundesarchiv: pp 39 (top rt), 43 (top left), 47 (center), 150-151, 152 (below), 154-155, 170, 175 (two pics), 211 (bottom), 225 (top), 227 (bottom left), 237 (top two), 241 (bottom two)
Cantiere Baglietto: pp 336-337, 338-339, 354-355, 356-357
Cantiere Navale Breda: p 378 (top)
Central Naval Museum, Leningrad, via Boris Lemarchko: p 34

Conway Picture Library: pp 56-57, 93 (center), 97 (below)
Stephen Cribb, Southsea: pp 210, 214-215
ECPA: pp 43 (top rt), 169, 237 (center), 327
Foto Drüppel: pp 40-41, 63 (top), 106 (top), 158-159, 178-179, 179 (center), 346 (bottom rt), 347 (top)
Aldo Fraccaroli: pp 32-33, 100 (top), 103, 159, 197, 239 (center left), 335, 358, 359
Shizuo Fukui: pp 108 (above), 160-161, 163 (upper), 166
General Dynamics: pp 259 (top), 262 (bottom rt)
Grumman: p 385 (bottom)
Robert Hunt Library: pp 79 (top), 80-81 (all three), 82 (all three), 84, 86-87 (below), 88-89 (below), 89 (top), 90-91 (below), 92 (top), 94-95 (below), 98-99 (below), 100-101 (below), 102, 104 (all three), 110, 111 (both), 117, 206, 280-281, 289
Imperial War Museum, London: pp 25 (top), 26, 26-27, 27 (top), 30-31, 41, 46-47, 47 (top left), 48-49, 50-51, 52-53, 56, 58-59, 78-79 (bottom), 95 (top), 177, 213 (bottom), 214, 215 (top left), 216-217, 218-219, 219 (top left), 229 (center), 231 (top rt), 233 (top), 240, 251 (top), 253 (center and bottom rt), 273, 274, 275, 284-285, 346 (bottom left), 347 (bottom two), 348 (top two), 348-349, 349 (top rt), 350-351, 353 (top)
Humphrey Joel: p 53
Norbert Krüger: pp 227 (top and bottom left), 228, 232
Lürssenwerf: pp 378-379, 382
Mainichi: p 120
Maps © Richard Natkiel: pp 34, 35, 47, 50, 51, 59, 62, 67, 97, 113, 150, 156, 157, 176, 180, 184, 284,

288, 292, 296, 298, 312
Marina Militare: pp 166-167, 168, 168-169
Marius Bar: pp 192-193, 207 (lower), 208 (two pics), 208-209
Ministry of Defence: pp 92-93 (below), 130-131 (main pic), 131 (left) 197 (top)
Ministry of Defence, London: pp 370-371, 372
Ministry of Defence, (Navy): pp 207 (top rt), 224-225, 232-233, 254, 257 (top), 258 (center), 260 (top), 262 (bottom left)
Musée de la Marine: pp 18, 44-45, 98 (top), 193 (top)
Museo Storico Navale, Venice: p 27 (center)
National Archives: pp 112 (top), 121, 125 (top), 126-127 (bottom), 128-129 (bottom), 132-133 (below), 188, 189 (bottom), 212, 222, 293, 296-297, 299, 300-301, 302-303, 304 (bottom), 306-311, 315, 317
National Maritime Museum: pp 14-15 (two pics), 24, 25 (lower), 28, 38, 38-39, 39 (top left), 54-55, 85 (bottom rt), 86 (top), 93 (top), 176, 209, 211 (top), 213 (top), 223, 229 (top), 243 (bottom), 255 (top left), 316 (bottom)
Naval Photographic Club: pp 152 (top), 182-183, 371, 373 (bottom), 375 (top rt)
Peter Newark's Western Americana: p 207 (top left)
Novosti: p 379
GA Osbon: pp 373 (top rt), 375 (top left)
Bengt Pettersson: pp 256-257
Antony Preston: pp 155, 162, 181 (top), 242 (top)
Real photographs: pp 352 (top), 352-353
Science Museum, London: pp 334-335

Staatsarchiv Dusseldorf: p 224
TASS: pp 384, 385 (top)
C & S Taylor: p 196
Ufficio Storica della Marina Militare: pp 336-340
Ullstein: pp 174-175, 179 (top)
USAF: pp 276-277, 278, 279
US Navy: pp 18-19, 19 (bottom two), 20 (two pics), 21, 31, 36 (lower), 43 (center), 54, 55 (top), 65 (two pics), 66, 66-67, 68, 69, 70-71, 85 (bottom left), 87 (top), 88 (above), 96, 98 (center), 105 (above), 106-107 (below), 107 (center and rt), 108-109 (below), 112-113, 114 (all three), 116, 118-119 (below), 119 (top), 122, 123 (all three), 124-125, 126 (top), 127 (top), 128-129 (top), 131 (bottom rt), 132 (above), 134-135 (all three), 142-143, 145 (two pics), 148-149, 161, 163 (lower), 164-165 (four pics), 172-173, 184-185, 185, 186-187, 189 (top), 190-191, 192, 193 (center), 194, 196 (top), 198, 199, 249 (top and center), 248-249, 250 (top and center), 250-251, 255 (top rt), 256-257, 257 (center), 258-259, 260 (bottom), 261 (top), 262-263, 268-269, 270-271, 272, 277, 278-279, 282-283, 286 (lower), 286-287, 288 (bottom), 290, 291, 292-293, 295, 296 (right), 298 (top), 298-299, 300, 301, 304 (top), 305, 313, 314-315, 316 (top), 318-327, 344-345, 360, 360-361, 362, 363, 364-365, 366-367, 368-369, 372, 380-381
P A Vicary: pp 152-153
Vosper Ltd: p 346 (top)
Vosper Thorneycroft: p 377 (top)
William J. Welch: p 381
Wright & Logan: pp 170-171, 374-375, 376-377, 377 (center)